Theodosia Burr Alston

THEODOSIA BURR
By C.B.J. Fevret de Saint-Mémin.

Theodosia Burr Alston

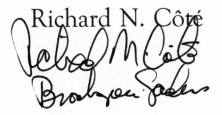

Portrait of a Prodigy

To John, with warmest lowcountry wishes

Richard N. Côté

CORINTHIAN
BOOKS

Mount Pleasant, S. C.

Publishers Cataloging-in-Publication Data
(Provided by Quality Books)

Côté, Richard N.
    Theodosia Burr Alston: Portrait of a Prodigy
    by Richard N. Côté.—1st ed.
    p. cm.
    Includes bibliographical references and index.
    LCCN: 2001127226
    ISBN: 1-929175-31-0 (hc)
    ISBN: 1-929175-44-2 (pb)

    1. Alston, Theodosia Burr, 1783-1813. 2. Women—United
    States—Biography I. Title.

E302.6.B9C67 2002   973.4'092
                                     QBI02-200505

First Edition:
    First printing, September 2002.

Corinthian Books
P.O. Box 1898
Mt. Pleasant SC 29465-1898
(843) 881-6080
http://www.corinthianbooks.com

To James L. Michie, a tireless archaeologist, brilliant scholar, and genial friend, without whose seminal research this story of Theodosia Burr Alston would have been woefully incomplete.

She was the soul of her father's soul.
—Charles Felton Pidgin

Contents

Chronology

Her age	Date	
	1756	February 6: Aaron Burr was born.
	1782	July 2: Burr married Mrs. Theodosia Prevost.
	1783	June 21: Theodosia Bartow Burr was born.
10	1794	May 18: Mrs. Theodosia Prevost Burr died.
17	1800	Burr was elected Vice President (1801-1805).
17	1801	February 2: Theodosia married Joseph Alston.
18	1801	Late July: the Alstons visited Niagara Falls.
19	1802	c. May 22: Aaron Burr Alston was born.
21	1804	July 11: Burr killed Alexander Hamilton in a duel.
22	1805	April 22: Burr departed on his first trip to the West.
22	1805	August 6: near death, Theodosia wrote her will.
23	1806	September: Theodosia, Joseph, and their son traveled down the Ohio River.
24	1807	February 18: Burr was arrested for treason and escorted to the Richmond, Virginia, state penitentiary.
24	1807	August 3: Burr's trial for treason opened in Richmond, Virginia.
24	1807	September 1: Burr was acquitted of treason.
24	1808	June 7: Burr began his European exile.
29	1812	May 4: Burr returned to America.
29	1812	June 30: Aaron Burr Alston died.
29	1812	December 31: Theodosia departed Georgetown, S. C., aboard the schooner *Patriot* and disappeared.
	1816	September 10: Joseph Alston died.
	1836	September 14: Aaron Burr died.

Preface

The diamond gives no indication of its worth until it has been
ground and polished and set in a manner worthy of its value.
                                                —Charles Felton Pidgin

From South Carolina on August 1, 1809, a slender, delicate young woman with large, expressive, dark brown eyes and dark auburn hair picked up her pen to profess her adoration for the man who was the center of her universe. Theodosia Burr Alston, who had just turned twenty-six, wrote to her twice-disgraced father, Aaron Burr, then in self-imposed European exile, "I witness your extraordinary fortitude with new wonder at every new misfortune. Often, after reflecting on this subject, you appear to me so superior, so elevated above all other men, I contemplate you with such a strange mixture of humility, admiration, love, and pride, that very little superstition would be necessary to make me worship you as a superior being, such enthusiasm does your character excite in me. When I afterward revert to myself, how insignificant do my best qualities appear. My vanity would be greater if I had not been placed so near you; and yet my pride is our relationship. I had rather not live than not be the daughter of such a man." It was the perfect match. Aaron Burr was Theodosia's god; Theodosia was Burr's prodigy and vision. They were far more than soulmates. Theodosia and her father were emotional Siamese twins who occupied separate bodies but shared a single heart.

Ovid's saying, "time devours all things," was never more true than when applied to Theodosia Burr Alston. During her life, her friends, family, and acquaintances knew her as a vivacious, mischievous little girl; a charming, intelligent young woman; a tender, loving wife; a caring, attentive mother; and a devoted daughter. In addition, she was trained by her obsessive but loving father as an intellectual prodigy and educational role model for women of the future. On the day of her marriage in 1801, Theodosia, aged seventeen years, seven months, and nine days, was without question the best educated woman in the United States. However, she was not being prepared solely for adulthood, marriage, and motherhood. Burr was grooming her to become a president, queen, or empress.

I first encountered Theodosia in 1990 while researching my biography, *Mary's World: Love, War, and Family Ties in Nineteenth-century Charleston* (Corinthian Books, 2001). Its subject was Mary Motte Alston Pringle of Charleston, whose elder brother, Joseph Alston, married Theodosia in 1801. Mary was nine years old when Theodosia died. Her story fascinated me, but since she played only a minor role in Mary Pringle's life, I had to wait until *Mary's World* was completed before I could research the life of Mary's intriguing sister-in-law. Although born to wealth and privilege and superbly educated, Theodosia led a tragic life that shackled and, ultimately, snuffed out her potential before she reached her thirtieth birthday. She faced a father who never gave up his emotional control of her. After her marriage to South Carolina rice planter Joseph Alston, she coped with a husband who adored her but could not meet any of her intellectual needs. In addition, she was transported from bustling, cosmopolitan New York to the slow-paced rural, agricultural South. She was cursed with incurable illnesses that severely damaged her health and drained her strength, yet she always pushed through the pain and moved on. Later, she suffered the social ostracism that grew out of her father's disgraces and was devastated by the loss of her only child to one of the many fevers that thrived in the South Carolina Lowcountry.

After her tragic disappearance at sea in the first days of 1813, she faced yet another cruel fate: the erosion and ultimate destruction of her identity. In the first stage of her descent into historical oblivion, she was simply lost in the shadows of her father's infamy. Then, as she was rediscovered, she was often portrayed as a South-hating northern society belle who had turned into a couch-ridden, neurotic victim of fate. In order to portray the real Theodosia, I first had to draw her out from under her father's shadow, and then deconstruct the accretions of fable and whimsey which had hardened into her "history."

As President Woodrow Wilson once remarked, Aaron Burr had "genius enough to have made him immortal, and unschooled passion enough to have made him infamous." Burr, the product of Calvinistic Puritan ministers, the diligent college student, the courageous Revolutionary War hero, the successful attorney, the able politician, the ambitious states-man, the vice president, the notorious duelist, and the man found not guilty—but not innocent—of treason, has been ana-lyzed and written about in extraordinary detail for many years. However, this book is not about Burr, but about Theodosia, the daughter he educated and adored. Burr is a key figure in this book, but he will be encountered chiefly as a private citizen and head of his household; the man who was Theodosia's father, teacher, counselor, confidante, soulmate, and shaper of her dreams.

The challenge of writing the biography of someone you can only get to know through studying incomplete collections of two-hundred year-old letters and reading thousands pages of conflicting opinions written by long-dead authors with heavy axes to grind is both daunting and extremely exciting. No one in their right mind would attempt such a task alone, but even with the help of the best experts and the oversight of the finest scholars and technical advisors, the outcome is al-ways the subjective product of the author.

Every biography ultimately consists of a large collection of facts, obtained from sources of varying quality, filtered through the sieve of the author's logic, arranged as artfully as possible, and, hopefully, reviewed by knowledgeable experts and specialists prior to publication. If the biographer does his work well, the reader gets to meet a realistic replica of the subject, with all his or her warts and haloes in their proper places. If done poorly, not only is the reader cheated of an accurate portrayal, but so is the subject.

James Parton, Aaron Burr's first serious biographer, faced the daunting challenge of writing a balanced story of a man whom America had come to despise almost as much as Benedict Arnold. Parton found his work easiest when he consulted the untainted, primary sources of information on Burr and ignored hearsay and conjecture. "The discordance and contradictions begin only when the inner circle of those who *knew* him is left, and the outer one of those who have *heard*, is entered," he wrote. Parton tried to ignore the pro- and anti-Burr partisans, read the historical record, and write what he found.

In writing this, the first biography of Theodosia, I have used the same approach. I have drawn chiefly upon Theodosia's personal correspondence with her father and her family and upon first-hand accounts by others who personally knew her. The primary challenge I faced was that she and her father were emotionally welded together to an extent rarely seen before or since their passing. Consequently, writing a book about Theodosia without spending half the pages talking about her father was similar to the challenge facing a surgeon trying to separate Siamese twins.

I had two goals in mind when I conceived this book. The first was to reveal Theodosia as a person in her own right. For this I used extensive quotations from her own writings. The Theodosia known to the majority of people today is a product of fiction and fancy; a doe-eyed pawn in her father's political intrigues or a pathetic, bed-ridden shadow of a woman who met a lurid death at the hands of pirates. Since these images bear little likeness to their subject, my second goal was to tear away the dense thicket of hearsay, mythology, and deliberate misinformation which, like the kudzu vines of her adopted South Carolina homeland, has overgrown and obscured Theodosia's true personality and achievements.

I drew my information from many sources. Most important were Theodosia's own letters, most of which are found with the papers of her father. Unfortunately, scholars have not yet focused the same attention on Aaron Burr the private citizen as they have on Burr the politician and statesman. A meticulously edited, two-volume edition titled *Political Correspondence and Public Papers of Aaron Burr*, edited by Mary-Jo Kline and Joanne Wood Ryan, makes these papers available in print, but, sadly, no printed companion edition exists for Burr's or Theodosia's personal papers.

Burr was planning to write an autobiography, and by 1807, had selected the most important of his letters and papers for that purpose. In his 1833 Revolutionary War pension application, Burr wrote, "when I had determined to go to Europe in 1807, I sent to my daughter then Mrs. Alston in South Carolina, all my private papers which were deemed of value carefully put up in boxes, to be kept until my return or further orders, which papers were shipped to me on my return in 1812, in a vessel which has never since been heard of." The documents were on board the *Patriot* with Theodosia when she was lost at sea in the first days of 1813.

The first fleeting record of Burr's relationship with his daughter appears in Samuel L. Knapp's *The Life of Aaron Burr* (1835), the first attempt at a Burr biography. From a research standpoint, Knapp's rambling, adoring book is useless except as a historical curiosity. Many letters between Theodosia and her father were first reproduced in Matthew L. Davis's two-volume *Memoirs of Aaron Burr* (1837) and in his *Private Journal of Aaron Burr During His Residence of Four Years in Europe* (1838).

Davis, Burr's close friend, was a sloppy and highly biased editor, who deliberately destroyed many of the papers entrusted to his care. Indeed, in the preface to volume I of the *Memoirs*, he sanctimoniously assured his readers, "I alone have possessed the private and important papers of Colonel Burr; and I pledge my honour that every one of them, so far as I know and believe, that could have injured the feelings of a female or those of her friends, is destroyed." That criterion alone would have led to the destruction of a sizable portion of Burr's letters. Nevertheless, the edited, abridged, revised, spliced, rewritten, or bowdlerized versions in the *Memoirs* are often the only surviving record of the documents that Davis subsequently destroyed, gave away, sold, or otherwise let slip through his fingers. Fortunately, the manuscript of Burr's European journal survived Davis's mindless editing. A diligently transcribed and annotated edition of 250 copies was published by William K. Bixby in 1903, who noted, "The liberties which Davis took with the journal were amazing and some of his changes were ridiculous."[1] The Bixby edition was used whenever possible.

Because many of Burr's papers were destroyed when the *Patriot* was lost, and because Davis was so negligent, there are major gaps in the Theodosia-Aaron Burr personal correspondence. One such void runs from May 23, 1805, to March 27, 1807, which covers the entire period when Burr's Western Conspiracy was peaking and Theodosia was preparing for the coronation she believed would soon follow. For these years, I relied chiefly on the reports of others for my information.

Theodosia herself complicated the role of her future biographers. In a letter dated August 6, 1805, she directed her husband to "Burn all my papers except my father's letters, which I beg you to return to him." In 1816, after Joseph Alston's death, a trunk of Theodosia's personal effects and letters—those she left behind at The Oaks while she was on her way to the 1812-1813 reunion with her father—was sent to Burr by William Algernon Alston, Joseph's brother. Given her penchant for writing, not to mention Burr's insistence that she do so, the relatively small quantity of her letters which have survived suggests that the burning may have taken place. Other letters written to her father may have been saved by him and sealed inside the tin boxes that went down with her ship. Most of the rest of her original correspondence is scattered among the manuscript collections of a dozen archives and libraries. Some letters are undoubtedly still in private collections. A professionally edited edition of her surviving papers would be a boon to future writers and scholars.

In the first century after Theodosia's death, two useful works appeared. The first was James Parton's 1857 *Life and Times of Aaron Burr*, expanded to two volumes in 1892. The other was Charles Felton Pidgin's *Theodosia: The First Gentlewoman of her Times* (1907), a compilation of the source material that he had collected while writing his two Theodosia novels, *Blennerhassett* (1901) and its sequel, *The Climax; Or, What Might Have Been* (1902). Pidgin gathered together a great deal of Theodosia fact and fancy, but the book was not a study of her life, and it asked no questions and sought no answers. Although it is idiosyncratic, speculative, redundant, partisan, often inaccurate, and must be used with great care, it is, nevertheless, a treasure chest of anecdotal material and Theodosia minutiae found nowhere else, especially concerning the provenance of the Nag's Head portrait.

The work of twentieth-century Burr scholars was an enormous help, as they used primary source materials, analytical skills, and literary and historical perspectives not available to their nineteenth-century predecessors to present the Burrian (but not the Theodosian) world to readers. My chief guides were Samuel H. Wandell's and Meade Minnigerode's *Aaron Burr* (1927); Nathan Schachner's *Aaron Burr: A Biography* (1937); Herbert S. Parmet and Marie B. Hecht's *Aaron Burr: Portrait of an Ambitious Man* (1967); Mary-Jo Kline and Joanne W. Ryan's *The Political Correspondence and Public Papers of Aaron Burr* (1983); Milton Lomask's *Aaron Burr* (1979 and 1982); Arnold A. Rogow's *A Fatal Friendship* (1998); Thomas Fleming's *Duel* (1999); Buckner F. Melton, Jr.'s *Aaron Burr: Conspiracy to Treason* (2000); and Roger G. Kennedy's *Burr, Hamilton, and Jefferson* (2000). On the artwork of John Vanderlyn, I was extremely fortunate to have two distinguished Vanderlyn experts, Dr. William T. Oedel of the University of Massachusetts,

Amherst, and Dr. Kenneth C. Lindsay, of the University of New York, Binghamton, as my advisors.

The next wellspring was the immensely useful archaeological and historical research performed at The Oaks in the early and mid-1990s by James L. Michie of Coastal Carolina University, Conway, South Carolina, and his devoted staff. In addition, I received great help and guidance from the staffs of The Hermitage, Ho-Ho-Kus, New Jersey; The Blennerhassett Island Historical State Park, Parkersburg, West Virginia; the Graveyard of the Atlantic Museum, Hatteras, North Carolina; and The Senate House Museum, Kingston, New York.

Finally, I drew upon the knowledge of South Carolina rice plantation life and culture acquired during the ten years it took to research, write, and edit *Mary's World*.

This book was written to restore to the daylight the flesh-and-blood Theodosia, the girl who giggled on her mother's knee; the thirteen-year-old who presided alone over a formal dinner for a powerful Indian chief; the young woman who pinned back the ears of her overbearing fiancé only days before their wedding; and the elegant lady who floated gracefully down the Ohio River on a flatboat, headed, she believed, on a one-way-trip to become Theodosia I, Empress of Mexico.

Now that I have mapped out the basic story of her life, I hope this book will be the front door through which the next generations of scholars and readers will pass to meet Theodosia and explore in detail the many facets of her heritage, personality, experiences, and destiny for themselves. And I also hope that their journey of discovery will be as fascinating as mine was.

Richard N. Côté
Mt. Pleasant, South Carolina
July 16, 2002

CHAPTER ONE

Good Stock, Deep Roots

A *perfect woman, nobly planned.*
–Grace Greenwood

Albany, New York
Summer 1783

Shouts of joy echoed through the house as the first cries of his new baby pierced the door of the bedchamber. Moments later, Col. Aaron Burr's best Madeira flowed like water as toasts were drunk to his wife, Theodosia, and their new daughter. Throughout the pregnancy, both parents had been anxiously counting the days until the birth of their first child. At the age of thirty-seven, Theodosia Bartow Prevost Burr was a full decade older than her husband. She had a "delicate constitution," and her health had been precarious for some time.[1] But the Fates had smiled, good luck prevailed, and Aaron and Theodosia's little girl was born healthy and vigorous on June 21, 1783.[2]

Her mother wanted to name her Sally, after her dear friend, Sally Reeve, Aaron's sister, in Litchfield, Connecticut. Theodosia wrote Sally's husband, Tapping Reeve: "Will you believe me, Reeve, when I tell you the dear little girl has the eyes of your Sally?"[3] Aaron was so excited when he wrote to Reeve that he used his business signature, "A. Burr." Theodosia added

1

a postscript, "Burr is half-crazy, pride at having a daughter & pursuit of the law divide his Attention—he mistook you for a client."[4]

Aaron, on the other hand, was determined to carry on the name of his beloved wife. On July 28, 1783, the one-month-old apple of Aaron Burr's eye was baptized in the Albany Dutch Reformed Church and christened Theodosia Bartow Burr.[5]

Burr would soon rise quickly to high office: from gentle-man volunteer to lieutenant colonel in the American Revolu-tion, to New York state attorney general, U.S. senator from New York, and, ultimately, vice president of the United States. But to read his letters to his wife and daughter is to see Burr in his finest role: that of a proud, doting father and loving husband.

Baby Theodosia—whom Burr soon dubbed "Miss Prissy" and "Our Miss Priss"—had a father who was totally devoted to her. Despite all the crises that would follow, Burr would never regret the affection and attention he had lavished upon his daughter. And he could not possibly have known how critical a part little Miss Priss would play in his soon-to-be notorious life.

Even though he had not yet reached the age of thirty when his daughter was born, Burr was already a rising, prosperous attorney, respected for his patriotism and heroism during the American Revolution. Through both his ancestry and his war-time experiences, Burr was well known and well connected throughout New England and New York.

Young Theodosia's birthright included a wide and admir-ing network of acquaintances. Her parents had intimate friend-ships with the most brilliant and talented men and women in the country and a heritage of intelligent, pious, and highly ac-complished ancestors. In short, Theodosia came from good stock with deep roots.

Two prominent traits of Theodosia's ancestors were their quirky courting habits and the propensity of their men to marry well educated women a generation younger than them-selves. Theodosia's grandfather, Rev. Aaron Burr, was a prime example. The son of Daniel Burr and his third wife, Elizabeth Pinckney, he was born in 1716 in Fairfield, Connecticut, where his Puritan family had resided for three generations.[6] Aaron senior graduated in 1735 from Yale College in New Haven in his nineteenth year. While there, he won one of three Berkeley scholarships, indicating that he had been a top scholar in Greek and Latin. The scholarship entitled him to financial support during two years of post-graduate study at Yale.

This third-generation Puritan, who served both church and state with distinction, was inspired to enter the ministry during a 1736 revival. He was licensed as a Presbyterian minister that same year; preached his first sermon in Greenfield, Massachusetts; and was stationed for a short time in Hanover, New Jersey. In 1737, after a town meeting in Newark, New Jersey, he was called to the pulpit of Newark's prominent First Presbyterian Church. In 1738, at the age of twenty-two, he was ordained as their settled minister and commenced an "eminently successful" ministry, for which he was paid an annual salary of £60 sterling.

Rev. Aaron Burr

He gained a commanding reputation as a pulpit orator and became known as "one of the most learned divines and accomplished scholars of his time."[7] His education made him the natural choice to start a school for boys, which allowed him to put his intelligence to good use and provided additional income.

Reverend Burr remained a bachelor until his mid-thirties. His sudden marriage to young Esther Edwards raised a few eyebrows but strengthened the family's already solid theological

Rev. Jonathan Edwards

connections. When they married in 1752, Esther was twenty-one; her husband was thirty-six. She was a daughter of the prominent divine, Rev. Jonathan Edwards, and his wife, Sarah Pierpont, who were then living in Stockbridge, Massachusetts.[8] Jonathan Edwards, a Connecticut native, had grown up on the Indian frontier. His father was the Rev. Timothy Edwards, M.A., a distinguished, Harvard-educated, minister-teacher-theologian.

Jonathan, the fifth child and only son, grew up with ten sisters—whom his father warmly described as his "sixty feet of daughters."[9] Today, Jonathan Edwards is looked upon as one of the greatest of America's colonial theologians.

Some look back at Jonathan's Puritan parents and see only joyless, austere souls, but that was not always the case. The journal of Jonathan's father, Rev. Timothy Edwards, noted that the double religious ceremony marking the completion of his new church and his formal ordination as its minister was followed by an "Ordination Ball" in the minister's house.[10] In addition, his daughters are known to have received two pairs of "heels"—the precursor of high-heeled shoes—to be attached to embroidered slippers.[11]

Sarah (Pierpont) Edwards, wife of the Rev. Jonathan Edwards

His mother, Esther (Stoddard) Edwards, had a strong effect on him. Unlike most of her gender, Esther had been sent to Boston to acquire a superior education. She was described as "tall, dignified, and commanding in appearance, affable and gentle in her manner, and regarded as surpassing her husband in native vigor and understanding."[12] Her father was the accomplished Rev. Solomon Stoddard of Northhampton, Massachusetts, a Harvard graduate and the school's first librarian.

Jonathan's father, Timothy, a revolutionary thinker for his time, educated his son and ten daughters identically—a practice Aaron Burr would adopt many years later. In a school conducted under his own roof, Timothy turned out scholars so well prepared that they could look forward to automatic acceptance at Harvard and Yale without the necessity of taking an entrance examination. His girls were so skilled in classical languages that "when called away from home, as he often was in his capacity of eminent divine, he left the instructions to his daughters in Latin and Greek, and particularly directed that they shall not fail to hear the recitations of the young men [his private students]."[13]

Jonathan Edwards grew into an outstanding preacher and scholar. As a young man, he was strongly influenced by John Locke's masterful "Essay Concerning Human Understanding," which discussed the nature of the self, the world, God, and the grounds of our knowledge of them. At thirteen, he entered Yale College and graduated with high honors in 1720.

A strict Calvinist, Jonathan devoted himself to "an awakening of zeal and restoration of strict devotional conduct," and wrote, "I made the seeking of salvation the main business of my life."[14] His crusade came to be known as the Great Awakening, and it laid the groundwork for the periodic religious revivals that continue today.

The tall, thin preacher was widely known for his "sermons of fire and brimstone in which, as the messenger of the Lord, he described the vast liquid mountains that would pour over the damned without mercy."[15] He promoted his ideals with such dedication, fervor, and lack of tact that his Northhampton congregation dismissed him in 1750. The censure had more to do with the declining power of strict Puritanism than with Jonathan's continuing obsession with it.

Jonathan's rigid Calvinism did not prevent him from bending his theological principles a bit when it came to matters of the heart. In 1727, he fell deeply in love with Sarah, the thirteen-year-old daughter of Rev. James Pierpont, whom he first met while studying at Yale. He pressed for an early marriage, but she stood firm. A heartfelt and eloquent love letter won her heart, but he still had to wait for her hand. Even after arguing that patience was not a virtue, Jonathan was forced to wait until she was seventeen to marry her. Ultimately, their union was both happy and fruitful.

Sarah was extremely pious, relished religious conversation, cared for the "weakly and infirm constitution" of her husband, and "bore her own troubles with patient cheerfulness and good humor." In the next twenty-two years, Sarah and Jonathan Edwards brought eleven children into the world. Like many of his neighbors, Reverend Edwards owned a slave, a horseman named Harry.[16]

In 1751, Jonathan was called to the pulpit of a Presbyterian church on the Indian frontier at Stockbridge, Massachusetts. There, among twelve white and 150 Housatonic Indian families, he wrote his "Essay on the Freedom of Will," a landmark metaphysical treatise noted for its brilliant reasoning. With so many children to clothe and feed, Jonathan was forced to write much of his essay on the backs of letters and on blank pages from discarded pamphlets. His daughter, Esther, made lace and painted fans and sent them to Boston to sell "to aid in the scanty support of the family."[17]

The man Esther would marry, Rev. Aaron Burr, was elected the second president of the College of New Jersey, later known as Princeton University, in 1748 at the age of thirty-two. Reverend Burr was described as having a "small and delicate frame, yet to encounter fatigue he had a heart of steel," and as being, like his future son and namesake, a "small man as to body, but of great and well improved mind."[18]

In 1752, Burr prepared a Latin grammar manual, the "Newark Grammar," which was used at the College of New Jersey for many years. He worked ceaselessly to improve and expand the young institution. During his tenure as president, he became known as one of the foremost men in the nation, not only for his leadership and intellectual achievements but also for "a certain grace and distinguished style of manner."[19]

Four years after assuming the leadership of the college, Burr was ready to marry. His courtship of Esther Edwards was as cordial as it was brief. Esther noted in her diary that when Burr came to visit her father in Stockbridge in the latter part of May 1752, he was already well known to the family, though he had not seen her for five years. "As a little girl [of thirteen] I have romped with him and sat on his lap," she wrote.[20]

After a stay of only three days, Burr was set to depart the next morning. The duty of preparing him a hearty breakfast fell to Esther. "Mr. Burr partook with the greatest relish, keeping up a current of gracious speech every moment; and finally, fixing his flashing eyes on me, as I sat rapt and listening at the other end of the board, he abruptly said: 'Esther Edwards, last night I made bold to ask your honored father, if I can gain your consent, that I might take you as Mrs. Burr, to my Newark bachelor's quarters, and help convert them into a Christian home. What say you?'"

The flustered young woman continued, "I was wholly unprepared for this sudden speech and blushed to my ears and looked down, and stammered out, as we are taught to say here: 'If it please the Lord.' I could not help asking myself, 'Has he been waiting for me all these years?'"[21]

Two weeks later, Esther made the long horseback ride from her parents' home in Stockbridge to Newark. She was accompanied by her mother, Sarah, and a young College of New Jersey graduate, who had been sent to escort them. It is likely that Burr's pressing duties as minister and college president kept him from escorting his future bride and mother-in-law to New Jersey. It is interesting to speculate about what the young bride-to-be might have contemplated as she made the long and tiring

175-mile ride to marry the affectionate and sincere older man she scarcely knew.

The Edwards party rode from Stockbridge to the Hudson River, traveled down the river on a sloop, and then crossed the bay to Newark.[22] At the time, Newark was still a small settlement totally surrounded by dense woods and farmlands. Because of the renown of the college's president and the age difference—fifteen years—between Reverend Burr and his bride, the impending marriage created a great deal of gossipy excitement in the sparsely populated New Jersey countryside.

The bride and her mother arrived on Saturday, June 27, 1752, and the couple was married two days later, on Monday evening. In a letter to the *New York Gazette* three weeks later, a student at the college wrote of Esther, "As I have yet no manner of acquaintance with her, I cannot describe to you her qualifications and properties. However they say she is a very valuable lady. I think her a person of great beauty, though I must say she is rather too young (being twenty-one years of age) for the President."[23]

Esther would later compare her husband to her father: "I think my father more impressive and solemn; but Mr. Burr is more ingratiating and captivating; has more of what people call eloquence.... Mr. Burr's nature seems to bubble up and overflow into expression."[24] Burr also superintended and encouraged his wife's continuing education—a rarity for the times. "My husband, Mr. Burr, has persuaded me to take up Latin with him," she wrote. "I had learned it a little in our home at Northhampton, where there was much teaching of the classics."[25]

Esther Burr became widely known for her attractiveness and even more so for her intellectual brightness. "She exceeded most of her sex in the beauty of her person, as well as in her behavior and conversation," wrote the editor of a book purporting to be Esther's journal. "She discovered an unaffected, natural freedom toward persons of all ranks with whom she conversed. She had a lively, sprightly imagination, a quick, penetrating discernment, and a good judgment."[26] Given her warm and welcoming personality and diligent work on behalf of the church and college, Mrs. Burr was quickly embraced by the community.

The Burrs made their first home in the handsome parsonage of the First Presbyterian Church at the corner of Broad and William Streets in Newark. There, in a second-floor bedroom, their two children were born. The first was Sarah (known throughout her life as Sally), on May 3, 1754. Their second child, Aaron, was born on February 6, 1756.[27] In her diary that day, Esther Burr wrote that she was feeling "very poorly, unable to write." She had no consolation from her husband, who was away on a trip in connection with his duties as pastor and university president. A few hours after writing her journal entry, she was surprised when the baby who would become the nation's most infamous, mysterious, and misunderstood vice president was born."[28]

The Parsonage of the First Presbyterian Church, Newark, New Jersey

As the student body of the college grew, the parsonage became too small to accommodate the scholars. President Burr looked to the town of Princeton, New Jersey, as a site for a new campus. Philadelphia architect Robert Smith designed Nassau Hall as the school's first permanent home. In 1756, Burr resigned the pulpit of his church, moved out of the parsonage, and relocated the college and his family to Princeton.

Prior to his giving up the pulpit, the twin roles of pastor of a large congregation and president of a college had taxed Reverend Burr in the extreme. By September 2, 1757, he was suffering from severe exhaustion and debilitating fevers.

Esther must have been extremely concerned, but she confined herself to writing descriptions of their two children that day. "Sally...is not much of a Baby, affects to be thought a Woman...we are about sending her to school, but Mr. Burr is expecting that she will prove a numbhead, but for my part I think her about middling on all accounts .... I have taken her to Meeting and she behaves very well and can give a good account of what Papa does there— She can say some of Doct. Watts verses by heart and the Lord's Prayer...but she is not over apt about the matter. Aaron is a little dirty Noisy Boy very different from Sally almost in everything he begins to talk a little is very Sly and mischievous Has more sprightliness than Sally and most say he is handsomer, but not so good tempered he is very resolute and requires a good Governor to bring him to terms."[29]

Rev. Aaron Burr died of exhaustion on September 24, 1757, at the age of forty-one. He was survived by his young widow, Esther, aged twenty-five; a three-year-old daughter; and a one-year-old son. In his will, Burr directed that his funeral be held at minimal expense and that the money thus saved be given to the poor from his estate. He was buried in the president's lot in the cemetery on the grounds of the university.

His hard work and frugality had resulted in the accumulation of a large and valuable estate, as shown by his account books. Starting with a salary of only £230 a year from his church, he used side businesses—such as translating books from Greek, selling stationery, and providing students with room and board for a fee—to amass an estate estimated to be worth £10,000 sterling by the time of his death. [30]

His father-in-law, Rev. Jonathan Edwards, succeeded him as president of the college. Edwards was inaugurated in February 1758, but he died on March 22 of that same year, after being inoculated for smallpox by Dr. William Shippen of Philadelphia, a friend of the Burr and Edwards families. In death, Edwards followed Burr's example, requesting burial with the least possible cost and ostentation. At his request, he was laid to rest in the president's lot near his friend, Burr.

In 1757, little Aaron, then twenty-one months old, fell seriously ill and nearly died. His mother was alarmed but turned to God for reassurance. She wrote to her father that November, "My little son has been sick with a slow fever ever since my brother left us, and has been brought to the brink of the grave; but I hope in mercy, God is bringing him back again. I was enabled, after a severe struggle with nature, to resign the child with the greatest freedom. God showed me that the children were not my own, but his, and that he had a right to recall what he had lent whenever he thought fit."[31]

The family experienced the bitter taste of death twice again in this same year. On April 17, 1758, just seven months after the death of her husband and two months after the death of her father, twenty-six-year-old Esther Burr also died of smallpox, leaving her children orphaned. After their mother's funeral, Dr. William Shippen, who had also inoculated Esther, took the children to Philadelphia.

The final blow fell when Sarah Edwards, now a widow, traveled to Philadelphia to collect her grandchildren from the Shippens. There she succumbed to dysentery and died on October 2, 1758. Her body was brought back to Princeton, where she was buried next to her husband. Thus did death unite two presidents of the College of New Jersey and their wives within the space of little more than a year.

Before he reached his third birthday, Burr and his four-and-a-half-year-old sister had experienced the deaths of their father, mother, grandmother, and grandfather. Given the amount of personal tragedy in his early life, it was only natural that Burr later found it difficult to form deep emotional bonds with those close to him, for as quickly as loved ones appeared, God seemed to whisk them away.

$\wp\!\!\ll$

The maternal branch of young Theodosia Burr's family tree was filled with men of arms as well as agents of the Lord. Her mother and grandmother each married military men. Theodosia's maternal great-grandfather was Rev. John Bartow, an intrepid Anglican missionary priest. In 1702, Bartow was sent by the Society for the Propagation of the Gospel in Foreign Parts (S.P.G.) to establish the Church of England in that part of the American wilderness known as Westchester County, New York.[32] At the same time, his fellow S.P.G. missionaries were bringing the gospel and the rites of the Church of England to the piney woods and marshlands of South Carolina, the homeland of young Theodosia's future husband, Joseph Alston. Reverend Bartow and his wife, Helena Reid, the daughter of a politically influential family of New Jersey landowners, produced at least one son, Theodosius.

Theodosius Bartow, a lawyer and resident of Shrewsbury, New Jersey, married Ann Stilwell in 1744. She was one of the "six beautiful daughters" of Richard and Mercy (Sands) Stilwell, of Long Island, New York, and Shrewsbury. Ann's writings indicated that she had "a well-rounded education, accomplished most likely with the help of tutors."[33] While she was expecting her first child, her husband was killed on October 5, 1746, in a carriage accident a few weeks before his daughter's birth.

Perhaps sensing the inevitable, Theodosius had requested that his child be named after him. A few weeks after his death, the baby girl who was to become Theodosia Burr's mother was christened Theodosia Bartow. Her name, like her father's, was Greek in origin and means "gift of god," from *Theos* (God) and the verb *dido* (to give).[34]

For five years, Ann Bartow raised Theodosia alone. Then, in 1751, when Theodosia was five years old, Ann married Capt. Philip DeVisme in Trinity Church in Manhattan. DeVisme was a New York merchant and former British army officer. From this second marriage, Ann bore three sons and two more daughters. Philip died in 1762, leaving Ann a widow again, this time with six children. Theodosia's younger half-siblings included Catherine DeVisme, Anne Bartow DeVisme, and three boys. "The ladies were accomplished and intelligent. For a long time their house had been the centre of the most elegant society of the vicinity."[35]

Theodosia grew up on the Bartow family's country estate in Shrewsbury and in New York City. "Her mother gave her the example of a woman who was well educated and taught her the social graces expected in a family of affluence and standing; female strength amidst losses and hardship; and a readiness to seize opportunities when and where they might appear. Her stepfather brought a European cosmopolitanism into the home with his London and French background and connections, and a military heritage, a merchant's acquisitiveness, a frequent use in the family of the French language, and an interest in books and ideas."[36]

When she was seventeen, Theodosia Bartow married twenty-nine-year-old Capt. (later Lt. Col.) James Mark Prevost, who used the anglicized version of his given name, Jacques Marc. The wedding took place on July 28, 1763, in New York's Trinity Church.[37] A native of Geneva, Switzerland, James served as His Britannic Majesty's commander of troops in New Jersey. He and his brother, Gen. Augustine Prevost, with whom he was sometimes confused, were both French Huguenots (Protestants) who had left their native country when the English Parliament authorized the king to grant officers' commissions to foreign Protestants.[38]

Shortly after his wedding, Prevost and his regiment were posted to Charleston, South Carolina, and Theodosia traveled with him. She soon became pregnant, and James arranged for a transfer to New York, where Theodosia stayed with her mother. Both Augustine and James were later posted to a frontier detachment of troops to fight Indians in Ohio during the French and Indian War.

In 1773, James was assigned to King George III's 60th ("Royal American") Regiment of Foot, and was promoted to major in 1775. That same year, he purchased what came to be known as "the Provost Patent in the Ramapo Tract," which included 240 acres in Orange and Bergen Counties in New Jersey, fronting on Ho-Ho-Kus Brook. The tract contained a newly built two-story Georgian style house that would come to be known as The Hermitage.[39]

By the time the American Revolution broke out, the parents-to-be of the future Theodosia Burr Alston were at radically different stages in their lives. Theodosia Bartow Prevost was the twenty-eight-year-old wife of a British soldier stationed in far-off Jamaica. Aaron Burr was an unmarried nineteen-year-old minister's son about to enlist in the Continental Army and serve under one of Gen. George Washington's talented officers, Col. Benedict Arnold.

As complicated as it was, the story of how Theodosia's parents were to meet and marry would pale in comparison to the complex, turbulent, and bizarre life that Aaron Burr would soon bring to his future wife, his daughter, her future husband, and the new nation.

CHAPTER TWO

Reverend Burr's Son

The death of their parents and maternal grandparents within the space of thirteen months was merciful only in that it happened while Aaron and Sally Burr were still toddlers. Nevertheless, these tragic events left young Aaron with emotional scars. Each of those who loved him, cared for him, and nourished him in his earliest years had been snatched away, and he was passed along to someone else. Burr learned the lesson early: no one could be relied upon for very long.

After Sarah Edwards died, she was laid to rest in the same cemetery at Princeton that cradled the remains of her three dearest relatives. Her two orphaned grandchildren remained with Dr. and Mrs. William Shippen in Philadelphia until 1759, when they became the charges of their twenty-one-year-old uncle, Timothy Edwards of Stockbridge, who was "the nearest relative by the mother's side."[1] He obtained formal guardianship of the two children on March 22, 1760.[2] A short time later he moved the family to Elizabeth Town, New Jersey. Young Edwards was a generous and loving family member by any standard, for he now had a wife, the former Rhoda Ogden, and eight children under the age of fifteen living with him.³ However, that did not mean that he was either soft or permissive.

A consummate Puritan, Edwards was uniformly strict with his young flock. Aaron and Sally Burr grew up in an age when elders were revered. Children rose when an adult entered the room. When young people met a clergyman or an older person in the streets, they were expected to stand aside, take off their hats, and bow or curtsey.⁴ Nevertheless, Uncle Timothy quickly learned that he had a precocious, high-spirited little boy on his hands who "had inherited much of the Edwards family's renowned intellect but little of their piety."⁵

In Elizabeth Town, Aaron Burr had two new playmates, Rhoda's brothers, Aaron and Matthias Ogden, both of whom were near Burr's age.⁶ From the anecdotes that survive about his childhood, we learn that Burr was a rambunctious but normal child whose greatest sin was to rebel several times against the rigid rules set by his uncle. At the age of four, he took offense at his tutor and ran away for several days. When he was eight, he sat in a tree and threw cherries at an "ancient maiden lady" whom he thought overly prim and odious. The woman promptly reported Burr to his uncle, who summoned him home, lectured him soundly about the enormity of his offense, subjected him to a lengthy session of prayer designed to induce contrition, and then, as Burr recalled, "licked me like a sack."⁷

Burr saved his most ambitious act of mischief for the year he turned ten, which came at a time in history when running off to sea was an achievable dream for a free-spirited young boy who lived on the Atlantic coast. Burr made his way across the bay to New York, where he finagled the position of cabin boy on an outbound ship. There he actually managed to serve his captain for several days before being tracked down by his eagle-eyed Uncle Timothy.

Seeing the furrowed brow on the face of his uncle as he strode toward the ship, Burr scrambled up into the rigging, a place where his dignified uncle would not follow him. Shouts and demands did nothing to bring him down, and the learned divine was ultimately forced to negotiate with the rebellious cabin boy. The standoff was resolved peaceably. After extracting a promise from his uncle that he would not be punished for his adventure, the little sea monkey climbed down from the masthead and went home to his books.[8] The episode clearly showed that Burr had an early taste for adventure. He would spend the rest of his life demonstrating the magnitude of his obsession with it.

Rev. Aaron Burr's handsome endowment made it possible for Timothy Edwards to secure excellent private tutors for young Aaron and Sally. Aaron proved to be a diligent scholar and studied late into most nights. Pierpont Edwards, the son of Rev. Jonathan and Sarah (Pierpont) Edwards, was six years older than Aaron, and studied with him for a time in Elizabeth Town.[9] Pierpont wrote to a family member, "Aaron Burr is here, is hearty, goes to school, and learns bravely."[10]

By the time Burr was eleven, he believed he had attained sufficient proficiency in his studies—and strength of ambition—that he applied for admission to the College of New Jersey at Princeton. At the time he was described as a "strikingly pretty boy, very fair, with beautiful black eyes and such graceful, engaging ways as rendered him a favorite."[11] Burr had studied Latin and Greek—prerequisites for admission to the freshman class—but he had a short and slender frame. The combination of his youth and small stature undoubtedly played a role in his being denied admission. Although many would later refer to him as "little Burr," they were referring only to his height and body build, not his intellect, energy, perseverance, or ambition.

Making a choice that would reflect a key component of his psychological makeup, Burr viewed the rejection as a personal challenge rather than a defeat. He redoubled his efforts and sought to master the classwork of the first two years of college at home. At the age of thirteen, he sought admission to the college's junior class. The college wisely rejected his cheeky application, as he rightfully should have been sixteen years old to become a junior classman. Nevertheless, more as a favor than

Nassau Hall, Princeton, New Jersey, 1764

a right, the college's president, the Reverend Dr. John Witherspoon, admitted his predecessor's precocious son as a member
of the sophomore class.

The young scholar threw himself into his studies with a
frenzy that would have intimidated or exhausted most students.
When Burr determined that he could not study as well in the
afternoon as in the mornings, he attributed the problem to too
much food. Thereafter, he reduced his diet to a minimum and
studied sixteen to eighteen hours a day. For the rest of his life,
he practiced a regimen of light eating and little sleep. This soon
left the slender boy looking decidedly thin and gaunt—some
thought him ill—but when he took his year-end examinations,
he found himself so far ahead of his classmates that he changed
course and later was described as being "as idle as he had formerly been industrious."[12] The quality of his scholarship never
faded, but he realized that he did not have to work as hard as
he previously thought necessary to achieve his scholastic goals.
This change of priorities permitted Burr to expand his world
past schoolbooks.

Despite his change of heart toward scholarly over-achievement, dissipation through vice was not often an option, as the variety of extracurricular activities available in the small village of Princeton was minimal. Burr played a game of billiards at a local tavern one night, but after winning a small wager, his Calvinistic indoctrination made him feel so degraded and guilty that he resolved never again to play any game for money. His Spartan regimen precluded enjoying much in the way of food or drink at the tavern, and his hormones were kept in check—for the time being, at least—by the college's Puritanical ethic. "It was not till after he had left college that he adopted the opinions which took the reins of passion out of the hands of conscience," wrote one of his early biographers.[13] Nevertheless, he is said to have spent his senior year in the "constant pursuit of pleasure" and may have seduced a local girl, Catherine Bullock, during that time. She died soon thereafter, not of a broken heart, as has been claimed, but of tuberculosis.[14]

Many of the views expressed in Burr's college essays were intimately connected to his future behavior, but not all. Burr, whose philandering later became legendary, wrote a paper on dancing, stating that "Many indeed are so full of idle scruples, and superstitious fancies that they number it among the deadly sins, and think no person can recommend [sic] it, who [has] religion really at heart."[15] In a paper entitled "Style," he argued that in writing, simplicity and conciseness were the hallmarks of quality. "A labored style is a labor even to the hearer," he wrote, "but a simple style, like simple food, preserves the appetite."[16] For the rest of his life, his writing style followed these guidelines.

In an ominously prophetic essay titled "Passion," written when he was a lad of fifteen, he clearly outlined the aspect of his character that would ultimately bring him to ruin. Burr held that "the grand design of the passions is to rouse to action the sluggish powers of the mind.... The passions, if properly regulated, are the gentle gales which keep life from stagnating, but, if let loose, the tempests tear everything before them." He continued, "Do we not frequently behold men of the most sprightly genius, by giving the reins to their passions, lost to society, and reduced to the lowest ebb of misery and despair?" Burr went on to note that: "In such cases, the most charming elocution, the finest fancy, the brightest blaze of genius, and the noblest bursts of thought, call for louder vengeance, and damn them to lasting infamy and shame." He concluded, "Permit me, however unusual, to close with a wish. May none of these unruly passions ever captivate any of my audience."[17] His reasoning was flawless, but his life—and the lives of his friends and family and even the life of the nation—would have been infinitely better had he heeded his own words and regulated his own passions after he reached adulthood.

The one thing Burr did indulge in to excess at Princeton was "multifarious reading." His school papers reflected his wide knowledge of contemporary literature, but he especially loved reading biographies and histories of great military men and their campaigns. He savored books on Prussia's King Frederick II, who came to be known as Frederick the Great, and works about The Seven Years' War (1756-1763), which involved most of Europe and began while Burr was still a toddler. Frederick—the champion of Protestantism—was greatly admired in the young American nation and may well have inspired Burr's visions of a military career. Furthermore, the American Revolution was only six years away when Burr entered college, and rumblings of discontent with King George III and the Mother Country were already making their way through the coffeehouses and church pews of the American colonies.

One of Burr's enjoyments at college was membership in a literary club known as the Cleosophic Society. Its members presided in rotation, and by chance, on the day it was Burr's turn to head the group, one of his least favorite professors stopped by to observe. Burr pulled himself up to his full (though meager) height, ordered the professor to rise, dressed him down for his failure to arrive on time, pointed out the necessity of senior members to set the proper example for his juniors, and then bade him sit. To the complete merriment of the society, the astonished professor did so. Burr's audacity, and the pomp and flourish with which he exercised it, made him a Princeton legend for years.[18]

A great religious revival swept through the college in 1771 and 1772, but the grandson of Rev. Jonathan Edwards and son of Rev. Aaron Burr remained unmoved. Like Princeton's president, Dr. Witherspoon, Burr viewed the hellfire-and-brimstone preaching as emotional frenzy, having little to do with useful religion and a great deal to do with spontaneous fanaticism.

In September 1772, Burr graduated from the College of New Jersey, receiving a Bachelor of Arts degree. Although he did not graduate at the top of his class, he nevertheless was chosen to give a commencement address. He titled it "Building Castles in the Air," a concept that was to be a recurring and cursed theme in his adult life.

Although he had completed all the requirements of his degree, Burr's patrimonial legacy permitted him the luxury of remaining at the college well into the next year to further his studies. He left Princeton in the summer of 1773 for Connecticut. He made leisurely stops along the way to visit the Ogdens in New Jersey and his uncle, Timothy Edwards, in Stockbridge. He then traveled to Litchfield, Connecticut, for a reunion with his sister. Sally, two years Burr's senior, had taken more than a scholarly liking to her tutor, Tapping Reeve.[19] Reeve, nine-and-a-half years older than Sally, married his pretty, adoring young student at Fairfield on June 24, 1773, just after she turned nineteen.[20]

Tapping Reeve

Burr's destination was the little village of Bethlehem, Connecticut, where, following in the theological footsteps of his father and grandfather, he enrolled in the most prestigious theological school in New England, which was run by the Reverend Doctor Joseph Bellamy. The learned divine had studied under Burr's maternal grandfather, Jonathan Edwards. As lackluster as Burr's theological commitments may have been, Bellamy's school was a logical choice—or so it appeared.

Burr, now seventeen years old, enjoyed the minister's library and the lively conversations that ensued there, but the boy who had tried to run away to sea and was enthralled with the exploits of Frederick the Great soon became disenchanted with the prospect of becoming a preacher. The fact that he was smitten with a girl from nearby Litchfield only accelerated his disinterest.[21]

To prevent his pupils from taking any dogma for granted, Bellamy encouraged Socratic dialogue, which was designed to question everything. As an intellectual exercise, where teacher and pupil were already in fundamental agreement on the outcome, it was all great sport. But with Burr, it was a dangerous game, for his faith was by no means solid and his capacity for analytical thought was prodigious. Before long, Burr found himself consumed with a full-blown crisis of faith. Burr was not the only one of his generation wrestling with these fundamental questions—or broaching radical concepts. At Oxford University in England, atheists' clubs had sprung up, and "infidelity" was fashionable. An outbreak of the same ideas occurred at Yale a few years later.

After a few months' residence with Dr. Bellamy, Burr was becoming a full-blown infidel. He wrote his friend and former classmate, Matthias Ogden, that after full and sober reflection, he had concluded, "the road to heaven was open to all alike."[22] With these sentiments, Burr had unequivocally rejected the gospel of redemption by grace as preached by his father and grandfather. Yet he had not jumped headlong into the atheists' camp. What he rejected was the "fear-inspiring, revengeful God" of his hellfire-and-brimstone preaching Puritan grandfather.

As a result, he—like many of the Founding Fathers—seems to have spent his life as a deist, but not an atheist. Nevertheless, he thought the Bible to be one of the most valuable of books, and particularly loved the Psalms of David.[23] In his last days, he was visited regularly by Rev. Dr. P.J. Vanpelt, a Dutch Reformed minister. When asked his views about the Holy Scriptures, Burr is quoted as having responded, "They are the most perfect system of truth the world has ever seen." But in his final hours, when Vanpelt asked if Burr expected to be forgiven by God for his sins and accepted into Heaven, Burr replied, "On that subject I am coy."[24]

Today, most Calvinistic denominations have long since progressed past Edwards' theology, as Burr did in his youth. In retrospect, Burr's concepts were ahead of his times, and he paid a high price for his radical beliefs, which were considered heresy among old-school Calvinists. Many of the local clergy damned him for forsaking the faith of his fathers and considered him an apostate and an infidel.[25] Burr, an intensely private man, did not try to influence others with his beliefs. They were personal, and he avoided discussions and disputes about religion for the rest of his life. He was tactful with those who abhorred his position, and to those who urged him to repent, he "neither resented nor regarded these well-meant endeavors; but waived them aside with good-humored grace, and sometimes even with tenderness."[26]

The College of New Jersey taught its scholars to be clear thinkers. Burr embraced all that his teachers had to offer. Then he took a giant step past his mentors and went on to become a total freethinker; a man of complete amorality. He set himself up as judge and jury of his undertakings, unbound by any rules except those of his own choice or making. In the years that followed, Burr would become involved in a bewildering array of controversial acts, many of which, on the surface, appeared inexplicable, irrational, and often contradictory. Indeed, by conventional standards of thinking, many would seem bizarre. However, viewed from the perspective of a perfectly amoral man, whose ethics were wholly self-defined, each made perfect sense—to Burr, at least.

This "perfect man of the world" found part of his new ethics embodied in the writings of Philip Dormer Stanhope, the fourth earl of Chesterfield, whose mastery of the social arts was the model for social deportment in London and elsewhere for a century after his death in 1773. Stanhope's lifelong mission was to lift his illegitimate son, Philip, "on a pedestal so high that his lowly origin should not betray itself." Stanhope sought to give his son's socially inferior blood a "true blue hue by concentrating upon him all the externals of an aristocratic education."[27] Lord Chesterfield's *Letters to his Son on the Fine Art of Becoming a Man of the World and a Gentleman* were based upon the concept that appearance and social polish could triumph where virtue alone might not.

This pragmatic—if cynical—philosophy found wide acceptance in the upper middle classes in the United States from the late eighteenth to the mid-nineteenth centuries. Theodosia's future husband, Joseph Alston, and all of his brothers were indoctrinated in Lord Chesterfield's code of deportment. Her future niece, Mary Motte Alston Pringle, owned Lord Chesterfield's *Letters* and used his teachings as a handbook for rearing her sons in Charleston during the first half of the nineteenth century.[28] Burr, the ultimate freethinker, adopted many—but not all—of Lord Chesterfield's ideas, although he would choose a totally different set of values as the ideals for his daughter.

Burr spent the summer of 1774 in the home of his sister and brother-in-law, Sally and Tapping Reeve. He was heartened to learn that Reeve was intensely devoted to Sally, as she was plagued with chronic asthma, which rendered her a virtual invalid for most of her married life. During this period, Burr spent much of his time playing the role of country squire, reading, riding horseback, hunting, and flirting with the neighborhood girls. Although he spread his charms far and wide, he did so evenly enough that no two girls could piece together any good case against him. It was a tactic that Burr would put to good use during his later romantic adventures. To his New Jersey crony, Matthias Ogden, he confessed that one of the Litchfield girls had actually made love with him. The result, Burr said, made him "feel foolish enough."[29]

Burr steeled himself against the temptations of the local ladies and decided to learn the practice of law from his brother-in-law, a "large, portly man known for his gentle and dignified manners." Reeve, already an eminent attorney, would later become a justice of the Supreme Court of Connecticut. He would also found the Litchfield Law School, which would soon become famous for its distinguished graduates. Burr was his first formal student.[30] The year 1774 passed along in an agreeable fashion for Burr. He was an affable, happy, hard-working eighteen-year-old, studying his future trade under an acknowledged master. Among his friends, he was known as high-spirited, fond of girls, and a fine horseman. Although younger than most of his colleagues, he was their acknowledged leader, and many predicted his future success.

In the midst of this reverie, serious problems were emerging. The friction between the American colonies and the Mother Country was producing serious confrontations. The British retaliations after the Boston Tea Party in December 1773 included closing the port of Boston, revoking self-government in the Massachusetts Bay Colony, and passing an act authorizing the British to quarter their troops in private homes. New Englanders were angry. Young patriot hotheads talked of rebellion against His Majesty's government. In 1774, delegates from twelve colonies convened the First Continental Congress in Philadelphia, the first display of American unity.[31]

Burr contemplated all the legalities and philosophical principles of the conflict and sided with the Whigs, the party opposed to the Crown and loyalist Tories. Eight months before blood was shed in neighboring Massachusetts, strife broke out near Litchfield. A patriotic mob tore down the house of a suspected Tory, and the sheriff arrested eight of the ringleaders. A band of patriots was poised to rescue its allies, but, to Burr's consternation, the men failed to act.

Burr was ready to jump into the fray.[32] He was still studying law with Tapping Reeve when the electrifying news arrived from Lexington and Concord of the minutemen's battle of April 19, 1775. His sister's health had improved so much that Burr had no further need to stay in Litchfield. At the age of nineteen, the adventurous young man closed his law books and prepared to join the revolution.

༄༅

The army was assembling in Cambridge, Massachusetts, when Burr wrote to his friend, Matthias Ogden, suggesting that Ogden join him in Litchfield. They would then march off together to volunteer for service. Ogden replied that he could not come immediately, so Burr went to see him in New Jersey. While in Elizabeth Town, the young men learned that the Continental Congress had met in Philadelphia and had voted to raise an army. They volunteered in June 1775 and prepared to join the army in Cambridge.[33]

Burr immediately proceeded to Philadelphia and met with William Bradford, a College of New Jersey graduate, and Col. Lewis Morris, a delegate to the congress. Soon thereafter, Burr met its president, John Hancock, who wrote an impressive letter of recommendation to General Washington for Burr and Ogden. Morris wrote another letter, specifically requesting that Washington grant officers' commissions to both young men.

In August 1775, Washington responded that officers were designated and

George Washington

paid by the provincial governments, not himself, and that he had no authority to grant the commissions that the two men sought. Burr, the son and grandson of prominent New England families, who held letters of reference from the highest echelons of the new government, took Washington's reply as a personal affront. This was the first in a series of unfortunate encounters between Burr and the commander-in-chief.

While serving as volunteers in Cambridge, Burr learned that a force of more than a thousand soldiers was preparing to march through Maine and attack the British fort at Québec City. To head the invasion of Canada, General Washington had selected Col. Benedict Arnold. Although Burr was ill, he immediately prepared to join the long and hazardous march. With no officer's commission, he served as an unpaid citizen volunteer.

The expeditionary force was assembled at Newburyport, Massachusetts in September 1775. Burr declined the opportunity to travel to the port by carriage, making the forty-five-mile trip on foot. The reason was simple: Burr wanted to test his physical capacity. He proudly wrote to his sister that he was "equal to the undertaking."[34] From Newburyport, the expeditionary force traveled by ship to the mouth of Maine's Kennebec River. There, they picked up two hundred bateaux (pine canoes) for the trip up the shallow waterway.

Benedict Arnold

Burr's clothing was quite different from that of his halcyon days at Princeton. "He wore a pair of coarse woolen trousers that covered the tops of his boots, and the same material had been used for his short double-breasted jacket. His fringed shirt had been a present from a Southern rifleman. About the hat, he wrote that it must have been 'meant to help my Deficiency in point of size,' for while the headgear itself was small, a large fox tail curled together with a black feather seemed to make him taller. Over his back he carried a blanket, 'as that's a thing I never trust from me," he informed Sally. A tomahawk, gun, and bayonet completed his regalia.[35]

He was also said to have taken one more accoutrement with him on the march: "a nineteen-year-old Indian mistress Jacataqua, from Swan Island on the Kennebec River, known to the men accompanying Burr as 'Golden Thighs.'" Whether Burr did or did not have an Indian lover in tow, armies on both sides of the conflict had camp followers during the Revolutionary War. Walter Blumenthal, author of *Women Camp Followers of the American Revolution*, noted that the 23,489 British soldiers in the New York area had 3,615 women with them.[36]

By the time they were halfway to Québec, many of the patriots were sick from the bad water. The heavy bateaux leaked, spoiling food and ruining gunpowder, and then snow started to fall. Food ran low, and the troops were forced to eat dogs, reptiles, shoe leather, and cartridge boxes.[37] Nevertheless, the expedition reached the outskirts of the city to find good news: American General Richard Montgomery had taken Montréal, and the British commander, General Guy Carleton, had fled to Québec. The bad news was that the 1,100-man American force had dwindled to 600 through sickness, death, and desertion.

In Québec, the British troops were surprised to see Arnold's forces. The Americans attacked but were driven off by British artillery and retreated to wait for reinforcements from Montréal. Matthias Ogden carried a message to Montgomery describing the emaciated condition of Arnold's remaining men and their pitiful lack of usable equipment, powder, and shot. Arnold's troops, too weak to attack and vulnerable to being attacked, waited it out. General Arnold chose Burr to take the next message to Montgomery. Using his knowledge of French and the garb of a priest to travel through the French Canadian countryside, Burr reached Montgomery, who immediately granted Burr a captain's commission and made him an aide-de-camp.

A view of Québec in 1775

Montgomery's reinforcements arrived about the same time that Arnold's troops received a supply of ammunition and clothing. On December 5, 1775, the combined forces of Arnold and Montgomery resumed the siege of Québec. On December 31, shielded from the enemy's view by darkness and a blinding snowstorm, the Americans attacked. Montgomery and his men, including Burr, scaled the walls of the city, only to be met by British cannons firing grapeshot. Montgomery, a huge man, took a ball to the head, and fell into the snow. After trying to rally the retreating American troops, Burr struggled to pull the general's massive body to safety through the ice and snow, but the disparity of their sizes made it impossible to do under heavy fire. That night, by moonlight, Burr returned to the battlefield and retrieved the general's body. Witnesses noted Burr's heroism in the face of almost certain death—a reputation that would withstand even the most controversial events of his later life.

The siege of Québec lasted another five months, during which Burr, the military greenhorn, matured into a respected officer and acknowledged hero. The assault on Québec failed when 900 British troops emerged from the walled city to find only 250 Americans. Arnold and the survivors in his company retreated.

During the siege, Matthias Ogden had received a commission from General Washington but decided he preferred a front-line post rather than a staff position. Ogden offered Burr the commission, and Burr took it, although he was not certain that Washington would accept the trade. When Burr reached Albany on his way home to Litchfield, he heard that Washington had approved his commission, and he immediately headed to New York to take on his new responsibilities.

Eyeing British warships in New York harbor in late June of 1776, Washington set up headquarters at Richmond Hill, a mansion on a hill two miles from the center of the city. When Burr, now a major, arrived, he found the general "unreceptive, stiff, and somewhat humorless."[38] Washington allowed himself no entertainment, and the same applied to his staff, who spent all their waking hours dealing with accounts, commissions, and the routine paperwork of war. Burr, expecting a return to urbane and civilized company, was disappointed. A man of action, he quickly grew unhappy over his new position and was reluctant to stay. A friend arranged for Burr to swap jobs with another officer on the staff of Maj. Gen. Israel Putnam, who lived in the city. The trade was greatly to Burr's liking, as he was then able to enjoy the pleasures of the city and the attention of General Putnam's wife and daughters.

When the Declaration of Independence was signed on July 4, 1776, the battle lines were clearly drawn: the British—the families and direct ancestors of a majority of the American colonists—were now officially the enemy. New York was a Tory stronghold, and many of its residents fled to Canada.

Burr again ran afoul of Washington when the general sent for Burr and another officer. When both arrived, the general, who was writing a letter at his desk, excused himself and left the room. Burr, overcome by curiosity, approached the desk and read the half-finished letter. When Washington abruptly returned, he caught Burr in the act and expressed his displeasure at great length.

Shortly after the letter incident, Washington sent Burr on a reconnaissance mission to Connecticut to scout the status of British troops and ships. Afterward, when Burr arrived in his native state of New Jersey, he was surprised to find that Washington had promoted him to lieutenant colonel. Instead of a polite letter of thanks, Burr wrote Washington a curt note expressing his disgust at having been passed over so many times before, while officers with less talent and experience had been promoted ahead of him. Washington subsequently blocked any further promotions for Burr, earning him Burr's enmity for the rest of both their lives.

Burr's first field command came in 1777, when he inherited the 260 men of Col. William Malcolm's New York regiment, then stationed in The Clove, above Ramapo, in New York. Malcolm, like many other gentlemen, had raised and equipped a battalion of troops to fight for the cause. He assumed the self-appointed title of colonel and then went home to his family, leaving the field command of the unit to a second-in-command. Because of his small stature, "Little Burr," as he was sometimes called, did not immediately impress the colonel, but he soon gained Malcolm's respect by quickly whipping the green recruits into shape and turning them into competent, disciplined soldiers. Twenty-year-old Burr commanded his troops with valor against the British as they foraged in Bergen County, New Jersey, in the fall of 1777—and also met his future wife.

South of The Clove, near Ramapo, lay The Hermitage, the well-known home of Theodosia Bartow Prevost. The land upon which The Hermitage stood had a history of European settlement. The pioneer Europeans to reside on the property were a Dutch family, the Traphagens, who started farming there in the early 1740s. About 1760, Henry and Elizabeth Lane bought the property and built the first stone section of what is now The Hermitage. When Henry Lane died in 1763, his wife sold the property. The buyer was Maj. (later Lt. Col.) Jacques Marcus (James Mark) Prevost. [39] Born in 1736, he was a Swiss native turned British army officer. He married Theodosia Stilwell Bar-tow, aged seventeen, in New York City in 1763. Then in 1767 he bought The Hermitage. His estate totalled 250 acres. Jacques was commissioned a captain in the British army on January 17, 1756 and was wounded in an attack on Fort Ticonderoga in 1758. Later he helped establish a British post at Fort Presque Isle (now Erie, Pennsylvania) and apparently spent time at Fort Niagara. [40]

The Hermitage, in Ho-Ho-Kus, New Jersey

Prevost served in the French and Indian War and was wounded at the Battle of Ticonderoga.[41] At the end of the war in 1765, he returned to New Jersey and was furloughed on half pay.

In the 1770s, the Hermitage was a relatively simple but commodious English-style farmhouse, built from red sandstone, oak, cypress, and chestnut. It was surrounded by trees, fields, orchards, and gristmills. The house was set back from the Hoboken-to-Albany post road (now the Franklin Turnpike) in Hopperstown (now Ho-Ho-Kus), near Paramus, New Jersey.[42] The Prevost family owned several slaves. In 1774, two of them—a man, aged forty, and his wife, aged about thirty-six—ran away, and Prevost offered a £5 reward for their return. The reward advertisement noted that the male slave was a "preacher among the negroes" and that both husband and wife knew how to read and write.[43]

The bustling, close-knit Prevost household included Theodosia's mother, Ann DeVisme. After the death of her first husband, Theodosius Bartow, in 1746, Ann had married Capt. Philip DeVisme, a British officer. When he died in the late 1760s, Ann, again a widow, moved to The Hermitage. The household also included Theodosia Prevost's half-sister, Catherine DeVisme.

In October 1763, Capt. Prevost was sent to Charleston, South Carolina by ship; Theodosia followed by land. She was pregnant by the end of January 1764, and he requested a transfer so that Theodosia could be with her mother when the baby arrived. No sooner did they reach The Hermitage than James was sent to the Pennsylvania frontier, from which his unit marched against the Native Americans. In 1765 he returned to his family. By James Prevost, Theodosia had five children. Of their daughters, Anna Louisa, Mary Louisa, and Sally Prevost, little is known. Their two boys, Augustine Frederick Bartow Prevost (known as Frederick)[44] and John Bartow Prevost (known as Bartow),[45] were described as "rollicking boys."[46] The ladies were accomplished and intelligent. For a long time their house was "the centre of the most elegant society of the vicinity, and after the Revolution had begun, officers of rank in the American army still visited them."[47]

When the war broke out, Major Prevost was living the life of a country gentleman. A staunch Loyalist, he requested to be called back into His Majesty's service at his former rank. He was, and fought as second-in-command to his brother, Gen. Augustine Prevost, in Georgia and South Carolina. Most of Theodosia's male relatives fought for the Crown, including two half-brothers, two uncles, and her two sons, Frederick and Bartow. This angered the New Jersey Whigs. On the Bartow side of her family, most of her Westchester relatives were Whigs, but even there, some were married to Tories. Theodosia's family exemplified the tortured and conflicting loyalties of many an American household during the revolution.

Had rebel zealots strictly enforced the laws of the newly formed state, the Prevost women would have had to move behind the lines of the British army. Indeed, some of the most vigorous Whigs wanted the law rigorously enforced, but the women had powerful allies in the wives of New Jersey's Governor Livingston and his brother-in-law, Lord Stirling. A galaxy of Revolutionary patriots and notables was entertained at The Hermitage, including Gen. George Washington; Washington's aide and later Secretary of War, James McHenry; Gen. William Alexander (who preferred being addressed as Lord Stirling, and whose nineteen-year-old aide-de-camp, Col. James Monroe, was charged with keeping his Lordship's wine glass full); Gen. Charles Lee; William Paterson; Commissary Gen. Jeremiah Wadsworth; Col. Robert Troup; Tench Tilghman; John Laurens; Alexander Hamilton; Col. Aaron Burr; and the Marquis de Lafayette.[48]

The fact that Theodosia Prevost was an American and entertained rebel officers put her and her family in a precarious position with the British, but most of the time the inhabitants of The Hermitage were respected—or at least tolerated—by both sides. Wisely, the ladies of The Hermitage countered the threat of having their property expropriated by behaving with grace, hospitality, tact, and propriety to officers from both sides.

James Monroe, who was in love with a "demanding young lady," at the time, wrote to her about Theodosia Prevost's many virtues. He described Mrs. Prevost as a woman "full of affection, of tenderness, and sensibility, separated from her husband, for a series of time, by the cruelty of war—her uncertainty respecting his health; the pain and anxiety which must naturally arise from it.... I then raised to her view fortitude under distress, cheerfulness, life, and gayety, in the midst of affliction."[49]

From the first moment Burr set eyes on Theodosia Prevost, he was convinced that she would be the love of his life. That she was ten years his senior; had four children, little money, and in frail health; and was already married to a British army officer were, for Burr, the perfect pragmatist, simply hurdles he had to clear in order to reach his objective. During his long and lusty life, Burr flirted with, wooed, and bedded countless women, but the only one he ever loved was, by his own free and frequent admission, Theodosia Bartow Prevost. It was said that she "first made him respect the intellect of women, and to whom he owed the happiest hours and happiest years of existence."[50]

Burr did not dally long in New Jersey. In November 1777, his regiment joined up with the main army near Philadelphia and went into winter quarters during the soul-wrenching encampment known as Valley Forge. There, once again, he served with Washington. At Valley Forge, Washington chose Burr to train and discipline the sentries who would warn of a British attack.

Burr enforced a rigorous discipline and personally inspected the pickets when they least expected him. The militiamen who served as sentinels resented him intensely and planned a mutiny. Burr secretly had the powder cartridges removed from their muskets, and when the mutiny commenced, he was able to end it quickly. In the spring, Burr and his troops fought with valor in the important Battle of Monmouth. Between the heat of the day and having had his horse shot out from under him, Burr was beyond exhaustion. He could hardly walk, and was soon stricken with heat stroke.

In the summer of 1778, the Continental Army rested for several days near Paramus, New Jersey. During the encampment, General Washington and his staff received a note from Theodosia Bartow Prevost, inviting them to visit. The invitation read: "Mrs. Prevost presents her best respects to His Excellency...requests the Honour of his Company as she flatters herself the accommodations will be more Commodious than those to be procured in the Neighborhood. Mrs. Prevost will be particularly happy to make her House Agreeable to His Excellency and Family [Washington's staff]—Hermitage Friday Morning eleven o'clock."[51]

After making a perfunctory visit to another family's home to which they had originally been invited, Washington and his staff quickly rode to The Hermitage. There, one of Washington's young aides wrote, "we talked and walked and laughed away the leisure hours of four days and four nights and would have gallanted and talked with them till now, had not the general given orders for our departure."[52]

Burr was not part of Washington's visit to The Hermitage, for the general had sent him to New York to spy on British activities there. After performing this reconnaissance, he took a short leave of absence in the autumn, spending a few weeks in his old home of Elizabeth Town, where his chief mission was to perform intelligence duties and set up a secret spy network

there and in New York City. He also spent a portion of his
rest and recuperation time at The Hermitage. Burr then applied to General Washington to retire for a time without duty
or pay, but Washington agreed only to a paid leave of absence. Sensing that this might later be held against him, Burr
declined the offer and returned to service.

In January 1779, Burr was appointed to an important duty:
defense of the front lines in Westchester County, New York.
With the British in command of New York City, the nearby
countryside was beset with lawlessness. The Whigs plundered
the Tories, the Tories attacked the Whigs, and flagless marauders
sacked and pillaged the homes of both. This military morass
became Burr's turf, and was known as "the Westchester lines."

After finding that the troops he now commanded were
among the most lawless, he laid down ironclad rules, which he
enforced with all the might of military law. He mapped the
area; made lists of friends, foes, and common criminals; and
organized a civilian intelligence service to communicate directly
with him. When the house of a Tory was sacked soon after he
took command, he had the guilty parties arrested within
twenty-four hours. He made them return the stolen property,
pay damages, and ask the Tory for forgiveness, and then he
gave the men ten lashes apiece. Like magic, plundering ceased
along the Westchester lines. Burr was as concerned with the
welfare of the men in his command as he was strict in their
regulation, and they repaid him with extraordinary service.
Later, when the British threatened to ransack the area, the handsome, young Burr was there to defend it, thereby falling neatly
into the role of protector of the women of The Hermitage. It
was about this time that Burr and Mrs. Prevost developed a
mutual admiration that ripened into love and passion.

In the spring of 1779, Theodosia Prevost's family faced a
serious threat: dispossession of their lands under a 1778 New
Jersey law which called for the confiscation of the property of
Loyalists and others acting against the Whig cause. Theodosia's
husband had been brought back from Jamaica to fight on American soil, and on March 4, 1779, he led his troops to their "final

victory" over the patriots in Georgia. He was quickly named lieutenant governor of the state's new royal government. After a time in that post he was sent to London but had returned to Jamaica by the spring of 1780.[53]

With Theodosia's husband actively fighting the patriots, the pressure to evict her and her family increased. Burr contacted his friend, New Jersey Attorney General William Paterson, asking him to intervene with the Bergen County Commissioners of Forfeited Estates. Paterson agreed to keep Burr informed of their proceedings. Paterson's prominence notwithstanding, the commissioners served notice to Theodosia that procedures were underway by the rebel government to seize all property listed in her husband's name. All of her many influential friends, including Burr, Paterson, and Troup, beseeched the commissioners to desist, citing the exemplary conduct of the Prevost and DeVisme women and their sympathy for the patriots' cause. By the fall of 1780, the confiscation proceedings were evidently dropped, as there is no further mention of them in official records or private correspondence.[54] The trials strengthened the bond between Burr and Mrs. Prevost.

Burr was as clever in the command of his romantic intrigue with her as he was adept in commanding his troops in the field. Despite the rigorous nature of disciplining and training his troops, which consumed a minimum of sixteen hours out of every day, he found ways to make brief visits to her. This was no small feat, as the Hermitage lay fifteen miles away from his post, across the Hudson River, which was "infested with the gun-boats and sloops of the enemy." The frequency of their meetings and the degree of the intimacy that Burr and his married love interest achieved are undocumented, but the relationship raised many eyebrows and gave birth to numerous tales of an illicit romance. One of the most eloquent—but unproved—legends of their alleged trysting was written by Edmund Clarence Stedman and published as "Aaron Burr's Wooing" in *Harper's New Monthly Magazine* in 1887.[55]

Burr's health, which had been deteriorating for the past two years, gave out in the spring of 1779, and he wrote to General

AARON BURR'S WOOING
by Edmund Clarence Stedman

From the commandant's quarters on Westchester Height
The blue hills of Ramapo lie in full sight;
On their slope gleam the gables that shield his heart's queen,
But the redcoats are wary—the Hudson's between.
Through the camp runs a jest, "There's no moon, 'twill be dark,—
'Tis odds little Aaron will go on a spark,"—
And the toast of the troopers is, "Pickets, lie low,
And good luck to the Colonel and the Widow Prevost!"

Eight miles to the river he gallops his steed,
Lays him bound in the barge, bids his escort make speed,
Loose their swords, sit athwart, through the fleet reach yon shore:
Not a word! not a plash of the thick-muffled oar!
Once across, once again in the seat, and away—
Five leagues are soon over when love has the say;
And "Old Put" and his rider a bridle-path know
To the Hermitage Manor of Madame Prevost.

Lightly done! but he halts in the grove's deepest glade,
Ties his horse to a birch, trims his cue, slings his blade,
Wipes the dust and the dew from his smooth handsome face
With the kerchief she broidered and bordered in lace;
Then slips through the box-rows and taps at the hall,
Sees the glint of a wax-light, a hand white and small,
And the door is unbarred by herself all aglow—
Half in smiles, half in tears—Theodosia Prevost.

Alack, for the soldier that's buried and gone!
What's a volley above him, a wreath on his stone,
Compared with sweet life and a wife for one's view
Like this dame ripe and warm in her India fichu?
She chides her bold lover, yet holds him more dear,
For the daring that brings him a night-rider here:
British gallants by day through her door come and go,
But a Yankee's the winner of Theo Prevost.

"Aaron Burr's Wooing"

Where's the widow or maid with a mouth to be kist,
When Burr comes a-wooing, that long would resist?
Lights and wine on the beaufet, the shutters all fast,
And "Old Put" stamps in vain till an hour has flown past—
But an hour, for eight leagues must be covered ere day:
Laughs Aaron, "Let Washington frown as he may,
When he hears of me next in a raid on the foe
He'll forgive this night's tryst with the Widow Prevost!"

Washington, resigning his commission for so long as it took for him to regain his health. Washington accepted with reluctance, noting that he "not only regretted the loss of a good officer, but the cause that made the resignation necessary."[56] It must have been hard for Burr to believe that four years in uniform had passed so swiftly. But as of March 10, 1779, he was again a civilian.

Eight days later, William Paterson penned a letter to Burr, commending him for having chosen such a fine woman as his intended bride. "I am married, Burr, and happy," he wrote. "May you be equally so. I cannot form a higher or a better wish. You know I should rejoice to meet you. Tell Mrs. Prevost that I shall take it unkindly if she does not call upon me whenever she thinks I can be of any service to her…. I congratulate you on your return to civil life, for which (I cannot forbear the thought) we must thank a certain lady not far from Paramus. May I have the occasion soon to thank you both in the course of the next moon for being in my line: I mean the married."[57] How Paterson, who knew Mrs. Prevost, failed to consider that she was still married remains unexplained.

At Westchester, Burr's presence was sorely missed. It was said that "when Burr left the [Westchester] lines a sadness overspread the country, and the most gloomy forebodings were too soon fulfilled."[58] Burr had no immediate plans, but he informed his sister, Sally, that he planned to travel to Boston prior to visiting her in Litchfield. The Boston trip was an attempt to secure the release of Theodosia Prevost's half-brother, Peter DeVisme, who had been captured at sea and imprisoned by the Americans, but Burr was unsuccessful in this mission.

While Burr was visiting a friend in New Haven in July 1779, British troops attacked and burned the town. Burr, still too weak to mount a horse, nevertheless rallied the local militia and Yale College students, who harassed the British troops long enough to enable the residents to flee with their children and valuables.[59] It was his last military act. He was weak and ill and had nearly exhausted the last of his inheritance, having generously spent much of it for the welfare of his troops. Although the adrenaline and excitement of battle had been his forte for four years, The Colonel, as young Burr was pleased to be known for the rest of his life, now sought enough rest to regain his health and enough preparation to make a living. Then, with his health and wealth restored, he would be ready to take on the challenge he truly savored: marriage to the object of his ardent affections, Mrs. Theodosia Bartow Prevost.

CHAPTER THREE

Courtship and Courtrooms

Every tender sensation is awake to thee.
—Theodosia Prevost Burr to Aaron Burr

Frustrated by the illnesses that had forced him off the battlefield in 1779, twenty-three-year-old Aaron Burr threw himself into the study of law and the pursuit of his intended bride. He felt certain that the law would provide him with a good income after the British were defeated and had left American shores. Fully half of the practicing lawyers were Tories and would either flee to England or be shunned if they were not barred from practicing law. In the relative isolation of Connecticut, under the tutelage of Titus Hosmer, a Connecticut delegate to the Continental Congress, Burr concentrated on regaining his health and resuming his legal education in Middletown.[1]

His physical recovery was slow and erratic. Each time that he seemed to make progress, he suffered setbacks. Some suggested that he take a long trip to the South to drain the ice and misery of Valley Forge from his bones. During the summer of 1780, Burr traveled to Ramapo, New Jersey, ostensibly to "take the waters," but his uncle, Thaddeus Burr, suspected that it wasn't the waters but the proximity of Theodosia Prevost in nearby Ho-Ho-Kus that would most benefit him. He wrote his nephew, "I wont Joke you Anymore about a certain lady. I wish however that your health was established, the Country was at an honourable peace, and you will meet with some fine agreeable Companion."[2] Theodosia's friends were very concerned—and the neighbors were soon gossping—that Mrs. Prevost was involved in a scandalous love affair while her husband was apparently alive and stationed in Jamaica.

Theodosia confirmed that her relationship with Burr had become quite close when she penned a letter to Burr's sister, Sally Reeve, in Connecticut that summer. Theodosia was concerned over Sally's health, and wrote, "Though I have not the happiness of a personal acquaintance, as the sister of my inestimable friend, you are justly entitled to my highest regard." She then invited the Reeves to visit the Hermitage, telling Sally that there they would find "a sympathizing friend."[3]

By the end of 1780, Burr had moved into the office of William Paterson, then New Jersey's attorney general. In Raritan, Paterson conducted Burr's training with great precision, but Burr was looking for a quick certification by the bar, believing that he could acquire the fine points of law later. Paterson understood and wished Burr well when he left to study under Thomas Smith. A New York lawyer, Smith had been forced to put his career aside when war broke out, but he was able to preserve his valuable law library. He agreed to turn Burr into a lawyer in six months, and Aaron threw himself into the work with vigor.

Burr moved into Smith's home in Haverstraw, New York, and reverted to the strict discipline that had served him so well at Princeton: small meals and long hours of study. He even rationed his correspondence to Theodosia, who in the spring of 1781, had been forced to move from The Hermitage to Sharon, and then Litchfield, Connecticut, to stay with the Reeves because of the scandal and pressure by the local Whigs. She understood how precious his time was and was aware of the goal he had in mind for the two of them when she wrote of their courtship, "I wish for you to study for your own sake; to ensure yourself respect and independence; to ensure us the comforts of life, when Providence deigns to fit our hearts for the enjoyment."[4]

The correspondence of the two lovers was both intellectual and playful. The Hermitage had an admirable library of French books, which Theodosia made available and which complemented Burr's decidedly republican tastes. In an age when women seldom read, much less studied, books, Theodosia was well-acquainted with history, philosophy, literature, biography "and could discuss the authors and subjects with authority."[5] She was the full equal of her future husband in literary matters and had much better judgment in ethical matters.

On the subjects of personal deportment and family management, Burr championed Voltaire[6] and Lord Chesterfield's *Letters to his Son*. Theodosia was delighted with his interest in Voltaire but was adamantly opposed to many of Lord Chesterfield's crass, artificial, and self-serving philosophies. Burr's appreciation of Voltaire, she believed, showed that he had an independent mind, but Theodosia was not carried away by Burr's sentimentality. "The English," she wrote, "from national jealousy and envy to the French, detract him [Voltaire], but, without being his disciple, we may do justice to his merit, and admire him as a judicious and ingenious author."

She championed Jean Jacques Rousseau's *Emile: Or on Education*. In Rousseau's book, his imaginary pupil, Emile, would "get his lessons from nature and not from men." Rousseau was not concerned with teaching Emile facts but with teaching the child to be able to think for himself. It would seem that *Emile*'s concept should appeal to Burr, but the extent of his disagreement with Theodosia on the subject is hard to judge.

From Litchfield on February 12, 1781, she wrote to Burr, "Your opinion of Voltaire pleases me, as it proves your judgment above being biased by the prejudices of others. I will not say the same of your system of education. Rousseau has completed his work. The indulgence you applaud in Chesterfield is the only part of his writings I think reprehensible.... If Rousseau's ghost can reach this quarter of the globe, he will certainly haunt you for this scheme," she chided him. "When [parents] wish to form a happy, respectable member of society—a firm, pleasing support to their declining life, [Rousseau's] Emilius [sic] shall be the model. A man so formed must be approved by his Creator, and more useful to mankind than ten thousand modern beaux." Although her husband, James, was presumably still alive in Jamaica, Theodosia felt it appropriate to sign her letter, "Affectionately, Theodosia Prevost."[7]

For Burr, his future marriage to Theodosia was a foregone conclusion, and his relationship with her two young sons proved it. As soon as he saw Theodosia warming to him, he embraced Bartow and Frederick as if they were his own natural children. Early in 1781, a year and a half before the wedding, Burr offered an old army friend, Major Alden, the position of tutor in the Prevost household. The position would have provided Alden, whose military pay had never come through, with £60 New York currency a year plus the use of Burr's office and library. "The two boys I wish you to instruct are of the sweetest tempers and the softest hearts," he wrote to his old friend. "A frown is the severest punishment they need. Four hours a day will, I think, be fully sufficient for their instruction."[8] For personal reasons, the major declined, but Burr's offer makes clear the strength of his devotion to Theodosia's family, even at that early stage of the relationship, and his assumption that he and Mrs. Prevost would soon be wed.

Burr's ardent wooing of her, the attention it attracted, and her strong affection for him were reflected in a letter that she penned in May 1781. "Our being the subject of much inquiry, conjecture, and calumny, is no more than we ought to expect," she wrote. "My attention to you was ever pointed enough to attract the observation of those who visited the house. Your esteem more than compensated for the worst they could say. When I am sensible I can make you and myself happy, I will readily join you to suppress their malice. But, till I am confident of *this*, I cannot think of our union. Till then I shall take shelter under the roof of my dear mother [at The Hermitage], where, by joining stock, we shall have sufficient to stem the torrent of adversity."[9]

Matters of health were frequent subjects of their correspondence. On December 5, 1781, Burr wrote to Theodosia, "A sick headache this whole day. I earned it by eating last night a hearty supper of Dutch sausages, and going to bed immediately after.... I took the true Indian cure for the headache. Made a light breakfast of tea, stretched myself on a blanket before the fire, fasted until evening, and then tea again. I thought, through the whole day, that if you could sit by me, and stroke my head with your little hand, it would be well; and that, when we are formally united, far from deeming a return of this disorder *un malheur* [a misfortune], I should esteem it a fortunate apology for a day of luxurious indulgence, which I should not otherwise allow myself or you."[10]

Theodosia's own health was then at a low ebb, at the midpoint of a lifelong decline. She wrote to Burr in 1781, "You speak of my spirits as if they were at my command, or depressed only from perverseness of temper. In these you mistake. Believe me, you cannot wish their return more ardently than I do. I would this moment consent to become a public mendicant [beggar], could I be restored to the same tranquility of mind I enjoyed this time twelvemonth [a year ago]."[11]

Burr's diligent studies under Thomas Smith paid off well and quickly. In October 1781, Burr applied to Richard Morris, Chief Justice of the Supreme Court of New York, asking that the honorable court waive the rule that required lawyers to study for three years before being admitted to the bar. He noted that he had been engaged in the study of law under Tapping Reeve "long before the existence of the present rule...surely no rule would be intended to have such retrospect as to injure one whose only misfortune is having sacrificed his time, his constitution, and his fortune to his country."[12]

The court agreed that Burr's four years of meritorious military service, which had interrupted his law education, and his recent stint of intensive preparation, constituted sufficient grounds to waive the three-year rule. They did not, however, waive the requirement of a rigorous examination, which Burr passed with distinction. On April 17, 1782, he was found "of competent ability and learning to practice as a counselor" and admitted to the New York State bar.[13] At the age of twenty-six, Aaron Burr opened an office in Albany and quickly set out to build what would become a large and profitable practice.

News did not travel quickly in the colonies during the war. Theodosia Prevost evidently never received an official notification of her husband's death, which occurred at the end of 1779. In December 1781, the news was printed in the *Royal Gazette*, a New York Loyalist newspaper.[14] Lt. Col. James Mark Prevost had died of wounds received while fighting the insurgents in the sun-baked, fever-infested British garrison known as Spanish Town, the colonial capital of Jamaica.[15] He had been the favored relative of Lt. Gen. Sir George Prevost, Baronet, who left a large legacy to Theodosia in his will, namely "One hundred pounds in Spanish Mill'd [milled] dollars, at eight shillings each, for the use of her children."[16] Theodosia's two sons, Frederick and Bartow, had enlisted as ensigns in their father's unit in 1780 at the "tender ages of sixteen and fourteen," but somehow avoided both bullets and fevers and "soon returned home to become citizens of the United States."[17]

The stage was now set for the event that both Burr and Theodosia had looked forward to for so long: their marriage. The three-month period between the commencement of his law practice and the day of their wedding in early July was one of furious activity for both of them. Burr was consumed by his work in Albany, but "schoolmaster Burr" was already laying down the strict patterns for the regulation and instruction of his future wife and children. "I am not certain I shall be regularly punctual in writing you in this manner every day when I get at business," he wrote his fiancée, "but I shall, if possible, devote one quarter of an hour a day to you. In return, I demand one half of an hour every day from you; more I forbid; less on special occasions. This half hour is to be *mine*, to be invariably at the same time, and, for that purpose, fixed at an hour least liable to interruption, and as you shall find most convenient. Mine cannot be so regular, as I only indulge myself in it when I am fatigued with business. The children will have each their sheet, and, at the given hour, write, if but a single word Burr, at this half hour is to be a kind of watch-word."[18]

Now the strict educator, five minutes later the doting hus-band-to-be, he recommended that Theodosia buy a Franklin stove to keep her house properly warm. His slave, Carlos, served as the messenger between Albany and Litchfield, Connecticut, where she was still living with Sally and Tapping Reeve.

After Cornwallis surrendered to Washington at Yorktown in October 1781, most of the British troops pulled back to the coast. Theodosia and her family felt sufficiently safe to reoccupy The Hermitage in early 1782.[19] The wedding took place on July 2, 1782, under a marriage license from Gov-ernor William Livingston. The bride was an Anglican, the groom a freethinker. Although the Dutch Reformed Church of nearby Paramus stood ready, Burr and his bride-to-be would not have made that church their first choice, for The Hermitage was both available and more hospitable. What-ever their theological differences, Burr and Theodosia put them aside for the occasion and were united in holy matrimony by the Reverend Benjamin Van Der Linde, most likely in the parlor of The Hermitage.[20] At the same ceremony, the minis-ter married Theodosia's half-sister, Catherine ("Caty") DeVisme, to Dr. Joseph Brown. Several bridesmaids and many friends added to the festive mood and helped celebrate the dual nuptials.

After their wedding, the Burrs left The Hermitage and set sail up the Hudson for their new home in Albany. From the state capital Theodosia wrote an apologetic letter to her sis-ter-in-law, Sally Reeve, noting that some of her trousseau and the refreshments for all of the events had been provided by the Browns.

> You had indeed, my dear Sally, reason to complain of my last scrawl. It was neither what you had a right to expect or what I wished. Caty's journey was not determined

on till we were on board the sloop. Many of our friends had accompanied us and were waiting to see us under sail. It was with difficulty I stole a moment to give my sister a superficial account.... You asked Carlos the particulars of our wedding. They may be related in a few words. It was attended with two singular circumstances. The first is that it cost us nothing. Brown and Catty provided abundantly and we improved the opportunity. The fates led Burr on in his old coat. It was proper my gown should be of suitable gauze. Ribbons, gloves, etc., were favors from Caty. The second circumstance was that the parson's fee took the only half Joe Burr was master of. We partook of the good things as long as they lasted and then set out for Albany where the want of money is our only grievance. You know how far this affects me. Our house is roomy but convenient. I have not been able to procure a good servant, though Burr has taken all imaginable pains, but we have one in prospect, if some evil does not interfere.... The Secret [their relationship] at length is revealed, and the Tongue of Malice dare not I think contaminate it.[21]

So the handsome, dashing, and brilliant Aaron Burr, age twenty-six, heir to an honored name and a hero of the Revolution—a man rising in his profession, with social entrées to the highest levels of New York society—was now married to Theodosia Bartow Prevost, ten years his senior, a widow in poor health with five children and no particularly advantageous political alliances. None of those things were drawbacks, for unlike Hamilton, Burr did not marry for wealth or the political advantage that would have come through an alliance with one of New York's ruling families. He had married for exactly two reasons: love and intellectual companionship.

No portrait of Theodosia is known to have survived, but she is variously described as a handsome or a plain woman. It didn't matter because her greatest charms for Burr were not physical but emotional and mental. Theodosia had what Burr craved in a companion: someone who could appreciate his own brilliance.

Theodosia Prevost Burr was one of the most cultivated women of her time and possessed a razor-sharp mind. A Burr scholar noted that "there is no record that [the elder] Theodosia ...had any extensive schooling, but her knowledge of languages, her analytic abilities, and her habits of reading indicate an education at home that was far above that received by most privileged women in the colonial New York / New Jersey area."[22]

As did Burr, she spoke fluent French, and The Hermitage was filled with books in that language, as well as fine prints and paintings. Her family home had been a center of New Jersey's most sophisticated society, and Theodosia was known as a consummate, graceful, and talented hostess with an "exceptionally luminous intellect." Her passions were grounded in her cultivated mind, making her the perfect companion for a man like Burr, whose mind was his pride and joy.

In the period just after the revolution, an educated woman was a rarity. The wives of the country's foremost men had been chiefly reared to be fertile mothers, nurturing parent-educators, and social ornaments to their husbands—but certainly not intellectual companions. Because few saw any value in educating women, Theodosia was a priceless gem for The Colonel. As a Burr biographer wrote, "The twelve years of his married life were his brightest and his best; and among the last words he ever spoke was a pointed declaration that his wife was the best woman and the finest lady he had ever known."[23]

The post-war law that banned former Tory lawyers from practicing their trade was a boon that young attorneys such as Burr and Alexander Hamilton fully exploited. Burr's practice grew rapidly—as did his pregnant wife's belly. The second exquisite delight in Aaron Burr's life occurred on June 21, 1783, when his first child, Theodosia Bartow Burr, was born in Albany. Both parents were concerned for the first few months because the little girl was sickly. From Albany, Theodosia wrote in distress to her husband, who was probably in New York:

How unfortunate, my dearest Aaron, is our present separation. I never shall have resolution to consent to another.... A few hours after I wrote you by Colonel Lewis, our sweet infant was taken ill, very ill. My mind and spirits have been on the rack from that moment to this. When she sleeps, I watch anxiously; when she wakes, anxious fears accompany every motion. I talked of my love towards her, but I knew it not till put to this unhappy test. I know not whether to give her medicine or withhold it: doubt and terror are the only sensations of which I am sensible. She has slept better last night, and appears more lively this morning, than since her illness. This has induced me to postpone an express to you, which I have had in readiness since yesterday. If this meets you, I need not dwell upon my wish. I will only put an injunction on your riding so fast, or in the heat, or dew. Remember your presence is to support, to console your Theo., perhaps to rejoice with her at the restoration of our much-loved child. Let us encourage this hope; encourage it, at least, till you see me, which I flatter myself will be before this can reach you. Some kind spirit will whisper to my Aaron how much this tender attention is wanted to support his Theo.: how much his love is necessary to give her that fortitude, that resolution, which nature has denied her but through this medium.[24]

Fate was kind. Little Theodosia's health improved quickly, and she turned into a bubbling, healthy little girl. Never had a child a more welcoming and adoring father than little Theodosia. As James Parton wrote, "She had a joyful welcome into the world, the beautiful child who was to have so terrible an exit from it. A father, ever fond, if not ever wise, received to his arms the infant who was to be to him so much more than a daughter, when her indomitable fidelity was all that linked him to the family of man."[25] Another said simply that she was "the soul of her father's soul."[26]

Burr knew that as good as his business was in Albany, the seaport of New York would be many times more fertile as soon as the British left. Long on plans and short on funds—a combination that would plague him for the rest of his life—he tapped the deep pockets of his uncle, Timothy Edwards, for the money he would need to move back down the Hudson.

The family moved from Albany to New York in December 1783, just as the British fleet left the harbor. They rented Mr. Verplank's house at #3 Wall Street, next to city hall, for £200 a year, "the rent to commence when the troops leave the city." Burr felt that he could afford the high rent and rightly so. He was an intelligent, well-prepared and ambitious man who was perfectly poised to acquire a good practice and a handsome income.

New York City had grown to 25,000 inhabitants but was still small enough that when John Adams passed through on his way to attend the first session of Congress, he "walked to every part of the city in one afternoon, and after seeing every thing in it worthy of a stranger's attention, went to the Coffee House and read the newspapers."[27] Burr handled as many or more cases than any other lawyer in the city and netted an annual income exceeding $10,000, a fine sum for the time. Seventy years after his death, a noted legal historian wrote of Burr, "as a lawyer who possessed all the legal weapons of offense and defense, and could use them with skill and daring, his equal has never lived."[28]

Although he was one of New York's most sought-after attorneys, Burr focused as much energy on his domestic life as possible. In 1785, the Burrs moved into a more commodious house on Maiden Lane and later into an elegant house on the corner of Nassau and Cedar Streets that boasted a fine garden and flowing grape arbors, all nestled in the center of the finest part of the city. Given his ancestry and military reputation, Burr could have moved easily within the highest social circles of New York society. However, because of Theodosia's fragile health, he remained somewhat reclusive and entertained and made social visits only on special occasions.

Because Burr was often away from home due to his travels as an attorney, he communicated his wishes and instructions through letters. All family members remained under strict injunction to write to him punctually every day he was gone. When they failed to write, they quickly heard from him. "By return of Mrs. Smith (who is obliging enough to deliver this), I expect much longer letters from our lazy flock," he wrote. "By the next opportunity I determine not to write you, but some others who deserve more attention than I fear they will think I mean to give to them. The girls must give me a history of their time, from rising to night. The boys any thing which interests them, and which, of course, will interest me. Are there any, or very pressing calls at the office? The word is given to mount. I shall have time to seal this and overtake them. Kiss for me those who love me."[29]

In April 1785, Theodosia was seven months pregnant with their second child when she wrote to her husband, "The family [is] as you left it. Thy Theodosia's health and spirits increase daily. Bartow's industry and utility are striking to the family and strangers.... Write when you have leisure; if it does not reach me immediately, it will serve to divert some tedious moment in a future absence; even when you are at home, engrossed by business, I frequently find a singular pleasure in perusing those testimonies of affection.... I take no walks but up one stairs and down the other. The situation of my house will not admit of my seeing many visitors."[30]

Burr was concerned for his wife's health, and reminded her, "Go to bed early, and do not fatigue yourself with running about the house. And upon no account any long walks, of which you are so fond, and for which you are so unfit. Simple diet will suit you best. Restrain all gôut for intemperance till some future time not very distant.... It is already late. I must be up at sunrise. Bon soir, ma chère amie."[31]

Burr reveled in the news that his daughter and stepchildren were being reared as he had dictated. "To hear that they are employed, that no time is absolutely wasted, is the most flattering of any thing that can be told me of them. It ensures their affection, or is the best evidence of it. It ensures, in its consequences, every thing I am ambitious of in them. Endeavour to preserve regularity of hours; it conduces exceedingly to industry."[32]

At the end of May, Burr combined his concern for his wife's health with a request. "Have you done running up and down stairs?" he wrote. "How do you live, sleep, and amuse yourself? I wish, if you had leisure for (or, if you have not, make it), you would read the Abbé Mably's little book on the Constitution of the United States.[33] St. John has it in French, which is much better than a translation. This, you see, will save me the trouble of reading it, and I shall receive it with much more emphasis *par la bouche d'amour* [from my love's own lips]. Adieu."[34]

Now in the last weeks of her pregnancy, Theodosia wrote Burr that she was feeling well and added that little Theodosia, then almost two years old, "waits with inexpressible impatience to welcome the return of her truly beloved. Every domestic joy shall decorate his mansion. When Aaron smiles, shall Theo. frown?"[35]

Indeed, another domestic joy soon appeared to decorate the Burr mansion: their second daughter, Sarah (whom they always referred to as Sally), born June 20, 1785. In the first months, all went well, and Theodosia wrote Burr, "Thy orders shall be attended to. Mamma joins in the warmest assurances of sincere affection. Theodosia and Sally [are] in perfect health."[36] Sally's health took a turn for the worse in the summer of 1786, and Theodosia wrote Burr, "by the advice of the physician, we have changed her food from vegetable to animal.... All good angels attend thee. The children speak their love." The fruit of Burr's rigorous educational program is evident when he heard from his wife that three-year-old Theodosia "has written to you and is anxious lest I should omit sending it. *Toujours la vôtre* [always yours], Theodosia."[37]

Burr was alarmed when Theodosia said no more about Sally's health and provoked over the diet the doctor had recommended. "Why are you so cautiously silent to our little

Sally?" he wrote in August 1786. "You do not say that she is better or worse; from which I conclude she is worse. I am not wholly pleased with your plan of meat diet. It is recommended upon the idea that she had no disorder but a general debility. All the disorders of this season are apt to be attended with fevers, in which case animal diet is unfriendly. I beg you to watch the effects of this whim with great attention. So essential a change will certainly have visible effects. Remember, I do not absolutely condemn, because I do not know the principles, but I am fearful."[38]

Despite the best intentions of their physician and the love of the family, the worst came to pass a short time later. Sally Burr died in October 1788, aged three years, four months.[39] Her mother wrote to the Reeves, "Variegated have been my scenes of anguish, but this exceeds them all—a tender, affectionate friend just opening into life...and flushed with health till the sly viper stole upon her vitals, there preyed unperceived...till too late. All aid proved vain—she passed gently from me to the region of bliss...yes, my Sally, she is...gone."[40]

Two stillbirths also saddened the Burr family. On August 3, 1788, Theodosia wrote to Tapping and Sally Reeve at Litchfield, "My health and spirits were in melancholy unison till the 9th of July [1788], when I had a most unfortunate lying-in, in every particular resembling the one in February [17]87— another lovely, beautiful boy expired seven hours before its birth. Its mother had nearly shared its fate, but Heaven in pity to her helpless family, to her daughter's tears, has deigned to restore her to them. During her illness she received every token of affection anxiety from those she loved."[41] Burr had lost three of his four children: Sally and two stillborn boys. The sole survivor was young Theodosia. She deeply missed her little sister, but her father's rigorous educational routine left her little time for grieving.

Burr fawned over his daughter but took equal delight in his two stepsons, Frederick and Bartow. After they returned from Jamaica and swore allegiance to the United States, Burr took both into his law offices as clerks. When he traveled on legal business, one or the other frequently joined him as his legal assistant. Burr was a generous and thoughtful stepfather to the two young men, and they revered him in return.

In October 1790, Bartow was admitted to the New York bar. He took over much of the work of his stepfather's law office when Burr was later elected to the Senate in 1791.[42] At home in New York City, Theodosia acted as the office manager for all the papers and duties required to carry out her husband's work. The following note to Theodosia was a typical one from Burr: "Tell one of the boys to send me some supreme court seals; about six. I forgot them. Write me what calls are made at the office for me. Distribute my love. Let each of the children write me what they do."[43]

In matters of the heart, the family, and the law office, Theodosia was treated as both a beloved companion and an intelligent adult as well. Even in routine business letters directed to her attention, Burr often showed his affection for his wife. He wrote from Philadelphia one day in 1785, "Unfortunately a gentleman with whom part of our business is has left town. If he should return to-morrow morning, I shall be the happiest of swains [suitors] on Wednesday morning.... I have been to twenty places to find something to please you, but can see nothing that answers my wishes; you will, therefore, I fear, only receive, Your affectionate A. Burr."[44]

Having spent so long waiting for him before their marriage, Theodosia did not welcome her husband's frequent absences and wrote to him almost every day. In April 1785, she penned a letter to him from New York, "I persuade myself this is the last day you spend in Philadelphia. That to-morrow's stage will bring you to Elizabethtown; that Tuesday morning you will breakfast with those who pass the tedious hours regretting your absence, and counting time until you return. Even little Theo. Gives up her place on mamma's lap to tell dear papa—'come home....' It is the last time of my life I submit to your absence, except from necessity to the calls of your profession.... The boys [are] very attentive and industrious; much more so for being alone. Not a loud word spoken by the servants. All, in silent expectation, await the return of their much-loved lord; but *all faintly* when compared to thy Theo."[45]

Reflecting on her health, Theodosia wrote to Burr in May 1785, "I anticipate good or evil as my spirits rise and fall; but I know no medium; my mind cannot reach that stage of indifference. I fancy all my actions directed by you; this tends to spur my industry, and give calm to my leisure. The family [is] as you left it. Bartow never quits the office, and is perfectly obliging. Your dear little daughter seeks you twenty times a day; calls you to your meals, and will not suffer your chair to be filled by any of the family."[46]

A few days later, she wrote, "Your dear little Theodosia can not hear you spoken of without an apparent melancholy; insomuch that her nurse is obliged to exert her invention to divert her, and myself avoid to mention you in her presence. She was one whole day indifferent to every thing but your name. Her attachment is not of a common nature."[47] Little Theodosia's health also wavered, but by the time she passed the toddler stage, she had left most of her childhood colds and fevers behind and had become an active, chubby, rosy-cheeked little girl.

Loving as he was, Burr was also extremely demanding and was quite capable of ignoring the burden of his wife's heavy domestic and business duties and the medical problems that complicated her life. In his letters, he lamented that she was not with him, but in the next sentence, he complained that she was not keeping in close enough communication. In the spring of 1785, he wrote to her from Albany, "I am vexed you were not of my party here—that we did not charter a sloop. I have planned a circuit with you to Long Island, with a number of pleasant &c.s, which are also reserved to a happier moment.... I feel impatient, and almost angry, that I have received no letter from you, though I really do not know of any opportunity by which you could have written; but it seems an endless while to wait till Saturday night before I can hear from you."[48] A few weeks later, he was again the loving, attentive husband. "Nothing in my absence is so flattering to me as your health and cheerfulness," he wrote. "I then contemplate nothing so eagerly as my return; amuse myself with ideas of my own happiness, and dwell on the sweet domestic joys which I fancy prepared for me."[49]

Burr's able legal work soon led to public office, although, in those early days, he evidently was not affiliated with any particular political party. He served two terms in the New York Assembly: 1784-1785 and1798-1799. During the first term, a bill was introduced to abolish slavery in the state of New York. There was no strong sentiment in support of the bill because New York State had, in 1800, the largest number of slaves—20,613—of any northern state.[50] Burr nevertheless allied himself with a small, but influential, group of men, that included John Jay and Alexander Hamilton, who were members of the Society for Promoting the Manumission of Slaves. Burr became their diligent advocate in the New York Assembly. He was so adamant that the state should immediately emancipate its slaves that he opposed even bills that called for gradual abolition.[51]

On the other hand, Burr's personal position on slavery was quite different from his public stance. He was a slave owner himself, and the son and grandson of slave owners. Even though he called for manumission, he continued to buy and sell slaves and managed his slaves like most other slaveholders. His early advocacy of manumission is even stranger in the light of an interview he held in Boston about 1831 with William Lloyd Garrison. Burr urged the prominent abolitionist and publisher of the *Liberator* to forsake the anti-slavery cause and cease publishing the newspaper."[52] These contradictions are explained by a basic characteristic of Burr's nature: he was a man of action, not philosophy; spontaneous but not principled. He often did what he thought best or advantageous at the moment, rather than making his choices based on an underlying philosophy. Therein lies the reason that so many of his actions seem mercurial or contradictory.

Having served out his second term as an assemblyman, he did not seek reelection and returned to private life and lawyering for the next two years. Burr entered the New York political arena again in 1789, joining forces with his future political rival and dueling opponent, Alexander Hamilton, to support the candidacy of Richard Yates for governor. Yates lost the election to the incumbent, George Clinton. Even though Burr had not supported him, Clinton realized Burr's potential and appointed him the state's attorney general in 1789, and he served until 1790.

The position of attorney general was extremely demanding. Burr had to consider and settle hundreds of large and small claims that resulted from the revolution. His work was so carefully crafted that it "met no opposition from any quarter."[53] His wife was overjoyed with the appointment because in 1789, the seat of government was still in New York City, and Burr's official duties seldom required him to travel away from home.[54] From 1790 to 1800, while the capital was under construction, the Congress sat in Philadelphia. Its first session in Washington opened in November 1800.

In 1791, Burr made a bid for the U.S. Senate. The Constitution had declared that the first body of senators would draw lots to see which of them would serve two-, four-, or six-year terms of office. After this first round of staggered terms, all future senators would serve for six years. In New York State, the Federalists controlled the state government and had installed their two choices for the U.S. Senate: Gen. Philip Schuyler and Rufus King. Schuyler had drawn the short term, which expired in 1791.

Prior to the 1791 election, the Federalists had made a gentlemen's agreement that Schuyler would be re-elected and James Duane, a prominent New Yorker who had married into the powerful Livingston family, would be elected as their other senator. However, the agreement faltered due to factional bickering and intra-family power squabbles within the party. Alexander Hamilton, then Secretary of the Treasury and head of the Federalist clan, unwisely stepped in and further muddied the waters. A convoluted series of proposals, private letters, and secret meetings followed. On September 19, 1790, the New York Assembly nominated Burr for Senator to succeed Philip Schuyler. The state senate concurred and he was appointed to serve a six-year term from March 4, 1791 to March 3, 1797.

Alexander Hamilton

"Panic coursed through the Federalist ranks," wrote historian Milton Lomask, "for Hamilton, through his own political ineptitude, had alienated a large part of the Federalist party and elevated Aaron Burr to a position of commanding influence on the national stage." Many of Hamilton's closest allies were aghast, and "his supporters bombarded him with letters black with prophesies of doom. The Secretary himself was stricken. "From this hour on, his own letters would be filled with excoriations of Burr, with those flashes of naked hate that would light the way to Weehawken."[55]

At home, Burr's wife was concerned for his health, which had still not fully recovered from his wartime problems. That summer she wrote, "It is of serious consequence to you to establish your health before you commence [becoming a] politician."[56] On October 24, 1791, when Congress convened in Philadelphia, then capital of the fledgling nation, Burr took his seat. Already an extremely private man, he became even more cautious and guarded in his political correspondence and often wrote in code. In a letter to his wife dated November 14, 1791, he wrote, "To the subject of politics I can at present make no reply. The mode of communication would not permit, did no other reason oppose." A short time later he wrote again, saying, "You will perhaps admire that I cannot leave Congress as well as others. This, if a problem, *can only be solved by a personal interview.*"[57]

The nation's early postmasters were not above opening personal mail for private advantage. As a result, businessmen often used secret codes, then known as ciphers, to keep private information private. The basic method used was a simple substitution code. The number 13 or "X" might stand for yourself, while 14 or "Y" would be your father, and 15 or "Z" the name of your political opponent. Both the writer and the recipient of a coded letter needed the decoding key, which told what number, letter, or symbol stood for what.

To a colleague in 1792, Burr wrote in cipher, "We may make use of both keys or cyphers, and if some of the persons or things are designated by different characters, no inconvenience will arise; if there should, we will correct it. *V* is to be the candidate, as my former letter will have told you. He has the wishes of *9* for his success, for reasons which will be obvious to you. Do you think that *8* would be induced from any motive to vote for him?"[58] The codes were easy to use but difficult to break.

Life in the provisional capital was not all lawmaking and ciphered letters for Burr. He lived in a pleasant boardinghouse

two blocks from the State House in Philadelphia. Two widows owned the house: Mrs. John Payne and her daughter, Mrs. Dorothea (Dolley) Payne Todd. Burr's wit and charm added to the congeniality of the boardinghouse, and he soon became Dolley Todd's close friend and advisor.

He was on good terms with two Virginia republicans: James Monroe and a fellow Princeton graduate, James Madison. Burr decided to play cupid. Dolley wrote excitedly to a friend, "Thou must come to me. Aaron Burr says that the great little Madison has asked to be brought to me this evening."[59] Although Madison was twenty years Dolley's elder, and their temperaments did not seem to be an obvious match (Madison was plain, short, and

Mrs. James (Dorothea "Dolley" Payne Todd) Madison

prim; Dolley was attractive, vivacious, and gregarious), the couple was married on September 15, 1794. To the delight of all parties, the union turned out to be both warm and successful.

Fourteen years later, James Madison was elected the nation's fourth president. His inauguration took place at the start of the darkest period in Burr's life, a time when he would be in dire need of Madison's help. The Madisons had the strongest possible confidence in him, and on May 13, 1794, Dolley Payne Todd, the future Mrs. Madison, named Burr as the person to care for her child in case she should die.[60]

During the six years that Burr served in the U.S. Senate, he was unable to see his family in New York for long periods. The trip from Philadelphia to his home took a minimum of three days and often longer. This prolonged absence from home probably gave free rein to one of Burr's favorite pastimes, flirting with the opposite sex.

For the rest of his life, Burr proclaimed his love for his wife, Theodosia. Nevertheless, his fondness for women was legendary, and his attractiveness to them was equally well known. Despite his short stature, he was dignified and commanding. "His speech sparkled with wit and was clear and melodious, one acquaintance commenting that 'honey trickles from his tongue.' Women were attracted by his interest in them almost as much as for his own charms. As they spoke, he stared with absorption, listening with attention and devo-tion."[61] West Virginia historian Ray Swick captured him perfectly when he wrote that Burr was "catnip to women."[62]

Aaron Burr as a young lawyer

Most of Burr's biographers portray him as a faithful husband to Theodosia, but that portrait may not be wholly accurate. Whether or not he strayed from the marital bed is difficult to determine with precision, because the handsome Burr was so often the target of jealous gossip, scurrilous innuendo, and salacious rumors.

Shortly after his marriage, for example, it was alleged that in the time between his bar examination in Albany (April 1782) and his wedding (July 1782), Burr allegedly slept with Maria Hoes Van Buren, the wife of Abraham Van Buren, a Kinderhook, New York tavern keeper and farmer. On December 5, 1782, a son was born to the Van Burens. They named him Martin, and he grew up to become the eighth president of the United States.[63] This allegation against Burr was never proven.

One alleged extramarital romance while Burr was in Congress was said to have been with Rebecca Smith, "one of the most admired beauties that ever adorned the drawing-rooms of Philadelphia." Sixteen years Burr's junior, his paramour was the daughter of Rev. William Smith, the first provost of the University of Pennsylvania. The romance, which had flowered in Rebecca's youth, rekindled, and she wrote, "my heart has never for an instant been estranged from you."[64] The first phase of the relationship ended with Rebecca's 1792 wedding to Samuel Blodgett, Jr. Then the romance resumed in Philadelphia in 1814, when Blodgett died and Burr, now a widower, became executor of his estate—and a frequent caller at the widow Blodgett's Philadelphia house.[65] These stories notwithstanding, most accounts of Burr during his marriage to Theodosia Prevost suggest that he was a devoted—if not totally faithful—husband. Most of his reputation as a wanton womanizer was earned later, after his wife's death.

No matter what woman Burr was romancing at any given time, the identity of his favorite child was never in question. It was young Theodosia, "Miss Prissy" or "my little Miss Priss," upon whom he lavished unending special attention. Just before Theodosia's second birthday, her mother wrote to Burr,

"Your dear little Theo. grows the most engaging child you ever saw. She frequently talks of, and calls on, her dear papa."[66]

In November 1787, during one of Burr's numerous trips, his wife wrote to him from New York: "What language can express the joy, the gratitude of Theodosia? Stage after stage without a line. Thy usual punctuality gave room for every fear; various conjectures filled every breast. One of our sons was to have departed tomorrow in quest of the best friends and fathers. This morning we waited the stage with impatience. Shrouder went frequently before it arrived; at length returned— *no letter*. We were struck dumb with disappointment. Bartow set out to inquire who were the passengers; in a very few minutes returned exulting,—a packet worth the treasures of the universe. Joy brightened every face; all expressed their past anxieties; their present happiness. To enjoy was the first result. Each made choice of what they could best relish. Porter, sweet wine, and sweet-meats made the most delightful repast that could be shared without thee. The servants were made to feel *their lord was well*, are at this instant toasting his health and bounty; while the boys are obeying thy dear commands, thy Theodosia flies to speak her heartfelt joys:— her Aaron safe, mistress of the heart she adores; can she ask more? Has Heaven more to grant?"[67] This was the warm, loving, and industrious household in which young Theodosia spent her childhood. She was thriving, and her mother told Burr that when he came home, he would find his little girl "rosy cheeked and plump as a partridge."[68]

By 1791, young Theodosia was eight years old, the pet of the household, and she exhibited a degree of fondness for her father that became a hallmark of their relationship. Burr's numerous letters to her were frequently playful and always interesting, and he always demanded in a loving, but direct, way that she pay more attention to her studies. In June of that year, Burr wrote his wife, "It is surprising that you tell me nothing of Theo. I would by no means have her writing and arithmetic neglected. It is the part of her education which is of the most present importance. If Shepherd [her tutor of writing and arithmetic] will not attend her in the house, another must be had; but I had rather pay him double than employ another."[69]

From Frederick Prevost's home in Pelham, Theodosia wrote back that Miss Priss "writes and ciphers [practices arithmetic] from five in the morning to eight, and also the same hours in the evening. This prevents our riding at those hours, except Saturday and Sunday.... I rise at five or six every day. Theo. makes amazing progress at figures. Though Louisa [one of her daughters by her first husband] has worked at them all winter, and appeared quite adept at first, yet Theo. is now before her, and assists her to make her sums. You will really be surprised at her improvement. I think her time so well spent that I shall not wish to return to town sooner than I am obliged. She does not ride on horseback, though Frederick has a very pretty riding horse he keeps for her; but were she to attempt it now, there would be so much jealousy, and so many would wish to take their turn, that it would really be impracticable."[70] Frederick soon became Theodosia's favorite sibling. She loved him intensely and confided in him her deepest feelings for the rest of her life.

The intellectual legacy young Theodosia had inherited from her parents and ancestors quickly became apparent, and she could write clear letters by the time she was five.[71] Her intellectual development and magnificent penmanship, with graceful, curling capital letters (but lack of periods) is evident in the following letter to her half-brother, Frederick, dated October 20, 1792, written when she was nine years old.

I hope the mumps have left you mine left me a week ago, Mrs. Allen is come from Philadelphia and talks no more of going to live there. Papa has been here and is gone again he and the frenchman has had a fray O he keeps in fine order the day before papa away we had your good pig for dinner mama was not very well that day we three dined upstairs and the frenchman below papa sent what he would have for diner he sent word

back again that all the diner should be brought before
him and he would see what he would have so papa
sent down beef and pig he said he did not understand
his dinig below without papa and me, Mr. Capron is in
Philadelphia at the point of death with the putrid fever
and Mr. huet [sic] an english music master had an
elegant fortepiano which papa bought for me it cost
33 Guineas and it is just come home I am tired of affectionate not being it but of writing it so I leave it
out, I am your sister Theodosia B. Burr.[72]

Burr created a progressive educational plan for her: the exact
same course of study that a bright boy her age would have
received. Theodosia was, in Burr's eyes, heir to the fourth generation of the Edwards-Burr intellectual dynasty. It had started
with his grandfather, Rev. Jonathan Edwards; progressed
through Edwards' son-in-law, Rev. Aaron Burr; then through
himself; and now, as he had no male child, through Theodosia
and then on to his grandson. Theodosia was Burr's blank slate,
upon which he was going to write the future of the Edwards-
Burr intellectual legacy in large, bold letters. He intended to
rectify Theodosia's failure in gender through rigorous academic and philosophical training. That was his goal, but it
still lacked a conceptual framework for her education; a
grand, noble vision suited for a female Aaron Burr. The structure he sought soon arrived courtesy of a woman whose revolutionary philosophies about the education of women were a
perfect match with Burr's plans for his daughter's destiny.

Burr found the map to guide his vision in the 1791 publication of a radical feminist book titled *A Vindication of the Rights
of Woman*, by Englishwoman Mary Wollstonecraft.[73] The author, a native of London, worked as a schoolteacher and head-
mistress of a private school. Wollstonecraft became convinced
that her young female charges had "already become enslaved
by their social training in subordination to men." In her previous book, *Thoughts on the Education of Daughters*, written in 1787,
she proposed the then-revolutionary concept that women had

rational natures "no less capable of intellectual achievement than are those of men." Her views on the equality of the sexes were further fueled by several years of observing the tumultuous political and social developments in France, after which she wrote her study, *A History and Moral View of the Origins and Progress of the French Revolution.*[74]

Known to many as one of the first mothers of feminism, Wollstonecraft believed that women had the same intel-

Mary Wollstonecraft

lectual capacity to exercise thought and reason as men and, therefore, should have the right to be educated in the same manner. From that education, she argued, would come the emancipation of women and their enfranchisement as equal citizens of the world. She felt that the right to an education stemmed directly from a woman's role as an educator. Wollstonecraft also wrote that equality in education would lead to a more stable marital relationship because that relationship would be based upon a partnership of equals. She went beyond Rousseau, who believed that only men could be trusted to exercise both thought and reason, be citizens, participate in the political world, direct their families, and lead their countries.

"Wollstonecraft, in her *Vindication*, makes clear her position: only when woman and man are equally free, and woman and man are equally dutiful in exercise of their responsibilities to family and state, can there be true freedom," wrote feminist historian Jone Johnson Lewis. "The essential reform necessary for such equality, Wollstonecraft is convinced, is equal and quality education for woman—an education which recognizes her duty to educate her own children, to be an equal partner with her husband in the family, and which recognizes that woman, like man, is a creature of both thought and feeling: a creature of reason."[75]

Burr came across *A Vindication of the Rights of Woman* by 1793. It had a profound effect on him, embracing and articulating, as it did, all of his convictions about the proper education of the woman of the future, the personification of whom would be his Theodosia. He proclaimed the book "awork of genius." Burr became Wollstonecraft's first prominent male supporter in the United States, and thereby, one of the first high-profile male proponents of female equality in America. Immediately upon finishing the book, Burr set out to shape Theodosia in Wollstonecraft's image. This did not, however, mean that he had adopted Wollstonecraft's model for male behavior—only her model for the education of women.

On February 16, 1793, Burr wrote to his wife about the book and its electrifying concepts. "You have heard me speak of a Miss Wollstonecraft, who has written something on the French Revolution;[76] she has also written a book entitled *Vindication of the rights of Woman*. I had heard it spoken of with a coldness little calculated to excite attention; but as I read with avidity and prepossession every thing written by a lady, I made haste to procure it, and spent the last night, almost the whole of it, in reading it. Be assured that your sex has in her an able advocate. It is, in my opinion, a work of genius. She has successfully adopted the style of Rousseau's Emilius; and her comment on that work, especially what relates to female education, contains more good sense than all the other criticisms upon him which I have seen put together. I promise myself much pleasure in reading it to you. Is it owing to ignorance or prejudice that I have not yet met a single person who had discovered or would allow the merit of this work?"[77]

As much as he embraced Wollstonecraft's concepts about the education of women, Burr's own libertine conduct demonstrated that he did not embrace her beliefs that chastity and sexual fidelity were virtues that both men and women must adhere to or that both must value duty over sexual pleasure.

Nevertheless, Wollstonecraft's influence on Theodosia's life, at least, was profound. Indeed, after encountering her book, Burr became a man with a mission. He wrote, "I hope by [Theodosia] to convince the world what neither sex seems to believe—that women have souls."[78] As a constant reminder for both himself and his daughter, Burr procured a copy of the portrait of the radical feminist author originally painted by John Opie.[79] He valued it so dearly that it was "one of the few possessions to which, in later life, he managed to cling through bankruptcy and poverty"[80] and only on his deathbed did he give it away to his "last and best friend."[81]

Burr's own chief personal deportment role model, Chesterfield, was clear on his perception of women: he had little use for them, save for their sexual services. "Women...are only children of a larger growth," he wrote. "They have an entertaining tattle and sometimes wit; but for solid, reasoning good sense, I never in my life knew one that had it... A man of sense only trifles with them, plays with them, humors and flatters them, as he does with a sprightly, forward child; but he neither consults them about, nor trusts them with, serious matters; though he makes them believe that he does both."[82] After his wife died, Burr followed Chesterfield in his treatment of women.

However, Burr wanted Theodosia to embody Wollstonecraft's philosophies, even though he had little intention of applying them to his own life. His position certainly seemed hypocritical, but he was always pragmatic in his actions. He generally held Chesterfield's opinions on the place of women, but may have supported Wollstonecraft's opposing philosophies when it came to his daughter because his lack of a male heir justified treating Theodosia as a boy.

Theodosia's education was a direct extension of Burr's. His intellectual and philosophical views had progressed from his youthful rebellion against Calvinistic Christianity, whose philosophies he replaced with those of the "pagan philosophers," the Greeks and the Romans. By the time he had finished college, he was a devoted freethinker, but even that was just a way-station on his intellectual and ethical evolution. Burr developed a thorough knowledge of ancient history through his readings of Pliny the Elder, whose *Natural History* explored the relationship between nature and what Pliny considered nature's greatest creation, humankind. Some of his other favorite classics were the *Annals* of Publius Cornelius Tacitus and the works of Suetonius Tranquillus and Titus Livius. He also enjoyed contemporary works, such as Edward Gibbon's *Decline and Fall of the Roman Empire*—which was based on the works of his favorite Roman authors. He read with pleasure the English translation of Miguel de Cervantes' novel, *Don Quixote de la Mancha*, which his wife also read—until she found that her husband had misplaced the third volume.[83]

His service in the American Revolution led to his sympathies for the French, their own revolution, and to the philosophies of The Enlightenment. Pushed on by a polished intellect and a massive ego, Burr progressed from the purely intellectual pleasures of freethinking to a life full of choices and actions based on a philosophy of total amorality. For the rest of his life, Burr blazed his own trail through all ethical, theological, and philosophical forests, living his life and making his decisions based solely on his own needs of the moment. The equanimity with which Burr bore his losses over the years shows the depth of his commitment to his totally pragmatic way of thinking. To have taken credit for his victories but blame others for his misfortunes would indeed have been hypocritical in Burr's eyes. However, as the sole creator of his own destiny, Burr knew that whatever came from his self-chosen actions was his alone to enjoy or suffer from. He did both without comment.

Burr was grooming his little girl for something much greater than childhood or even her approaching adolescence. A master plan for the education of his soul-child was already in the advanced stages of evolution in his mind—a grand vision of womanhood that could only be conceived by someone with Burr's prodigious intellect and ravenous ambition.

The rigorous discipline and educational schedules set by Burr, and enforced in his absence by his wife, might have seemed obsessive or oppressive to some, but Burr was as loving, caring, and attentive as he was demanding. He was a formidable teacher, and his letters abounded in good advice. His discipline and methods created no resentment in his children and drew no reproach from his wife. On the contrary, Theodosia wrote to him, "O! my love, how earnestly I pray that our children may never be driven from your paternal direction. Had you been at home today, you would have felt as fervent in this prayer as your Theo.... I really believe, my dear, few parents can boast of children whose minds are so prone to virtue. I see the reward of our assiduity with inexpressible delight, with a gratitude few experience. My Aaron, they have grateful hearts."[84]

Following her father's rigorous plan, with the help of her wise and intelligent mother, young Theodosia's education progressed rapidly. Her father scoured every city he visited for new books to bring her. From Westchester, New York, he wrote to her in 1792, when she was nine, "I rose up suddenly from the sofa, and rubbing my head—'What book shall I buy for her?' I said to myself. 'She reads so much and so rapidly that it is not easy to find proper and amusing French books for her; and yet I am so flattered with her progress in that language, that I am resolved that she shall, at all events be gratified. Indeed, I owe it to her....' I went into one bookseller's shop after another. I found plenty of fairy tales and such nonsense, fit for the generality of children nine or ten years old. 'These,' said I, 'will never do. Her understanding begins to be above such things;' but I could see nothing that I would offer with pleasure *to an intelligent, well-informed girl of nine years old.* I began to be discouraged. The hour of dining was come. 'But I will search a little longer.' I persevered. At last I found it. I found the very thing I sought. It is contained in two volumes octavo, handsomely bound, and with prints and registers. It is a work of fancy, but replete with instructions and amusement. I must present it with my own hand."[85]

The astonishing degree to which Burr was devoted to Theodosia's education is evident in a letter written to his wife from Philadelphia in 1793, when Miss Priss was ten. Reporting on a recent visit to the homes of two of their friends in Philadelphia, Burr wrote, "I am more and more struck with the native good sense of one of that family, and more and more disgusted with the manner in which it is obscured and perverted: cursed effects of fashionable education! of which both sexes are the advocates, and yours eminently the victims. If I could foresee that Theo. would become a mere fashionable woman, with all that attendant frivolity and vacuity of mind, adorned with whatever grace and allurement, I would earnestly pray God to take her forthwith hence. But I hope by her, to convince the world what neither sex appear to believe—that women have souls!"[86] He laid out his philosophy at greater length—and paid his wife a great compliment—in his letter to Theodosia on February 15, 1793:

> It was a knowledge of your mind which first inspired me with a respect for that of your sex, and with some regret, I confess, that the ideas which you have often heard me express in favor of female intellectual powers are founded on what I have imagined, more than what I have seen, except in you. I have endeavoured to trace the causes of this *rare* display of genius in women, and find them in the errors of education, of prejudice, and of habit. I admit that men are equally, nay more, much more to blame than women. Boys and girls are generally educated much in the same way till they are eight or nine years of age, and it is admitted that girls make at least equal progress with the boys; generally, indeed, they make better. Why, then, has it never been thought worth the attempt to discover, by fair experiment, the particular age at which the male superiority becomes so evident?[87]

In every available moment, Burr poured his attention into young Theo's education, even writing letters to her from the floor of the Senate while a dull speech was being given.

Demanding as he was, he was also free with compliments and encouragement for her good work. Indeed, he went out of his way to make her feel special. He wrote to his young lady from Philadelphia one day, "In looking over a list made yesterday (and now before me), of letters of consequence to be answered immediately, I find the name of T. B. Burr. At the time I made the memorandum I did not advert to the compliment I paid you by putting your name in a list with some of the most eminent persons in the United States. So true is it that your letters are really of consequence to *me*. I now allude to that of the 19th instant, covering a fable and a riddle. If the whole performance was your own, which I am inclined to hope and believe, it indicates an improvement in style, in knowledge of the French, and in your handwriting. I have therefore not only read it several times, but shown it to several persons with pride and pleasure."[88]

Of his daughter, he demanded eternal educational discipline. In 1793, just before Christmas, he wrote to her from Philadelphia, "Every hour of your day is interesting to me. I would give, what would I not give to see or know even your most trifling actions and amusements? This, however, is more than I can ask or expect. But I do expect with impatience your journal. Ten minutes every evening I demand; if you should choose to make it twenty, I shall be the better pleased. You are to note the occurrences of the day as concisely as you can; and, at your pleasure, to add any short reflections or remarks that may arise. On the other leaf [of this letter] I give you a sample of the manner of your journal for one day."[89]

But the shadow of the Earl of Chesterfield clearly loomed over Burr's pen when he wrote to her about how she should appear to others. "There is nothing more certain that you may form what countenance you please. An open, serene, intelligent countenance [such as she displayed for the painter, Stuart], a little brightened by cheerfulness, not wrought into smiles or simpers, will presently become familiar and grow into habit. A year will with certainty accomplish it. Your physiognomy has naturally much of benevolence, and it will not cost you much labor, which you may well spare, to eradicate it. Avoid, forever avoid, a smile or sneer of contempt; never even mimic them. A frown of sullenness or discontent is but one degree less hateful. You seem to require these things [e.g., observations] from me, or I should have thought them unnecessary."[90]

Burr's ambitious educational plan seems to have paid off. At the age of nine and a half, Theodosia's letters looked as if they had been written by a trained calligrapher. By 1793, when she was ten years old, Theodosia had gained a solid command of French and Latin and was studying Terence and translating forty lines of Virgil a day. Two years later, she started learning Greek. Burr wanted her to devote more attention to geography but had concluded that her tutor, Mr. Gurney, was a poor teacher of the subject and that he would be forced to accept slow progress until he could be replaced.

Burr, the product of three generations of teachers and an educational prodigy in his own youth, often sounded like a relentless and demanding taskmaster; a martinet with an insatiable mania for teaching. Theodosia was his advanced experiment in education, his prototype for the ideal woman of the future. Her education followed the pattern laid out by a contemporary French writer, Joseph Joubert, who stated, "Education ought to be tender and severe, not cold and soft."[91] But even given these high goals, few fathers in the post-Revolutionary period included fencing and pistol marksmanship in their daughter's course of studies as Burr did.[92] Burr wasn't educating some rich man's future wife. He had bigger plans.

Burr's relentless emphasis on their daughter's intellectual development and his all-too-frequent absences from home occasionally provoked a reaction from his wife. Theodosia observed that their daughter was overloaded with responsibilities—as was her mother. She wrote on July 2, 1791:

> Theo. never can or will make the progress we would wish her while she has so many avocations. I kept her home a week in hopes Shepherd would consent to attend

her at home, but he absolutely declined it, as his partners thought it derogatory to their dignity. I was therefore obliged to submit, and permit her to go as usual. She begins to cipher. Mr. Chevalier attends regularly, and I take care she never omits learning her French lesson. I believe she makes most progress in this. Mr. St. Aivre[93] never comes; he can get no fiddler, and I am told his furniture &c. have been seized by the sheriff. I don't think the dancing lessons do much good while the weather is warm; they fatigue too soon. I have a dozen and four tickets on hand, which I think will double in value at my return. As to the music, upon the footing it now is she can never make progress, though she sacrifices two thirds of her time to do it. 'Tis a serious check to her other acquirements. She must either have a forte-piano at home, or renounce learning it. For these reasons I am impatient to go in the country. Her education is not on an advantageous footing at present.... The moment we are alone she tries to amuse me with her improvement, which the little jade knows will always command my attention; but these moments are short and seldom. I have so many trifling interruptions, that my head feels as if I had been a twelvemonth at sea. I scarcely know what I speak, and much less what I write. What a provoking thing that I, who never go out, who never dress beyond a decent style at home, should not have a leisure moment to read a newspaper. It is a recreation I have not had since you left home, nor could I get an opportunity by water to send them to you. Albany will be a more favourable situation for every conveyance. But I don't understand why your lordship can't pay your obeisance at home in this four week vacation. I think I am entitled to a reason.[94]

In the hands of a less loving father, young Theodosia could have become a resentful, cranky, belligerent little tyrant; a monstrously spoiled child; or just the opposite: a rigidly molded, finely chiseled educational savant, created in the image of her father and denied her own personality. None of these were her fate. Because Burr's endless expectations were balanced with massive doses of love and approval for her efforts, young Theodosia became a charming child prodigy instead of a rebellious tyke, spoiled brat, or educated robot.

Outside the sphere of her education, she was a normal, impulsive little girl who loved spending countless hours with her best girlfriend, Natalie de Lage; playing with dolls; enjoying social and ballet dancing and ice skating; and acquiring skills in horsemanship.[95] "The moral precocity, which is so much more deadly than mental," wrote a Burr biographer, "she escaped, as it appears she told fibs, begged off from practicing, and was excessively fond of a holiday; which may have kept Horace and Gibbon from destroying her."[96]

While his daughter flourished, Burr's wife declined. Despite her chronic health problems, which were growing worse, Theodosia continued to run the Burr household and supervise the training and education of her children. "Theo. has begun to write several letters," she noted in 1791, "but never finished one. The only time she has to write is also the hour of general leisure, and, when once she is interrupted, there is no making her return to work."[97]

Burr's wife was often vexed at the combination of his frequent absences and his proclivity for taking under his wing—and into his house—the young children of clients who were often "the products of unhappy circumstances."[98] When the soft-hearted Burr was away, the care of these children fell to his overburdened wife. On one particularly exasperating day, Theodosia wrote to Burr, "If I pass thro' a day without being heart-sick with the noise & different little calls from one triffle to another I think myself fortunate."[99]

Burr responded to her descriptions of physical afflictions with his own recommendations. "You seem fatigued and worried," he wrote in July 1791, "your head wild and scarcely able to write, but do not name the cause. Whatever it may have been, I am persuaded that nothing will so speedily and effectually remove such sensations as gentle exercise (or even if it is not gentle) in the open air. The extreme heat of the weather, and the uncommon continuance of it, have, I fear, interrupted your good intentions on this head, especially as you are no friend to riding early. I wish you would alter this part (if it is any part) of your system. Walking early is bad on account of the dew; but riding can, I think, in such weather, be only practised with advantage early in the morning. The freshness of the air, and the sprightliness of all animated nature, are circumstances of no trifling consequence."[100]

He frequently showed his concern. In October 1789, Theodosia had injured her left hand and had received a burn on her face, which left a scar.[101] Burr had evidently scolded her—as he often did—for some trifling thing in a previous letter, for when he wrote after the accident, he said, "When I was complaining and accusing you of neglect, you were suffering the most excruciating pain; but I could not have imagined this unfortunate reverse. Impute my impatience to my anxiety to hear from you…. Frederic [sic] is the laziest dog in the world for not having written me of your situation."[102]

By the end of 1793, Burr's wife, Theodosia, was forty-seven years old, and her health was declining rapidly. Burr frantically consulted his knowledgeable friends, especially the noted Philadelphia physician, Dr. Benjamin Rush, who had recently been proclaimed a medical genius. Rush had achieved amazing cure rates during the Philadelphia yellow fever epidemic of 1793. Burr felt fortunate to be able to see him, but his description of his wife's medical problems and the treatments that had been prescribed by several previous physicians demonstrated forcibly the depth of ignorance that prevailed in the medical community at the time and the ghastly effects of that lack of knowledge. Burr wrote to Rush on August 20, 1793:

Mrs. B[urr] still continues to be weak & low, and to suffer much— But either her disorders, or their symptoms have essentially changed— In five or six months past she has been afflicted with an almost constant choke; which is supposed to be Nephritic [of the liver], & which indeed assumes all the appearances of a nephritic complaint—at Intervals of three of [or] four weeks she has returns of Nausea and Vomiting, which have sometimes lasted six & eight Days & with such Violence as to threaten life—when these abate, the Cholic [abdominal pain], from which she is never wholly free, returns with greater severity— [Dr. Samuel] Bard thinks that these arise out of, and are immediately produced by, the old Complaint— Browne [Dr. Joseph Brown, her brother-in-law] is of opinion that they [are] original & independent disorders, and that the former one has been stationery for some Months past— Their joint and their separate prescriptions have at different times been faithfully followed, but in no Instance with any sensible good effect,—Sometimes indeed, they appear to have provoked the Nausea and at others, to have brought on a most tormenting and obstinate tenesmus [inability to urinate or defecate]— Her diet does not appear to have the smallest influence upon the Cholic— She eats with impunity whatever appetite or whim suggests— fruits, Vegetables, fresh or Salted Meats— Her pulse varies from 90. to 110 a Minute, seldom passing those limits—frequent chills & flushes of heat— Perhaps your inventive Mind may sieze some Idea that you may throw light on her Case.[103]

On December 24, 1793, Burr wrote to his wife, "[Dr. Rush] has this evening called on me, and given me as his advice that you should take hemlock [a poisonous plant]. He says that, in the way it is usually prepared, you should commence with a dose of one tenth of a grain, and increase as you may find you can bear it; that it has the narcotic powers of opium, superadded to other qualities. When the dose is too great, it may be discovered by a vertigo or giddiness; and that he has known it to work wonderful cures. I was the more pleased with his advice, as I had not told him that you had been in the use of this medicine;

the concurrence of his opinion gives me great faith in it. God grant that it may restore your health."[104]

Unfortunately, the extract of hemlock—which Socrates drank to take his own life rather than be executed for corrupting the youth of Athens with his rigorous methods of philosophical inquiry—led instead to Theodosia's death. In January 1794, Dr. Rush suggested that the dosage be increased, and Burr prepared to leave Congress if his wife did not improve. Rush also prescribed doses of laudanum and advised Theodosia to cut back on "animal foods."

Because his wife was too sick to write, Burr asked young Theodosia to report on her mother's health in every letter. He gave serious consideration to resigning his seat in the Senate to care for his wife, but Theodosia refused to let him. Young Theo wrote him on January 1794, "Ma begs you will omit the thoughts of leaving Congress."[105] In his customary stoic fashion, Burr ignored the powerful emotional implications of the statement and, instead, corrected his daughter's grammar. "'Omit' is improperly used here," he responded. "You mean '*abandon, relinquish, renounce,* or *abjure* the thoughts,' etc. Your mamma, Mr. Leslie, or your dictionary (Johnson's folio) will teach you the force of this observation. The last of these words would have been too strong for the occasion."[106]

In the next months, the noted Philadelphia physician, Dr. Benjamin Rush, and other doctors prescribed everything they could think of, including small amounts of milk, port wine, sweet oil, molasses and milk, milk punch, chocolate, bark (quinine, effective against malaria), and the continued use of hemlock. Burr was worried when his physician prescribed mercury. He wrote, "I hope the mercury, if tried, will be used with the most vigilant caution and the most attentive observation of its first effects. I am extremely anxious about the event of such an experiment."[107] Although the dangers of mercury were unknown in his time, Burr's concern was well founded. Mercury is a virulent poison, readily absorbed by the body, which can cause serious and permanent nerve and kidney damage.

While Burr was agonizing over the rapid decline in Theodosia's health, he was also being considered for a position of high honor: U.S. Minister to France. A caucus of Democrats resolved to recommend Col. Burr for the post, and Burr's friends, Madison and Monroe, took the recommendation to President Washington. At the time, Burr was at the height of his esteem in the eyes of the young republic. Washington quickly reviewed the recommendation and refused it, saying he had "made it a rule of life never to recommend or nominate any person for a high and responsible situation in whose integrity he had not confidence."[108] Because of his long-standing aversion to Burr, Washington appointed Monroe instead. Monroe was placed in a delicate position. As Burr's friend, he wished to decline unless Burr formally decided not to accept his party's nomination for the post.

Ultimately, the entire matter was superceded by Theodosia Burr's health. All the best medical treatments of the time were of no avail. For Burr's beloved wife, the end came in their New York home on Sunday, May 18, 1794. Burr, in Philadelphia, learned of it via an express letter the next day. In a letter to his uncle, Pierpont Edwards, dated May 24, Burr described her passing: "You have for two years past heard of the Sufferings of Mrs. Burr during her painful Illness—& Before this you have probably heard of the fatal event of it. It was announced to me at Philadelphia on Monday last (the 19th) that she had died on Sunday—But one hour before the arrival of this express, I recd. the letters by the post dated the Saturday preceding, advising me that she was easier & apparently better than for some weeks before. Indeed so sudden & unexpected was her death that no immediate Danger was apprehended untill the Morning that she was relieved from all earthly Cares."[109] He went on to say, "Though her situation had long been considered as helpless, yet no apprehension was entertained of any immediate danger until a few hours before her death; she then sank calmly and without pain into her last sleep. My little daughter though much afflicted and distressed, bears the stroke with more reason and firmness than could have been expected for her years."[110] The cause of death appears to have been cancer of the stomach. Theodosia Bartow Prevost Burr is believed to be interred in one of Trinity Church's New York burial grounds, but the exact place is still being sought.

Burr had left the heavy emotional burden of nursing her dying mother to young Theodosia, who was not yet eleven years old. No written record of her feelings about her mother's death has survived. Certainly the loss of her mother was both tragic and unfortunate for young Theodosia. She was free from the responsibility of caring for her mother in her father's absence, but she had lost her mother's companionship and the emotional support that her father was seldom around to bestow. Her mother had brought a sense of balance to the entire family.

With his wife's passing, the guiding light was permanently extinguished in Aaron Burr's heart. Many years later, as Burr himself was contemplating his journey to the Great Beyond, some of the last words he spoke were this testimony to the wife of his youth: *"The mother of my Theo was the best woman and finest lady I have ever known."*[111]

Had Theodosia lived to a full, mature age, Burr's later life might have been completely different. However, even though she loved him intensely, Theodosia probably would have been unable to curb Burr's immense appetite for power and intrigue because she was a woman. Even a Burr woman had traditional roles to play and lines she dared not cross. Nevertheless, Theodosia's death was a profound blow that left her husband emotionally crippled for the rest of his life. In future years, Burr sought the consolation, companionship, and beds of countless women, but none could compare to his late wife.

Stoic Burr, unwilling and unable to show any public display of emotion, returned to the Senate and threw himself into his work. Within a short time, he was again lecturing young Theodosia about every detail of her education, but the emotional subject of their shared loss was never mentioned on paper. Burr's emotional world had been shaped by his love for a woman of great intelligence. With his wife gone, Burr focused all of his love on his daughter. With the exception of her mother, Burr never loved any woman as he did his daughter, and Theodosia never loved any man—even her future husband, Joseph Alston—nearly as much as Aaron Burr. The intensity and devotion of their relationship has few parallels and no equal in the history of the nation. Their incredible closeness ultimately gave rise to rumors, but neither father nor daughter evidently knew or cared about them—yet.

To Burr, as the only surviving female in the family, Theodosia's duty was clear. She inherited her mother's mantle and quickly assumed the role of her father's confidante, closest companion in his leisure hours, and mistress of his New York City townhouse on Partition Street and his new and elegant country estate, Richmond Hill, just outside the city.

Now there was no one to check or balance Burr's overwhelming influence. "The little Theodosia was now beginning her education, every step of which was thoughtfully superintended by her father, " wrote James Parton. "From her earliest years, she began to manifest a singular, almost morbid fondness for her father, who, on his part, was resolved that she should be peerless among the ladies of her time."[112] Father and daughter became the center of each other's universe.

For Burr, rearing his little girl and giving her an extraordinary education became a lifelong obsession. But his desire to rear a superior woman-child went far beyond mere education. Burr had envisioned an incredible goal for her and crafted a master plan to achieve it. He would direct her every waking moment to shape Theodosia into something new, radical, and monumental.

As he demonstrated throughout his life, Burr was no petty theorist. He was a passionate, egotistical visionary on scale that made the gods cringe. He wanted to push mortal achievement to its absolute limit. His plan was to turn Theodosia into the nation's shining new model; a protototype for the super-woman of the future. Theodosia was not being reared to assume the mundane role of a smart girl, a dutiful daughter, or a charming rich man's wife. She was being groomed to become a female Aaron Burr, prepared to take her rightful place in the world as a future president, queen, or empress.

CHAPTER FOUR

The Mistress of Richmond Hill

So like a vine the father-love entwined
Her and grew strong...
                              —Alexander T. Ormond

In May 1794, Theodosia, who was a month shy of turning eleven years old, came home from her mother's funeral with a heavy heart and a long list of challenges. She had lost her mother, whose chief companion she had been during the last two years of her slow and agonizingly painful death. The physical distance between Philadelphia and New York had deprived her of her father's company most of that time, and his stoic nature severely limited the amount of emotional support he was capable of giving her. Theodosia's two devoted half-brothers, Frederick and Bartow, no longer lived in the family home. Frederick was married and had a place at Pelham, New York. In 1795, the year after his mother's death, Bartow left for France as secretary to James Monroe, the American ambassador in Paris. The last mention of any of Theodosia's stepsisters occurred in 1791.[1] She no longer had any girls of her own age at home to talk to.

The loss of her mother must have been a dreadful blow for such a little girl. The result was that it brought Theodosia and her father even closer together—and they were already incredibly close. While Theodosia was entering her teenage years in the mid-1790s, Burr was serving out his six-year term in Congress. A year after his wife's death, Burr and his daughter moved into a new house at 30 Partition Street (now part of Fulton Street), in the heart of New York City. Burr wrote to Theodosia on January 5, 1795, "our house in Partition-street is very neatly finished, and pleases me much; so much that I propose to inhabit it upon our return from Philadelphia, at least until the hot weather."[2] At the same time, Burr was preparing their new home at Richmond Hill for occupancy. As one writer noted of the mansion, "few houses in America have sheltered so many prominent men and women, or experienced more vicissitudes of fortune and use."[3]

Burr's expansive country manor stood near the present corner of Varick and Charlton streets, in the heart of downtown New York.[4] It was built on a lofty hill then known by the Dutch settlers as *Zandt Berg*, or Sand Hill, a range of hills which once ran across part of the city. The house was constructed in 1760 for Maj. Abraham Mortier, Commissary (Paymaster General) of the British forces in New York. He surrounded his "noble mansion" with "broad lawns and pleasant walks and gardens" and was known as "a cheerful old gentleman, but the leanest of all human kind. He was almost diaphanous."[5]

Mortier was displaced by the revolution, and Richmond Hill's next visitor of note was George Washington, who arrived in 1776 and made Richmond Hill his headquarters and the home for his wife, Martha.[6] Col. Aaron Burr first saw the mansion on May 20, 1776, when he arrived from Canada and reported to Washington's headquarters there. Washington remained at Richmond Hill until his army retreated to Harlem Heights, where he set up his headquarters in the Roger Morris House—subsequently known as the Jumel Mansion, where Burr was to live in his dotage with his second wife, the rich, notorious widow, Madame Eliza Bowen Jumel. During the British occupation of the city, Richmond Hill was occupied by a succession of general officers, including Lord Dorchester and Sir Guy Carleton, the last commander of British forces in the city.

When peace came, Richmond Hill reassumed its role as a center for New York's high society. In 1789, it became the home of the new nation's first vice president, John Adams. His wife, Abigail, was in love with the mansion. That September, she wrote a glowing description of the property:

> I write to you, my sister, not from the disputed banks of the Potomac, the Susquehanna, or the Delaware, but from the peaceful borders of the Hudson—a situation where the hand of nature has so lavishly displayed her beauties that she has left scarcely anything for her handmaiden, art, to perform. The house in which we reside is situated upon a hill, the avenue to which is interspersed with forest trees, under which a shrubbery rather too luxuriant and wild has taken shelter, owing to its having been deprived by death, some years since, of its original proprietor, who kept it in perfect order. In front of the house the noble Hudson rolls its majestic waves, bearing upon his bosom innumerable small vessels, which are constantly forwarding the rich products of the neighboring soil to the busy hand of a more extensive commerce. Beyond the Hudson rises to our view the fertile country of the Jerseys, covered with a golden harvest, and pouring forth plenty like the cornucopia of Ceres [the goddess of agriculture]. On the right hand, an extensive plain presents us with a view of fields covered with verdure and pastures full of cattle. On the left, the city opens upon us, intercepted only by clumps of trees and some rising ground, which serve to heighten the beauty of the scene, by appearing to conceal a part. In the background is a large flower-garden, enclosed with a hedge, and some very handsome trees. On one side of it is a grove of pines and oaks, fit for contemplation.[7]

When Burr moved into Richmond Hill, his family consisted of himself, his ailing wife, young Theodosia, and his stepsons,

Frederick and Bartow Prevost. On May 1, 1797, Burr assumed the remaining portion of a 99-year lease on the estate, which was part of the glebe lands belonging to New York's Trinity Episcopal Church.[8] The stately two-and-a-half story, wooden-frame mansion was set on brick piers, which raised the entry level a half story off the ground. It measured fifty by sixty feet, featured two and a half stories, ornate exterior moldings, Chinese Chippendale porch railings, and a two-story portico supported by Ionic columns and topped by a pediment featuring a Palladian eyebrow fanlight. The top floor had gabled windows and gave entrance to a rooftop widow's walk, which was surrounded by matching Chinese Chippendale railings.

Inside, the house featured mahogany staircases and rooms full of elegant, expensive furnishings designed to display Burr's social status and surround his family with comfort and splendor.[9] Like his arch-rival, Alexander Hamilton, Burr was a conspicuous consumer. The social dueling with the fineness of their homes—Richmond Hill vs. Hamilton's "The Grange"—led both to financial hardship. Burr's house was filled with inlaid card tables, mahogany chairs, ornate mirrors, and a pianoforte.[10] A tall candelabrum on rollers illuminated the mansion's fine paintings, Wedgwood china, fine silver, and cut glass.[11] One of Richmond Hill's chief features—as might be expected from a man like Burr—was its splendid library. He started to collect books as a boy, and when he reached maturity, he turned to his London bookseller to send him the latest editions of books that suited his wide-ranging tastes.

During Burr's residence, the grounds consisted of 160 acres that extended to the Hudson River and broad savannahs and salt marshes known as Lispenard's Meadows. Through the property and into the Hudson ran a pretty, curving little stream whose Dutch name was Bestaver's Killetje, later Minetta Creek, which Burr dammed to create a pond, which provided a visual delight during the summer and a fine place to skate in the winter.[12] Within months of moving in, Burr promised to send his daughter "a most beautiful assortment of flower-seeds

The Richmond Hill Mansion

and flowering shrubs" to expand the gardens.[13] He was soon busy planting trees and shrubs, hollyhocks, snowballs, tulips, and Jerusalem cherries.

The cream of New York society flocked to the mansion on the hill to mingle with the nation's foremost men and women and enjoy Burr, his Theodosias, and their stunningly elegant dinner parties. Like his colleague, Thomas Jefferson, Burr was a knowledgeable wine fancier and a well-stocked wine cellar. To young Theodosia in 1794, he wrote from Philadelphia, "I despair at getting genuine Tent wine [a Spanish red wine] in this city.[14] There never was a bottle of real unadulterated Tent imported here for sale. Mr. Jefferson, who had some for his own use, has left town. Good Burgundy and Muscat, mixed in equal parts, make a better Tent than can be bought. But by Bartow's return you shall receive what I can get—sooner, if I find a conveyance."[15]

Burr's use of wine at the family table followed the French tradition; children were allowed to drink it. Burr imbibed modestly but never to excess. It wasn't his Calvinism, for he had banished that, or his age, for he was only thirty-eight, that limited his drinking, but his lingering health problems from the war.

"I cannot drink a single glass of wine without serious injury," he wrote, "still less ardent spirits."[16]

In August 1794, when Theodosia was eleven years old and was invited to attend a dinner, her Spartan father gave her the following advice: "Be careful…to eat of but one dish; that a plain roast or boiled: little or no gravy or butter, and *very sparingly* of dessert or fruit: no more than half a glass of wine; and if more of anything to eat or drink is offered, decline it. If they ask a reason—*'Papa thinks it not good for me,'* is the best that can be given."[17]

As quickly as Burr's many clients filled his pockets with money, he filled his house with handsome portraits by the nation's finest artists. As a gift to himself, and as a token of affection for his wife, Burr commissioned an enameler to paint facing twin miniature portraits of himself and her on the face of a pocket watch in 1792. The resulting tiny portraits were cartoonish and bore no resemblance to either Burr or his wife, but they symbolized the depth of his love for the elder Theodosia.[18]

Aaron Burr's pocket watch, c. 1792

One of the first true portraits he commissioned was a life-size, three-quarter-length study of his daughter, painted late in 1794 and dated 1795. The artist was Rhode Island native Gilbert Stuart, one of the most brilliant portraitists this nation has ever produced. Three years earlier, Stuart had painted a sensitive bust portrait of Burr that reflected "more the dreamy look of an artist and poet …rather than the astute look of the lawyer and politician, which Burr was known to be."[19]

Theodosia Burr, about eleven years old

Stuart's portrait of Theodosia was considerably less successful. Much less sophisticated than the painting of her father, it reflects few of the master artist's considerable talents. It can best be described as a simple, pleasant picture of a sweet, tranquil, young girl. Executed with little detail or psychological insight, Stuart captured none of Theodosia's enthusiasm, intelligence, inquisitive nature, or emotional vitality. The plainness and simplicity of its background and unimaginative use of broad-lighting do nothing to compensate the viewer for the uninspired snapshot he presents of a generically pretty, demure, and placid child.

Burr had mixed feelings about the painting. From New York on January 5, 1795, he wrote, "Your picture is really quite like you; still it does not quite please me. It has a pensive, sentimental air; that of a love-sick maid! Stewart [sic] has probably meant to anticipate what you may be at sixteen; but even in that I think he has missed it."[20]

Throughout her life, Theodosia often spoke fondly of Richmond Hill, where she lived from 1795, when she was twelve, until she married in 1801 and departed for South Carolina. The household servants consisted of approximately ten African-American slaves. Burr's ancestors owned slaves as far back as 1735, when his maternal great-grandfather, Rev. Timothy Edwards, of East Windsor, Connecticut, noted that the cost of his Negro slave had been £90 when purchased in 1694, but that, by 1735, the cost of a Negro woman had risen to £200. His notation demonstrates that slaveholding by a New England clergyman was not considered inappropriate.[21]

In addition to unnamed cooks and maids, Burr's staff included Alexis, the doorman, jack-of-all-trades, and *major domo* of the mansion; Harry and Sam, coachmen; Carlos and Caesar, both of whom often served as messengers; Peter Yates, Burr's mulatto valet who often traveled with him; Mat; Anthony; and Tom. Females included Eleonore, a maid; Nancy; and a small girl of about eleven.[22] One favored Burr slave, Peggy Gallatin, showed exceptional writing skills in a series of four letters she wrote to her "honoured master," in which she reported on the state of his household at Richmond Hill while he was away. She also applied for, and was granted, permission to attend "a day-school, kept by an elderly man and his wife, near our house."[23] Although Burr saw to it that his slaves were taught to read and write, he reserved other traditional slaveowners' privileges for himself and his family. He wrote to Theodosia in

1796, "Mat's child shall not be christened until you shall be pleased to indicate the time, place, manner, and name."[24]

Death had robbed Burr of his wife and stole Theodosia's mother, but salvation arrived in 1793 in the form of three aristocratic refugees from the French Revolution. In September 1793, Natalie de Lage de Volude, not yet eleven; her governess, Madame de Senat;[25] and her governess' daughter, sailed from France to New York.[26] Natalie was a child of privilege, born at the palace of Versailles, the godchild of Louis XVI and Marie Antoinette, and a member of the French nobility. The family departed just steps ahead of enraged revolutionaries, who ultimately executed about 2,600 real or suspected royalists in Paris and another 50,000 throughout the countryside. The revolution forced most of France's nobility to flee for their lives. Many emigrated to Holland and England; some came to America because France had strongly supported America in its revolt against the British.

As the French monarchy was crumbling, Natalie's mother, Stephanie d'Amblimont, Marquise de Lage de Volude, a devoted royalist, "ran hither and thither across Europe to give the comfort of her presence to her friends and relatives in distress."[27] During that time, Natalie and her sister, Stephanie, lived with their grandmother in Bordeaux. Natalie was described as "a slender girl with bright blond hair flowing below her shoulders, warm brown eyes, and a radiant face."[28]

When King Louis XVI and Marie Antoinette were arrested and beheaded in 1793, Natalie's parents realized that they must leave France or face certain death. Her father joined a royalist army encampment; her mother was left to determine the fate of

Natalie de Lage de Volude, about 13 years old

the children. The plan evolved quickly: Natalie, the eldest, was evacuated to America in care of a governess, Madame de Senat, to wait there for the arrival of her parents and two sisters. Her father and grandfather considered offers of asylum as officers of the Russian navy.

Life was made more perilous when her mother's best friend, the Princesse de Lamballe, was beheaded at the guillotine and her head was paraded around Paris on a pole. After twice escaping arrest and certain death by only minutes, Natalie's mother obtained a forged passport and fled for America by ship, forced to leave her two girls in France with their grandmother. Natalie's younger sister, Stephanie, lived out her life in France, and the youngest daughter, Calixte, died in Spain at the age of ten. The ship never saw New York. It was captured by the British, then nearly sunk in a storm, and finally limped into a Spanish port in the spring of 1794. Natalie's parents and grandfather eventually reunited in Spain, with the hope that they could somehow find a way to bring Natalie to rejoin them.

And so the little French girl found herself a stranger in a foreign country, deprived of her father, mother, sisters, and grandmother, whom she would probably never see again. Natalie arrived in New York sometime near Christmas 1793, with no family member to guide her life. She, Madame de Senat, and Madame's young daughter were exiles in a new land, scared and very lonely.[29]

Determined to survive, Madame de Senat and her two young charges quickly set down roots in New York's French refugee community. Madame found a teaching position at the Ecole Economique on Anthony Street, but she wanted to open her own school. With her teaching background and ties to the royal court, and her correspondingly high cultural status, she soon opened the de Senat Seminary. Her first pupils consisted chiefly of French émigrés who wanted a French education for their children. This small group of young scholars was soon joined by the children of prominent and influential New York families, including the Livingstons, Hamiltons, Schuylers, and

Bossards, all of whom wanted to give their children a proper European education.

The father of one new student offered Madame de Senat the use of his New York townhouse in Manhattan as both a school and a residence for herself, her daughter, and her young charge. This well-known gentleman, an avowed Francophile and a United States Senator from New York, was Aaron Burr. As proof that he held Madame de Senat in the highest possible esteem, he chose her to be his daughter's teacher. Madame provided Theodosia two things of immense value: a sophisticated French education and a substitute mother who would care for her during Burr's long absences from home. In addition, Natalie's age—she was only nine months older than Theodosia—and intimate connections with the French nobility made her the perfect companion for Burr's daughter. Father and daughter Burr gained much from Natalie's grace, warmth, and beauty.

Natalie, who had been without a father for several years, was immensely grateful for the fatherly affection Burr showered on her. Burr was thoroughly infatuated with the beautiful little French girl and may have been tempted to carry the welcome too far. In November 1795, Burr wrote to his friend, Dr. William Eustis, "At my side, in my library, in the country [Richmond Hill], at the table at which I sit this dark, stormy night, sits reading, but more than half the time laughing & talking, the loveliest creature that I know of her age (now in her 14th)."[30]

Theodosia Burr, about 13 years old

Burr's devotion to his daughter did not stop him from comparing her to Natalie—sometimes unfavorably. "Observe how Natalie replies to the smallest civility which is offered to her,"

Burr wrote to Theodosia. He noted that Natalie's letters were "full of good sense, of acute observation, of levity, of gravity, and affection," whereas a recent letter from his daughter was pronounced to be "pleasant and cheerful. Careless, incorrect, slovenly, illegible. I dare not show a sentence of it even to Eustis. God mend you."[31]

Theodosia showed signs of jealousy when her father started spreading his affection between herself and Natalie, but Burr soon explained away her fears. Theodosia accepted Natalie, and the two soon became best friends. Within the same brief period, Madame de Senat became Theodosia's French teacher; harp, piano, and dancing instructor; role model; and, for all intents and purposes, stepmother. In turn, Natalie was treated exactly as if she were Burr's adopted daughter, and indeed, that is how Burr described her to his friend, Eustis.[32] Nevertheless, the adoption was based purely on sentiment and generosity, and was never formalized.

As the two girls entered their teenage years, they took long walks among Richmond Hill's fragrant gardens and rode along the banks of the Hudson, probably daydreaming and giggling about local boys and talking about Natalie's faraway friends and family. In New York, the two were virtually inseparable as they enjoyed the many parties, dances, and other soirées hosted by New York's social elite.

As he had done a decade before with his wife's two sons, Burr had again shown how quickly and fully he could open his heart to those in need—a concept Lord Chesterfield would never have embraced. According to Dr. Johnson, Chesterfield demonstrated an "insolent lack of kindness, or consideration." Although Burr embraced many of Chesterfield's ideas, he was always his own man and a slave to no one's philosophies. Burr displayed another obvious sign of kindness in 1795, when he invited his friend, Col. Ward, and his family to temporarily move into Richmond Hill to escape a fever epidemic then raging in New York City.[33]

Burr, who was a better businessman on a small scale than large, directed that his business agent, Roger Strong, should always settle Madame de Senat's accounts with him promptly. A perennial teacher, Burr also stressed that Theodosia spend as much time as possible with her Latin tutor, Mr. Martel.[34]

Phase One of Burr's master plan for Theodosia's education had consisted of highly structured, straightforward instruction received at home. Now she had entered Phase Two: intensive instruction in specific subjects by specialized tutors, such as Mr. Martel and Madame de Senat. The third phase would commence upon her marriage to an appropriate man with suitable potential. By the time Theodosia reached the age of twenty-one, The Colonel planned to have created the ultimate woman of the future: nothing less than a female Aaron Burr.

Burr and Madame de Senat shared the use of 30 Partition Street. Burr used it as his office, while Theodosia's mentor used the rest as a school and residence for herself, her daughter, and Natalie. The arrangement pleased Burr, for the school also attracted other children of like-minded families for Theodosia to get to know. Across the street was another school, run by Benjamin Romaine. One of his students, Washington Irving, became friends with Theodosia and Natalie. Irving, who went on to become one of America's first internationally famous writers, was a frequent guest at Richmond Hill, which lay a mile or so from Burr's office and Madame de Senat's school.

The de Senats and Natalie were well ensconced in their new home when Burr wrote to Theodosia, aged eleven, in August 1794, "Your manners are not yet quite sufficiently formed to enable you to do justice to your own character, and the expectations which are formed of you, or to my wishes. Improve, therefore, to the utmost the present opportunity; inquire of every point of behaviour about which you are embarrassed; imitate as much as you can the manners of Madame De Senat, and observe also every thing which Mrs. Penn [Theodosia's original governess][35] says and does. You should direct your own breakfast. Send Cesar every morning for a pint of milk for you; and, to save trouble to Madame De Senat, let her know that you eat at breakfast only bread and butter."[36]

The degree to which Burr embraced all things French was exhibited in a letter he wrote to Theodosia just after Natalie and Madame de Senat moved in. "The account of your time is very satisfactory," Burr wrote in reference to the portion of Theodosia's journal that she had enclosed. "You really get along much better than I expected, which is infinitely to the credit of your good sense, that being your only guide. From the attentions you receive from Mrs. Penn and her family, I judge you have been so fortunate to gain her esteem, and that her prejudices are turned into prepossessions, which I assure you gratified me not a little. Your invitation to the Z.'s was, I confess, a very embarrassing dilemma, and one from which it was not easy to extricate yourself. For the future, take it as your rule to visit only the families which you have known me to visit; and if Madame de Senat should propose to you to visit any other, you may tell her what are my instructions on the subject.... This direction about your visits applies only to the citizens or English families. You may, indeed it is my wish, that you should visit with Madame de Senat all her French acquaintance."[37]

The perennial schoolmaster closed his letter with a typical set of instructions to his eleven-year-old scholar. "Set apart every day half an hour or an hour to write to me, and I must again entreat you to write at least legibly: after great pains, I am wholly unable to decipher some of the hieroglyphics contained in your last [letter]. Four pages in Lucian was a great lesson; and why, my dear Theo., can't this be done a little oftener? You must, by this time, I think, have gone through Lucian. I wish you to begin and go through it again; for it would be shameful to pretend to have read a book of which you could not construe a page. At the second reading you will, I suppose, be able to double your lessons; so that you may go through it in three weeks. You say nothing of writing or learning Greek verbs;—is this practice discontinued? and why?"

In addition to Madame de Senat, Theodosia continued to receive daily instruction from her chief tutor, Mr. Leslie, whose availability was a recurring source of concern to Burr. "I am very sorry to see so many blank days with Mr. Leshlie," he wrote. "If he is not at your room within a quarter of an hour of his time, Cesar should be forthwith sent off express for him. Let Cesar, therefore, call on you every morning at the hour Mr. Leshlie ought to come."[38]

Whatever problems Burr might have occasionally had with Theodosia's handwriting or other educational trifles, it is clear that by the time she was eleven-and-a-half years old, Burr was enormously proud of his young prodigy. In December 1794, he wrote to her, "I obeyed faithfully the command in your letter which bade me read the journal first, and I read it with great eagerness, hoping to find what I did find in the last sentence. That 16th [of December] was really a surprising day. Three hundred and ninety-five lines, all your exercises, and all your music. Go on, my dear girl, and you will become all that I wish."[39] By the time she was twelve, he was prompting Theodosia to read Homer's *Iliad* and *Odyssey*.

Burr was clearly a century ahead of his time in theories about educating women as the equals of men. What troubled observers even more, though, was the total absence of Christianity and the Bible as the foundation for her education. In 1864, Burr biographer James S. Parton wrote, "His system of training, with many excellent points, was radically defective. Its defects are sufficiently indicated when we say that it was pagan, not Christian. Plato, Socrates, Cato, and Cicero, might have pronounced it good and sufficient; St. John, St. Augustine, and all the Christian host would have lamented it as fatally defective."[40] As late as 1900, Burr was still being faulted for the lack of any theological structure in his daughter's intellectual growth plan. In 1908, a female critic wrote, "One thing seems to be lacking to render it symmetrical, lovable, and happy—the religious element. If the Edwards faith and spirituality [the Calvinism that Burr had rejected] had descended to her with the Edwards will and intellect, she would have been, indeed, 'A perfect woman, nobly planned.'"[41] In discussing Burr's relationship with God and religion after the theological torment he went through in his last year at Princeton, Parton and other of his biographers went so far as to label him a total infidel and an active opponent of organized religion. Neither accusation has any basis in fact. What Burr had rejected was solely the barnacle-encrusted doctrines of Calvinistic Puritanism.

Burr never picked any fights with God, and never wrote a word that could be construed as atheistic. In fact, Burr, raised a Protestant, was clearly in favor of the practice of religion by others and was a strong supporter of religious plurality. This is unambiguously evident in a letter he wrote to his daughter while on the legal circuit at Troy, New York, on August 21, 1794. "The business I have undertaken here will, contrary to all expectation, detain me till Saturday night," he lamented. "I hope to be on my return Monday, when you must begin to pray for northerly winds; or, if you have learned, to say mass, that the French Roman Catholics rely on to procure them all earthly and spiritual blessings. By-the-bye, if you have not been to the Roman chapel, I insist that you go next Sunday, if you are not engaged in some other party."[42]

Like his countrymen, Washington and Jefferson, Burr had little enthusiasm for the practice of Christianity, although none of them were atheists. All three were Deists—men who believed in a Divine Being of some sort. Despite Washington's extensive correspondence, he said hardly a word about his practice of religion. Jefferson went further, and actively cut all references to the divinity of Jesus out of his Bible. Burr, on the other hand, was a quiet, non-militant deist.

Not content to guide only Theodosia's intellectual development, Burr also lectured her about her health. "Your habit of stooping and bringing your shoulders forward on your breast not only disfigures you, but is alarming on account of the injury to your health. The continuance of this vile habit will certainly produce a consumption: then farewell papa; farewell pleasure; farewell life! This is no exaggeration; no fiction to excite your apprehensions. But, setting aside this distressing consideration, I am astonished that you have no more pride in your appearance. You will certainly stint your growth and disfigure your person."[43]

To some extent, a competitive relationship developed between Theodosia and Natalie for Burr's affections and approval, and Theodosia sometimes came up short by Burr's standards. When Theodosia was twelve, he wrote to her that she often ignored Madame de Senat's attentions, commenting, "you appeared scarcely sensible that she was speaking to you."[44]

Minor jealousies aside, the two girls studied hard and made great merriment as they developed into teenagers. Far beyond virtually any other girl her age, Theodosia had the opportunity to socialize with some of the most extraordinary men and women of her time. By the time she was sixteen, she was the official mistress of Richmond Hill, responsible for the complete operation of the house in her father's long absences. She was also the official hostess when friends of the family—or heads of state—came to visit.

Theodosia as a teenager

The guest lists were impressive. There were always the leading political lights: Revolutionary War heroes, founders of the nation, and distinguished statesmen, including President George Washington, Vice President John Adams, Thomas Jefferson, James Madison, Alexander Hamilton, and Mayor Edward Livingston.

In addition, the constant flow of distinguished Frenchmen and women were a special delight to Natalie, who accepted their kind offers to relay messages and letters back to her mother, sisters, and grandmother. One such gentleman was Charles Maurice de Talleyrand-Périgord, Prince de Bénévent, a "first-rate genius" and consummate political manipulator. A former bishop under the monarchy, he turned Republican and was sent to London by the French National Assembly to seek Britain's neutrality during the French Revolution. However, his mission failed due to events at home. When the French monarchy fell, he sought refuge first in England and then in America. He shared with his host, Burr, fine manners and a talent for conducting engaging discourse and seducing women. The revolution having succeeded, he returned to Paris in 1796.

A theological fellow traveler of Burr's was Constantin François de Chassebœuf, Count de Volney, a French historian whose expertise was gained through travels in Egypt and Syria. He opposed the Reign of Terror and was imprisoned. When liberated, he visited the United States as a senator under Napoléon, who made him a count. His best-known book was *The Ruins, or, Meditations on the Revolutions of Empires* (1791), an influential work that popularized religious skepticism on both sides of the Atlantic.

Louis Philippe, who succeeded Louis XVIII as King of France, was known as the "Citizen King," because he was elected king by the citizens of Paris. He came to the United States with two younger brothers in 1796 and returned in 1800. He reigned from 1830 to 1848.

Jérôme Bonaparte, the brother of Emperor Napoléon Bonaparte, was nineteen when he arrived in America. Here he met, fell in love with, and married Elizabeth Patterson of Baltimore. They sailed for Lisbon, but she was not allowed to land. Napoléon opposed the marriage, annulled it, and gave her a pension. In order to become a king, Jérôme married a daughter of the King of Würtemburg. After he assumed the throne, he invited his semi-ex-wife to come to Westphalia, where he offered her a home and a pension of two hundred thousand francs a year. She is said to have stated that "Westphalia was not large enough for two queens, and as she had already accepted

Napoléon's annuity, she preferred 'being under the wing of an eagle, than to being suspended from the bill of a goose.'"[45]

As exotic as were Theodosia's European guests, none could top William Brant Thayendanegea, a Native American of the Mohawk tribe and leader of the Iroquois confederation known as the Six Nations. Brant, who was educated in Connecticut, was a Christian, and he translated portions of the Bible into his native language. His sister was married to a baronet, Sir William Johnson of Johnson Hall, and Brant's son-in-law was frontier magnate George Croghan.[46]

Although Brant's component of the Six Nations had remained loyal to the crown and fought against the Americans, Brant—like Burr—was no friend of the English, who wanted control of Upper Canada (now Ontario), which was a hotly contested territory in the late 1790s. In response to advertisements placed in U.S. newspapers by the governor of Upper Canada, thousands of American speculators purchased large tracts of land there. Burr himself had had borrowed a huge sum—$23,000—from a wide range of friends to invest in the Canadian lands.[47] In 1797, Robert Liston, the British envoy to the United States, wrote to William Wyndham, Lord Grenville, that men who were hostile to England's control of the region were plotting to purchase much of Upper Canada. Burr was one of two named conspirators.

Joseph Brant Thayendanegea, about 1776

Burr had developed a strong friendship and rapport with Chief Brant while serving as a U.S. Senator, and had invited the chief to Philadelphia. There, Burr assembled a collection of distinguished foreign guests, including the minister of the French Republic, Count de Volney; Charles de Talleyrand-Périgord; and other expatriates. The result, according to Burr, was an evening where Brant "contributed his full share to the conversation, exhibiting at all times sterling good sense, and enlivening the hours with sallies of pleasantry and wit which 'set the table in a roar.' The result was not only an agreeable, but highly intellectual entertainment."[48]

But Burr was not a man to settle for idle chatter. He always had big pots to stir. The intellectual entertainment he mentioned centered around the Count de Volney's planned invasion of Upper Canada, which would presumably be supported by (and benefit) all the recent land investors—such as Burr.[49] "Brant's Mohawk Indians were, at the time, ripe for French overtures," a historian wrote, for although they had remained loyal to the Crown during the revolution, Canadian land granted to them by the British did not come with clear title, thus frustrating Brant's plan to sell land to white settlers.[50]

When the chief left Philadelphia for New York, Burr gave him the following letter of introduction to take to Theodosia, then only thirteen-and-a-half years old: "This will be handed to you by Colonel Brant, the celebrated Indian Chief. I am sure that you and Natalie will be happy in the opportunity of seeing a man so much renowned. He is a man of education—speaks and writes English perfectly—and has seen much of Europe and America. Receive him with respect and hospitality. He is not one of those Indians who drink rum, but is quite a gentleman; not one who will make you fine bows, but one who understands and practices what belongs to propriety and good breeding. He has daughters—if you could think of some little present to send to one of them—a pair of ear-rings, for example—it would please him. You may talk to him very freely, and offer to introduce him to your friend, Mr. [Thomas L.] Witbeck, at Albany."[51]

Theodosia, with Natalie's help, rose to the occasion in exactly the manner her father would have expected. She hosted the chief at a formal dinner party in the spring of 1797, to which she invited fourteen of the most eminent men of the city, including New York's Bishop Benjamin Moore, Dr. Samuel Bard, and Dr. David Hosack.[52] Bard had been one of Theodosia Bartow Prevost Burr's physicians during her final months, and, seven years later, Hosack would attend Alexander Hamilton as he lay dying from Burr's bullet.

Brant's biographer, Col. William Leete Stone, wrote, "Miss Theodosia received the forest chief with all the courtesy and hospitality suggested, and performed the honors of her father's house in a manner that must have been as gratifying to her absent parent as it was credible to herself."[53] Stone went on to say that in writing Burr of the event, Theodosia "gave a long and sprightly account of the entertainment. She said that, in making the preliminary arrangements she had been somewhat at a loss in the selection of such dishes as would probably suit the palate of her principal guest. Being a savage warrior, and in view of the many tales she had heard, of

> The Cannibals that each other eat,
> The anthroppphagi, and men whose heads
> Do grow beneath their shoulders—

"She added, sportively, that she had a mind to lay the hospital under contribution for a human head, to be served up like a boar's head in ancient hall barbaric. But, after all she found him a most christian and civilized guest in his manners."[54] Brant was so delighted with his treatment that he extended an invitation to Theodosia to visit him and his family in Canada, an offer that she and her future husband later accepted.

Col. Burr's senatorial term of office expired in 1797. To his surprise, the very man he had previously defeated, Gen. Phillip Schuyler, soundly trounced his re-election bid. He took the loss in stride, returned to his lucrative law practice, and was soon appointed to the New York Assembly. For Burr, who found the everyday practice of law a tedious pastime and gross underuse of his talents, it was simply a time to take stock, make plans, and survey the national political landscape for new opportunities. They were not long in appearing.

While Burr was in the assembly, Theodosia was nearing her sixteenth birthday. The charming and talented daughter of the wealthy New York lawyer did not lack for admirers or suitors. When Edward Livingston, then the mayor of New York, escorted Theodosia aboard a French warship visiting the city, he warned her, "You must bring none of your sparks on board, Theodosia. We have a [gunpowder] magazine here, and we shall all be blown up."[55]

In 1798, John Davis, an Englishman visiting New York, wrote, "Mr. Burr introduced me to his daughter [then fifteen], whom he has educated with uncommon care; for she is elegant without ostentation, and learned without pedantry. At the time she dances with more grace than any young lady of New York. Miss Theodosia speaks French and Italian with facility, is perfectly conversant with the writers of the Augustan age, and not unacquainted with the language of the Father of Poetry." Davis then went on to add, "Martel, a Frenchman, has dedicated a volume of his productions to Miss Burr, with the horatian epithet of '*dulce decus.*'"[56]

Harman Blennerhassett, Jr. wrote of Theodosia, "Her person was small, while to its enchanting symmetry and expression of countenance illuminated by vast reading and general knowledge, her imposing mien and flashing wit made her the ruling spirit to every circle."[57]

Not everyone was as impressed with Theodosia's diverse accomplishments as was young Blennerhassett. In 1801, the year of Theodosia's marriage, Burr's close friend, Robert Troup, wrote disapprovingly to a friend that while Theodosia appeared "handsome round faced and black eyed... Her acquaintance say her reading has been wholly masculine, that she is an utter stranger to the use of the needle, and quite unskilled in the different branches of domestic economy."[58] Burr would have been proud. Theodosia's masterful blend of the feminine graces with his own intellectual capacity and unconventionality shocked and amazed all of their contemporaries, male and female alike.

One of her oddest potential marriage candidates—though evidently not so odd in young Theodosia's eyes—was none other than Burr's old Revolutionary War friend, Dr. William Eustis, of Cambridge, Massachusetts. Three years older than her own father, Eustis was, at least temporarily, a fantasy figure in Theodosia's life. Sometime during her teenage years, she wrote to him, "Your visit appears to me like a dream, and Every Night I wish to dream it over again, for according to modern superstitions after three times it would be verified; It is, however, I believe, better for me, that you should be absent, for in one day your pretty flatteries almost turned my head; it is only since your departure that I have recollected the folly of putting faith in anything uttered by a gentleman, even by Dr. Eustis in these matters. But great as the danger is and conscious as I am of it, in the true spirit of my sex, it is one which I sincerely wish to risk whenever you choose. Goodbye, we shall leave Providence tomorrow."[59]

Eustis had served in Congress together as an Anti-Federalist, and the two men often discussed their relationships with women. Burr often mentioned Theodosia in his letters to his friend and would later ask Eustis to evaluate Burr's potential son-in-law. There is no evidence that Eustis was either aware of or encouraged Theodosia's affection for him, but the physician did correspond with Theodosia later in life about her medical problems.

Another rumored candidate for Theodosia's heart was Washington Irving, the future literary lion, who was about fifteen months older than she. Although some characterized Irving's family as "middle class," the children grew up in New York not far from Burr's close friend, Commodore Nicholson. Irving's brother, Peter, was inspired by Burr's politics and later became the editor of *The Morning Chronicle*, a pro-Burr newspaper.[60] Washington Irving had become acquainted with Theodosia in 1794, when Madame de Senat was operating her private school across the street from the one he attended.

It was reported that Irving squired Theodosia and Natalie to many a dance and party, but the relationship seems to have been socially cordial but not romantic. Burr genealogist Charles Burr Todd wrote, "Irving and lovely Theodosia were acquaintances, it is true, but there is no proof of any intimacy between them."[61] Much the loss, wrote Theodosia's first biographer, Charles F. Pidgin. He was no supporter of Joseph Alston, and stated, "We wish that Theodosia had become mistress of Sunnyside [Irving's home]." Had Theodosia married the author and not the planter, Pidgin wrote, "she would somehow have been spared the wrangle with Jefferson, the deadly affair at Weehawken, and the mystery of the Ohio River Island." Pidgin's curious logic supposes that the blame for all of those disasters originated with Theodosia's future husband, Joseph Alston, rather than with Burr himself. Irving became one of Burr's intimate friends. He was also a close friend of Judge William Van Ness, Burr's second in the duel with Alexander Hamilton, and later traveled to Richmond to stand by Burr during his trial for treason.[62]

John Vanderlyn, a handsome young artist from upstate New York, has been suggested as a possible candidate for Miss Burr's heart and hand. Vanderlyn came to New York in 1792, where he studied at the Colombian Academy of Painting and worked at an artists' supply shop run by Thomas Barrow. Gilbert Stuart left two paintings, including one of Aaron Burr, for framing and gave Vanderlyn permission to copy them. The young painter ran out of money after two years and returned to Kingston, his hometown.

In 1795, Burr, his greatness now in blossom, saw the copy portrait, concluded that Vanderlyn "might eventually do honor to his country as an artist," and became his patron. The artist met Theodosia and Natalie at Richmond Hill. He resided there during the spring and summer of 1796, where he painted portraits of many of Burr's friends, as well as a half-length profile portrait of Theodosia, facing to the left. Then he headed for the shop of Gilbert Stuart, where he helped block in copies of Stuart's portrait of George Washington.

In 1796, when Theodosia was twelve or thirteen, Burr provided Vanderlyn with funds and letters of introduction to

Aaron Burr in 1802

several of his prominent friends in France. The artist fell in love with Paris, where he painted full time until he returned to New York in 1801. In 1802, he painted a portrait of Theodosia, which Burr later took to Europe and showed widely to his friends. Burr always considered that portrait his favorite. Vanderlyn also painted a portrait of Burr and started another of his patron, which he completed in Europe two years later.

Vanderlyn never married. It has been suggested that he had developed a great fondness for Theodosia, while Burr allegedly wanted to nourish a budding romance that she had struck up with the son of a powerful southern family "as a means of gaining political support there for his presidential ambitions." In 1801, the handsome and talented painter was twenty-six, and the beautiful Theodosia, eighteen. When Burr became aware of Vanderlyn's romantic attentions to his daughter, the story continues, Burr packed the lovestruck artist off to study in Europe again. "Heartbroken and true to the memory of his great love," the story goes, "the artist lost himself in his art." After recounting this story, Vanderlyn expert Kenneth Lindsay

Theodosia Burr Alston in 1802

carefully noted that "there is not a single word in the extant letters of Theodosia, her husband, her father, or the artist which alludes to a thwarted love affair."[63] Vanderlyn returned to Paris in May 1803 and remained in Europe until 1815."[64]

One beau was supposed to have been Virginian Meriwether Lewis, the skilled army officer of Lewis and Clark fame. However, Lewis could not have courted Theodosia because he was serving on the Indian frontier under Gen. James Wilkinson in 1800. Lewis was selected by Jefferson to be his secretary, but he did not arrive in Washington until March 1801, when Jefferson moved into the executive mansion—and Theodosia was already one month married to Joseph Alston.[65] During her October 1803 visit to the capital, Lewis was already heading West. Two of Lewis's biographers put him at the scene of Burr's 1807 trial, and Claude G. Bowers, author of *Jefferson in Power*, put a scholar's blessing and exclamation point on the unfounded gossip that during her father's trial, with her son and husband both in Richmond, Lewis and Theodosia "dance together, dine together, and together they canter over the Virginia hills on horseback. And she a married woman!"[66]

While Theodosia was coming of age, Burr was finishing his term as senator. When his re-election bid failed, he cast his eyes elsewhere—and upward. In two years, the nation would elect a new president and vice president. And who else, in Burr's ambitious mind, was better suited for either role? His plan, which evolved over the next year, was straightforward: first build a strong support base in New York City and the state legislature, and then use that base as the springboard for the presidential election.

By orchestrating the election of thirteen Republican assemblymen from New York City to the state legislature in 1800, Burr proved that he had the ability to run a masterful campaign against Alexander Hamilton's slate of Federalist candidates. The Republican assemblymen, he assured Jefferson, would be the key to assuring Jefferson all of New York's electoral votes when the presidential election was held. A problem arose when Burr went to ask former governor George Clinton to run for one of the assembly seats. Clinton held no affection for Jefferson, and stated that if Burr were to be the presidential candidate, he would serve. Burr ultimately negotiated an agreement with Clinton to run, with the condition that he would not have to officially or publicly support Jefferson in the coming election. The deal was done.

When the election results were announced on May 2, 1800, Burr's entire slate of Republicans was elected to the assembly, and his political stock soared. He had proven himself an able strategist, a wise politician, and an indefatigable party worker. Thanks to Burr, Jefferson was assured all twelve of New York's electoral votes in the coming election. "The Victory is complete," Burr wrote to Jefferson, "and the manner of it is highly honorable."[67]

With Jefferson now slated to become the Democratic-Republican presidential candidate, Commodore Nicholson, the father-in-law of Burr's friend, Albert Gallatin, was sent on a mission to sound out possible vice-presidential candidates from New York. First, he spoke with former governor Clinton but found him reluctant to accept because of his age and the recent death of his wife. Richmond Hill was Nicholson's next logical stop. Who better to choose as the runningmate than Burr? Jefferson was a southerner; Burr was from New York. Burr had made Jefferson's nomination a virtual certainty, and the two had been on cordial—if not warm—terms for many years, despite differences over individual matters of policy and preference.

In their discussions, Burr shared his concern that if the Republican ticket did not prevail, Burr would lose his opportunity to become New York's governor, a position for which he was virtually a shoo-in candidate. Two of Burr's closest friends, John Swartwout and Matthew L. Davis, then joined the meeting. They reminded Burr that he "should accept and that he was obliged to do so upon principles which he had urged at the late election that called for the subordination of all personal considerations for the good of the party."[68] Burr looked past his reservations, set aside his gubernatorial ambitions, and accepted his party's choice as the candidate for Vice President of the United States.

During the summer of 1800, when Burr was busy preparing for the coming election, Theodosia turned seventeen. Burr paid his daughter his highest possible compliment: he made her privy to a great many of the intimate details of his political—and personal—intrigues. As a precautionary measure, he also groomed her to be both circumspect and cautious in all things. From Albany in 1800, he wrote in a coded letter:

> You reflect, and that is a security for your conduct. Our most humiliating errors proceed usually from inattention, and from that mental dissipation which we call heedlessness. You estimate your situation with great truth. Many are surprised that I could repose in you so great a trust as that of yourself; but I knew that you were equal to it, and I am not deceived. You do right to stay much at home. It will scarcely be worth while to go to **V.P.'s C.** is excluded from all rule. I am quite oppressed with the kindness and friendship of **b. b.** towards you. How fortunate you are in such a friend. If their invitations should be so frequent as to interrupt your lessons, you will do well to refuse even them. There is a measure to be observed in the acceptance of the good offices even of our best friends; and at your age, to prefer duty to pleasure when they are in collision, is a degree of firmness rarely exhibited, and, therefore, the more calculated to inspire respect. I perceive that I am not very explicit; but you will *reflect* and discern my meaning. Montesquieu said he wrote to make people think, and not to make them read."[69]

Burr spent the summer of 1800 with Theodosia, enjoying the pleasures of Richmond Hill. Upon his arrival, he discovered that she had a serious suitor, a South Carolinian by the name of Joseph Alston, then twenty-one years old. Joseph—styled by some as a "Palmetto Plutocrat"—was a wealthy rice planter of Georgetown District, South Carolina, one of the most fertile places in the world, and valued his considerable property at

£200,000 sterling.[70] His paternal grandfather, Joseph Allston, had bequeathed him 100 slaves and The Oaks, a flourishing rice plantation with a somewhat dilapidated mansion on the Waccamaw River, in the heart of the state's flourishing rice coast. The Alstons headed the list of the richest of South Carolina's planter-aristocrats, and young Joseph was the favored son among his numerous cousins.

A miniature portrait painted when he was in his early twenties showed that Joseph had dark brown, curly hair; short side-whiskers; gray-blue eyes; and brown eyebrows.[71] The son of William Alston, Joseph had the finest education that his father's considerable wealth could buy. All of William Alston's sons attended private school in Charleston from early fall through December, when they moved to Joseph's father's residential rice plantation, Clifton, on the Waccamaw. There, Col. Alston's boys had first-class tutors. One such educator was Connecticut native John Pierpont, who had graduated from Yale in 1804 and tutored the younger Alston children in Charleston and at Clifton from 1805-1810.[72] After finishing his private schooling and briefly attending the College of Charleston, Joseph entered Aaron Burr's *alma mater*, the College of New Jersey, as a junior in 1795. A classmate, E. S. Thomas, wrote that some of his contemporaries considered him

Joseph Alston

talented but autocratic and overbearing. Alston departed a year later and did not graduate. He returned to his father's home, the Miles Brewton House on King Street, where he lived until he married. The miniature painting shown here is the only image of him known to survive.[73]

Upon his return to South Carolina, young Alston prepared for the same career that Burr had chosen: the law. Alston studied under Charleston's distinguished Edward Rutledge, a signer of the Declaration of Independence, a British prisoner of war, a South Carolina legislator, and an attorney. Alston was admitted to the South Carolina bar in 1799, but the law did not hold his attention for long. He spent the better part of 1800 traveling the country, and embodied the type of person of whom South Carolina historian, George C. Rogers, Jr., wrote, "Only the very rich could move so slowly and elegantly."[74]

Joseph ultimately owned about 6,287 acres and 223 slaves on his Lowcountry rice plantations, plus thirty more slaves upstate. This made him one of the largest planters in a region full of large planters, and Joseph ranked in the top one-half of one per cent of the South Carolina plantation aristocracy.[75] About 1810 he built a summer residence near Greenville, South Carolina, which burned after Alston's death.

At some point during his travels in the North, Alston had been introduced to Theodosia. By the summer of 1800, it was evident to Burr that the young gentleman was smitten with his daughter, and she seemed to encourage his attentions. Burr seemed pleased with the match, but was cautious. Both Burr and Alston had planned trips to New England that summer. Burr was traveling to solidify support for the Republicans, an act of which Federalist leader Alexander Hamilton was well aware. Hamilton wrote that Burr's election would bring an attempt "to reform the Government *a la Bonaparte*. He is as unprincipled and dangerous a man as any country can boast—as true a Catiline [conspirator] as ever met in midnight conclave."[76]

Alston was simply continuing his leisurely tour to acquaint himself with the region and its leaders. Burr gave Alston a letter of introduction to his close friend, Dr. William Eustis. In advance of Alston's expected arrival, Burr asked Eustis to scrutinize his would-be son-in-law carefully when he arrived. "Joseph Alston, a young man of very respectable family & fortune from S. Carolina will hand you a letter from me (of mere introduction).... I beg your particular attention to him—but more—

I beg you to analyze and anatomize him soul & heart & body, so that you may answer me all questions which I may put to you on that head when we meet in Providence—Mr. A. will probably attend you to Providence for I have told him that I should expect to meet you there.... P.S.: Mr. A. *is republican.*[77]

Alston evidently acquitted himself well in New England, as Burr quickly took him into his confidence. During his return trip to South Carolina, Alston served as Burr's personal messenger. The Virginians were anxious to hear the most recent political news from the North (and New York City in particular), where they desperately needed a victory if the Republicans were to have a chance of gaining the presidency. Therefore, Alston was directed to Virginia with letters of introduction to Jefferson at Monticello. From there he carried letters from David Gelston, a New York political friend of Burr's, and to Vice President James Madison at Montpelier.[78] In his letter to Madison, Burr described Alston as "intelligent, sound in his principles, and polished in his manners."[79] This mission was the first in a lifetime of personal, political, and financial favors that Joseph Alston would perform for his future father-in-law.

The love letters exchanged during Joseph's courtship of Theodosia are his earliest surviving correspondence. They provide an interesting, amusing, and intriguing window into the minds of Theodosia, Burr's prodigy modeled on Mary Wollstonecraft, and Joseph, William Alston's eldest son, who had been poured directly into the Chesterfieldian mold. On January 13, 1801, Theodosia replied to a relatively recent letter from Alston, which must have been a virtual proposal of marriage. In her feisty reply, Theodosia made it clear that she was ready to be wooed and won—but made it equally clear that she was still waiting for more of both.

I have already written to you by the post to tell you that I shall be happy to see you *whenever you choose;* that I suppose is equivalent to *very soon;* and that you may no longer feel doubts or suspicions on my account, I repeat the invitation by a packet as less dilatory than the mail; but for all these doubts and suspicions I will take ample revenge when we meet. I yesterday received your letter of the 26th of December, and I am expecting your defence of early marriages to-day. My father laughs at my impatience to hear from you, and says that I am in love; but I do not believe that to be a fair deduction, for the post is really very irregular and slow—enough so to provoke anybody. We leave this for Albany on the 26th inst., and shall remain there until the 10th February. My movements will after that depend on my father and *you*. I had intended not to marry this twelvemonth, and in that case thought it wrong to divert you from your present engagements in Carolina; but to your solicitations I yield my judgment. Adieu. I wish you many returns of the century."[80]

The next day she added a postscript: "I have not received your promised letter; but I hope it may be long in proportion to the time I have been expecting it. The packet has been delayed by head-winds, but now that they are fair she will have a quick passage; at least such I wish it. Adieu, encore. Theodosia."[81]

Her wish was granted. On December 28, 1800, Joseph wrote a response phrased more like a lawyer pleading a shaky case to a jury than a love letter to an intended bride. On the other hand, he was bidding for the hand of the highly intellectual daughter of a masterful attorney. In his tome, written from Charleston, he refuted Theodosia's quotation from Aristotle that "a man should not marry before he is six-and-thirty." Then he went on to quote Benjamin Franklin; defend South Carolina's treatment of slaves against the claims of the northern abolitionists; praise his native state; assure Theodosia that, contrary to northern rumor, the rice swamps of South Carolina were not unhealthful; and reassure his fiancée that South Carolina women were intelligent and well educated. It was an amazing dissertation, which started off with a spirited defense of marrying young.

[You wrote that] Aristotle says 'that a man should not marry before he is six-and-thirty:' pray, Mr. Alston, what arguments have you to oppose such authority? Hear me, Miss Burr.

It has always been my practice, whether from a natural independence of mind, from pride, or what other cause I will not pretend to say, never to adopt the opinion of anyone, however respectable his authority, unless thoroughly convinced by his arguments; the 'ipse dixit,' [Latin for "he, himself, has spoken it"] as logicians term it, even of Cicero, who stands higher in my estimation than any other author, would not have the least weight with me; you must, therefore, till you offer better reasons in support of his opinion than the Grecian sage himself has done, excuse my differing from him.

Objections to early marriages can rationally only arise from want of discretion, or want of fortune in the parties; now, as you very well observe, the age of discretion is wholly uncertain, some men reaching it at twenty, others at thirty, some not till fifty, and many not at all; of course, fix such or such a period as the proper one for marrying is ridiculous. Even the want of fortune is to be considered differently according to the country where the marriage is to take place; for though in some places a fortune is absolutely necessary to a man before he marries, there are others, as in the eastern states, for example, where he marries expressly for the purpose of making a fortune.

But, allowing both these objections their full force, may there not be a single case that they do not reach? Suppose (for instance, merely) a young man nearly twenty-two, already of the *greatest* discretion, with an ample fortune, were to be passionately in love with a young lady almost eighteen, equally discreet with himself, and who had a "sincere friendship" for him, do you think it would be necessary to make him wait till thirty? particularly where friends on both sides were pleased by the match.

Were I to consider the question personally, since you allow that 'individual character' ought to be consulted, no objection certainly could be made to my marrying early.

From my father's plan of education for me, I may properly be called a hot-bed plant. Introduced from my infancy into the society of men, while yet a boy I was accustomed to think and act like a man. On every occasion, however important, I was left to decide for myself. I do not recollect a single instance where I was controlled even by advice; for it was my father's invariable maxim, that the best way of strengthening the judgment was to suffer it to be constantly exercised. Before seventeen, I finished my college education; before twenty, I was admitted to the bar.[82] Since that time I have been constantly travelling through different parts of the United States; to what purpose, I leave you to determine.

From this short account of myself, you may judge whether my manners and sentiments are not, by this time, in some degree formed. But let us treat the subject abstractedly; and, as we have shown that under particular circumstances no disadvantages result from early marriages, let us see if any positive advantages attend them.

Happiness in the marriage state, you will agree with me, can only be obtained from the most complete congeniality of mind and disposition, and the most exact similarity of habits and pursuits; now, though their natures may generally resemble, no two persons can be entirely of the same mind and disposition, the same habits and pursuits, unless after the most intimate and early association; I say *early*, for it is in youth only the mind and disposition receive the complexion we would give them; it is then only that our habits are moulded or our pursuits directed as we please; as we advance in life, they become fixed and unchangeable, and instead of our governing them, govern us. Is it not, *therefore*, upon every principle of happiness, that persons should marry young, when, directed by mutual friendship, each might assimilate to the other, than wait till a period when their passions, their prejudices, their habits, etc., become so rooted that there neither exists an inclination nor power to correct them? Dr. Franklin, a very strong advocate for my system, and, I think, at least as good authority as Aristotle, very aptly compares those who marry early to two young trees joined together by the hand of the gardener.[83]

Those on the other hand, who do not marry till late, say 'thirty,' for example, he likens to two ancient oaks:

> Use all your force, they yield not to your hand,
> But firmly in their usual stations stand;
> While each, regardless of the other's views,
> Stubborn and fix'd, it's natural bent purses!

But this is not all, it is in youth that we are best fitted to enjoy that exquisite happiness which the marriage state is capable of affording, and the remembrance of which forms so pleasing a link in that chain of friendship that binds to each other two persons who have lived together any number of years. Our ideas are then more refined; every generous and disinterested sentiment beats higher; and our sensibility is far more alive to every emotion our associate may feel. Depend upon it, the man who does not love till 'thirty' will never, never love; long before that period, he will become too much enamoured of his own dear self to think of transferring his affections to any other object. He may marry, but interest alone will direct him in the choice of his wife; far from regarding her as the sweetest friend and companion of his life, he will consider her but as an unavoidable encumbrance upon the estate she brings him. And can you really hope, my Theodosia, with all your ingenuity, to convince me that such a being will enjoy

equal happiness in marriage with me? With me, about
to enter into it with such rapture; who anticipate[s] so
perfect a heaven from our uniting in every study, im-
proving our minds together, and informing each other
by our mutual assistance and observations? No—I give
you full credit for your talents, but there are some causes
so bad that even you cannot support them. Enough,
however, of this topic till we meet; I have already given
you a volume of nonsense upon it.

Then the determined swain set out to combat the negative
portraits that some of Theodosia's northern friends had
painted about his beloved South Carolina, starting with allegations that it was hot, humid, and unhealthy. He replied
that Charleston was no hellhole but "the most delightfully
situated city in America, which, entirely open to the ocean,
twice in every twenty-four hours is cooled by the refreshing
seabreeze." He went on to call it "the Montpelier of the south,
which annually affords an asylum to the planter and the West
Indian from every disease."[84] Here Alston is describing the
city of Charleston, which, unlike the rice plantations, received
a direct sea breeze, and was not as problematic a place to live
as the rice plantations, which were the best possible breeding
pond for fever-infested mosquitoes. Alston's was quite a
different picture than the one painted by a fellow South
Carolinian, who described the rice plantations of Georgetown
District as one of the "deadliest, most disease-ridden places
on earth this side of the Black Hole of Calcutta."[85]

Next, Joseph refuted the belief that South Carolinians were
uncultured and boorish, noting that although the men did engage in hunting and horse-racing, neither were injurious to the
character. As to the ladies of the Lowcountry (who, he certainly
hoped, would never see the letter), he admitted to his intended
New York bride that Carolina women were "not generally as
handsome as those of the Northern states.... Their education is
perhaps more attended to than anywhere else in the United
States," he wrote. "Many of them are well informed, all of them

accomplished." Given that he was writing to one of the brightest and best educated women in the nation, it is doubtful that she found the statement impressive.

"They are perfectly easy and agreeable in their manners," he wrote, "and remarkably fond of company; no Charleston belle ever felt 'ennui' in her life," the planter's son stated boldly. Joseph had evidently had never discussed this subject with any Lowcountry woman who had to spend her winters on the plantations. Many South Carolina planters' wives and daughters complained to each other about the sheer boredom and "everlasting routine" of plantation life, the isolation from city life and each other, and the endless domestic duties expected of them, such as finding work for all the household slaves and then supervising them.

"In the richness of their dress and the splendour of their equipages they are unrivalled," he wrote to the New York socialite, who knew no other kind of society. Joseph evidently had great confidence in his ability to learn languages rapidly. "You wish me to acquire French. I already understand something of it," he stated, "and, with a little practice, would soon speak it. I promise you, therefore, if you become my instructress, in less than two months after our marriage to converse with you entirely in that language. I fix the period *after* our marriage, for I cannot think of being corrected in the mistakes I may make by any other person than my wife. Suppose, till then, you return to your Latin, and prepare to use that tongue with me, since you are adverse to one understood by all the canaille [rabble]. Adieu. I have literally given you a folio volume.... P.S. The arrangement you speak of proposing in your letter for an interview [e.g., meeting her soon] has determined me. I shall therefore sail certainly in a few days. Winds be propitious!"[86]

If not the winds, then it must have been all the Fates working in unison who were propitious. Theodosia, in New York, had written her last letter to Joseph on January 13, 1801, and his letter of December 28, written from Charleston, had not yet arrived. However, in writing, "to your solicitations I yield my judgment," it is clear that she had already chosen to marry. That was just as well, because a furious flurry of activity commenced almost immediately. In the nineteen days between January 13 and February 2, Theodosia had received Joseph's great treatise on the matrimonial estate, and Joseph had sailed from Charleston to New York to Albany, where Burr was serving in the state legislature.

Burr and Theodosia had set off for Albany earlier in a sleigh. From Poughkeepsie, New York, on January 24, Theodosia wrote a sarcastic and indignant letter to Alston, upbraiding him, the Southern hothouse product, for predicting—with no knowledge of snow, sleigh travel, the terrain, or any other good reason— that the trip to Albany would be highly problematic.

"Thus far we advanced on this *terrible* journey, from which you predicted so many evils, without meeting even with inconvenience. How strange that Mr. Alston should be wrong. Do not, however, pray for misfortunes to befall us that your character may be retrieved; it were useless, I assure you; although I am very sensible how anxious you must now be to inspire me with all due respect and reverence, I should prefer to feel it in any other way."[87]

The letter must have come as a total shock to Alston, because no well-bred woman of South Carolina would ever have pinned her fiancé's ears back as Theodosia had done with this letter, written as it was just eight days before their wedding. In it, Alston learned—or should have learned—that he was not dealing with a meek, submissive Southern belle, but with the intellectual, outspoken daughter of Aaron Burr; the philosophical embodiment of Mary Wollstonecraft. Theodosia's masculine education and indoctrination had made her both independent and quite willing to think and speak for herself.

Nevertheless, in barely three weeks, Alston, Theodosia, and Burr had formally agreed upon the marriage and planned the wedding. *The New York Commercial Advertiser* of Tuesday, February 7, 1801, announced, "Married—At Albany, on the 2nd instant, by the Rev. Mr. Johnson, Joseph Alston, of South Carolina, to Theodosia Burr, only child of Aaron Burr, Esq."

Following the precedent of her father, Theodosia and Joseph's marriage ceremony was conducted by a minister of the Dutch Reformed Church.[88] The place of the ceremony in Albany was not stated.

The wedding was not the only thing Burr had on his mind in January 1801. He had campaigned hard in 1800 to organize the precincts, turn out the vote, and assure that Thomas Jefferson received all of New York's electoral votes. In the general election, the Republicans won, but when it came to the Electoral College, Burr and Jefferson tied for the highest number of electoral votes. The tie threw the election into the hands of the House of Representatives. The winner would be inaugurated president and the loser, vice president.

Burr had accepted the secondary role in advance. Jefferson was in a good mood and was already picking out his cabinet. Because the office of the vice president was not considered part of the president's cabinet, Burr had not even planned to be present for the inauguration.

As the day of the vote neared, the threat of chaos heightened. Both Jefferson and Burr had their supporters, and the Federalists had two options: seek to maintain a deadlock and thereby frustrate the entire election process or try to throw support to either Jefferson or Burr to promote whichever of the two might best destabilize the Republican administration.

On January 2, 1801, the votes were counted in the Electoral College. For the Democratic-Republicans, Jefferson and Burr tied at seventy-three votes each. The Federalists' candidate, John Adams, got sixty-five votes, South Carolina's Charles Cotesworth Pinckney received sixty-four, and John Jay, one. The top two candidates would become president and vice president, but which man would take which office? That would be determined by the House of Representatives.

Burr remained in New York while the debate raged, but his enemies charged him with politicking to have himself chosen over Jefferson. A letter he wrote to Joseph Alston on January 15, after nearly two weeks of balloting had taken place, clearly shows that Burr had no such notion. "My dear Sir," he wrote to his future son-in-law, "Your two letters have been received, and gave me great pleasure. We are about to begin our journey to Albany. I propose to remain there till the 10th of February; possibly till the 20th. If you should come northward, you will find a letter for you in the postoffice of this city. The equality of Jefferson and Burr excites great speculation and much anxiety. I believe that all will be well, and that Jefferson will be our next president."[89] Hamilton dove directly into the fray, slandered Burr, and did everything he could to defeat him. Had Burr been the political megalomaniac and manipulator that his opponents and some biographers have painted him, he might easily have become America's third president. In reality, he held himself back, out of the fray, and let history take its course. His forbearance cost him the presidency.

After an agonizing seven-day struggle that ended on February 17, 1801, after thirty-six rounds of voting, Jefferson was elected president, Burr became vice president, and the nation could breathe again—or so it seemed. However, behind his back, Jefferson and his Virginia friends were already at work, digging up scurrilous gossip which was printed and distributed as pamphlets to weaken Burr's credibility and power.

Back in Albany, Joseph and Theodosia rejoiced over their new state of matrimony and the forthcoming inauguration. The newlyweds spent the first week of their honeymoon with Burr in Albany while he completed his work in the assembly. From there, they traveled down the Hudson to Richmond Hill for a brief visit and then went on to meet up with Burr at Baltimore on February 28.

The three then traveled to Burr's new quarters in Georgetown, by then a settlement of five thousand people, three miles from the capital.[90] There, Burr received a constant flow of foreign visitors, all ready to congratulate him or seek favor with the incoming administration. On March 4, 1801, in the chamber which then served as the meeting place of the Senate, the Alstons and a thousand other dignitaries watched as the tall, red-headed Jefferson and the diminutive, black-haired Burr were sworn in as the third president and vice president of the United States, their term to expire March 3, 1805.

Burr now faced a bittersweet future. Within two weeks, he had gained his high office, but he had lost his daughter. As for Theodosia, she had gained a good husband, but in doing so, she had chosen to leave behind her father—the mirror of her soul—and the sleighs, apple orchards, and rolling hills of New York for a new home and way of life in a place nearly as foreign to her as Russia, Brazil or Mexico. Little did she know that in a few years, she would be on a one-way voyage to become the empress of one of those exotic places.

CHAPTER FIVE

The Yankee Belle

To womanhood she grew a fair young queen,
Who by her graciousness all hearts subdued,
And held them chained by her enthralling charm.
                                        —Alexander T. Ormond

The year was 1801, the dawn of a new century. Although Theodosia Burr, aged seventeen and a half, loved Joseph Alston, she probably had little comprehension of the lifestyle she was marrying into. Nevertheless, she had a fine education, a father who loved her, and a wonderful future to look forward to. It was a time for great expectations. Joseph, aged twenty-one and a half, loved Theodosia Burr—although he probably had little idea what a volatile, unconventional father-daughter team he was joining. Aaron Burr, almost forty-five, loved everything he saw before him—with the exception of the fact that he might now be separated from his Theodosia for long periods of time. Nevertheless, his beloved daughter had made a good marital match. His new son-in-law was rich and Republican. His daughter's new father-in-law was very rich, very influential, Republican, and a personal friend of Jefferson. Burr himself had just been inaugurated Vice President of the United States and held the second-highest office in the land. Certainly his loss of the presidency to Jefferson had been a blow, but nevertheless, Burr must have thought, life was good.

Not everyone agreed with him. Natalie de Lage was dejected and dismayed, for she had just lost the companionship of her dearest friend. Northern gossips had little use for Alston and his Southern ways. "The aristocratic Alstons may have been one of South Carolina's greatest planter families," wrote historian Ronald Ray Swick, "but Theodosia's choice for a husband left her woman friends aghast."[1] Four days after the wedding, Maria Nicholson wrote to her sister, Hannah Gallatin, wife of Jefferson's Secretary of the Treasury, "Report does not speak well of [Alston]: it says that he is rich, but he is a great dasher, dissipated, ill-tempered, vain, and silly. I know that he is ugly and of unprepossessing manners. Can it be that the father has sacrificed a daughter to affluence and influential connections? They say that it was Mr. A[lston] who gained the eight votes in Carolina at the present [presidential] election, and that he is not yet relieved from pecuniary embarrassments."[2]

Robert Troup, one of Burr's closest friends from the revolution and a law student with Burr under William Paterson, wrote Rufus King, U.S. Minister to Great Britain, on May 27, 1802, that "the marriage was an affair of Burr, and not his daughter, and that the money in question was the predominating motive." He described Alston as "Ordinary—his manner pedantic—his temper not very soft—his politics violent on the democratic side," but Troup was far from unbiased. He had no use for Theodosia's "masculine education."[3]

Theodosia's husband clearly did not make a favorable impression every

Theodosia Burr Alston
at the time of her marriage

place he visited, yet those who objected to him rarely gave any specific reasons why. George Washington's step-grand-daughter, Nelly Custis, speaking of a fashionable dance at Williamsburg in 1801, wrote to a friend, "Colonel Burr, his daughter, and her husband were there. Mrs. Alston is a very sweet, little woman, very engaging and pretty—but her husband is the most intolerable mortal I ever beheld. I cannot enough congratulate dear Eliza [her sister] on escaping a union with him. I think he is more calculated to break a Wife's heart than any other person I have ever seen."[4] Despite these observations, Mrs. Custis grudgingly admitted that Alston had good sense, though "it is securely locked in the recesses of his brain."[5]

A miniature portrait shows him as a young man with a slight smile who appears to be in his early twenties. He has dark brown curly hair, short side whiskers, gray-blue eyes and brown eyebrows, a fresh complexion with red lips and cheeks, clean-cut features, wearing a dull blue coat with gilt buttons, a white vest, and an elaborate pleated neck-cloth.[6] Whatever impressions he made upon people, two things are certain. The first is that Joseph Alston has remained a hazy figure. Seldom the master of his own destiny, Alston's life always seemed to be the aftereffect of choices made by Burr and Theodosia, rather than his own. His second feature was equally clear: he was a solid, respectable man who deeply and sincerely loved his wife and son and served his state well. Nevertheless, the relative impact made by Theodosia versus her husband can easily be seen in the sea of words devoted to her and the paucity of material on him.[7]

The allegation that Burr had bartered off the maidenhead of his only daughter to Alston in return for money and South Carolina's eight electoral votes in the 1800 presidential election probably started as a rumor spread by his Federalist competition. As a political smear made during a viciously partisan election, it had every natural advantage, including logic. The tales spread further when rumors circulated—and were later proven true—that Burr was borrowing large sums of money from his wealthy new son-in-law.

Nevertheless, Theodosia and Joseph's marriage, which had begun so quickly, thrived on mutual love and admiration, despite its curious roots, the wails of political and anti-Southern rumormongers, and its obvious political and financial advantages for Burr. In the end, it was Theodosia, not her father, who chose Joseph Alston as her husband. In their twelve years of marriage, although Alston was often away from his wife when she needed him most, he treated Theodosia with love and respect. She loved him in return, never regretted her choice of marriage partners. Nevertheless, Joseph Alston always seemed to stand in the shadow of his exotic wife—just as Theodosia had always stood in the huge shadow cast by her father.

From Washington, the newlyweds headed south by carriage on the twenty-day trip that separated the nation's capitol from Theodosia's new home on the Waccamaw River in All Saints' Parish, near Georgetown, South Carolina. Burr had provided them with a long list of friends and colleagues—people who would become links in the new world of national power politics into which he was directing Alston—to visit along the way, and thereby strengthened bonds of acquaintance and loyalty for Burr. In Philadelphia they were to see Charles Biddle, a former sea captain, merchant, and Burr's loyal friend; to ask a Dr. Edwards to give Mr. Alston a letter of introduction to Caesar A. Rodney, of Wilmington, Delaware, "a very respectable young man" who served as a U.S. Representative. He would then introduce Alston to "the venerable" John Dickinson, a great Revolutionary statesman of Pennsylvania.[8] Aaron Burr was nothing if not well connected.

Yet it was clear from his first letter after Theodosia's departure that the light of his house had departed. On March 8, 1801, Burr wrote to her, "Your little letter from Alexandria assured me of your safety, and for a moment consoled me for your absence. The only solid consolation is the belief that you will be happy, and the certainty that we will often meet." Then, out of the blue, he had an intriguing question: "Would Mr. Alston be willing to go as secretary to Chancellor Livingston? I beg his immediate answer."[9]

Thomas Jefferson had recently appointed Chancellor Robert R. Livingston, a prominent New York equity court judge, as U.S. Minister to France, and he was searching for a chargé d'affaires to head the legation. Burr promptly nominated his new son-in-law. If Alston took the post, it would serve two purposes. First, it would further Theodosia's exposure to the social and intellectual elite of the continent, thereby continuing Burr's educational plan. Second, it would enable Alston to make important business and political contacts for Burr.

The decision was far from certain. Alston had not yet made a start in politics, and he had a substantial equity in his plantations. Furthermore, he was a newlywed. Although he knew that Theodosia would have relished spending several years in France—partly because her dear friend, Natalie de Lage, would undoubtedly accompany her—Alston opted to stay the course, return to the Waccamaw, and take up the planter's life as he had planned. Theodosia told her father that she understood, and Burr wrote to her, "The reasons which you and your husband give against the voyage to France concur with my judgment. You can go a few years hence more respectably, more agreeably. Adieu, cher enfant."[10]

On March 24, 1801, Jefferson contacted Gen. Thomas Sumter, the newly elected Senator from South Carolina, offering the position to his son, Thomas Sumter, Jr. The younger Sumter, a bachelor, accepted and proceeded to New York to join Livingston for the voyage.[11] This was to be a life-altering decision for Theodosia's dear friend Natalie.

The 1790s were painful enough times for the French royalists, but three somber blows befell Natalie de Lage in addition to the storms in the political climate. In 1797 came the news that her grandfather, Admiral d'Amblimont, had been killed in a naval battle. Two years later, her father died of yellow fever in Puerto Rico, and then an uncle died in Europe. Now, with her closest friend, Theodosia, gone to live in far-away South Carolina, Natalie's yearning to reunite with her mother was overwhelming. The new policies of Napoléon Bonaparte opened the door to reunification of the French people and the return of former royalists. For the first time in years, Natalie saw hope that she might see her mother and *la belle France* again.

Natalie heard about the Livingston appointment and the young South Carolinian who was to accompany him, and she consulted her surrogate father, Burr, about making the trip in their company. Burr was torn between the further emptiness such a move would bring and the young woman's desire to reunite with her only surviving parent. Knowing how badly Natalie wanted the reunion, he agreed, and he commissioned John Vanderlyn to make a portrait of her before she left.

Natalie had first met Thomas Sumter at Frederick Prevost's house in Pelham, New York. Although reluctant to leave the man who had provided her with both love and comfort, the thought of making the trip to France with handsome Sumter was quite appealing. Burr gave Natalie a letter of credit for five hundred dollars, and she and America's French legation sailed from New York on October 15, 1801.[12] There was insufficient room aboard the ship for Madame de Senat and her daughter, who were forced to stay behind.

Sans chaperone, love blossomed quickly aboard ship between Natalie, then nineteen, and Sumter, thirty-three. The legation reached French soil in twenty-six days and arrived in Paris on December 3, 1801. By that time, Sumter had already proposed marriage to the young French girl, and there was little doubt about her response.[13] One formidable impediment would be Natalie's mother. A prominent royalist, she was unlikely to agree to her daughter's marriage to a hated Jeffersonian Republican like Sumter. Worse, Sumter's father, the general, had started life as a common man, working his way up the ladder of agricultural success, all without a drop of noble blood in his veins. Even worse, Sumter was an Episcopalian, not a Catholic. Thence began the matrimonial battle royal.

For Stephanie d'Amblimont, Marquise de Lage de Volude, a match between her daughter and a Protestant Republican commoner from America simply would not do. Not only would Natalie not have the advantage of the education, social status, and privilege that a marriage to a proper French Catholic would provide, but her eventual return to the backwoods cotton fields of rural America would permanently separate her from her mother, who had already felt her loss for eight years. Only after extensive, volatile, and highly complex negotiations, which were facilitated by the ambassador himself, were Mlle. Natalie de Lage de Volude and Mr. Thomas Sumter, Jr. married on March 20, 1802. The nuptial vows were exchanged in a Roman Catholic ceremony authorized by the archbishop of Paris and with at least the consent—if not the enthusiastic blessings—of her mother.[14]

Back on the other side of the Atlantic, Theodosia and Joseph Alston had reached their temporary new home, Hagley plantation, which Joseph's father, Colonel Alston had purchased for them in 1801 as a wedding present. With little pleasure, they lived there with Joseph's brother and sister-in-law, John Ashe Alston and his wife Sally, while Joseph's house at The Oaks was being renovated. In November 1802, Theodosia wrote Burr, "It might appear ill-natured and ungrateful for the kindness John and Sally show me to regret residing at Hagley. But you, who always put the best construction on my words and deeds, will allow, that a place in which we have suffered much and run a risk of suffering more must be unpleasant."[15] To cope with the tight quarters at Hagley, Theodosia and Joseph made long and frequent visits to Clifton, a more commodious plantation belonging to Joseph's father, Col. William Alston.

About 1800, Col. Alston had built a large, unpretentious, and airy beach house on Debordieu Island that the family jokingly referred to as "The Castle."[16] Jacob Motte Alston, a grandson of Col. William Alston and nephew of Joseph Alston, provided a good description. "It was here that my grandfather lived in summer," he wrote in his memoir. "His house was built to stand the hurricanes which would now and then sweep the southern coast. An under-ground frame of heavy timber on which the house was built protected it from the winds and waves of a century.... The great storm of October 1822, which caused such destruction of life and property, did not

"The Castle" on Debordieu Island

injure this house."[17] Theo-dosia, Joseph, and their son spent many happy days at The Castle and at their oth-er favorite seashore retreat, Sullivan's Island, located about seven miles north of Charleston.[18]

As the daughter of the Vice President of the United States and, more important to the South Carolinians, the wife of an Alston, Theodosia stood "at the head of fashion, and sustained herself with great dignity."[19] Theodosia wrote to her father that she had received a warm and enthusiastic reception from her new in-laws and the other Lowcountry rice barons. She wrote in the same vein to her sister-in-law, Frances Ann Prevost, noting that "so hospitable had everyone been that she questioned Northern notions about the alleged reserve and coldness of Carolina women."[20]

Burr replied, "The cordial and affectionate reception which you have met consoles me, as far as any thing can console me, for your absence."[21] Indeed, all of the Waccamaw Neck planters, as well as the bluebloods of Charleston, welcomed the vice president's daughter, who had demonstrably embraced their heritage by marrying into the vast cousinage of South Carolina's wealthiest and most influential families.

Even though she was fully accepted by her new family and soon became the darling of two states, Theodosia never bonded with the South. She stayed in South Carolina only as long as she had to and left as often as possible for the greatest period of time she could justify. Despite her kind treatment by her new friends and neighbors on the rice plantations and in Charleston, Theodosia forever considered herself a citizen of Richmond Hill and New York, not of The Oaks and South Carolina. Her husband was in South Carolina, but her home and heart were with her father.

The distance between Burr and his daughter only strengthened his devotion to her. "You know," he wrote after she had gone south, "that you and your concerns are the highest, the dearest interest I have in this world, one in comparison with which all others are insignificant."[22] Even before the newlyweds arrived in South Carolina, Burr wrote that he was "preparing with all imaginable zeal for a voyage to Charleston. One obstacle interposes; that you can conjecture. That removed, and I shall be off in forty-eight hours."[23] Theodosia did not need to conjecture about anything, as she had been the recipient of detailed accounts of her father's amorous adventures for years. The "obstacle" Burr referred to was just one more of his numerous romantic liaisons.

Ultimately, he was unable to free himself from the demands of his office and his mistress long enough to visit the Alstons in 1801. Instead, he urged them to come back north and spend the summer in New England. Burr wondered, "How can Mr. Alston, consistently with his views of business, leave the state for five or six months, as you have proposed, for your northern tour?" Burr went on to say that he had recently shipped her two dozen pairs of long, colored kid gloves and a half-dozen pairs of short ones (for horseback riding) and asked her to please send him orders, "that I may have the pleasure of doing something for you or your amiable family." Burr alluded to the chance that he might marry soon, almost on a whim, to a woman now engaged to someone else. "If I should meet her, and she should challenge me, I should probably strike at once," Burr wrote, but like so many of his many hormone-fueled dalliances, it amounted to nothing.[24]

Theodosia was serious about getting her married life in the South off to a good start, even if her house at The Oaks was still not fit for habitation. On June 10, 1801, she wrote to her half-brother, Bartow Prevost, "The necessary preparations for entering on my new & important station of housekeeper have absorbed all my soul. My only friends & companions of late have been masons & painters &c."[25]

Soon after her arrival on the Waccamaw, Theodosia started to learn the details of plantation life and the Alston family history. The immigrant founder of what later became the Allston/Alston rice dynasty, John Allston, was born in England in 1666 and came to America between 1685 and 1694. He had six children, one of whom was William Allston, who married Esther Labrosse de Marboeuf, a French Hugue-not, in 1721. William and Esther moved to All Saints Parish, on the Waccamaw River, in 1730 and purchased The Oaks, a 1,000-acre plantation, from Percival Pawley. It proved to be a purchase "that would keep his descendants in possession of the land for the next 138 years."[26]

William and Esther Allston's thirteen children included Joseph Allston, who married Charlotte Rothmahler. Upon his father's death in 1744, Joseph inherited The Oaks, its house, and a marsh island of 129 acres. He took control of these when

he came of age in 1756. Joseph and Charlotte had six children, including William Allston. Destined to become both a military and agricultural leg-end in his own time, William was born in 1756 at The Oaks, where he spent much of his childhood. Wil-liam's first wife was Mary Ashe, the daughter of General John Ashe of North Carolina. She bore him five children before her death in 1789. Theodosia's future husband, Joseph Alston, was the second child and first son of that marriage. As the el-dest son, Joseph received special attention and privileges.

Joseph Alston was born on August 15, 1779, in the middle of the broiling South Carolina summer. He was not born at The Oaks or any other Georgetown District rice plantation, as has often been stated, but rather in one of the Alston townhouses in Charleston.[27] The reason is simple: the threat of contracting a fatal disease. As Joseph Alston's nephew wrote, "the first question asked of one who had visited Georgetown in the sickly months of August and September, was 'who was dead?'"[28] The fear of malaria and yellow fever from the mosquito-infested rice fields was so great that one planter wrote, "I would as soon stand fifty feet from the best Kentucky rifleman and be shot at by the hour as to spend a night on my plantation in the summer."[29]

The threat of disease gave rise to what became known as the "planters' migration." The wealthy South Carolina rice planters moved their households from the city to their plantations in late November or early December, after the first hard frost had killed the disease-carrying mosquitoes. There they resided as country gentlemen until the late spring, when the heat, humidity, and insects drove them back to the city, from whence they frequently traveled to spas in North Carolina, New England, or abroad. During the summer, the only whites left on the plantations were the small planters, who couldn't afford to leave, and the overseers, who ran the day-to-day operations of the plantations for the absent owners of the large plantations. The slaves were left to suffer through the heat and fever-infested rice fields year-round.

Col. William Alston
of Clifton Plantation

Col. William Alston's wealth and influence had earned him the nickname, "King Billy." About 1792, he became the first of the family to adopt the "one-L" spelling of his surname, in order to distinguish himself from a kinsman of the same name. Thus, his son was known as Joseph Alston, rather than Allston. Joseph's mother died when he was ten years old. Two years after her death, his father married twenty-three-year-old Mary Brewton Motte, the daughter of Revolutionary War heroine Rebecca Motte and her husband Jacob. On Friday, April 29, 1791, Colonel Alston and his new bride entertained President George Washington at Clifton "in a style which the president pronounced to be truly Virginian." The president declared that he had seen "nothing in all his travels so justly entitled to be styled a fairy land, as the rice fields of Waccamaw in the genial month of May."[30] When asked how she dressed to meet the President, Col. Alston's wife told Jacob Motte Alston that she wore a band on her forehead that was emblazoned, "Hail to the Chief."[31] President Washington was so pleased by his warm reception at Clifton that upon his return to Mt. Vernon, he sent Col. Alston an imported mare and a young jackass.[32]

In 1792, when Joseph was thirteen, Colonel Alston bought out the interests of his new wife's mother and aunt and moved into the Miles Brewton House, the most beautiful and tasteful residence in Charleston. For £7,000 sterling, he received title to the stunning Palladian townhouse and its enormous 149 foot x 473 foot double lot, which embraced the house, a brick-paved courtyard, and extensive formal fruit and flower gardens. Tucked away behind a privacy wall stood the working buildings: a two-bay coach house, a tack room and

Mary Brewton Motte Alston

the coachman's quarters, the kitchen, a cistern for drinking water, another cistern under the kitchen and coach house for agricultural and animal watering, servants' quarters, another tack room, three double-tie stalls for coach and riding horses and two cows, and last, but not least, two privies.[33]

The Miles Brewton House, 27 King St., Charleston

Miles Brewton, the man for whom the house was built, was one of Charleston's wealthiest merchants and slave traders. Born in Charleston in 1731, he worked his way up through the ranks and invested his wealth in "ships, land, and conspicuous consumption." The house he built on King Street was a visible reflection of his wealth. Brewton entertained often and on a grand scale. In 1773, he had as his dinner guest the Boston lawyer and patriot, Josiah Quincy, Jr., who marveled at the opulent display:

> Dined with considerable company at Miles Brewton, Esqr's, a gentleman of very large fortune: a most superb house said to have cost him 8000£, sterling. The grandest hall I ever beheld, azure blue satin window curtains, rich blue paper with gilt, mashee borders, most elegant pictures, excessive grand and costly looking glasses etc.... A most elegant table, three courses, nick-nacks, jellies, preserves, sweetmeats, etc. After dinner, two sorts of nuts, almonds, raisins, three sorts of olives, apples, oranges, etc. By odds the richest wines I ever tasted.... At Mr. Brewton's side board was very

magnificent plate: a very large exquisitely wrought goblet, most excellent workmanship and singularly beautiful. A very fine bird kept familiarly playing over the room, under our chairs and the table, picking up crumbs, etc., and perching on the window, side board and chairs: vary [sic] pretty.[34]

Despite his status as a wealthy businessman, Brewton placed his principles and the welfare of his countrymen above the interests of his purse and became one of the colony's foremost early patriots—albeit a conservative one. Miles Brewton esteemed both his American countrymen and his British king, and fervently hoped that bloodshed might be avoided. Despite his close ties to the Mother Country, when it came time to stand and be counted, he stood with the patriots, not the Tories. Miles Brewton did not live to see the fruit of his patriotism. In the summer of 1775, he and his wife packed their trunks. On August 24, they and their three children took ship for Philadelphia, where Brewton evidently planned to leave his family with relatives while he returned to his business and patriotic duties in Charleston. They never arrived. The entire family was lost at sea and never seen again.[35] Theodosia would come to know this house well, because in her time, it was the home of her father-in-law, Col. William Alston, and the place where she would give birth to her only child.

The Lowcountry rice planters did not lack in cultural sophistication, but their agricultural society and the wide distances between their plantations made social intercourse more difficult and less frequent than in large cities. In describing America in 1800, Henry Adams said "The small society of rice and [sea island] cotton planters at Charleston, with their cultivated tastes and hospitable habits, delighted in whatever reminded them of European civilization. They were travelers, readers, and scholars; the society of Charleston compared well in refinement with that of any city of its size in the world, and English visitors long thought it the most agreeable in America.... The

Duc de Liancourt in 1796 found that nowhere in the world was hospitality better exercised than in South Carolina."[36]

Moving from the fast-paced urban North to the slow-moving rural South was a major transition for Theodosia, and it probably induced a severe case of culture shock. When she arrived in South Carolina, she faced a daunting set of challenges. She had just moved from a large city to a rural plantation, and now she had to integrate her life with that of her new in-laws, adapt her northern habits and behaviors to those of the South, adjust her relationship to slaves and their owners, and assume her roles as the mistress of a large plantation and as a woman in southern society.

The first hurdle was the relative isolation of her new home. She had left the excitement of post-Revolutionary New York, the nation's first temporary capital, for life on an agricultural plantation ten miles from the small village of Georgetown, South Carolina. The sudden lack of companionship would have been hard for any young woman.

In terms of social status, Theodosia and Joseph Alston were on an equal footing. Both were descendants of multiple generations of hard-working and respected ancestors who had served their country nobly in the revolution. In terms of money alone, Theodosia had "married up." Joseph Alston had a great deal more wealth—land, annual income, and money in the bank —than Aaron Burr. The only area where Alston fell short was the size and quality of his house at The Oaks. Tara it wasn't.[37]

The Oaks house that Theodosia knew was the second to sit on a small knoll that commanded a view of Oaks Creek and the Alston rice fields. The plantation itself extended from the edge of the Waccamaw River to the salt marsh on the lower extremity of Murrell's Inlet, thereby forming a cross-section of the Waccamaw Neck.[38]

The first house on the site had a dirt floor and is believed to have been constructed in the early 1730s by William Allston. In 1744, at the age of 11, Joseph Allston inherited the house from his father, William. Sometime after Joseph reached legal age in 1756, Joseph took down the original 1730s house and built a more permanent house over the remains. By the 1760s, The Oaks had been developed into a handsome and productive plantation. When Josiah Quincy visited in 1773, he recorded the following description:

> Spent the night with Mr. Joseph Allston, gentleman of immense income all of his own acquisition. He is person between thirty-nine and forty, and a very few years ago begun the world with only five negroes—has now five plantations with an hundred slaves on each. He told me his neat [net] income was but about five or six thousand pounds sterling a year, [but] he is reputed much richer. His plantation, negroes, gardens, etc. are in the best order of any I have seen! He has propagated the Lisbon and Wine-Island grapes with great success. I was entertained with more true hospitality and benevolence by this family than any I had met with.[39]

Joseph "of The Oaks" Allston died in 1784, leaving the plantation and its house to his grandson, Joseph Alston (the second generation of the "one-L" Alstons and the future governor), when he reached the age of twenty-four. That happened in 1803, two years after his marriage to Theodosia. At that time, the house was about forty years old. Young Joseph had lived with his father, William Alston, in his Charleston townhouse and at his Clifton and Fairfield plantations. Who actually lived at The Oaks between 1784 and 1803 is not certain. By the time of Joseph's marriage to Theodosia, the house had seriously deteriorated. There were numerous cracks and openings in the wall planking, making the house both drafty and a haven for insects. In short, it was in need of substantial renovation and nowhere near fit to welcome a new bride.

No image of The Oaks house is known to exist, but extensive archaeological research carried out by James L. Michie in the 1990s tells us a great deal about Joseph and Theodosia's residence. The Oaks that they finally moved into in 1804 was a wooden frame house, thirty-two feet deep and forty-two feet wide, with a pair of end-gabled chimneys. The front porch faced the entrance road; the back porch faced the rice fields and the kitchen building. The Waccamaw River was out of sight, and only Oaks Creek was visible from the house.[40] The out-of-the-way location and unimpressive vista of The Oaks house—facing, as it did, on a simple road, rather than on one of the prestigious rice rivers—reinforced its modest social status. It was a relatively unpretentious farmhouse of moderate size, probably one-and-a-half stories high, set on brick piers, and built chiefly of longleaf pine. The interior walls had been coated with a thick application of yellowish-orange, shell-based plaster, covered with a thin coat of white plaster, which filled in the cracks left by three different patterns of crude and irregular wooden siding.[41] It was perhaps a third the size and nowhere near as sophisticated as Burr's ornate mansion, Richmond Hill. A double row of slave quarters stood behind and to the east of the house. Compared to the many large and elegant plantation houses that lined the Georgetown District rice rivers, The Oaks was no showplace.

Theodosia was distinctly unimpressed with the house at The Oaks, and the datelines of her letters indicate that she spent most of her time at Hagley and Clifton instead. The letters she wrote expressing her reservations have not survived, but one of her father's replies reflects them. "I am gratified that you do not begin with splendor," he wrote. "To descend with dignity is rare."[42]

Even if the house was not in the same class as Richmond Hill or the Miles Brewton House, its contents reflected the opulent lifestyle that the Alstons embraced in Theodosia's time. The tables at The Oaks were set with fine Chinese porcelain, stenciled creamware, blue transfer-printed pearlware, silver- and bone-handled knives, engraved punch bowls, small engraved bowls, faceted and clear leaded-glass decanters and tumblers, and stemmed wine glasses.[43]

Theodosia and Joseph enjoyed a variety of brewed beverages (such as cider, porter, beer, and ale), distilled spirits (such as gin), and wines. The house at The Oaks had a garret, which was ideal for the storage of Madeira.[44] This fortified Portuguese wine is similar to port and sherry. It was a favorite of the planters in eighteenth- and nineteenth-century South Carolina because it would age perfectly when stored in their hot garrets. The production of "Lisbon and Wine Island grapes," which Josiah Quincy noted in 1773, demonstrates that Joseph Alston of The Oaks was attempting to produce his own Madeira. Like their president, Thomas Jefferson, and Burr himself, Theodosia and Joseph enjoyed champagne. That, however, may have been the end of the similarities that Theodosia shared with her new family and neighbors.

In New England, Theodosia was the daughter of a free-thinking, opt-out descendant of generations of Calvinist ministers. Although she had not burned as many theological bridges as her father had, there is no record that she attended church in the north and it is unlikely that she attended public worship services on any regular basis after she moved south. In South Carolina at the time, religion was chiefly a woman's sphere, one to which men gave approval but little presence, except for service on the vestry. However, even that was a civic, rather than religious, duty. Theodosia's absence from worship at either of the nearby parish churches would have been noticed and discussed by the other plantation wives and would have served to estrange her from the local community rather than help her bond with it.

Despite the fact that her father was a slaveowner during Theodosia's childhood, and she was accustomed to seeing slaves at Richmond Hill, nothing could have prepared Theodosia for the sea of black faces that confronted her when she arrived at Clifton. In 1820, blacks outnumbered whites by a ratio of more than eight to one in Georgetown District.[45] With more than two hundred slaves, Joseph Alston had double the quantity necessary to be designated one of the "great planters" by agricultural historians. Nevertheless, a number of his Georgetown District friends owned many more. They included his Waccamaw Neck neighbor, Joshua John Ward, who in the 1850s owned the largest number of slaves in America—nearly

1,100—who produced an annual crop of 4,500,000 pounds of rice for him.[46]

Burr's position as a strong and early supporter of abolition, and of teaching slaves to read and write, could not have sat well with the Alstons, who were among the largest slaveowners in the state. Indeed, one of Joseph Alston's nephews, Edward Jenkins Pringle, became one of the South's chief apologists for slavery when he published his carefully written defense of the "peculiar institution" entitled *Slavery in the Southern States* in 1852.[47] However, in 1801, the full force of Northern Abolitionist pressures had yet to be felt by the Southern planters, and Burr's status as a slaveowner may have mitigated some of their apprehension of his abolitionist views.

Theodosia's new role as mistress of a large plantation was a significant change from that of socialite mistress of Richmond Hill, for she was now responsible for the medical welfare and provisioning of over 200 slaves; twenty times as many as at Richmond Hill.[48] Then there was the climate. In New England, people adapted to each of the four seasons as they came and went. In South Carolina, the planters made annual migrations from their city homes to their plantations around the end of November, lived there until late March or April, and then moved back into their city homes or off to cool resorts and spas in the North or abroad.

For the women, plantation life frequently meant drudgery, isolation, and boredom. To see another white person besides her husband and son, Theodosia would have had to travel more than a mile by carriage to the next plantation. In New York, she needed only to look out the window or next door. Being stranded on the Georgetown District rice plantations along the Santee, Waccamaw, or Black Rivers for five or six months meant being cut off from the social intercourse, genteel refinements, and innocent pastimes to which Southern women were supposed to confine themselves. One of Theodosia's young relatives by marriage poignantly expressed this sense of isolation at the age of eleven, when she wrote about winter at Beneventum Plantation on the Black

River, "I do not like the country as well as town, as I find it too dull, particularly, situated as we are, so far from all our little friends."[49]

Jane Lynch, mistress of Greenfield, a large rice plantation on the Black River near Georgetown, described the "everlasting routine of plantation life": "Boxes of stores to be opened, and tidily put away (N.B. that last I confess to not doing) negro breeches that must be cut out, and coat sleeves that 'won't come out' (6 yds. to the contrary notwithstanding)—Cows that will not find their calves...and lavish their milky and maternal treasures on the wrong ones—oxen that run away in the swamp and are never to be coaxed back—invisible stomach aches and visionary pains in the side etc etc etc etc etc etc."[50]

For the planters and their sons, the mild winters on the plantation offered hunting deer in the pine forests; shooting snipe and waterfowl; shrimping amidst the rich, odorous pluff mud of the tidal marshes; fishing and crabbing in the creeks; and living out their fantasies of being English country gentlemen. Intemperance was a major vice. Many a night in the great Alston mansion on King Street, parties were held where the doors were locked after the ladies had been sent off to the withdrawing room to talk and sew, and no man was permitted to leave until he was roaring drunk.

What little entertainment the planter families did have in the country came from visiting each other. They traveled by carriage or by boats rowed by slaves, who transported the families between the plantations that lined the tidal rivers like pearls on a necklace. Entertaining at the evening dinner table was the chief form of social life. The planters had plenty of time to enjoy themselves, as the slaves did all the heavy work, and the overseers took care of most of the on-site management. The plantation mistress managed the house slaves—the chambermaids, nursemaids, wet nurses, cooks, seamstresses, and butlers. The oversight of the hostelers (horse handlers) and carriage drivers was considered "mens' work," and those tasks fell to her husband.

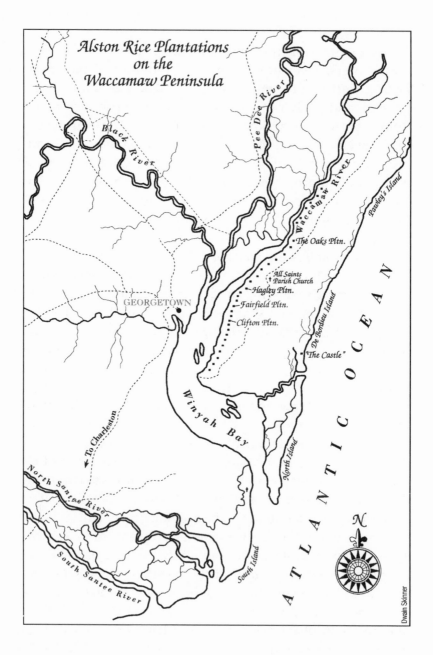

Alston Rice Plantations
on the
Waccamaw Peninsula

Theodosia also had to rise to the challenge of being the chief public health officer for the slaves. It was her job to visit their houses frequently, observe and inquire about their health, and monitor the state of their pregnancies. She also had to maintain an adequate stock of medical supplies and remedies, visit the slaves' infirmary when notified that someone was ill, and determine whether to summon the professional attention of a local doctor. In addition, she was the plantation's quartermaster and commissary, with the biannual role of distributing "Negro cloth," needles, thread, and shoes to the slaves. These duties would have come as a surprise to any young woman from New York City.

While she had the duties of plantation mistress added to her life, she suffered the loss of intellectual stimulation she was accustomed to at Richmond Hill. For Aaron Burr's daughter, this would have been an enormous letdown. Of all the cultured and refined women who wintered on the rice rivers, there was none who could match Theodosia's prodigious education or acquaintance with the foremost men or women of her time. Mary Wollstonecraft and her radical feminist theories were virtually unheard of in South Carolina, and even if they had been better known, they would have been discounted or derided. On the other hand, the concepts of Lord Chesterfield, which stressed courtly civility, social gloss, and the dominance of men, had deep roots in the Southern soil.

Loving and solicitous as they were, Joseph Alston and his extended family were no substitute for the brilliance of her father, the sophistication of Natalie de Lage and Madame de Senat, or the excitement of conversing at Richmond Hill with Presidents Washington, Jefferson, and Madison; Vice President Adams; Alexander Hamilton; Mohawk Chief Joseph Brant Thayendanegea; and Frenchmen cut from the cloth of Charles Talleyrand, Count de Volney, and Louis Philippe. For Theodosia, what passed for social life on the Waccamaw must have been painfully dull and a great disappointment. Her boredom was apparent to Burr, for he wrote to her, "Go to the races, and appear to be amused. Be more social."[51]

Theodosia coped with her father's absence through frequent correspondence and long, annual trips to the North. Upon learning that Burr would be unable to visit them that spring after their wedding, Theodosia immediately began preparing for a trip to see him. On May 26, 1801, her bags were nearly packed. Burr wrote that he was making camp in Broadway and that Richmond Hill would be vacant until their arrival. Besides the reunion with her father, Theodosia also had her friend, Natalie de Lage, close to mind. That summer, she knew, would be the last chance she would have to see Natalie for... who could tell how long?

The boat trip to New York City commenced in June, just as Theodosia was turning eighteen. She and Joseph had a warm reunion with Burr in the city and at Richmond Hill. In late June or early July, "the Little Matron," as Burr referred to her, and her husband used the mansion as their base camp for an extraordinary expedition into the backwoods of New York State.[52] They set out to visit Niagara Falls, one of the greatest natural wonders of North America, and to accept the invitation of Chief Joseph Brant Thayendanegea, who had invited her to visit his home and nation four-and-a-half years earlier.

Author Dwight Whalen wrote that the Alstons set out on their adventure with a party of servants and hostellers and nine packhorses. After reaching the frontier town of Buffalo, they pushed on and arrived at Niagara several days later, at the end of July.[53] Theodosia wrote to her sister-in-law, "If you wish to have an idea of real sublimity, visit the Falls of Niagara—they are magnificent; words when applied to express their grandeur appear to lose half their significance—to describe them is impossible; they must be seen."[54]

The bridal tour of the early nineteenth-century was much different than the honeymoon of present times. In Theodosia's time, the bride and groom, often accompanied by female family members, spent their time visiting friends and relatives who could not attend the ceremony. Theodosia's bridal tour started in Albany and wound its way south via Washington, giving the Alston and Burr friends along the way the opportunity of

The Falls at Niagara

meeting the new spouse. The Alstons' visit to Niagara was the second leg of their nuptial tour.

Theodosia and Joseph were the first recorded couple to have made the Falls of Niagara part of their bridal tour, and their example started a trend. In December 1803, Jerome Bonaparte, a younger brother of Napoléon and a guest of Aaron Burr's at Richmond Hill, married an American, Elizabeth Patterson. In the first summer of their married life, they also visited Niagara. With these wealthy luminaries setting the example, a national tradition—honeymooning at Niagara Falls—was born.[55] Burr was elated. On August 20, he wrote to Theodosia, "I was so very solicitous that you should see Niagara, that I was constantly filled with apprehension lest something might prevent it. Your letter of the 29th July relieves me. You have actually seen it."[56]

Burr also encouraged his young painter friend, John Vanderlyn, to visit the Falls. On September 18, 1801, Burr wrote to Thomas Morris that Vanderlyn was preparing to return to France and wanted to take with him some American scenes. "For this purpose he is now on his way through your country to Niagara. I beg your advice and protection. He is a perfect stranger to the roads, the country, and the customs of the people, and, in short, knows nothing but what immediately concerns painting."[57] Vanderlyn completed his trip to Niagara in the fall of 1801, taking a steamboat from Kingston, his home on the Hudson River, upstream to Albany, and then made the rest of the trip by stagecoach and horseback. At Niagara, he stayed on the British shore for twelve days and made many sketches, although he was "initially disappointed at the lack of mountains and hills that he thought would be a part of his composition."[58] He finished the sketches when he returned to his New York studio that fall and began working on his paintings the next summer. He took the sketches to London in 1803 in search of an engraver.[59] He subsequently returned to Niagara in 1827 and 1837, and his Niagara paintings are among the best known of his works.[60]

From Niagara, Theodosia and Joseph traveled on to visit Chief Brant at Burlington Bay, Ontario. Since the chief had not seen her since she was a little girl, Gov. George Clinton gave the young married couple a cordial letter of introduction.[61] Brant's home was an impressive sight in the middle of the wilderness: a five-bay Georgian manor house with a Palladian fanlight above its portico.[62]

The meeting was fascinating for all parties, and Burr wrote to Theodosia, "Your determination to visit Brandt [sic] gives me great pleasure, particularly as I have lately received a very friendly letter from him, in which he recapitulates your hospitality to him in *ancient days*, and makes very kind inquiries respecting you; all this before he could have entertained the remotest idea of seeing you in his own kingdom."[63] The newly-weds proceeded on to York, Kingston, Montréal, and Québec, and then turned south. On the last day of September, the Alstons had the honor of dining with President Jefferson, an event that Theodosia enthusiastically described in a letter to Frederick Prevost and his wife, Frances. The delight she took in Frederick's friendship is evident in the playful tone of her letter. From Dumfries, Virginia on October 18, 1801, she wrote:

I sat down with a determination to scold you for breach of promise as to your second visit, but you are, I believe, too far off—there are two disadvantages which attend venting one's passion at so great a distance, the first is that the pleasure of witnessing its effects can not be enjoyed, & as that, with me, is the principal charm of scolding, I will not for the present be in good humour; but woe be unto you when we meet. Thus far, we have come more rapidly than we at first intended, for our plan was to have passed two or three days in Philadelphia; but the good people there have taken it in their heads that there was literally a plague in N[ew] York and thus excluded all coming thence from the city & county of Phila[delphia]—under a fine of five hundred dollars & they placed guards round the town & sent health officers about the county to enforce the law—we got into the latter by stealth and rode round the city—then we determin[e]d to indemnify ourselves at Baltimore but hearing on our arrival that there were some good races &c. were soon to take place at Richmond, we ate a hasty dinner & set off for Washington, where we remained yesterday & had the felicity of dining with

the President—it became lawful for me as my friend
Mrs. Maddison was there—the house [i.e., the executive mansion] is really superb; it is built with a white
stone which gives it an elegant appearance outside, inside it is well divided, but not as elegantly furnished as
it ought to be.[64]

In New York in early October, Theodosia bade a tearful
farewell to Natalie de Lage, after which she and Joseph took
ship for Charleston.[65] Natalie sailed for France the following
week.

Burr was enormously pleased with Theodosia's trip. From
New York on November 3, 1801, he wrote, "You made two,
perhaps more conquests on your Northern tour—King Brandt
and the stage-driver; both of whom have been profuse in their
eulogies. Brandt has written me two letters on the subject. It
would have been quite in style if he had scalped your husband
and made you Queen of the Mohawks."[66] Burr could make
jokes of the event because he and Brant were good friends.

Brant had written Burr in 1801 supporting the ordination
of Davenport Phelps as an Episcopal priest and missionary to
the Mohawks in the area of Niagara. The application was successful, and the missionary was ordained in New York in 1801.
Whether Burr was involved in facilitating the ordination is not
known. However, he wrote Theodosia in December 1801, "Yesterday, Mr. Phelps, mentioned in the enclosed, delivered to me
two pair of moccasins, directed—'From Captain Joseph Brant
to Mr. And Mrs. Alston.' Your ship having sailed, I don't know
how or when I shall forward them to you; but we will see. I
send the original of Captain Brant merely to show you how an
Indian can write. It is his own handwriting and composition.
Upon this notice of his attention you should write him a letter
of acknowledgment for his hospitality, &c."[67]

The Alstons had just passed through North Carolina when
Burr wrote to Theodosia, "This fine day brings me to your
two letters from Raleigh and Fayetteville, 28th and 30th of October. It is quite consoling to find that you will have taken the

precaution to inquire the state of health before you venture your precious carcass into Charleston. A fever would certainly mistake you for strangers, and snap at two such plump, ruddy animals as you were when you left New-York." Burr went on to say that treats would soon be in store for them after they reached home. "You shall have apples, and nuts, and a cook, and lucerne [alfalfa] seed. As to femme de chambre [a chamber maid], I cannot speak with certainty. I have put in motion the whole French republic on the occasion." Burr continued, expressing his affection for Natalie. "A letter received from Madame d'Lage since Natalie sailed, advises us that she is there waiting for her, which is indeed most fortunate, and relieves me from a small portion of the anxiety which I suffer for that charming girl."[68]

With Theodosia and Natalie gone, and Burr serving his four-year term as vice president in Washington, he gave serious consideration to selling Richmond Hill. The reason had nothing to do with his feeling for the place or his need of it. Burr was searching for funds to pay his debts. A proposed sale for $140,000, which Burr described as "though not half the worth, is enough and more," fell through, and the mansion remained in his hands for several more years.[69] In retrospect, he would have been fortunate had he sold it at that price.

Whether he was in debt or not, nothing was too good for his Theodosia. In the winter of 1801, he sent her a new maid and cook. He wrote that the maid was, "a good, steady-looking animal, agée vingt trois [age 23]. From appearance, she has been used to count her beads [pray the rosary] and work hard, and never thought of love or finery. The enclosed recommendations of Madame Dupont, the elder, will tell you more. You are in equal luck with a cook. I have had him on trial for a fortnight, and he is the best I have ever had in the house; for cakes, pastry, and jimcracks, far superior to Anthony. In short, he is too good for you, and I have a great mind not to send him; you will be forever giving good dinners. He has something of the manner and physiognomy of Wood, your teacher. M'lle la femme de chambre and Monsieur le Cuisinier [the maid and the cook] are both pure French (not creole), and speak well the language. He will take with him a quantity of casseroles dishes and other implements of his etat [trade]."[70]

As soon as Joseph Alston returned to his native state, he traveled to Columbia on business. In a letter to his new bride dated November 25, 1801, he showed his tender affection for Theodosia when he closed his letter with the words, "Adieu, ma femme—Je t'embrasse [I do nothing but think of thee]."[71]

Three weeks later, Burr took up an increased correspondence with him, with the aim of drawing Alston deeper into the world of national politics—and fatherhood. On December 13, 1801, Burr wrote "Herewith is enclosed a duplicate of the bill of lading, specifying the articles shipped for you on board the Protectress—She sailed this afternoon. The president's message, of which a copy was sent to you by this ship, will have reached you through other channels long before her arrival. One idea contained in this message is applauded by our ladies. They unite in the opinion that the 'energies of the men ought be principally employed in the multiplication of the human race,' and in this they promise an ardent and active co-operation.... I hope the fair of your state will equally testify their applause of this sentiment; and I enjoin it on you to manifest your patriotism and your attachment to the administration by 'exerting your energies' in the manner indicated."[72]

Burr was thrilled when, in late January 1802, he learned that his son-in-law, aided by the romantic powers of Lelawala, the original "Maid of the Mist," and He-no, the "Thunder God" of Niagara, who lived in a cave behind the Horseshoe Falls, had worked their magic. Theodosia was pregnant, and the vice president was about to become a grandfather. He immediately dashed off a congratulatory letter to Alston. "The successful 'execution of your energies,'" Burr wrote, "is highly grateful to me. It seems probably that I shall pronounce, in person, on the merit of the workmanship somewhere about May day."[73]

Burr wanted to roam the mountains of North Carolina when he came to visit. But most of all, he wanted a healthy child and daughter. "You must walk a great deal," he instructed

Theodosia. "It is the only exercise you can take with safety and advantage, and, being in Charleston, I fear you will neglect it. I do entreat you to get a very stout pair of over shoes, or short boots, to draw on over your shoes. But shoes to come up to the ankle bone, with one button to keep them on, will be the best; thick enough, however, to turn water. The weather has not yet required this precaution, but very soon it will, and I pray you to write me that you are so provided; without them you will not, cannot walk, and without exercise you will suffer in the month of May. To be at ease on this subject, you must learn to walk without your husband—alone—or, if you must be in form, with ten negroes at your heels. Your husband will often be occupied at the hours you would desire to walk, and you must not gener [distract] him: oh, never."[74] A few days later he added the caution, "Do not suffer a tooth to be drawn, or any operation to be performed on your teeth." [75] With the baby due in late spring, the proud almost-grandfather immediately set out to arrange his trip to the South.

It was clear that Theodosia missed her home. Thinking already about a return trip to the North, Theodosia wrote to Frances Prevost in March that it would be wonderful to see their *two sons* playing together. With her characteristic tact and charm, she also noted that if the child were to be a daughter, "my only wish is that she may be the Frances of her day."[76]

Theodosia was no longer a girl but a married woman and an expectant mother. The next phase of Burr's master plan for her education consisted of broadening her knowledge of the world. Until her marriage, her education had consisted of instruction in languages, literature, philosophy, and European history, with each subject being taught by a specialized tutor. Now Burr set her out to become a woman who was broadly informed in all areas of world geography and current events. In this quest, her tutors were going to be the world's journalists.

"I wish you would learn to read newspapers; not to become a partisan in politics, God forbid; but they contain the occurrences of the day, and furnish the standing topics of conversation," Burr wrote. "The reading of newspapers is a knack which you will acquire in six weeks, by reading, during that time, every thing. With the aid of a gazetteer and an atlas, you must find every place that is spoken of. Pray, madam, do you know of what consist the 'Republic of the Seven Islands?'"[77] Do you know the present boundaries of the French republic? Neither, in all probability. Then hunt them."[78]

Burr was never satisfied with the volume of correspondence that he received from her. After joking that she was a lazy correspondent, he wrote facetiously, "I wish you would teach a half dozen of your negroes to write; then you might lay on the sofa, and if you could submit to the labor of thinking and dictating, the thing would go on." From the eternal taskmaster he turned a few lines later into an amorous widower on the prowl and asked Theodosia if she had given any thought to seeking out some female companionship for him when he came south.[79] Burr then returned to the subject of writing, but this time, he spoke of his future grandchild, which he guessed would be a boy. "If you will have Pet or Peet, Peter, Peter Yates, Peter Alston, Petrus Burr (or by every other name he may be known) taught to write a good hand, and make me a present of him, I will subscribe myself your very much obliged and humble servant."[80]

The date on which Congress would adjourn kept changing, and now Burr was predicting that the twenty-day carriage trip would not happen until May. "I could, with pleasure, have passed the summer with you in the mountains; but the heat and dissipation of Sullivan's Island is not so inviting," he wrote.[81] However, nothing was going to stop him from meeting his first grandchild. He wrote to Alston a few days later, "Nevertheless, I shall come, though *at your hazard*, which, you know, would be a great consolation to me if I should be caught by a bilious fever in some rice swamp." Of Theodosia, he wrote, "With her Northern constitution she will bring you some puny brat that will never last the summer out; but, in your mountains, one might expect to see it climb a precipice at three weeks old."[82]

As the time to depart from Washington drew near, Burr passed along further details of his trip. He planned to take coaches to Charleston via Richmond to Fayetteville and from there to Georgetown and Clifton. "I have ordered Vanderlyn to send you, from New-York, both his and Stuart's pictures of A. Burr; and have told him to ship himself for the port of Charleston on the 1st of May.[83] I have also desired that my beautiful little bust of Bonaparte be sent to Mr. William Alston."[84] That bust graces the mantle in the withdrawing room of the Miles Brewton House to this day.

So great was Burr's desire to be present for the birth of his grandson that he left Washington while Congress was still in session. The vice president arrived in the rice country on Friday, April 30, where he received the hospitality of Mr. Kinloch, a fellow rice planter and neighbor of Joseph's father. Burr found transportation to Clifton on Saturday, May 1, only to find that Theodosia and Joseph were in Charleston. The next day he tried to engage a stage to take him and his baggage to Charleston, but he wrote from Clifton, "Unfortunately, the stage was full— not even a seat vacant for the vice-president. I am, therefore, doomed to remain here one day longer, and to be two days on the road. My horses not having arrived, Mr. [William] Alston will, on Wednesday morning, set out with me in his curricle [a two-person, open carriage]. We shall dine and stay the night of Wednesday at Mrs. Mott's, and on the day following, Thursday evening, reach Charleston."[85]

The news of his impending arrival had already reached Charleston, and the Charleston *Times* announced, "The Vice-President of the United States is expected in town, this evening. The Federalist Artillery Company have orders to salute him on his landing." The arrival actually took place on the 6th, when his carriage was floated across the Cooper River from Mt. Pleasant to Charleston. The joyous reunion of father and daughter was further enhanced by the splendid reception given the vice president by the city. On Friday evening, May 7, Burr attended the presentation of a play entitled "Lovers Vows," the proceeds from which went to benefit the city's orphans. A week later, the newspapers noted, "the Vice-President of the United States dined with the citizens of this place at the

Carolina Coffee-House. The arrangements made by the committee merit the approbation of the company; nothing was wanting to secure the most perfect harmony and satisfaction. Captain John Blake presided. On entering the room to dinner, Burr's march, by Mr. Foucard, was performed by the band." Eighteen toasts were drunk during the festivities.[86]

With the birth of his grandchild seemingly not imminent, Burr made a short trip to Savannah, where he also found an extremely warm and formal welcome. But the most important celebration came the next week. Back in Charleston, Aaron Burr Alston was born about May 22, 1802, just over nine months after his parents had explored the natural wonders of Niagara Falls.[87]

The painful and extensive consequences of her son's birth were to define Theodosia's physical existence for the rest of her life. Theodosia's agony peaked and ebbed, but never left her in comfort for long. The physicians of her day had neither the ability to properly diagnose illness nor the means to treat it. Consequently, Theodosia was in constant pain.

No one knows where in Charleston Aaron Burr Alston was born. Three possible sites have been proposed: the luxurious, three-story townhouse belonging to Joseph's brother, Charles Cotesworth Pinckney Alston, at 21 East Battery Street; Joseph Alston's three-story single house at 94 Church Street; and his parents' home, the Miles Brewton House, at 27 King Street. Upon examination, the choice quickly narrows.

The birth could not have taken place at Charles Alston's house, because he was only six years old when his nephew was born and did not buy the splendid mansion on East Battery until 1838. Joseph Alston's own house at 94 Church Street is a possibility. His father, Col. William Alston, purchased the house after 1799 and, in 1805, gave it to Joseph, who sold it the same year. Depending upon how Colonel Alston was using the house in the summer of 1802—it may have been occupied by renters or other family members at the time—it is theoretically possible that Aaron Burr Alston was born there. However, a better candidate exists: the Alstons' stately Palladian mansion on King Street.

In 1792, Joseph's widowed father, Col. William Alston, remarried, and purchased The Miles Brewton House at #27 King Street from his new wife's relatives. Joseph and all of his brothers and sisters grew up there, and Joseph lived there until his marriage. In 1802 one would have found William Alston, aged 46; his second wife, Mary Brewton Motte Alston, aged 33; and five or six children from toddlers to their late teens living there. It provided an ideal environment for childbirth. Numerous servants and wetnurses were available, and the city's best physicians stood at the ready. The withdrawing room, on the second floor just off the ballroom, had long been used as the "birthing chamber," a family tradition that originated before the revolution and continued into the 1880s.

The Alston plantation houses at Clifton and Hagley (but not The Oaks, then under renovation), would have been totally unsuitable because of the threat of summer fevers. After considering all these factors, the "ancient family homestead" on King Street seems to be the most likely birthplace for Aaron Burr Alston. Burr was in Charleston for the better part of May and early June, except for the few days spent in Savannah. What finer residence in the city was available to accommodate the visiting vice president than the Alston family mansion on King Street?

Surrounded by her loving mother-in-law, sisters-in-law, and numerous black maids, Theodosia went through an unusually painful delivery.[88] It was a difficult birth, but mother and child survived. Aaron Burr Alston grew into a healthy, normal little boy, but the aftereffects of the difficult birth took a heavy toll on his young mother. At the time, the magnitude of her gynecological problem—a prolapsed uterus—could neither be properly diagnosed nor treated, so Theodosia's only alternative was to bear the pain and hope it would go away. She was cursed to seek the counsel of esteemed and learned physicians who did not know how to examine her, how to determine what was wrong with her, or how to treat her. In this light, it is not hard to see why neither her husband's wealth nor her father's influence could bring her any relief from what would be a full decade of physical agony and emotional despair.

Burr, who had been only a door away from his daughter during the agonizing birth, immediately wanted to whisk his ailing daughter and new grandson away from Charleston's oppressive summer heat. Although he was busy minding the affairs of his large plantation and campaigning for a seat in the South Carolina legislature, Joseph Alston objected, but he ultimately agreed because of the presumed advantage the change of climate would bring to his wife's health.

One June 16, when her son was barely three weeks old, and a week before she turned nineteen, Theodosia boarded the brig *Comet* in Charleston harbor. With her sailed her father, her son, and her sister-in-law, Maria Alston, wife of Sir John Nisbet. They arrived in New York a week later. With this trip, Theodosia established a new variation on the planter's annual migration. Starting in 1802, she and her son would spend five or six months each summer and fall with her father in New York, with or without her husband. This demonstrated an astonishing degree of female independence; something totally without parallel in the South, but Theodosia was nothing if not unconventional.

The day after their arrival in New York, Theodosia reached Richmond Hill and composed a long, heart-felt letter to her distant husband. After describing the beauty and grandeur of her beloved northern home, she wrote, "How much did I wish for you to join with me in admiring it. With how much regret did I recollect some rides we took together last summer. Ah, my husband, why are we separated? I had rather have been ill on Sullivan's Island with you, than separated from you. Even my amusements serve to increase my unhappiness; for if anything affords me pleasure, the thought that, were you here, you also would feel pleasure, and thus redouble mine, at once puts an end to enjoyment." Theodosia envisioned a four-month stay and assured her new husband, "God knows how delighted I shall be when once again in your arms."[89]

Joseph had evidently complained about the poor quality of the cigars available in Charleston, for on June 26, Theodosia wrote, "I send you a box containing a thousand; the seller took some trouble to choose the best for me, and I have added some

Vanilla and Tonka beans to them."[90] She was concerned that "the filth of the streets in Charleston" might be the cause of the disease there, and added, "Perhaps I am wrong in both my reason and opinion. If so, you are able to correct; only do as you think best, and be prudent. It is all I ask. I imagine the subject worth a reflection, and you cannot err. Montesquieu says he writes to make people think; and why may not Theodosia?" She closed her letter with the fond observation, "our son looks charmingly."[91]

In July, wonderful news arrived at Richmond Hill: Natalie de Lage was about to be married to none other than to Thomas Sumter, Jr., the South Carolina gentleman she had met aboard ship on her way to France. "Nothing could be more grateful to me than your proposed connexion with Mr. Sumter," Burr wrote to his expatriate darling girl, now almost twenty years old. Burr noted that although he knew little about the young man, he had a fine reputation, and he (Burr) would "most cordially take him to my bosom as a son." Burr went on to say that he and the elder Sumter had "long been acquainted" and that they had been "fellow-soldiers during our revolutionary war, in which he acted a most distinguished part." Burr promised to divide his time in South Carolina equally between Natalie and Theodosia. "Which is my favourite daughter I have not yet been able to decide," he told Natalie. "We must not, however, abandon New-York. I will have you both there, if possible, every year, and at Richmond Hill you shall renew the recollection of the happy hours of your childhood."[92]

Theodosia expressed her inherent fondness for New York over any other place in a letter to Joseph two days later. "With the beauty of the country it is impossible not to be delighted, whether that delight is confessed or not; and every woman cannot fail to prefer the style of society, whatever she may say. If she denies it, she is set down in my mind as insincere and weakly prejudiced."[93]

Theodosia's warm and endearing letters in the summer of 1802 masked the shocking realities of her medical condition. Burr suggested that she spend time "taking the waters" at the spa in Ballston, New York, a favorite summer watering hole for the affluent families of both the North and the South. In fact, the waters of the spa could have little effect on her health. Her prolapsed uterus had rendered her incapable of having more children. Soon, gruesome recurring uterine infections greatly added to her misery, as well as making marital sexual relations impossible. For the rest of her days, these plagues constantly sapped her strength, threw her into bouts of depression, and several times threatened her life.

In literature written after her death, Theodosia was frequently painted as being neurotic, a hypochondriac, or suffering from a "frail or delicate constitution" or "nervous fevers." Many writers gave the impression that she was somehow medically or psychologically defective, but nothing could have been further from the truth. Theodosia had a highly trained mind and never failed to exercise full command of her considerable senses. Although frequently in agonizing pain, she faced and fought her medical challenges at every juncture. She forced her mind past the limitations of her body to carry out her duties— and destiny—despite the severe limitations imposed upon her by the primitive state of medical knowledge and the men who exercised it.

In desperation over her agony, but constrained even from accurately describing her symptoms to her male physician, she told her dear sister-in-law, Frances Prevost that she was about to "lay a very heavy tax" upon her. Theodosia's physician in New York, Dr. Samuel Bard, had prescribed "partial cold bathing" as a cure for her severe gynecological infections. The doctor's prescription made it obvious that he had no idea what was wrong with her or if by some chance he did, he had no treatments that could address her specific medical problems. Theodosia wrote that "after making use of this prescription for a day or two I was troubled by violent pains beginning sometimes at my back or side and going through me....A horrible sensation like a spike running up me worried me all yesterday."

Theodosia, not wanting to offend the doctor, asked Frances to discretely contact Dr. Bard and ask him what she should do next. "I know I am asking you to do a very unpleasant thing, but where can I apply, what can I do?" Theodosia wrote. Frances rose to the occasion, and Bard's new prescription brought some temporary relief. In profuse gratitude, Theodosia wrote to Frances, "Never, never, my best friend, shall I forget this mark of your affection. How few women are there who could have risen superior to all the false delicacy in which our sex in general rather pride themselves."[94]

Whatever the problems Theodosia might be laboring under, she knew how thrilled Burr was to have his grandson by his side. Grandfather Burr was ecstatic when the boy could finally gurgle out "gamp" or "gampy" for "grandfather," and from that point on, Burr called him by those two names, as well as the "heir apparent," "the V.P.," or "The Vice President." Abigail Adams, who often ran into Burr in Washington, complained at length to her sister, Mary Cranch, that Burr was so proud of talking about his grandson that "You would think to hear him that no man in the world had ever been a grandfather before."[95]

The spas had no curative effects on Theodosia, whose health careened wildly during the fall. On one day Burr would learn that she had recovered her appetite and spirits, and on the next that she was suffering again. Three physicians whom Burr had consulted decided in September, in their collective wisdom, that Theodosia's ills would be alleviated if she stopped nursing her baby. Theodosia "peremptorily refused," Burr wrote to Alston, "and the bare proposition occasioned so many tears and so much distress that I abandoned it. Within the last three days, however, she has such a loss of appetite and prostration of strength, that she is satisfied of the necessity of the measure for the sake of the child, if not for herself, and I have this day sent off a man to the country to find a suitable [wet] nurse."

Burr went on to say that Theodosia had left Ballston Spa, and he was certain that had she stayed there two weeks longer, "the cure would have been radical. The ride to [the] Hudson, only thirty miles, brought on a relapse," he wrote, "and, with slight variations, the affliction was increased and her strength diminished. [Dr.] Bard advised the Springs, and was quite angry that she left them," Burr reported. "There is nothing in this disorder," Burr pronounced, "which immediately threatens life; nor is it, at present, attended with pain; but if it should become fixed upon her, of which there is danger unless speedily cured, it will unfit her for every duty and every enjoyment in life. The medicines, which under the direction of Bard she used at Lebanon [another spa], have hitherto proved ineffectual since her return. I have written fully to Eustis, and expect his answer within two or three days."[96]

At the end of September, Theodosia heard that her husband was ill. Ignoring her own medical predicaments, she wrote to him, "You have been imprudent, and all my fears are fulfilled. Without any one near you to feel for you, attend to you, to watch every change and share every pain. Your wife only could do that. It is her whose soul clings to yours, and vibrates but in harmony with it; whose happiness, whose every emotion, more than entirely dependent on yours, are exchanged for them." Theodosia had yet more love to share with her husband. "Your son, too, were we with you, would charm away your cares. His smiles could not fail to soothe any pain. They possess a magic which you cannot conceive until you see him."[97]

Theodosia missed her husband as much as she enjoyed being near her father. In September 1802, while Alston was assiduously campaigning for a seat in the South Carolina legislature, Theodosia wrote to show her concern for his career and well-being. "How does your election advance? I am anxious to know something of it; not from patriotism, however. It little concerns me which party succeeds. Where you are, there is my country, and in you are centered all my wishes. Were you a Brutus, I should be a Roman. But were you a Caesar, I should only wish glory to Rome that glory might be yours. As long as you love me, I am your wife and friend: contented and proud to be that." In closing her letter, she showed her teasing wit. "I am very happy you have chosen chess for your amusement. It keeps you constantly in mind how poor kings fare without their queens."[98]

A month later, Theodosia was no longer capable of writing in the role of the loving, attentive wife. She was desperate and in fear for her life. "You already know the result of my confinement in bed," she wrote to her husband on October 30, 1802. "It certainly relieved me for some time, which proves how easily that cure would have succeeded at first. I have now abandoned all hope of recovery. I do not say it in a moment of depression, but with all my reasons about me."

Then her letter turned eerily prophetic. "I am endeavouring to resign myself with cheerfulness; and you also, my husband, must summon your fortitude to bear with a sick wife the rest of her life. At present, my general health is very good; indeed, my appearance so perfectly announces it, that physicians smile at the idea of my being an invalid. The great misfortune of this complaint is, that one may vegetate forty years in a sort of middle state between life and death, without the enjoyment of one or the rest of the other. You will now see your boy in a few days, and you will really be very much pleased with him. He is a sweet little rascal. If Heaven grant him but to live, I shall never repent what he has cost me."[99]

In another month, the fates again intervened, this time for the better. In November, Burr wrote to Alston, "The cold weather of the last ten days has had a happy effect on Theodosia. She is so far restored that I can with confidence assure you that she will return in health. The boy, too, now grows fat and rosy with the frost. They have taken passage in the brig Enterprise, Captain Tombs, the same with whom we came last June."[100]

Theodosia, her son, and Lady Nesbit arrived home on November 24, just after her newly elected husband traveled to Columbia to take a seat in the South Carolina House of Representatives for the first time. Inspired in part by ambitions fueled by his father-in-law, Alston was elected as a Democratic-Republican member representing Christ Church Parish, which lay between his home parish, All Saints, and the city of Charleston. It was the first of ten two-year terms that he served in the state legislature, the last three of which (1805-

1809) he served in the additional capacity of Speaker of the House.

Burr welcomed the news of Theodosia's safe arrival. "All of this I learned last night," he wrote on December 4. "Vanderlyn and I drank a bottle of Champagne on the occasion." He went on to note that Vanderlyn had finished the portrait he had started while Theodosia was last there, and the artist exclaimed with enthusiasm, "This is the best work I have ever done in America."[101]

Joseph Alston had spent time the previous year buying new furniture for The Oaks, but the place was nowhere near ready for habitation, so the young family continued to spend the winters at Clifton. It is somewhat of a mystery where they lived while in Charleston, for on January 26, 1803, Burr wrote, "I can't conceive how you all stow yourselves into that little wreck of a mansion." He may have been jokingly referring to the Miles Brewton House. But if so, it was neither little—it had three floors, fifty-four by sixty-five feet, versus Richmond Hill's fifty by sixty feet—nor a wreck, as it was widely known then, as now, as one of the finest residences in America. Burr made it clear that the summer of 1803 was to be reserved for visiting him in New York or, perhaps, joining him for a "tour through the western country."

From Clifton in March, the middle of the South Carolina springtime, bad news arrived for Burr. Theodosia's health had again plummeted. She was delirious with fever and near death. Once again, she valiantly showed her resilient spirit:

> I have been quite ill till within these two or three days totally unable to write. The whole family, as well as myself, had begun to think pretty seriously of my last journey; but fortunately, I have had the pleasure of keeping them up a few nights and drawing forth all of their sensibility, without giving them the trouble of burying, mourning, &c. I was one night so ill as to have lost my senses in a great measure; about daylight, as a last resource, they began plying me with old wine, and blisters to my feet. But, on recovering a little, I kicked off the

blisters, and declared I would be dressed; be carried in the open air, and have free use of cold water. I was indulged. I was carried below, where I drank plentifully of cold water, and I had my face, neck, and arms bathed with it, and it assisted most astonishingly in recovering me. The day before yesterday I was put on a bed in a boat and brought up here [to Clifton]. The change of air and scene have assisted me wonderfully. I am again getting well. Indeed, the rapidity with which I gain strength surprises the whole family. The secret is, that my constitution is good. I exert myself to the utmost, feeling none of that pride, so common to my sex, of being weak and ill. Delicacy and debility are sometimes fascinating when affected by a coquette, adorned with the freshness of health; but a pale, thin face; sunken, instead of languishing eyes; and a form, evidently tottering, not gracefully bending, never, I suspect, made, far less could they retain a conquest, or even please a friend. I therefore encourage spirits, try to appear well, and am rewarded. In a few days I shall be on the high road to health. Mari [French for husband and her nickname for Joseph] is well, and the boy charming."[102]

Theodosia and Joseph spent the summer and fall of 1803 in New York, visiting the spas, staying at Richmond Hill, and making a trip to Washington to see Burr. There Theodosia exchanged visits with her friend, Dolley Madison, of whom she noted, "she is still pretty; but oh, that unfortunate propensity to snuff-taking." Theodosia also reported taking tea with the Secretary of the Treasury and his wife, Albert and Hannah Gallatin, noting "nobody asked us to eat."[103]

Two Alstons—husband Joseph and, perhaps, one of his brothers—had accompanied them to the North on this trip. The return trip by carriage seemed to drag on forever, and Theodosia was becoming cranky from being cooped up for so long with them and her two-year-old. After nearly three weeks of travel, she wrote to Burr, "Thank Heaven, my dear father,

I am at Lumberton, and within a few days of rest. I am sick, fatigued, out of patience, and on the very brink of being out of temper. Judge, therefore, if I am not in great need of repose. What conduces to render the journey unpleasant is, that it frets the boy, who has acquired two jaw teeth since he left you, and still talks of *gampy*. We travel in company with the two Alstons. Pray teach me how to write two *A*'s without producing something like an *Ass*. We expect to reach Georgetown the 1st of November. There we shall remain three or four days, and then proceed to Charleston."[104]

Much to the delight of the vice president, his little Gampy grew like a weed. Much to Joseph's delight, Gampy also recognized Col. Alston as "grandfather." Burr had returned to Washington after Gampy's birth only to be inundated with political brushfires, vicious partisan attacks and backbiting, and the appearance of scurrilous newspaper articles and books. He rose to face each challenge in turn, always calm, ever resolute, and thoroughly disciplined. All the while he presided over the Senate, showing a thorough knowledge of the bills as they made their way through the legislative process, exercising firm and impartial discipline upon the speakers, and generally seeking to carry out the nation's business without undue favoritism.

In his letters to Theodosia, he regularly commented upon his long-standing affair with Céleste, a high-born Philadelphia society woman with whom he narrowly avoided committing matrimony. Theodosia knew and liked her and thought that Burr had made a serious mistake in not pursuing her with less intrigue and more forthrightness. But Burr was an incorrigible flirt, who "distracted himself with many women, and committed himself to none."[105] Whether by chance or by choice, the opportunity to marry Céleste slipped through his fingers.

Theodosia and her family returned to Clifton early in November 1803 so that Joseph could attend to his legislative duties. Theodosia seems to have moved back and forth between Clifton and Hagley that winter. She would have preferred to be moving into their permanent home, The Oaks. There, work progressed at a snail's pace, exasperating Theodosia. At the rate things were going, she must have thought, she would be an old woman before she ever lived in her own house. From Clifton on November 8, 1803, she wrote to Burr, "We have visited the Oaks house since our arrival. The lazy workmen have been wasting their time, and have not yet finished what two Northern workmen could have done in a month. They are in the act of plastering, and that will not be dry enough to admit us in some time. Thus I will remain with John [John Ashe Alston] till Mr. Alston returns from Columbia. Do you think we may safely enter the house then? The plastering will be finished in less than a week hence; and the legislature, you know, adjourns at Christmas. I am particular on this subject, because I have known persons to suffer from inhabiting a house too newly finished, and I wish to have your opinion."[106]

Burr wrote back on December 6 with practical advice. "Your house will not be a fit or healthy residence for your boy before the middle of April or 1st of May," he said. "The walls may, to the touch, appear dry in three or four weeks; but shut up any room for twelve or twenty-four hours, and enter before it be aired, you will meet an offensive, and, as I believe, a pernicious effluvia; an air totally unfit for respiration, unelastic, and which, when inhaled, leaves the lungs unsatisfied. This is the air you will breathe if you inhabit the house. I could, perhaps, show chymically how the atmosphere of the closed rooms becomes thus azotic, but I prefer to submit to the test of your senses."[107] The Alstons heeded Burr's advice. They didn't move into the house at The Oaks until March 1804. Burr replied to the notice that they had moved by saying "the pretty description of your house and establishment, and all, were very amusing."[108]

In November 1803, Theodosia received news that in order to pay off debts, Burr had finally sold most of the land surrounding Richmond Hill to John Jacob Astor, but that "the house, outhouses, and some three or four acres remain. Enough to keep up the appearance, and all the pleasant recollections of your infantine days, and some of your matronly days also, are reserved with interest. This weighty business, however, is completed, and a huge weight it has taken from the head and shoulders, and every other part, animal and intellectual, of A.B." Then Burr's pen turned to his grandson. "If little *gamp* could read, I should write him volumes. I find my thoughts straying to him every hour in the day, and think more of him twenty fold than of you together."[109]

When Theodosia and Gampy returned home in the winter of 1803-1804, Burr constantly inquired about him. "Of the boy you never say enough," he wrote of his twenty-month-old grandson. "Nothing about his French in your last. I hope you talk to him much in French.... You do not say whether the boy knows his letters. I am sure he may now be taught them, and then put a pen into his hand, and set him to imitate them. He may read and write before he is three years old. This, with speaking French, would make him a tolerably accomplished lad of that age, and worthy of his blood."[110] A few months later, he wrote again with great impatience, "Does he yet know his letters? If not, you surely must want skill, for, most certain, he can't want genius."[111]

By December, Theodosia evidently had found some way to get the toddler to put marks on paper, which Burr pronounced to be a letter. He wrote to her, "Tell dear little gampy that I have read over his letter a great many times, and with great admiration. Mrs. Law, to whom I showed it, thinks it a production of genius."[112] Another effort a few months later produced more adulation. "The letter of A.B.A at the foot of yours, was far the most interesting. I have studied every pothook and trammel of his first literary performance, to see what rays of genius could be discovered." [113]

More good news came just before Christmas. Natalie de Lage—now Mrs. Thomas Sumter, Jr.—had a baby of her own, a daughter named Natalie Annette, nicknamed "Nat." Her mother had kept in regular contact with Burr and Theodosia during her French sojourn. After spending several months in England, where they acquired two English maids to help Natalie make the transition to the world of plantation mistress, the Sumters departed England on October 2, 1803. They

arrived in Charleston on November 20, just in time for the
Christmas social season. Theodosia had planned to meet them
at the docks, but after waiting several days, departed for
Clifton just three hours before their ship landed. When she
received word that they were indeed in Charleston, she and
Joseph hastily returned to the city, where the two women
celebrated a joyous reunion, and the two South Carolinians
met for the first time.

On December 10, 1803, Theodosia gave the following report to her father: "I found Natalie delighted to see me, and
still pretty. She has grown thinner, much thinner; but her complexion is still good, though more languid. The loss of her hair
is, however, an alteration much for the worse. Her crop is pretty,
but not half so much as her fine brown hair. I write you all
these foolish little particulars because you enter into them all,
or, rather, are sensible of all their importance to us. Natalie has
a lovely little daughter called after her. Mr. Sumter is very affectionate and attentive to her, and polite to me. I like him infinitely better than I did. He is an amiable, good-hearted man,
with talents to render him respectable."[114]

The Alstons took the Sumters to their home at 94 Church
Street, just a few blocks from the docks, where the Sumters spent
several weeks as their guests. After rounds of festivities, where
Theodosia noticed that Natalie was getting more than her share
of the attention, the Sumters moved on to their new home in
Stateburg, South Carolina, in the district named after her father-in-law's ancestors.[115]

Burr wrote to Natalie, "Your safe arrival, my dear Natalie,
gave me the greatest joy. Theodosia has given me a detailed
account of yourself and your lovely little girl. All as I could
wish. I could never realize that you were not lost to me till I
heard that you were actually on American ground. Your letter relieved my anxieties and fulfilled my hopes, by assuring
me of your unabated affection. But when or where, I pray,
are we to meet? Engage Mr. Sumter to come and pass the
summer [of 1804] with me at New-York; by the summer I
mean from the 1st of May till the middle of November.... You

will review with pleasure the scenes of your sportive childhood, and you will gratify the fondest wishes of your affectionate friend and father."[116]

Burr had the same plan for seeing the Alstons that year. Joseph Alston had recently purchased a tract of land called Montalto, near Richmond Hill, which he planned to develop as their summer residence. At the time, Burr had his New York headquarters in John Street, from which he was actively running his campaign for governor of New York. Burr painted a lavish and inviting picture of how the Alstons should spend their summer with him.

> You take Richmond Hill; bring no horses or carriage. I have got a nice, new, beautiful little chariot, made purposely to please you. I have also a new coachee, very light, on an entirely new construction, invented by the vice president. Now these two machines are severally adapted to two horses, and you may take your choice of them. Of horses I have five; three always and wholly at your devotion, and the whole five occasionally. Harry and Sam are both good coachmen, either at your orders. Of servants there are enough for family purposes. Eleonore, however, must attend you, for the sake of the heir apparent. You will want no others, as there are at my house Peggy, Nancy, and a small girl of about eleven. Mr. Alston may bring a footman. Anything further will be useless; he may, however, bring six or eight of them, if he like. The cellars and garrets are well stocked with wine,[117] having had a great supply last fall. I shall take rooms (a house, &c.) in town, but will live with you as much or as little as you may please and as we can agree; but my establishment at Richmond Hill must remain, whether you come or not. Great part of the summer I shall be off eight or ten days at a time, but no long journeys. You will have to ride every day or two to Montalto to direct the laying out of the grounds &c. In this way you cannot, without wanton extravagance,

expend more than four hundred dollars. If you insist on bringing your horses, there is now room for them, and plenty of provender. You ought to come by water, but not to be swindled again by taking a cabin. Bring your Ada ["dah," a black nursemaid], if you please, to finish her education.[118]

1804 was the defining year in Burr's life. It had certainly started off well. On January 3, he had written to Peggy Gallatin, one of his servants at Richmond Hill, "to assure you that I am in perfect health.... that I have had no duel or quarrel with anybody, and have not been wounded or hurt."[119] In February, he was nominated as a candidate for governor of New York, running against Judge Morgan Lewis. Soon after this, he was inviting the Alstons and the Sumters to spend the summer and fall with him at Richmond Hill and celebrate a grand reunion.

Then in April, things began to sour. The election campaign turned incredibly vicious and personal. In the same month, Burr wrote to Theodosia that his plan to become governor of New York had been "lost by a great majority."[120] From that point on, Burr's life spiraled totally out of control. Three months after the lost election, Burr and his arch-rival, Alexander Hamilton, would meet with pistols on a dueling field at Weehawken, New Jersey, across the harbor from New York City. The outcome would seal the fates of both men.

CHAPTER 6

The Clouds of Weehawken

The flame of daughter-love
Burned bright as erst and her sweet loyalty
Was a pure fire untouched by evil breath
                                    —Alexander T. Ormond

The historic duel at Weehawken, New Jersey, in the early hours of July 11, 1804, was the start of the most bizarre period in Theodosia's life. It unleashed a cornucopia of fantasies and set into motion an array of plans that launched her, her husband, her father, and a long, odd cast of characters on a vision quest so grandiose, complex, and mysterious that no one other than Burr himself could possibly have conceived it. The immediate outcomes were the end of Hamilton's life and Burr's reputation. The less obvious result was that after Hamilton's death, Burr—an enterprising man now without hope for a respectable career in the East—was forced to seek other, less orthodox ways to occupy his extraordinary mind and prodigious energies.

In South Carolina, Theodosia knew nothing of her father's plans. Only Burr; Hamilton; Nathaniel Pendleton, Hamilton's second; William Van Ness, Burr's second; and a few close friends knew about the duel in advance. Indeed, on June 23, two days after Theodosia's birthday, while the final dueling formalities were being arranged, Burr wrote to her about the birthday party held for her *in absentia*. "The Laights and half a dozen others laughed an hour, and danced an hour, and drank [your] health at Richmond Hill. We had your picture in the dining-room; but, as it is a profile, and would not look at us, we hung it up, and placed Natalie's at table, which laughs and talks with us."[1] No mention was made of an impending crisis.

Burr deliberately kept Theodosia in the dark until the last possible moment. On the evening of July 10, the night before the mortal combat, he sat down and quietly composed a long letter to her, written in the most matter-of-fact manner. He started out with a chivalrous request designed to protect any of those closest to him—notably his lovers—from harm.

"Having lately written my will, and given my private letters and papers in charge of you, I have no other direction to give you on the subject but to request you to burn all such as, if by accident made public, would injure any person. This is more particularly applicable to the letters of my female correspondents," he wrote.[2] Burr had planned that his son-in-law someday would write his biography, and he told Theodosia, "All my letters, and copies of letters, of which I have retained copies, are in the six blue boxes. If your husband or anyone else (no one, however, could do it so well as he) should think it worth while to write a sketch of my life, some materials will be found among these letters."[3]

To Natalie de Lage Sumter, he could afford to leave nothing, "for the very good reason that I had nothing to leave any one. My estate will just about pay my debts," he wrote, "and no more." But nevertheless, he wanted to leave his almost-daughter something precious to remember him by. "Give Natalie one of the pictures of me. There are three in this house; that of Stuart, and two by Vanderlyn. Give her any other little tokens she may desire. One of those pictures, also, I pray you to give to Doctor Eustis."

He directed that his stepson, Bartow Prevost, receive "something—what you please," and later awarded him his watch. Burr evidently thought that his other stepson, Frederick, was a more likely future dueling candidate than Bartow and left to him his wearing apparel and "a sword or pair of pistols." Burr later instructed his daughter, "When you come hither you must send for Frederic, and open your whole heart to him. He [Frederick] loves *me* almost as much as Theodosia does; and he does love *you* to adoration."

Burr's last requests tell us more about his slave-owning philosophy. He asked Theodosia to convey to Peggy Gallatin, a favored slave at Richmond Hill, "the small lot, not numbered, which the fourth article [of his will] mentioned in my list of property. It is worth about two hundred and fifty dollars. Give her also fifty dollars in cash as a reward for her fidelity," he wrote. "Dispose of Nancy as you please," he continued. "She is honest, robust, and good-tempered. Peter [Yates] is the most intelligent and best-disposed black I have ever known. (I mean the black boy I bought last fall [1803] from Mr. Turnbull.) I advise you, by all means, to keep him as the valet of your son. Persuade Peggy to live with you if you can."

Then Burr moved on to his most important treasures: his intellectual property. "Burn immediately a small bundle, tied with a red string, which you will find in the little flat writing-case—that which we use with the curricle [carriage]. The bundle is marked '*Put.*'[4] The letters of *Clara* (the greater part of them) are tied up in a white handkerchief, which you will find in the blue box No. 5.[5] You may hand them to Mari [Joseph Alston], if you please. My letters to Clara are in the same bundle. You, and bye-and-by Aaron Burr Alston, may laugh at *gamp* when you look over this nonsense. Many of my letters of *Clara* will be found among my ordinary letters, filed and marked, sometimes '*Clara*,' sometimes 'L.'"

Burr, the father-teacher-taskmaster of her life, closed with a heartfelt message that expressed his total satisfaction with his daughter—and urged her to keep striving for the goals that he expected her to achieve. "I am indebted to you, my dearest Theodosia, for a very great portion of the happiness which I have enjoyed in this life. You have completely satisfied all that my heart and affections had hoped or even wished. With a little more perseverance, determination, and industry, you will obtain all that my ambition or vanity had fondly imagined. Let your son have the occasion to be proud that he had a mother. Adieu, adieu. A. Burr."[6]

Burr also had some parting instructions for his son-in-law. Along with John Swartwout and William P. Van Ness in New York, Joseph and Theodosia were co-executors of his estate. Burr left his bills and his estate to Joseph Alston. The latter included Richmond Hill, its furniture, paintings, library, maps, and wine. Burr suggested that the fully furnished Richmond Hill would be a "more convenient residence" than Alston's partially completed New York country estate, Montalto, "particularly as no expense will be necessary for buildings or improvements."

Then Burr made the purpose of his letter perfectly clear to Theodosia's husband. "I have called out General Hamilton, and we meet to-morrow morning. [William] Van Ness will give you the particulars. The preceding has been written in contemplation of this event. If it should be my lot to fall, * * * * * * * * [sic] yet I shall live in you and your son. I commit to you all that is most dear to me—my reputation and my daughter. Your talents and your attachment will be the guardian of the one—your kindness and your generosity of the other."[7]

Always the master of destinies, Burr then added, "Let me entreat you to stimulate and aid Theodosia in the cultivation of her mind. It is indispensable to her happiness and essential to yours. It is also of the utmost importance to your son. She would presently acquire a critical knowledge of Latin, English, and all branches of natural philosophy. All this would be poured into your son." Lest Alston dismiss his request, Burr pressed on with an emotional appeal. "If you would differ with me as to the importance of this measure, suffer me to ask it of you as a last favour. She will richly compensate your trouble."[8] After finishing his letter, Burr lay down on a couch in his library and fell into a deep sleep.[9]

This letter to Alston gives us insights into the puzzling dichotomy of Burr's intentions for his daughter. He hides the facts of his upcoming duel from Theodosia, but reveals them to her husband. Then he tells Alston how he (Burr) will live on through his son-in-law and grandson, without mention of his daughter. Burr has educated her to the utmost degree, but based on his actions immediately prior to the duel, the question arises: was it Burr's intent to create through Theodosia's education a prototype for generations of women to come, or just to produce a suitable super-teacher for his grandson?

The roots of the duel lay in Burr's politics. He was a skilled master at building support bases for his plans. In New York, one of his Federalist opponents admitted that Burr, "by his arts & intrigues...[has] done a great deal towards revolutionizing the State."[10] From New York, Burr built the political base that would substantially help his national career. In 1800, Hamilton actively opposed Burr and attempted to convince his colleagues that Burr was a man whose "public principles have no other spring or aim than his own aggrandisement." He stated that Burr's "insatiable appetite" and "personal financial irresponsibilities" would lead to "corrupt expedients" and the use of "unprincipled men" of all parties to "overrule the good men of all parties." Hamilton stated that Burr's career "proves that he has formed himself upon the model of a Cataline, and he is too cold blooded, and too determined a conspirator ever to change his plan."[11]

Despite Hamilton's opposition, Jefferson was elected president and Burr vice-president on the thirty-sixth vote in the deadlocked House of Representatives. Burr went on to be sworn in as the nation's third vice president and took his seat as president of the Senate. Pressured by his friends for political appointments, he passed the names of many cronies along to Jefferson for approval, but the Virginian vetoed many of them. Jefferson's final insult to Burr came when he rejected Burr's campaign to have his ally (and future biographer), Matthew L. Davis, appointed to a naval post in New York. Burr's access to Jefferson was virtually closed, and Jefferson turned to George Clinton or his nephew, DeWitt, for advice about appointments.

As president of the senate, Burr, a skilled parliamentarian, earned high marks from virtually all of his colleagues. "Mr.

The scene of the duel, overlooking New York City

Burr, the Vice President, presides in the Senate with great ease, dignity & propriety," wrote Senator William Plumer, a Federalist from New Hampshire. "He preserves good order, silence— & decorum in debate—he confines the speaker to the point."[12]

Nevertheless, the Clintons, aided by James Cheetham, publisher of New York's *American Citizen*, waged a vicious war against Burr in the newspaper and through flyers. "The handbills were numerous…uniform however in Virulent and indecent abuse… I discover that to villify A.B. was deemed of so much consequence, that packages of them were sent to Various parts of the country…. These papers were exhibited as being characteristic of the party by which they were issued."[13] That party was, of course, Hamilton's Federalists.

Burr also had problems within his own party, who came to regard him as an "unprincipled opportunist who would stop at nothing to rebuild his shattered political and personal fortunes."[14] As a Jefferson biographer noted, Burr "offended one side without satisfying another."[15] Jefferson refused to support Burr on his second-term ticket, replacing him with George Clinton.

When Burr's term as vice president was about to expire, he paid a rare visit to Jefferson. His request, couched in a diplomatic tone, was simple: he wanted Jefferson to acknowledge his service to the Republicans by offering him a diplomatic post or by backing him for governor of New York. "He seemed in effect to be offering to go into exile quietly," wrote Buckner F. Melton, "if only Jefferson would grant him a last political wish."[16] As he had so many times before, Jefferson gave Burr an enigmatic response and then ignored him. Rebuffed, Burr threw himself into the 1804 New York gubernatorial race as an independent candidate.

In this contest, Alexander Hamilton put forth his utmost energies against Burr and was soon "intriguing for any candidate who can have a chance of success against A.B." Though the relations of these political leaders had remained outwardly friendly, Hamilton had not hesitated to express in private his distrust of Burr and to block several of his ambitious projects.

The campaign soon turned bitter, and there were many flagrant attacks on Burr. Broadsides in both English and German titled *Poor Behrens!* claimed that he had cheated a man out of his inheritance of $30,000; *Poor Morgan!* said that Burr had ordered a man whipped thirty-nine times for no good reason while he commanded the Westchester lines. Another alleged that he had lured and kept the daughter of a Washington tradesman in his Partition Street house for nefarious purposes; yet another insinuated that Burr had consorted with prostitutes while his wife lay dying. As he had when encountering personal attacks in the past, Burr said nothing.

Even though Burr threw himself into the fray with great vigor, he lost by an overwhelming 8,000-vote margin to the Federalist candidate, Morgan Lewis, Chief Justice of the New York Supreme Court. Burr had now been shunned by his own party and trounced by the Federalist opposition. He was a man with nowhere to go—except after his nemesis, Alexander Hamilton.

A crisis was quickly at hand, fueled by Hamilton's chronically loose tongue. In the spring of 1804, Judge John Taylor of Albany gathered a group of Federalists for dinner at his home on State Street. They included Hamilton, Judge Kent, and Dr.

Charles D. Cooper, a passionate admirer of Hamilton. The discussion soon turned to the upcoming election, whereupon Hamilton let loose with his views. Cooper wrote to Philip Schuyler that "Gen. Hamilton and Judge Kent declared, in substance, that they looked upon Mr. Burr to be a dangerous man, and one who ought not to be trusted with the reins of government." Then he went on to say, "I could detail to you a still more despicable opinion which General Hamilton has expressed of Mr. Burr."[17] The letter was published in the *Albany Register* on April 24, 1804.[18] The four words, "still more despicable opinion," published for the world to see, were the straws that broke the camel's back.

When he heard of the statements made by Hamilton at the dinner party, Burr insisted on "the necessity of a prompt and unqualified acknowledgment or denial of the use of any expressions which could warrant the assertions of Dr. Cooper."[19] But just what was Hamilton's "still more despicable opinion?" This question, which remains unanswered, has fascinated historians since the day it was uttered. A number of opinions have been voiced. Not surprisingly, given the two men involved, they all revolve around politics or women.

Burr's perceived threat to the Union as a potential secessionist is cited as one possibility for the "still more despicable opinion" that Hamilton could have expressed. If this is true, Hamilton would have had to pick Burr out of a long lineup of outspoken secessionists, many of whom were New Englanders of Hamilton's own party. In 1803, Jefferson completed the Louisiana Purchase, which doubled the size of the United States. He quickly filled the new government posts with Republican officials, whose influence over the newly enfranchised voters was obvious. New England—the only place where the Federalists held sway—was reduced to a minority section of the country. A collection of anti-Jefferson fanatics known as the Essex Junto saw the nation's westward expansion as the death knell for the power of New England. They proposed to carve off the New England states, plus New Jersey and New York, and, with Hamilton's leadership, secede from the union.

"Secession of the New England states, a new Northern federal union, seemed the only way out to some."[20]

Hamilton turned them down, so in 1804, New Hampshire senator William Plumer and two other New England proto-secessionists, Timothy Pickering and James Hillhouse, dined with Burr. Plumer recalled, "Mr. Hillhouse unequivocally declared that is was his opinion that the United States would soon form two distinct & separate governments. On this subject Mr. Burr conversed very freely—& the impression that his observations made on my mind was, that he not only thought such an event would take place but that it was necessary that it should."[21] Hamilton made public Burr's secessionist sentiments in a letter to Robert G. Harper on February 19, 1804. If Burr won, he announced, "a dismemberment of the Union is likely to be one of the first fruits of his elevation."[22]

If Burr were proposing secession, it would be a direct violation of his oath of office to "protect and defend the Constitution of the United States" and, therefore, a treasonable action. Was holding secessionist tendencies Hamilton's "still more despicable opinion" of Burr? That is unlikely, for to pillory Burr for secessionist leanings would mean that dozens of other New Englanders—Federalist and Republican alike—would have to be locked into the stocks with him. And to admit that Burr had been conspiring over secession with Federalists would have been just the thing Jefferson would have jumped on and made public, as he hated both Burr and the Federalists.

The first speculation of a feminine impetus for the duel appeared in an 1860 pro-Burr novel by Jeremiah Clemens, entitled *The Rivals: A Tale of the Times of Aaron Burr and Alexander Hamilton*. This tale has Burr issuing the challenge because Hamilton had allegedly driven a woman named Adelaide to insanity and death and had destroyed the reputation of Margaret Moncrieffe, later Mrs. Croghan (later divorced), a mistress of Frederick Augustus, the Duke of York, and several other British aristocrats and politicians. She later wrote a book about giving her "virgin love" to "an American colonel" on General Putnam's staff—who may or may not have been Burr—whose caddish conduct when she was a teenager nudged her down the slippery slopes which led to an immoral life.[23] Was this example of Burr's alleged profligacy the "still more despicable opinion" that triggered the duel? Given that both Burr and Hamilton were known womanizers, it hardly seems likely.

In a 1902 novel, *The Conqueror*, Gertrude Atherton suggested that both Hamilton and Burr were lovers of Madame Eliza Bowen Jumel, the rich and notorious widow who, in 1833, became Burr's second wife. In the novel, Jumel, in love with Hamilton, but angry that he broke off the affair, tells him the night before the duel, "when you die, it will be by the hand of my deputy [Burr]. I tell you because I am determined that your last earthly thought shall be of me."[24] However, there is no evidence that Hamilton was ever Jumel's lover, so this theory from fiction must also be discarded.

In 1791-1792, Hamilton had conducted an adulterous relationship with Mrs. James Reynolds, which he admitted to three congressmen. One theory, advanced in 1976 by Hamilton biographer Robert Hendrickson, was that Hamilton thought the affair was a case of sexual entrapment engineered by Burr— who represented Reynolds in her divorce suit—to discredit him. Was this the "still more despicable opinion?" There is no documentary evidence that Hamilton or his descendants thought so.[25]

In his popular 1973 novel, *Burr*, Gore Vidal introduced the most incendiary possible reason for the duel. In his book, a fictional journalist named Charles Schuyler has ingratiated himself with the aged Aaron Burr in order to learn the intimate details of his life and write Burr's biography. When interviewing Burr's close friend, Samuel Swartwout, half drunk and loose-lipped at the time, Schuyler asks him, "What was it that General Hamilton said of Colonel Burr that was so 'despicable'? That made him fight the duel?"

"Swartwout said, 'An ugly story, and it was typical of Hamilton to spread it about…. he said that Aaron Burr was the lover of his own daughter, Theodosia.' Swartwout continued, 'Not until I was half-way home did I begin to wonder whether or not what Hamilton had said might, after all, be true.' Swartwout then reflected on what Burr's second wife, Eliza Jumel, had said of Burr and his daughter, *'He loved no one else.'"*[26]

Vidal, whose historical research for his book was prodigious, later admitted that he had made up the entire concept. "The incest motif," he said, "is my invention. I couldn't think of anything [else] of a 'despicable' nature that would drive AB to so drastic an action."[27] Despite being born of a novelist, and disowned by its own author, the incest motif quickly entered the realm of Burrian folklore. Burr scholars gave it serious consideration for one simple reason: it made sense and had a ring of truth about it.

In 1979, Milton Lomask pointed out that Hamilton might well have believed in the possibility of an incestuous relationship between Burr and his daughter. On June 22, 1792, Hamilton had written a confidential letter to Gouverneur Morris in which he proposed carefully selected Roman code names for the persons to be discussed under the seal of confidentiality. Washington was to be *Scavola*; Jefferson, *Scipio*; and Hamilton himself was to be *Paulus*. For Burr he chose the code name *Savius*, after Plautus Savius, who is known to history solely for the fact that he seduced his nine-year-old son and then "was ordered by a court to take his own life."[28]

In 1998, Arnold A. Rogow addressed the concept and concluded, "It is, indeed, difficult to imagine any other remark of Hamilton's that could have had a similar result. Nor can anyone be certain that the relationship, whatever its nature, between Burr and his daughter was not believed by Hamilton and others to be incestuous." If that were the case, said Rogow, "Burr could never have let a comment like that go unpunished." Rogow also suggested that "Hamilton so loathed Burr—and himself—that he sacrificed his life in order to destroy Burr's future in politics."[29]

Whether or not Burr had a physically incestuous relationship with his daughter cannot currently be proven for want of documentation. Neither Burr nor Theodosia hinted of it on paper, and no third party ever wrote that it was so. However, there is ample evidence, through Burr's pattern of behavior, that Burr was guilty of *emotional* incest. Dr. Patricia Love, author *of The Emotional Incest Syndrome: What to Do When a Parent Rules Your Life,* wrote that "Human beings have an innate need for companionship and intimacy, and when those needs are not met by [an adult] partner, the natural tendency is to turn to a child." She goes on to say that "emotional incest takes place when a seemingly loving parent gives a child messages that make him or her think that she is responsible for filling the parent's emotional needs at an adult level of participation."[30]

Was Burr guilty of emotional incest? This profile accurately describes his relationship with his daughter after his wife died. As the "chosen child," Theodosia became his wife substitute, and even after she married, her primary emotional relationship was with her strong-willed father, not her comfortable and undemanding new husband. Emotionally, Theodosia never left her father's home.

We know that Burr was a lusty lad from his teenage years on and that he had made the gift of his virginity to a New England lass by the time he was seventeen. At Princeton, he is said to have bedded a local girl during his senior year. At the age of twenty-one, Burr carried on his well-known affair with a married woman: his future wife, then Mrs. Theodosia Bartow Prevost. After his wife died, Burr invested all of his emotional energy in his daughter, Theodosia, with whom he had an "uncommon attachment." There is no doubt that his daughter became his substitute wife and confidante after 1794, when she was eleven. Burr constantly reminded Theodosia that she was the center of his universe and that without her, he would be emotionally devastated. Theodosia, in turn, showed an "almost morbid" affection for her father.

Theodosia's relationship with her father was at least, puzzling, and at worst, troubling. Burr often held up Natalie—in whom Burr took a somewhat lascivious interest—as the superior example of deportment, but Theodosia's feelings or objections, if any, are not recorded.

The strangeness of their relationship increased as Theodosia grew up. While she was still a teenager, Burr regaled Theodosia with stories of his mistresses and other amorous affairs. Later, during his European self-exile, when Theodosia was a newlywed in her twenties, he kept a journal for her and occasionally sent her copies. In addition to detailing his daily errands and professional meetings, the journal carefully documented his affairs with women of substance, as well as the whores he regularly rented. For a father to share the intimate details of his sex life with his daughter is certainly bizarre, and well beyond the normal bounds of the father-daughter relationship. It is not hard to imagine that Theodosia, who was intensely in love with, and devoted to, her father, had strongly conflicting feelings when he spoke and wrote this way: arousal, guilt, revulsion, curiosity, and, even, perhaps, fears of her own incestuous desires. Granted, the time period in which they lived was lusty, but nevertheless, Theodosia was young and vulnerable, and her father had no right to violate the intergenerational boundary.

Theodosia was married at a relatively young age (though not unusually so) and to her first serious suitor. Joseph Alston was a perfectly normal and suitable man but not one that a woman who was being brought up to be an intellectual prodigy would logically fall madly in love with. Was Burr pairing her off with a politically useful and wealthy husband or was it a perfectly suitable love match for his upper-class daughter? Viewed from the perspective of an emotionally incestuous relationship, Alston was the perfect husband for Theodosia. His work as a planter and politician was the main focus of his existence. To Theodosia, he was warm, supportive, undemanding—and willing to let Burr remain the primary man in her life.

Theodosia was emotionally welded to Burr, but the marriage he supported would take her far away from him. When Theodosia left with her husband for South Carolina, Burr several times expressed a sense of profound loss that bordered on grief. To compensate, he soon induced her to make annual visits to New York that lasted up to five or six months. He does not seem to have seen his son-in-law as a rival but rather as a con-federate. After Burr's remark to Alston about "exerting his en-ergies" to increase the population, it almost seems as if he was prying between the sheets of their marital bed, wishing in some way to participate vicariously.

Theodosia seemed to experience little conflict about the move south, although she missed her father once they were separated. Why was she willing to endure the foreseeable bore-dom of South Carolina plantation life that her friends had warned her about? If she really was a female Aaron Burr, she would not want to be tied down, yet she had contracted a thor-oughly conventional marriage. Was it because the separation from Burr brought her some psychic space in which to think—and feel—for herself?

Her husband was a warm and supportive man, neither in-vasive nor emotionally needy, but not someone a highly intel-ligent woman would fall deeply in love with. Perhaps she loved him as a rescuer. She probably felt both guilty and relieved about leaving her father. Then, when she became ill, she was once again dependent on her father. Could this have added to her distress? For Theodosia, her relationship with her father may ultimately have been an unavoidable attraction that brought her no real joy; one with a deep sense of obligation and an undercurrent of emotional co-addiction.

The case for emotional incest is substantial. The question that remains unanswered is whether Burr's passion for his daughter extended beyond his heart and mind. At a minimum, Burr's relationship with his daughter was uncommonly intense and filled with eroticism. Whether it literally broke the ulti-mate father-daughter taboo remains a matter of conjecture.

When Cooper's letter alluding to the "despicable opinion" was published in the *Albany Register*, Burr demanded that Hamilton denounce the statement. Hamilton replied with sev-eral letters that obfuscated, waffled, evaded, nit-picked, and ultimately, failed to give Burr the satisfaction he demanded.[31] In June 1804, the month Theodosia turned twenty-one, Burr challenged Hamilton to obtain satisfaction through a duel of honor. Hamilton, knowing Burr's position to be justified, accepted. The weapons would be pistols. The detailed procedures were described in detail by the *Code Duello*, to which most gentlemen of Burr's and Hamilton's class subscribed.

It was an age of dueling. Neither Burr nor Hamilton was a stranger to the deadly sport. In 1799, John Barker Church, Hamilton's brother-in-law, alleged that Burr had taken a bribe. Burr challenged him. On the dueling ground, Burr's first shot missed Church, but Church's ball snapped a button off Burr's coat. As their seconds reloaded the pistols, Church had a change of heart. He apologized, and the duel ended without bloodshed. Hamilton had stood as a second for South Carolina's John Laurens in his duel against Gen. Charles Lee, and Hamilton's son, Philip, died in a duel in 1801, using one of the set of pistols Burr and Hamilton used.

The night before the duel, as Burr was writing instructions for Theodosia and Joseph Alston, Hamilton sat at home, writing a letter to his wife, Elizabeth, to be opened in case the worst came to pass. In it he stated, "it is not to be denied, that my animadversions on the political principles, character and views of Col. Burr have been extremely severe, and on several occasions, I, in common with many others, have made very unfavourable criticisms on particular instances of the private conduct of this gentleman." Then Hamilton created the controversy that would forever surround the duel by stating that he proposed to "throw away" his first fire, and even had thoughts of "reserving my second fire—and thus give a double opportunity to Col. Burr to pause and reflect."[32]   Did Hamilton simply have a death wish?

Why Hamilton did not apologize and, thereby, render the duel unnecessary will never be known. Should he die, his family, which consisted of his wife and seven children, would be at the mercy of relatives for their support. Burr, on the other hand, was a widower with one married daughter. In 1889, one historian proposed that Hamilton, who had lost his son to a duel and had recently witnessed the alarming decline of the Federalist party, "deliberately provoked a duel to end his life without the taint of suicide."[33]

Why Burr carried out his challenge is easier to grasp. His career had been thwarted at every turn by Hamilton and his allies. In addition, Hamilton had slandered his name in public and had refused to acknowledge or retract the statements. By the standards of the day, the duel was fully justified. It was a matter of honor. Burr had no knowledge that Hamilton might be thinking of holding his fire.

The date was the morning of July 11, 1804. The place was the top of the New Jersey cliffs at Weehawken, which offer a spectacular view of New York City. Judge William Van Ness, Burr's second, and his friend, John Swartwout, woke Burr from a sound sleep at Richmond Hill just before daybreak. By prearranged plan, Burr and Hamilton departed the city before daybreak, at about 5:00 A.M., with Burr scheduled to arrive first. John Gould rowed Burr and Van Ness across the Hudson to the dueling ground. As previously agreed upon, Hamilton and his second, Nathaniel Pendleton, arrived a short time later, accompanied by Dr. David Hosack, a physician, who remained a discreet distance away so that he could later state under oath that he did not witness the duel.

After the seconds counted off the ten paces and loaded the specially made, hair-triggered, .54-caliber pistols, which Hamilton, by agreement, furnished, the rivals took their weapons and stood ready. At the command, "Present!" Burr and Hamilton both fired. Hamilton missed; Burr's aim was true. His bullet struck Hamilton in the right side of his abdomen. He fell immediately and died the next afternoon. When Hamilton lost his life, Burr lost his reputation and career. Later, Burr reflected that had he let wisdom prevail, he might have seen that the world was large enough for both him and Hamilton.

Hamilton's death elevated him to instant martyrdom and relegated Burr to eternal infamy. His funeral in New York was "almost Wagnerian" in its scope and drama. In the press and the pulpits, Hamilton was eulogized and his virtues extolled, while Burr was excoriated, even though all of the rules required by the dueling code had been scrupulously observed. All flags in New York flew at half-staff; all businesses were ordered

The duel, as imagined by an early illustrator

closed; and British and French warships in the harbor fired their guns in salute.[34] Burr was literally dumbfounded by the reaction to the duel. As one historian noted, the duel had been "conducted with the utmost propriety, the participants took equal chances of life or death, and, according to the ethics of that age, though not of this, neither was in the slightest degree censurable."[35]

At Richmond Hill, Burr remained secluded. Shortly after he returned from the duel that morning, he was visited by a cousin from Connecticut. Burr received him cordially, invited him to take breakfast with him, inquired about his friends, and exchanged pleasant conversation. The duel was never mentioned. When the young man reached the city, the news was being shouted from every streetcorner: "Colonel Burr has killed General Hamilton in a duel this morning." The relative was dumbfounded. Burr had not seemed the least out of sorts, an indication of the total control he exercised over his actions and emotions.[36]

Although dueling was not uncommon at the time, it was a felony offense in New York and New Jersey, and murder was a crime in all states. The coroner of the city and county of New York sought out witnesses to testify against Burr, but his friends remained loyal, even after the coroner threw Burr's friend (and future biographer) Matthew L. Davis into jail for refusing to testify. Burr was soon indicted for murder in both New York and New Jersey.

The second day after the duel, he wrote to Joseph Alston, "General Hamilton died yesterday. The malignant federalists or tories, and the imbittered Clintonians, unite in endeavouring to excite public sympathy in his favour and indignation against his antagonist. Thousands of falsehoods are circulated with industry.... I propose leaving town for a few days, and meditate also a journey for some weeks, but whither is not resolved. Perhaps to Statesburgh [S.C.]."[37] Burr obviously thought that Natalie Sumter's home on the high hills of the Santee would be a good place to lie low until passions cooled in New York.

The news of the duel came as a heavy blow to the Alstons, then summering in Charleston. Theodosia had just turned twenty-one, her marriage was in its third year, and her son was two years old. She did not yet have a house of her own, her health vacillated between bearable and severely painful, and now her father had been indicted and was being hunted down as an accused murderer. She longed to see and comfort him and be comforted in return. As painful as the news of the duel was to her, she bore it with the unflinching fortitude she had learned from her father. As Pidgin said of her trials and heartbreaks, "one such would have unnerved an ordinary woman, but her teacher had made her a combination of velvet and steel."[38] She was his creation. She accepted his view of the affair verbatim and never blamed him for the duel or its aftereffects. Nevertheless, the day before she heard of the duel was the last truly happy day Theodosia Burr Alston spent on the earth.

Burr started his flight from the ghost of Alexander Hamilton on Saturday evening, July 21, when he and his friend, young Samuel Swartwout, brother of John, and Burr's mulatto servant, Peter Yates, stepped aboard a barge at a little landing behind Richmond Hill. The oarsmen turned downstream and rowed all night. By 9:00 on Sunday morning, they had arrived at the home of his friend, Commodore Thomas Truxtun, at Perth Amboy, New Jersey. After furnishing Burr with overnight accommodations, Truxtun took him twenty miles to a place where he could rent a carriage and horses for his trip south. Burr traveled incognito to Philadelphia, where he arrived on July 24. There, to his amazement, he found that that news of the duel, which had been fought thirteen days earlier, had not yet reached the city.

Burr, Swartwout, and Yates remained in Philadelphia, waiting for news of the coroner's inquest. Burr spent his time enjoying the hospitality of his friend, Charles Biddle; holding mysterious talks with Jonathan Dayton, a former U.S. senator from New Jersey; and trysting with his paramour, Céleste. The news he had feared arrived on August 2: warrants had been issued by the coroner's jury for the arrest of Burr and the two seconds for murder. On August 14, a New York grand jury indicted the three for dueling. Finally, on October 23, a New Jersey grand jury indicted Burr for murder, despite the fact that Hamilton died in New York.[39]

The Vice President of the United States was now a fugitive from the law. He wrote to Theodosia on August 3, "You will have learned, through Mr. Alston, of certain measures pursuing against me in New-York. I absent myself from home merely to give a little time for passions to subside, not from any apprehension of the final effects of proceedings in courts of law.... You will find the papers filled with all manner of nonsense and lies. Among other things, accounts of attempts to assassinate me. These, I assure you, are mere fables. Those who wish me dead prefer to keep at a respectful distance."[40] A week later, just before departing for the South, he wrote to her again and joked, "If any male friend of yours should be dying of ennui, recommend to him to engage in a duel and a courtship at the same time."[41]

Burr's destination could not be Charleston, for he was now subject to arrest and extradition to New York or New Jersey if he showed his face in a major metropolis. Instead, using the alias Roswell King, he headed for Hampton Plantation on remote St. Simon's Island, Georgia, the home of his friend, Pierce Butler. Twelve years Burr's elder, Butler, the son of an Irish baronet, had served in the British army but resigned in 1773 to become a gentleman planter in South Carolina and Georgia. He served as an officer in the Continental Army and as a U.S. Senator from South Carolina. Burr, still accompanied by Yates and Swartwout, departed from Philadelphia on a small schooner on August 11 or 12 and reached Butler's plantation on August 25.

Burr had two goals for his trip. The first was straightforward and tactical: lie low and avoid contact with the law until the hysteria over the duel cooled in New York and New Jersey. The second was strategic: explore Spanish Florida and take the pulse of the people who lived there. Spanish Florida extended south from a line just south of St. Mary's, Georgia, to the tip of the Florida peninsula and west to New Orleans, where the Spanish held a stranglehold on travel and trade on the Mississippi River. Westward expansion by the Americans made Spanish Florida a territory of immense strategic value, and Burr wanted to learn all he could about it. Tensions were running high with Spain, and many Americans expected war to break out at any time. Forced to flee New York, Burr made the best of his time by using it to scout and make friends in this part of what might become his and Theodosia's future empire.

Burr was as welcome in Georgia as he had been demonized in New York. Dueling was more prevalent and accepted in the South. People were genuinely glad to see him. To his friend Biddle, he wrote on September 1, "In this neighbourhood I am overwhelmed with all sorts of attention and Kindness—

Presents are daily sent [;] things which it is supposed I may want so that I live most luxuriously."[42]   Butler's plantation, and that of his neighbor, John Cooper, provided him with accommodations and a lifestyle that were close to paradise.

On August 31, 1804, Burr wrote to Theodosia, "I am now quite settled. My establishment consists of a housekeeper, cook, and chambermaid, seamstress, and two footmen. There are, besides, two fishermen and four bargemen always at command. The department of laundress is done abroad [i.e., nearby]. The plantation affords plenty of milk, cream, and butter; turkeys, fowls, kids, pigs, geese, and mutton; fish, of course, in abundance. Of figs, peaches, and melons there are yet a few. Oranges and pomegranates just begin to be eatable. The house affords Madeira wine, brandy, and porter. Yesterday my neighbor, Mr. Couper, [sic] sent me an assortment of French wines, consisting of Claret, Sauterne, and Champagne, all excellent; and at least twelve months' supply of orange shrub, which makes a most delicious punch. Madame Couper added sweetmeats and pickles.... We have not a fly, moscheto, or bug. I can sit a whole evening, with open windows and lighted candles, without the least annoyance from insects; a circumstance which I have never beheld in any other place. I have not even seen a cockroach." A visiting French girl also provided him with an interesting conversation partner. "Now, verily," he continued, "were it not for the intervention of one hundred miles of low, swampy, pestiferous country, I would insist on your coming to see me, all! Little *gamp*, and Mademoiselle Sum*tare* [Natalie], and their appendages; for they are the principals."[43]

On September 7, St. Simon's was struck by a violent hurricane, which destroyed much of his hosts' rice and long-staple cotton crops. Burr had planned to visit "the Floridas" for five or six weeks but that could not be achieved. Departing on the 15th, he made it as far as the St. Johns River, thirty miles from St. Augustine, and returned to Butler's plantation on the 25th. Despite the luxuries of the island and the copious supply of champagne, Burr's goals were set: bring Theodosia to Natalie's home in Stateburg, where he could visit them both, and then return to Washington to his post as President of the Senate in November. Burr departed St. Simon's on September 28 and arrived in Savannah on October 1, where he was serenaded that evening by a band of musicians and residents eager to greet and talk with him.

Burr had to make a detailed study of maps and gazetteers to reach Stateburg from Savannah. The hurricane had destroyed "every bridge and causeway." A small tornado hit the city on October 1, adding to the damage. Georgetown seemed to be the nearest port to his destination. Charleston was to be avoided, but Sullivan's Island was on his approved list. He proposed to travel from there up the Cooper River to Strawberry Chapel, "where there is the best tavern in the state," and from there up a "very direct and beautiful road" to the high hills of Santee. But this was all guesswork. "Now, for aught which I as yet know, it will be as easy for me to get to the mountains, or to the Alps, or the Andes, as to Statesburgh."[44]

Through the generosity of Savannah residents, Burr obtained horses for himself, Swartwout, and Yates. They departed on October 5 and reached Stateburg on October 13. To prepare them for the shock of seeing him after his exposure to the Southern climate, he wrote ahead to Theodosia, "Pray let A.B.A. know that gamp is a black man, otherwise he may be shocked at the appearance of A.B., who is now about the colour of Peter Yates. Not brown but a true quadroon yellow; whether from the effects of the climate, or traveling four hundred miles in a canoe, is no matter." [45]

The pride Thomas Sumter took in his home town was evident in a letter he wrote to a friend in Paris: "I believe if you could be once settled at Stateburgh you would never wish to abandon it—its neighborhood is flourishing faster than almost any place I ever saw & the healthyness of the climate has made it the residence of many charming families & the resort of great numbers from the low countries in summer who wish to procure or preserve health-come & see it."[46] The records are mute as to Thomas Sumter's feelings about the duel, but Burr received a warm welcome and enjoyed a splendid and heartwarming reunion with Theodosia, Gampy, Joseph, and Natalie under the eaves of Thomas and Natalie's beautiful plantation residence, Home House. The day after his arrival, Burr wrote Charles Biddle, "I arrived here yesterday and have the Satisfaction to find my daughter & her son in the Most perfect health—my young friend & fellow traveller, Sam. Swartwout, leaves me at this place.... My present plan being to attend the Senate at the opening of the Session."

Burr's budding vision of a Western empire was still a closely guarded secret—probably not even known to Theodosia at the time—that did not intrude upon the heartfelt Southern hospitality extended to him by the Sumters. He may or may not have known that his beloved Richmond Hill, the house that had sheltered his wife, witnessed the birth of their four children, and welcomed Natalie de Lage, had been seized and sold for $25,000 to pay some of his creditors. The sale left $7,000 - $8,000 in unpaid debts. If he knew, he didn't communicate the news to Theodosia and Joseph until his return to Washington in November.[47]

After a stay of six days, Burr bid farewell to his Palmetto State hosts and rode to Fayetteville, North Carolina. From there, he made his way to Petersburg, Virginia—"Jefferson country"— and was, to his great surprise and delight, given a hearty, three-day welcome by the citizens, which included an "elegant supper," and a "public dinner." From Richmond, he wrote to Theodosia on the last sheet of paper that she had given him in Stateburg. He told her that it had been reserved for "The Travels of A. Gamp, Esq., A.M., LL.D, V.P.U.S., which will appear in due time." Amazed by the warmth and civility of his reception so close to the capital, he wrote, "Virginia is the last state, and Petersburgh the last town in the state of Virginia, in which I should have expected any open marks of hospitality and respect. You will have seen from my note of this morning to Mr. Alston how illy I have judged."[48] After passing through Richmond, he reached Washington on November 4, just in time to attend the opening session of the Senate the next day.

Many senators were totally astonished to see Burr enter the chambers and take his place at their head that day, but courage and fortitude were among his core characteristics. Although shunned by most of the Federalists and given a cool, if proper, reception by his own party, Burr conducted the remainder of his vice-presidential term with dignity and great professionalism. In the spring of 1805, he presided over the Senate impeachment trial of Judge Samuel Chase. For these duties, he earned notice as a wise and able jurist. On March 2, he informed his colleagues that the time had come for him to say goodbye. After noting several items of business that the Senate might wish to attend to, he made a brief but moving speech about his love for his country, the Constitution, and the noble role of the Senate. He then rose, turned, and left the hall for the last time.

"In the chamber behind him," wrote Milton Lomask, "grown men wept. Senator Mitchell shared the moment with his wife. 'There was a solemn and silent weeping for perhaps five minutes,' he told her. 'For my own part, I never experienced anything of the kind so affecting me.... My colleague, General Smith, stout and manly as he is, wept as profusely as I did.'"[49]

Many men have been disgraced, paid their penance, worked hard, and resumed their professions and regained high office. If his departure from the Senate in 1805 could have been the last they saw of Burr as he slipped into quiet obscurity for a while, the world might ultimately have forgiven him for the duel. Given the healing power of time, Burr might have been able to move to the West, establish a good law practice, get himself elected a senator from a frontier state, and quickly return to Washington. It could have been, but he had something much more ambitious —more Burrian—in mind.

His Senate colleagues, who wept when he exited the chamber on March 2, might not have been so deeply moved had they known of a communication dated August 6, 1804, less than four weeks after the duel and six months before he left them weeping. The ciphered letter was written by Anthony Merry, British minister to the United States, to his superior, Lord Harrowby, the British Foreign Secretary in London. Marked "Most Secret," it read:

My Lord, I have just received an offer from Mr. Burr
the actual Vice President of the United States (which
Situation he is about to resign)[50] to lend his assistance
to His Majesty's Government in any Manner in which
they may think fit to employ him, particularly in endeavouring to effect a Separation of the Western Part
of the United States from that which lies between the
Atlantick and the Mountains, in its whole Extent. His
Proposition on this and other Subjects will be fully detailed to your Lordship by Col: [Charles] Williamson
who has been the Bearer of them to me, and who will
embark for England in a few Days. It is therefore only
necessary for me to add that if, what is generally
known of the Profligacy of Mr. Burr's Character, His
Majesty's Ministers should think proper to listen to his
offer, his present Situation in this Country where he is
now cast off as much by the democratic as by the Federal Party, and where he still preserves the Connections
with some People of Influence, added to his great
Ambition and Spirit of Revenge against the present
Administration, may possibly induce him to exert the
Talents and Activity which he possesses with Fidelity
to his Employers.[51]

While Vice President of the United States, Burr had secretly notified the British government that he was developing
plans to split off the western states from the rest of the United
States and secede. In this, he asked for the political and financial support of the Crown. This was clearly a violation of his
sworn oath to "support and defend the Constitution of the
United States." For Burr, the perfectly amoral man, the end
justified the means. The outcome would probably be welcomed
by the majority of people in the region, and that was that.

Burr had been a traitor once before, when he forsook his
allegiance to his king, George III, joined the American rebellion,
and took up arms against the Mother Country as an officer
in the Continental Army. For that act of conscience and his

bravery under fire, he came to be revered by his countrymen, who elected him to the second-highest office of the nation.

Now, less than three years into that position of public trust, he not only stood accused of murder but had apparently betrayed his nation by seeking an unholy alliance with the British to bring about the secession of the Western states. The duel had clouded him with dishonor. Now this act, and the bizarre events that would soon follow, would finish the job and leave him shrouded in total infamy. Killing a man in a fair duel of honor in broad daylight in front of two official witnesses was something Americans could at least debate from different perspectives. However, Burr's fellow citizens would have little tolerance for a man who would secretly collude with England out of anger or for personal gain. This is the way his Western Conspiracy would ultimately be viewed by many of his countrymen, if not by Burr, Theodosia, and her husband. They had obvious reasons to view it favorably.

At The Oaks in South Carolina, Theodosia got the first hints about her father's new plans in a letter he wrote on March 10, 1805, from Washington. "On the 13th I shall leave this [place] for Philadelphia. There is no reason to think I shall this season visit either New-York or New-Jersey. The plan of summer operations is for me to go from Philadelphia to Fort Pitt (Pittsburg), thence through the states on each side of the Ohio. To visit St. Louis and the mouth of the Mississippi; thence through Tennessee (where [to] pass a month) to Orleans; and thence, either by water or land, to the Atlantic coast, not far from Yarnaco or the mouth of the Waccama[w]. Thus you see that you are the end of all plans, and wherever they may begin, the termination is the same. This tour has other objects than mere curiosity. [It is] an operation of business, which promises to render the tour both useful and agreeable." He ended the letter on a pragmatic note. "My right of franking letters [sending free of postage] will cease on the 23d of this month, so that you are not to expect pamphlets, &c., by the mail. God bless thee."[52]

Theodosia, her health having again taken a drastic turn for the worse, could not have been comforted to read that her beloved father would be touring the wilderness and out of touch for nearly half a year. Although she was accustomed to a life where the men she loved were frequently absent, it must have been especially painful at that moment, for on August 6, 1805, Theodosia thought that her death was imminent. A heart-rending letter showed the depths to which her never-ending medical problems had dragged her body and spirit. The letter, written immediately after her husband's departure from The Oaks on a trip, was nothing less than Theodosia's last will and testament and contained instructions to her husband on how to distribute her earthly goods and how to regard and care for her son and father. The envelope bore the inscription, "To my husband. To be delivered after my death, and before my burial."

> Whether it is the effect of extreme debility and disordered nerves, or whether it is really presentiment [a premonition], the existence of which I have often been told of, and always doubted, I cannot tell; but something whispers me that my end approaches. In vain I reason with myself; in vain I occupy my mind, and seek to fix my attention on other subjects; there is about me that dreadful heaviness and sinking of the heart, that awful foreboding, of which it is impossible to divest myself. Perhaps I am now standing on the brink of eternity; and, ere I plunge into the fearful abyss, I have some few requests to make.
>
> I wish your sisters (one of them, it is immaterial which) would select from my clothes certain things which they will easily perceive belonged to my mother. These, with whatever lace they find in a large trunk in the garrett-room of the Oaks house, added to a little satinwood box (the largest, and having a lock and key), and a black satin embroidered box, with a pincushion; all these things I wish they would put together in one trunk, and send them to Frederic [Bartow], with the enclosed letter. I prefer him, because Bartow's wife

would have little respect for what, however trifling it may appear, I nevertheless deem sacred.

I beg Sister Maria [Alston][53] will accept of my watch-ring. She will find a locket which she gave me, containing the hair of her mother; she had better take it. If the lace in my wardrobe at the Oaks will be of any use to Charlotte [Alston],[54] I beg she will take it, or anything else she wishes. My heart is with those dear amiable sisters, to give them something worth preserving in recollection of me; but they know that a warm friendship is all I have to give.

Return to mamma [Mary Brewton Motte Alston] the eagle she gave me. Should an opportunity to Catherine Brown[55] ever occur, send her a pearl necklace, a small diamond ring, a little pair of coral tablets, which are among my trinkets at the Oaks. I pray you, my dear husband, send Bartow's daughter some present for me, and to himself and Frederic [Bartow][56] a lock of my hair. Return Natalie [Sumter] the little desk she gave me, accompanied by assurances of my affectionate recollection, and a ring of my hair. Remember me to Sally [Reeve],[57] who is truly amiable, and whom I sincerely esteem.

I beg, also, you will write immediately to New York, forwarding some money for the comfortable support of Peggy [Gallatin][58] until my father can provide for her. Do not permit grief at the loss of me to render you forgetful of this, for the poor creature may expire of want in the mean time. I beg this may be attended to without delay.

To you, my beloved, I leave our child; the child of my bosom, who was once a part of myself, and from whom I shall shortly be separated by the cold grave. You love him now; henceforth love him for me also. And oh, my husband, attend to this last prayer of a doting mother. Never, never listen to what any other person tells you of him. Be yourself his judge on all occasions.

He has faults; see them and correct them yourself. Desist not an instant from your endeavors to secure his confidence. It is a work which requires as much uniformity of conduct as warmth of affection toward him. I know, my beloved, that you can perceive what is right on this subject as on every other. But recollect, these are the last words I can ever utter. It will tranquillize my last moments to have disburdened myself of them.

I feel you will scarcely be able to read this scrawl, but I feel hurried and agitated. Death is not welcome to me. I confess it is ever dreaded. You have made me too fond of life. Adieu, then, thou kind, thou tender husband. Adieu, friend of my heart. May heaven prosper you, and may we meet hereafter. Adieu; perhaps we may never see each other again in this world. You are away, I wished to hold you fast, and prevent you from going this morning. But He who is wisdom itself ordains events; we must submit to them. Least of all should I murmur. I, on whom so many blessings have been showered—whose days have been numbered by bounties—who have had such a husband, such a child, and such a father. Oh, pardon me, my God, if I regret leaving these. I resign myself. Adieu, once more, and for the last time, my beloved. Speak of me often to our son. Let him love the memory of his mother, and let him know how he was loved by her. Your wife, your fond wife, Theo.

[Postscript]: Let my father see my son sometimes. Do not be unkind towards him whom I have loved so much, I beseech you. Burn all my papers, except my father's letters, which I beg you return to him. Adieu, my sweet boy. Love your father; be grateful and affectionate to him while he lives; be the pride of his meridian; the support of his departing days. Be all that he wishes; for he has made your mother happy. Oh! My heavenly Father, bless them both. If it is permitted, I will hover round you, and guard you, and intercede for you. I hope for happiness in the next world, for I have not been bad in this.

I had nearly forgotten to say that I charge you not to allow me to be stripped and washed, as is usual. I am pure enough thus to return to dust. Why, then, expose my person? Pray see to this. If it does not appear contrary or silly, I beg to be kept as long as possible before I am consigned to the earth."[59]

Theodosia had a right to be depressed. She was weak in body and spirit, stranded on the Waccamaw with her three-year-old son. After the news of the duel reached South Carolina, a subtle chill had descended over her already limited social relationships. Her husband was busy managing his extensive plantations and was often away in Columbia on legislative business, and her father was roaming the West. Had Burr been in closer contact with her and known the extent of her debilitated condition, he might have told her more details of his bold plan for himself, Theodosia, and Gampy. If so, she might have felt better, knowing that if all went well, in eighteen months, she could be sitting next to her father on a golden throne, gazing down at her subjects as Theodosia the First, Empress of Mexico.

CHAPTER SEVEN

Codeword: Emperor

And so she gave
A true heart's fealty and a woman's craft
To further his designs, dazzled, mayhap,
By the richest stake for which his subtile mind
So deeply prayed; an empire in the South,
Where she, in regal splendor by his side,
The sceptre of a gracious realm should wield.
                              —Alexander T. Ormond

In the mind of a man like Aaron Burr, making the transition from Vice President of the United States to Emperor of Mexico was not a great leap. Indeed, in his eyes at least, it was simply a logical career move. Viewed from the perspective of a pragmatic man, the employment contract with his present employer—the United States government—was not going to be renewed by its C.E.O., Thomas Jefferson. The forty-nine-year-old vice president was financially embarrassed because of his lavish lifestyle, his involvement in several failed speculative ventures, and his consistent generosity to others—which included the support of orphaned children of several friends and, it is rumored, some illegitimate offspring of his own. He needed to find a new position suited to his talents and ambitions. Since his present employer no longer wanted him, Burr did the logical thing: he sent out feelers to the competition and looked to the West for his next career opportunity.

Two major legal obstacles stood in his way, both of which he would have known about, given his familiarity with the law and his high position in government. First, he was not simply contemplating the lateral career move of a high-level business executive to a competing company. Had Burr been an ordinary man of commerce, that would have been perfectly acceptable, but he was not. He was a sitting Vice President of the United States. The ambitious plan Burr contemplated included collusion with a foreign power—in this case, Great Britain—to assist in the invasion of Nueva España (New Spain, or Spanish Mexico) by his private army. It may also have included encouraging the secession of the western states, which might then attach themselves to Burrian Mexico and form a single new country with Burr as its monarch and New Orleans as its capital. What Burr proposed was not a mere corporate spin-off or merger with another corporation. If his plan included the invasion of Mexico—still technically, at least, the territory of a friendly country—it was, at a minimum, illegal. Then there was his second objective, if one were to believe the worst claims made against him. That allegedly included inciting secession of the western states, which would have been an act of treason.

The Spanish laid claim to all of present-day Florida, plus a strip of the Gulf Coast that ended at the Mississippi. Spanish territory resumed as Nueva España at the Sabine River, two hundred miles west of New Orleans and about fifty miles northeast of present-day Galveston, Texas. The United States was expanding rapidly in the first years of the nineteenth century, and Spain stood directly in the way.

Fueled by the Louisiana Purchase in 1803, westward expansion of the United States had the will of the people solidly behind it by 1805. Along with many other Americans, Burr was certain that a war with Spain was imminent. If the conflict broke out spontaneously—or with a little help—Burr was certain that he could land his private army in New Orleans, proceed to Vera Cruz, and conquer Mexico in a matter of weeks. On this, Burr and his detractors were in full agreement: Burr was prepared to invade Mexico with a private army and seize its government.

Where Burr and his critics differed was solely over the question of whether or not it was also his plan to incite the secession of the western states, namely Ohio, Kentucky, Tennessee, the Indiana Territory, the Mississippi Territory, and the city of New Orleans. All were sparsely populated and had loosely structured governments without strong ties to the eastern power structure.

After capturing Spanish Mexico, some said, Burr planned to weld this territory together with Spanish Florida. He would then rule as emperor of the enormous new nation, whose capital would be New Orleans. Theodosia would become Empress upon Burr's death, and her son would take the throne when he came of age. Thus, Burr's goals for Theodosia would be fulfilled; his money problems would be solved by seizing the gold of Montezuma; and at the diplomatic level, Burr would at last stand on equal terms with the President of the United States. That was the grand plan. His enemies damned him for his secessionist intrigues, but Burr always denied publicly that he had any such intentions and consistently stated that his only goal was to invade and conquer Mexico. Scholars today are still debating the unresolved question of Burr's alleged treason.

As outlandish as it seems in retrospect, the whole scenario might have worked. Even Jefferson had admitted that the country might become too big to govern as a single union and indicated that he might countenance the separation of the western half. He wrote to Dr. Joseph Priestly in 1804, "Whether we remain in one confederacy, or form into Atlantic and Mississippi confederacies, I believe not very important to either part."[1]

In retrospect, it boggles the mind to contemplate what Jefferson was tacitly assenting to. What are now the 48 contiguous states would be split into two separate nations. A puny United States of America, consisting of the original thirteen colonies, would extend from the Atlantic coast to the Allegheny mountains, north to Canada, and south to Georgia. The new nation—let's call it "Burrania"—might well grow to include what are now the other 35 states and could stretch west from

A.B URR.ESQ.

Aaron Burr in 1805

the Alleghenies to California, north to Canada, and south to include Florida, the Gulf Coast, all of Mexico—and perhaps, all of Central and South America!

After he left the Senate chamber for the last time, Burr had but one viable option: look west. He was confident that he could carry out what ultimately came to be known as the "Western Conspiracy" or the "Burr Conspiracy" with the help of the right friends and allies, and he had many. From his service in the army and his time spent presiding over the senate, Burr had numerous professional friends, old army comrades, social acquaintances, and senators that he could call upon. When they heard about Burr's plan, many good, intelligent men agreed that it was feasible.

To recruit confederates for the Mexican scheme or to convince the leaders of the western states to join him, Burr first had to do what he did best: make allies and build a constituency for his plan, even though its exact goals were not yet clear. Nevertheless, the agenda was truly Burrian in scope. He would make a reconnaissance trip of the entire western frontier. Starting from Philadelphia, he planned to travel by horseback to Pittsburgh, then float down the Ohio River to the Mississippi, and then journey past Natchez to New Orleans, making friends and recruiting sympathizers, financial backers, and co-conspirators at every stop.

"The West" in 1805 was quite different from the cowboys-and-Indians stereotype that would dominate the tabloid press seventy years later. When Burr embarked upon his adventure, the American West was any place west of the Appalachian Mountains. Organized white settlements essentially ended on the west bank of the Mississippi. After the revolution, people moved west, but political and economic power remained concentrated in the New England states, New York, and Virginia. Federal influence west of Appalachia was so weak that the settlers of Tennessee and Kentucky gave serious thought to allying themselves either with France's Louisiana or Spain's Florida long before hearing Burr's scheme.

Conspiracies are hazardous, and depend on men willing—as Burr was—to take huge risks in return for the promise of large rewards. Pulling off a grand conspiracy takes a large cast of characters, some of whom are often a little shady or, at least, a bit odd around the edges. The perfect hunting ground for Burr was the western frontier, which was full of rough-and-tumble men who admired his spirit, did not condemn him for his duel, and generally made their own rules.

When it came to recruiting odd and shady fellows for his project, Burr started at the top of the list. His chief co-conspirator was Brig. Gen. James Wilkinson, then commander of all U.S. military forces in the West and soon to become governor of the Louisiana Territory. A Maryland native, Wilkinson had served with Burr in 1775 during the Québec campaign, where he discharged his obligations with courage and tact. His marriage to Charles Biddle's cousin, Ann, gave him entrée into that wealthy and powerful Philadelphia merchant family and to Burr, who was

Gen. James Wilkinson

Biddle's close friend. In 1784, Wilkinson moved to Kentucky and provided numerous kind and generous services to his neighbors. He earned their respect, became popular, and soon became involved in several nefarious separatist movements. 1787 saw him at the mouth of the Mississippi, seeking to negotiate with the Spanish governor of Louisiana, Esteban Rodríguez Miró, for the rights to free navigation of the river and to market his goods. Instead, Miró threatened to seize his two boatloads of tobacco and flour and summoned him to a meeting.

The Spanish governor found Wilkinson open to making mutually profitable agreements. Wilkinson walked out of the room with permission to bring any goods he chose into Louisiana, free of duty. In return, Miró now had Wilkinson, known in subsequent coded letters to Madrid as Agent Number 13, on his payroll at $2,000 per year as a frontier informant for Spain.[2] The next year, Wilkinson also endeared himself to the British government, gaining from that connection information that he immediately bartered to the Spanish. To the British, he bartered information gained from the Spanish, and *voila*, a double agent was born!

Wilkinson returned to active U.S. military service in 1791 and was regularly promoted, largely due to the lack of competition on the frontier. By 1796, he was the highest-ranking officer in the U.S. Army. He was also wily, resourceful, greedy, and fat. He drank too much and was good at getting into and out of trouble. Nevertheless, in Washington, Jefferson, Madison, and Hamilton all took him seriously because what he boasted of was true. Having lived on the frontier for twenty years, Wilkinson knew more about the western lands "than any Christian in America."[3] Burr's lack of judgment in choosing Wilkinson as his chief co-conspirator bore out Andrew Jackson's later observation that "Burr is as far from a fool as I ever saw, and yet he is as easily fooled as any man I ever knew."[4]

Napoléon had acquired Louisiana from the Spanish and sold it to the United States in 1803 for $13 million. In December of that year, Wilkinson watched as the Stars and Stripes was raised in New Orleans. Spain still owned Florida, a strip along the coast of the Gulf of Mexico, and Nuevo España, but its boundaries on both sides of the Louisiana Territory were vague.

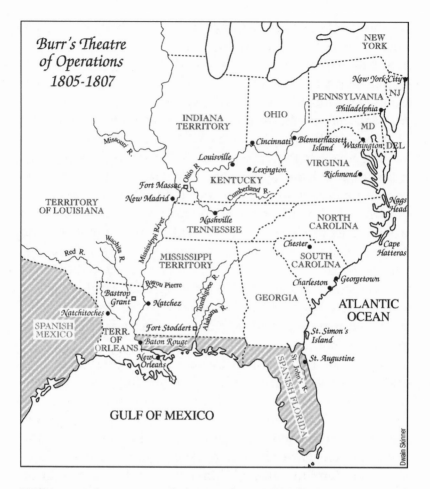

Burr's Theatre of Operations 1805-1807

Dwain Skinner

Wilkinson, the man on the spot, demanded $20,000 in unpaid pension funds from the Spanish administrator who had supervised the transfer of Louisiana from Spain to France. He settled for $12,000—and reconfirmed his status as a Spanish secret agent.

In April 1804, Wilkinson sailed from New Orleans to New York and a rendezvous with Burr, who had just lost his bid for governor. Their meeting at Richmond Hill on May 23, 1804, probably marked the start of the operation to invade Mexico. Strong moral support from Charles Williamson—a British officer during the revolution, a secret agent for His Majesty thereafter, and a ten-year friend of Burr's—greatly augmented Burr's plan to liberate the Spanish territories.[5]

Burr's covert contact with the British ambassador in August 1804 was intended to solicit support, both naval and financial, for his plans to oust the Spanish from their Florida and Gulf Coast territories. With the assistance of the British navy to keep the Spanish from attacking his expeditionary force when it reached New Orleans, Burr could move straight into Mexico. However, Burr's "feeler" to the British ambassador was thought by many to be an act of outright treason.

While serving out his term of office, Burr had serious planning to do. On April 10, 1805, he left Washington on horseback, headed for Pittsburgh. He was concerned about his son-in-law's apparent lack of vision. Burr was on the road to becoming Emperor of Mexico; Theodosia would become Empress; and Gampy, heir apparent. But what was Burr supposed to do with Joseph Alston, whose ambition for power and high office was only lukewarm?

From Philadelphia on March 22, he wrote a frank letter to his son-in-law, upbraiding him for his lack of ambition. "I am not wholly free from apprehension that you take no interest in anything but a rice-field," Burr scolded. "Fame says that you are about to degenerate into a mere planter. If so, it is to be lamented that you have any thing above common sense, and that you have learned any more than to read and write, for all above common sense and school education spoils the planter. Though in my former letters I did not, in express terms, inform you that I was under ostracism, yet it must have been inferred. Such is the fact. In New-York I am to be disenfranchised, and in New-Jersey hanged. Having substantial objections to both, I shall not, for the present, hazard either, but shall seek another country."[6]

Theodosia then received counseling from her father about her failed health. "I am apprehensive that your milk diet will not carry you through the summer," he wrote. "You will want stimulus of some kind. For this purpose something is used in all warm countries. In the West Indies they drink rum and they die. In the East Indies and China, ginseng is the panacea. Try ginseng. Some decoction or (bitter) infusion. When my stomach is out of order or wants tone, nothing serves so effectually as a cup of chamomile tea, without sugar or milk. I think this would give you an appetite. Make the experiment. Bathing in seawater is a grand preservative. If your bath be in the house, the best time is an hour or two before dinner. Tepid bath; none of your cold baths for such a machine as yours. If you have no convenience for a warm bath in the house, set a mason to work to-morrow and make one in each of your country houses. It is high evidence of the barbarism of our Southern states that, in an extent of three hundred miles, filled with wealthy people, and in a hot climate, there should not be, in any one private family, a convenient bathing-room."[7] With a few more words of concern over the health of little Gampy, Burr closed his letter and set off to seek his fortune in the West.[8]

From Pittsburgh on April 30, he wrote to Theodosia about his new "ark," the flatboat that would carry him down the Ohio and the Mississippi. "My boat is, properly speaking, a floating house, sixty feet by fourteen, containing dining-room, kitchen with fireplace, and two bedrooms; roofed from stem to stern; steps to go up, and a walk on the top the whole length; glass windows, &c. The edifice costs one hundred and thirty-three dollars, and how it can be made for that sum passes my comprehension."[9] That same day, he and his traveling companion, New Yorker Gabriel Shaw, set off down the Ohio River in search of Burr's destiny.

By May 5, they had reached Marietta, Ohio, where they paused to tour prehistoric earthworks. Continuing their journey, they, like many other travelers on this western edge of nowhere, rounded a bend in the river and beheld an amazing sight. On the serpentine island before them was a magnificent, gleaming white Palladian mansion, "from which wings extended like welcoming arms toward approaching boats."[10] Burr carried with him a letter of introduction from Dr. Robert Wallace of Marietta, to the owners of the island paradise, Harman Blennerhassett and his beautiful wife, Margaret.[11]

The Blennerhassetts were a study in contrasts. Harman Blennerhassett was forty years old at the time; his wife, just

Blennerhassett Island

thirty-three. The youngest son of Irishman Conway Blennerhassett and his wife Elizabeth, Blennerhassett was born in England in 1764. In 1792, when his father died, he inherited the
family fortune: Castle Conway and its 7,000-acre estate at
Killorglin in County Kerry, Ireland. By that time, Blennerhassett
had earned multiple academic degrees and was a practicing
member of the Irish bar. He was also an outspoken member
and officer of the secret patriotic (and anti-British) Society of
United Irishmen, which was considered treason by the British.

In 1794, thirty-year-old Blennerhassett married Margaret
Agnew, aged twenty-three, the daughter of Capt. Robert Agnew
and his wife, Catherine. The age difference, though substantial, was not all that unusual for the times, but their relationship was. Catherine Agnew was Blennerhassett's sister.
Blennerhassett had married his niece.

It was a scandalous union, forbidden by the church both in
England and Ireland, permissible there under civil law, but an
anathema to the family. To escape the wrath their incestuous
marriage had fueled, and to avoid having his estate confiscated by the English, Blennerhassett sold his patrimony for
£28,000 (about $140,000) in 1795. In May 1796, the wealthy
Blenner-hassetts boarded the *Harriet* in Gravesend and set

The Blennerhassett Mansion

sail for America. From New York they proceeded on to its western frontier, where they could hide their shamed relationship and "pass their days in an idyll, he in his botanist's garden, she on horseback, studying nature, and lavishing their attentions on each other."[12] Eventually, two sons were born to them in their utopia in the middle of a rapidly expanding nowhere.

Harman Blennerhassett was tall, stoop-shouldered, and awkward, and he had a condition known as "dancing eyes." He was also extremely nearsighted and couldn't tell a man from a horse at ten paces. Although genial and generous to a fault, Blennerhassett was prone to snobbishness, had a fiery temper, and was impractical, naive, and a poor manager of his once-considerable fortune. A versatile and well-educated man, he accumulated a huge library; was fascinated with science and astronomy; played and composed music for the base viol, cello, and lute; and was trained in the classical languages. It was said of him that his "intellectual tastes and aristocratic training were not the qualities needed for success in a pioneer community" and that he had "every sense but common sense."[13] Clearly, Harman Blennerhassett was not cut out for life on the frontier.

Harman Blennerhassett

Margaret Blennerhassett was. At 5'7", she "towered over most of her lady friends and looked their husbands straight in the eye."[14] She also vaulted over fences with one hand and often ferried across the river, walked the twelve miles to Marietta, Ohio; took breakfast there; and then walked back. On horseback, she raced so quickly through the forests that her servants were hard pressed to keep up. She was also very easy on the eyes, "with a slim waist and superb bust," and graced with blue, almond-shaped eyes; fair skin with ruddy cheeks; and glossy brown hair. She spoke fluent French, was extremely well read, and, like Burr himself, oozed sophistication and charisma. It was said that no one could be in her company, even a few minutes, without being strongly attracted by her fascinating manners.[15]

The Blennerhassetts welcomed Burr as he stepped off his ark, delighted and flattered to have the former vice president as their guest. Their dinner conversation lasted until eleven o'clock that evening. Although it went unrecorded, their discussion probably included more than social pleasantries and cultured discourse

Margaret Agnew Blennerhassett

in French. Based on later correspondence, Burr probably brought up his plans for Mexico, as he would certainly have eyed Blennerhassett's island paradise as a fine staging ground for future military operations. Burr would also have noted his host's deep pockets —or so they must have looked—as assets to be mined.

Whatever Burr said to them that night, it worked. "From that moment on, the Blennerhassetts, man and wife, were as fascinated by the little colonel as a pair of cukoos by a snake."[16] The price they would pay for their fascination was Blenner- hassett's indictment for treason. Despite the offer of a soft bed in a lavishly furnished guestroom, the Spartan colonel slept on his flatboat that evening, breakfasted with the cosmopolitan couple, and then moved on.

In Cincinnati, he met with Kentucky senator John Smith and former senator Jonathan Dayton. The three had earlier formed the Indiana Canal Company, from whose coffers Burr borrowed the huge sum of $25,000 for his "other" project: the invasion of Mexico. Dayton, an old friend of Burr's from Princeton and the march on Québec, became one of Burr's chief lieutenants.

At almost every stop, Burr was greeted like a conquering hero. Bands played for him, parades were arranged on short notice to celebrate his arrival, and balls and fancy dinners were held in his honor. Burr was euphoric. He knew that he had found the proper stage for his grand play.

On May 30, Burr met up with General Andrew Jackson in Nashville, where the little colonel's arrival was greeted with a cannon salute. In full dress uniform, Jackson invited his friends from throughout the region to meet Burr at his home, known, like Theodosia Bartow Prevost's home in New Jersey, as The Hermitage. After rounds of talks and endless fes- tivities, Burr borrowed one of Jackson's boats and floated down the Cumberland River. Just south of its junction with the Ohio, he rendezvoused with his military ally, General Wilkinson. After much discussion and planning, Wilkinson sent Burr forth down the Mississippi with "an elegant barge, sails, colours, and ten oars, with a sergeant, and ten able, faithful hands."[17]

After stopping in St. Louis and Natchez, Burr arrived in New Orleans on June 25, 1805, four days after Theodosia's twenty-second birthday. The city was the key to the entire Mississippi trade and the gateway to Mexico and the Spanish-held lands along the Gulf, with their enormous production of sugar cane and cotton. Again, Burr was welcomed with banquets and balls. His negotiations with his future allies lasted three weeks.

Burr found New Orleans, the intended capital of his planned empire, much to his liking. "The inhabitants of the United States here are called Americans," he wrote. "I have been received with distinction." The warm reception included congratulations and a warm invitation to visit by a convent of Ursuline nuns, who feted him with "a repast of wine, fruit, and cakes." Before he left, he asked the sisters to remember him in their prayers. He also noted that at the many dinners held in his honor, *A la santé Madame* Alston [to the health of Mrs. Alston] is generally the first toast at every table.[18]

Mrs. Alston desperately needed more than toasts to her health. Because Burr's access to mail was so irregular, he had no idea that Theodosia desperately needed medical assistance—treatment that no doctor of the time could administer. In fact, Theodosia was then at her lowest physical and emotional ebb; reduced to despair over her failed health and the apparent hopelessness of ever recovering it. Indeed, she feared that her death might come at literally any hour. On August 6, 1805, in deep agony and profound depression, she sat at a desk and wrote what would be her last will and testament. In it, she prayed that her husband, who had just left on a business trip, would care for their son and ensure that he and his grandfather would always be able to visit each other.[19] Burr did not hear of her near-death condition until his return to Washington months later.

From July through September, Burr traveled throughout the sparse settlements in Tennessee, Kentucky, and Missouri, where he continued to be welcomed. He recruited potential allies and often spoke contemptuously—sometimes too contemptuously—of the federal government. Given the hundreds of people Burr met and discussed his ideas with between Philadelphia and New Orleans, it was not surprising that his objectives did not remain secret.

On August 2, 1805, a Federalist newspaper, the *Gazette of the United States,* asked the question, "How long will it be before we hear of Col. Burr being at the head of a revolution party on the western waters?" The newspaper laid out a full array of accusations: that Burr was recruiting men to settle Louisiana, was planning to entreat the states bordering on the Mississippi to secede, and was preparing to collude with the British navy and take Mexico.[20] Burr might have heard about the charges in Lexington, Kentucky. The newspaper there reprinted the entire article while he was visiting.

Despite what others were speculating, Burr had not yet committed a provable treasonous act. Not a man had been signed up to fight against the Union; not a rifle had been purchased; and not a single agreement had been drawn up. Along the entire route, Burr had given each man only a piece of the puzzle, plus whatever he believed they wanted to hear. If called to task for his words during the trip of 1805, Burr could claim that they were but castles in the air, and no one could prove otherwise. That, however, was not the case. In September 1805, he and Wilkinson had "settled the plan for an attack on Mexico," Burr later told Andrew Jackson.[21] In the fall and early winter, he returned east, and, to the surprise of many, dined with President Jefferson in Washington.

To Theodosia, he wrote sporadically, telling her where he had visited, describing the interesting sights he had seen, and portraying the people he had met. His letters were, however, simply a travel journal for his daughter's edification and amusement, not an insider's guide to an international conspiracy. Burr's writings to her show that in 1805, Theodosia was completely unaware of the nature of any Mexican or secessionist plans and the fact that they were being financed with substantial amounts of her husband's money.

From the capital city on November 29, 1805, Burr wrote to Alston, "My solicitude about the health of Theodosia is no way relieved by the sort of recovery of which she advises me. The boy, too, has a relapse of the ague [fever, accompanied by chills, probably malarial], a disease of all others the most fatal to the infant constitution. Great God! what sacrifices do you make, and to what end? These solicitudes poison all my enjoyments, and often unfit me for business. Being apprized from recollection of our personal communications last autumn, and of our correspondence last winter, of the engagements and ties which will prevent you, at least for some months, from leaving South Carolina, I determine, at any sacrifice, to rescue Theodosia and son."[22] Once again, father-protector Burr swooped in and took control of Alston's wife and child. By then, Alston had become so accustomed to having Burr make the critical decisions for Theodosia and Gampy that he probably didn't even put up even token resistance.

Overall, Burr's reconnaissance trip of 1805 was a success. He had met most of the influential men in the western half of the country and had charmed, intrigued, or seduced many of them with visions of adventure, glory, wealth, power, and position. Everywhere west of the Alleghenies, Burr was a rising star. East of the mountains was a different story. By the time he reached Washington, he was under wide suspicion as being a threat to national security. On December 1, 1805, just a few days after Jefferson and Burr dined together, the President received an anonymous letter warning him of Burr's conspiracy.[23]

Burr was then moving from strategy to action. He wintered in Philadelphia, laying out tactical plans to invade Mexico. Britain was a problem. On January 6, 1806, the British agent, Williamson, sent a letter to London, outlining England's proposed contribution to the conspiracy, which he saw as an effective way to counter the French influence in the region. Williamson proposed that if the British government would support Burr with encouragement and £200,000, he foresaw Burr leading 50,000 American troops to Mexico City before August of that year.[24]

The British seemed sympathetic but had not yet given Burr any commitment or money. Indeed, the entire 1805 trip had been financed by Joseph Alston and the funds Burr had borrowed from the Indiana Canal Company. Because that company's one-time money supply was now exhausted, Theodosia's husband remained the conspirators' chief financier.[25]

Fortunately, Blennerhassett was still under Burr's spell, but by the end of 1805, he, too, was running low on money. Burr had revisited Blennerhassett Island in October 1805, but the Blennerhassetts were away on a trip in the East. Burr wrote to him, suggesting that the talented aristocrat deserved a bigger, more prestigious role in history than the proprietor of a fancy house in the middle of nowhere. By dangling the prospect of riches and a title in Mexico in front of the myopic gentleman, Burr found his mark. "Blenny," as his neighbors fondly called him, immediately took the bait.

He replied on December 5, 1805, explaining his financial situation, and then closed his letter with relish. "Having thus advised you of my desire and motives to pursue a change in life, to engage in any thing which may suit my circumstances, I hope, sir, you will not regard it indelicate in me to observe to you how highly I should be honored in being associated with you in any contemplated enterprise you would permit me to participate in.... Not presuming to know or guess at the intercourse, if any, subsisting between you and the present government, but viewing the probability of a rupture with Spain, the claim for action against the country will make upon your talents, in the event of an engagement against, or subjugation of, any of the Spanish territories, I am disposed, in the confidential spirit of this letter, to offer you my friends, and my own services to cooperate in any contemplated measures in which you may embark.... I shall await with much anxiety the receipt of your reply, and with warm interest in your success and prosperity."[26]

In his desperation to improve his financial lot, Blennerhassett was a chicken waiting to be plucked, but a lust for money was not his only reason for his willingness to join Burr. The Ohio River was becoming ominously busy, and with the encroachment of an ever-growing population expanding westward, the Blennerhassetts' darkest secret was threatened. With no wish for his growing boys to learn of their parents' dubious marriage, an escape to the wilds of a foreign country would have been a powerful inducement to join Burr on his search for the Golden Fleece in Mexico.

Blennerhassett's letter did not reach Burr until February 1806. In the full glow of his ambition, and with British funds nowhere to be seen, Burr was in dire need of financial resources. Blennerhassett and Burr were a perfect match, but the former heir to Castle Conway would pay a high price for his naïveté.

In spring 1806, Burr set his plan into action. He spent several months contacting prominent people, soliciting financial aid for an expedition against Mexico. Despite a Spanish incursion across the Sabine River on the Mexican border, war between the United States and Spain did not seem imminent, and Burr despaired. Indeed, he seems to have been willing to give up the whole plan if Jefferson would have granted him an ambassadorship, for which purpose Burr visited the president about March 22. Nothing between the two men had changed. Jefferson still considered politics a matter of the public good; Burr still considered it nothing more than an amusing game. Jefferson declined his request, forever ending the possibility of Burr's participation in Jefferson's administration. Burr had but one choice left: return to "Plan A," the West.

In February 1806, Burr had received Blennerhassett's letter and, by implication, a blank check. In the spring and summer, Burr negotiated the purchase of about 350,000 acres of the "Bastrop Grant," a 1,200,000-acre tract on the Ouichita (Washita) River, for $50,000, paying $5,000 immediately, assumed $30,000 of debts, and promised to pay off the balance later. With the land in his control, Burr now had a "Plan B": if war did not break out, or if the Mexican invasion fell through, he had a huge colony he could populate, farm, or sell for profit. The promise of land grants in the fertile river valley also gave him an incentive that he could dangle in front of potential recruits for his army.

Even while he was buying land to give him a fallback position, Burr proceeded full speed ahead with the invasion plans. He drew three maps of the region that showed beyond any doubt that his goal was the conquest and acquisition of all of Spanish Mexico. It was illegal, but it was not treason.[27]

In the last week of July, Burr's associate, Jonathan Dayton, wrote General Wilkinson an encoded letter that would become the "smoking gun" in the government's prosecution of Burr for treason. The "ciphered letter" was originally attributed to Burr and purported to outline in detail the grand plan of the Mexican invasion.[28] It stated that Burr had the funds he needed and had actually commenced the operation. Troops would rendezvous in Ohio at Blennerhassett Island in November 1806. The letter went on to say that the "naval protection of England is secured" and that U.S. Navy Commodore Thomas Truxton would coordinate efforts of the British and U.S. naval forces to assist them. Burr was to act as supreme commander, with Wilkinson as second in command, to name all subordinate officers. "Burr will proceed westward 1 August—never to return," the letter stated. "With him go his daughter and grandson. The Husband [Alston] will follow in October with a corps of worthies."

The plan allegedly was to leave Blennerhassett Island on November 15 with the first 500 or 1,000 men in boats then under construction and to arrive at Natchez between December 5 and 15, where they would meet up with Wilkinson and decide the final details of the Mexican invasion. The letter said of the Mexicans, "if we will protect their religion and will not subject them to a foreign power, that in three weeks it will all be settled." The letter closed by stating, "The Gods invite us to glory and fortune. It remains to be seen whether we deserve the boons."[29]

The letter was not what it seemed to be. Not only had Burr not written it, but some of the statements were erroneous and ludicrous. Dayton, who would also be charged with treason, had written it, and had exaggerated many parts of the plan, evidently in an attempt to lure Wilkinson, who was having second thoughts, into carrying out his part of the operation.

Back on his island, Blenner-hassett had been busy. Using the pen name "Querist," he wrote articles for the Marietta newspaper advocating peaceful separation of the West from the Union.[30] Next, he financed the construction of fifteen riverboats and gathered large quantities of provisions for Burr's army. These included pork, flour, whiskey, bacon, and several hundred barrels of dried cornmeal. In addition, Blennerhassett acted directly as a recruiter for the expeditionary force. Not to be out-

Margaret Blennerhassett on the Marietta Trail

done, Margaret Blennerhassett helped the cause at a ball one night when she "interrupted the dancing and entertainments to make a speech urging the young men present to seize the opportunity to go south with Burr and his men."[31]

In answering the question, "Who were his confederates?" Burr's early biographer, James Parton, stated unequivocally, "Before all others, his daughter, who was devoted to the scheme heart and soul." He then went on to list the reasons why. "To achieve a career, and a residence, which she, her husband, and her boy could share were the darling objects with which Burr had gone forth to seek a new country. She caught eagerly at his proposal. She saw in it a means whereby her father could win a glorious compensation for the wrongs she felt he had endured, and obtain a conspicuous triumph over all his enemies."[32] Visualizing herself as Empress of Mexico would not have been difficult for a young woman whose mother had spent evenings telling her wondrous stories about the glories of Russia's imperial court and the triumphs of Catherine the Great.

In the summer of 1806, Theodosia turned twenty-three, and Gampy, aged four, was in grave danger. Theodosia had taken him to the North in the middle of May, "moving frantically from place to place seeking professional help for him."[33] On August 18, 1806, she wrote to Frederick Prevost from Bedford Springs, Pennsylvania:

> My boy has been quite in ill health. For sometime after your departure from Falsington [Pennsylvania] I continued in the application of your recipe, & at first it appeared, with success; but after some time, to my astonishment, I found there was a tumor forming under his chin, which increased rapidly, & though accompanied with fever, caused no pain.— We hastened to Philadelphia where I consulted every one celebrated for medical skill, and agreed that it was a remote effect of fever & ague, & calomel;—but my son grew worse,— I verily believe that had he continued there much longer he would have had his constitution so much debilitated as never to have recovered from it. So after spending a fortnight in anxiety & suspense I determined in disgust to leave Phila[delphia] & physicians:— my father's affairs were such as to detain him, but convinced that country air would benefit my child I could not hesitate to set off accompanied by my servants only, & after a fatiguing journey behold we arrived. We reached this place on the 21st July & since that day my son has been gaining strength and health: the tumor has dispersed without forming a hole & the boy now looks better than he did in N. York. I too have been ill in Phila[delphia] but that is of little consequence in comparison to the ailments of the poor little Gampy.[34]

With Gampy's health improved, the three Alstons returned to Philadelphia. What adrenaline must have been coursing through Theodosia's veins the day she arrived there with her father. The shunning Burr and, to a lesser extent, the Alstons, had received since the duel would be a thing of the past. The opportunity for imperial greatness lay before them.

From the City of Brotherly Love, Burr and Col. Julien De Pestre, Burr's expeditionary chief of staff, began their dangerous, exhilarating one-way trip down the Ohio River to the Mississippi, where they would proceed to New Orleans and then on to Mexico City, their ultimate destination. Theodosia and Gampy waited for Alston to join them in Philadelphia. She was clearly excited by the prospects of things to come. In August 1806, Theodosia wrote to Frederick Prevost, referring to the project with zest as "the new settlement which I am about to establish."[35]

Burr and De Pestre reached Pittsburgh on August 21, 1806, where Burr recruited men and ordered provisions for his army. The newspapers of the day turned a spotlight on their activities, and Burr's "secret" plans were now everyday news. Even the Spanish minister, the Marqués de Casa Yrujo, knew about them and sent his own spy, José Vidal, down the Ohio and Mississippi Rivers to monitor Burr and report back.[36]

Burr pressed on, confident that the population would welcome him again as they had in his earlier visits, now that the planned invasion of Mexico was front-page news. The first major problem arose when Burr visited the extensive estate of Col. George Morgan, an Indian trader, land speculator, and, like General Wilkinson, friend of the Spaniards. That evening, Burr quipped once too often about how easy it would be to overthrow Jefferson's government. Burr's host promptly fired off a letter to Jefferson, suggesting that Burr had a plan for the separation of the Union. In fact, Jefferson had been receiving such letters since December 1805.[37] Burr's conspiracy had deteriorated into one of the worst-kept secrets in American history.

Burr and Colonel De Pestre again set off down the river. Their first stop south of Pittsburgh was Blennerhassett Island. The Blennerhassetts were delighted to see him again and learn the new details of his plans. Although Burr's visit lasted only two days, from August 31 to September 1, 1806, he and Blennerhassett accomplished a great deal. First, he told Blennerhassett the details of the fairytale kingdom he was about to establish in Mexico. Blennerhassett's role? Ambassador to the court of St. James, of course. Or, if the plan floundered or war between the U.S. and Spain could not be brought about, there were always the rich lands of the Bastrop Grant to exploit. Either way, Blennerhassett would be part of the grand and glorious adventure, and he was thrilled.

Then there was the money. Alston was one of the chief financiers, Burr told Blennerhassett, but he had suffered two bad crop years in a row and was temporarily short of funds. Could Blennerhassett cover some bills with drafts of his own, backed by Alston's pledge to make them good? Yes? Well, fine. With those details out of the way, it was time for serious work. Burr and Blennerhassett traveled to Marietta, Ohio, where they commissioned the construction of fifteen large bateaux, capable of holding 500 men, and a keelboat for carrying provisions. The delivery date was December 9, 1806, and Blennerhassett paid the $1,319 cost. One of the boats, it was noted, was fifty feet long and was "fitted with partitions, fireplace, and glass windows for the Blennerhassett family."[38] The Blennerhassetts thought of the voyage as a one-way trip.

Blennerhassett wasn't the only one building boats for the Burr expedition. Near Nashville, General Andrew Jackson had received $3,500 from Burr and started immediately to have five large boats constructed and provisioned.[39] Thus, Jackson, who hated the Spaniards, became a collaborator in the Mexican invasion plan, although he later withdrew his support when he became concerned that Burr's plan included instigating the secession of the western states.

After two days, Burr moved on, but the Blennerhassetts were not alone for long. Sometime in September, Theodosia, Joseph, Gampy, their carriage, and their entourage of servants came ashore, much to the delight of the Blennerhassetts. Theodosia and Margaret formed an immediate, powerful bond, based on their sophistication and common interests—not to mention the destiny they had now agreed to share. Theodosia was twenty-three; Margaret, thirty-three. Both of them spoke several languages, including fluent French; had extensive knowledge of European affairs and customs; and had received liberal and aristocratic educations.

In Margaret Blennerhassett, Theodosia must have seen a woman who could replace the mother she had lost, the favorite aunt she never had, or the best friend who had slipped away when Natalie de Lage went abroad with Thomas Sumter. For Margaret, the cultured and sophisticated New Yorker, described as "the paragon of brains, beauty, and wit that her father had long ago made up his mind she would be," must have been a breath of fresh air.[40] Parton wrote that Margaret, "happy in the company of Theodosia, full of confidence in her father's talents, was a-glow with pleasant expectation."[41] There is no record of what Harman Blennerhassett thought of Joseph Alston, but Margaret was not thrilled with him. "I never could love one of my own Sex as I do her," she said of Theodosia, but "how can she live with such a man as Alston?"[42] For whatever reasons, Alston, though totally devoted to his wife and son, seldom gained the respect of Theodosia's women friends, and he remains a wispy shadow, tagging dutifully along like a coal car fueling the mighty, Burr-powered steam engine.

One of the few other observations of the Alstons' visit was recorded by Morris B. Belknap of Marietta. On October 27, 1806, he wrote, "Mr. Alston of South Carolina, lady, & suit[e] passed through this place last week—stopped at the island—revisited this—and have now gone for Kentucky— He is son in law to Mr. Burr—a man of immense possessions— From my intimacy with Blennerhassett I had the honor to be introduced to him and lady— He appears like a man of excellent understanding and high spirits— Nothing superfluous in his manners or equipage— Notwithstanding the gentlemanlike conduct he displayed while in Marietta, there as a loud talk of him being mobbed by the rabble Capt. E. Hill at their head. These same mad rabble swear in their wrath they will tar and feather Burr should he make his appearance at Marietta."[43]

Towards the end of September, the Alstons and Harman Blennerhassett were preparing to leave the island to join Burr in Kentucky. They all met in Lexington, but then the Alstons turned east and returned to South Carolina. Was the Alstons' 1806 trip down the Ohio not designed to be a one-way trip to Mexico after all? Was it planned that Alston would return to his legislature, thereby preserving the appearance of normalcy, while the Mexican operation was advancing? Or did Burr sense that his mission would soon fall apart and wanted to evacuate his daughter and grandson before it all came crashing down? Whatever the reason, the timing was fortunate. Within weeks, Burr's entire plan crumbled into dust, and Theodosia and her husband did not have to personally witness it. The Blenner-hassetts were far less lucky.

In October 1806, Wilkinson, fearful of being exposed as a co-conspirator, turned against Burr and informed Jefferson of the Mexican plan, carefully exculpating himself, of course. Wilkinson told Jefferson that Burr planned to take New Or-leans, sail from there on February 1, and land in Vera Cruz to begin his march on Mexico City. Spanish Secret Agent No. 13 then told his president that he would move his troops away from the Mexican border and fortify his positions in and upriver of New Orleans, to save the nation from the "thousands" of zealous Burrites who were imminently expected to invade from the North. Wilkinson was nothing if not an audacious schemer and a bombastic liar. At the time, Burr's "revolutionary army" numbered perhaps a hundred men, women, and children, half of whom probably thought they were headed to take up homestead claims on the Bastrop Grant.

Coincidentally, on October 6, the citizens in the neighbor-hood of Blennerhassett's estate held a mass meeting and or-ganized themselves to defend their property from "any threatened attack."[44] They obviously meant Burr and Blennerhassett, whom they pronounced "enemies of the Republic." President Jefferson, who was already aware of what was going on, issued a proclamation on October 27, 1806, denouncing Burr's plan and warning the people against it. Burr's vision of empire started unraveling almost immediately.

In November, Joseph Hamilton Daviess, a Federalist dis-trict attorney in Kentucky, hinted that Burr was committing treason and asked for a court order to compel him to answer questions before a Kentucky grand jury. Although the motion was denied, much to Daviess' surprise, Burr nevertheless appeared in Frankfort and agreed to appear before the grand jury. After Daviess could not procure his star witness, the prosecutor moved that the grand jury be dismissed. To the thorough approval of the crowds outside, and with a smile on his face, Burr departed. The smile would not remain for long.

Later in the month, Jefferson sent a confidential agent to meet with Blennerhassett to determine Burr's intentions. Blennerhassett believed the agent to be a Burr confederate and revealed the Mexico plan, thus sealing both Burr's fate and his own. On November 27, Jefferson publicly announced that a plan to attack Spanish Mexico was underway and directed that the conspirators, whom he did not name, be arrested by either civil or military authorities.

A second federal grand jury in Frankfort commanded Burr's presence on December 2. After hearing the prosecution's witnesses, the grand jury signed a written declaration on December 5, exonerating Burr of any activities improper, injurious, or inimical to the peace and welfare of the country. Afterward, the former defendant was made the guest of honor at a giant public ball in his honor. Then Burr departed for Nashville.

In Ohio, Blennerhassett quickly concluded his preparations to join Burr, including selling his half of his mercantile business and appointing an overseer to manage the rental of his property on the island. His affairs, however, were falling apart, and back at the island, chaos was setting in. On December 6, Governor Tiffin of Ohio told the legislature that a hostile expedition was preparing to leave from Marietta, bound for the capture of New Orleans. In response, the Ohio General Assembly authorized him to use the state militia to capture the conspirators. That same day, Blennerhassett returned from Marietta, profoundly disappointed that the bateaux were not finished.

The next day, on December 7, his spirits rose when four boats and thirty-two men, led by Burrite Comfort Tyler, arrived from Pennsylvania, but two days later, the local Washington County,

Ohio militia seized eleven of the boats that Burr had commissioned and Blennerhassett had paid for. A party of Burrites sneaked into Marietta to recover them, but after a violent fistfight with the militiamen, they got away with only one boat.

On December 10, when word of the imminent arrival of the militiamen reached the island, Blennerhassett chose flight over fight. He had good reason: the militia had threatened to kill him and burn his house. However, he thought that ice on the river would make his family's trip on a flatboat unsafe and decided that Margaret and their sons should temporarily stay behind. He departed the island about 1:00 AM on the 11th. After she was certain that her husband was safely underway, Margaret rode to Marietta, where the family boat was moored. There, she learned that all the boats had been impounded, and she headed back for home.

When the militia arrived on the morning of December 11, they found the island empty and sent a patrol downriver to intercept Tyler and Blennerhassett's five boats. The nights were cold, and the sentinels consumed so much brandy and whiskey to keep warm that they dozed off, and the boats slipped silently past them.

When Margaret arrived back on the island on December 13, she found wanton destruction. The militia had arrested some followers of Burr, young Pittsburgh men of good families, and had taken them to the mansion to be tried on the spot. There, the militiamen found Blennerhassett's ample wine cellar, got thoroughly drunk, and shot up and ransacked the mansion. After apologizing to Margaret the next day, the militia commander permitted her to depart on her family's flatboat with the young Pittsburgh men. With her house in ruins and her neighbors an angry mob, she and her two boys left the island on December 17 for the final time. After again being detained by the militia and stuck on a Mississippi River sandbar, she was finally able to join her husband at Natchez on January 24, 1807.

At the time it was happening, Burr had no way of knowing about the catastrophe at the island. While Margaret Blennerhassett was fleeing the island, Burr was in Nashville, trying to pacify Jackson and lay claim to the boats Jackson was having built for him. After signing a loyalty oath to the United States, Burr convinced Jackson that he was not trying to dismember the Union and went

Margaret Blennerhassett's flight from the island

to see his new boats. To his dismay, only two were ready, but eight days later, all were completed. Burr and a few recruits headed down the Cumberland River to join Blennerhassett's fifteen boats on the Mississippi.

He and Blennerhassett met on January 27, where Burr learned the bad news. Most of the boats had been confiscated, and militias all over the West were rising against him. At Nashville, Burr had discovered that Wilkinson had negotiated an agreement with the Spaniards, and not only would there be no war, but Wilkinson was now his enemy. By the third week of 1807, Burr had only a handful of boats and perhaps sixty to a hundred men at most. His former collaborator, General Wilkinson, commanded the forces of the U.S. Army to block, rather than lead, his entry into New Orleans. It was clear to Burr that the invasion of Mexico was no longer possible.

Events quickly went from bad to worse. Two Burrites, Dr. Justus Bollman and Burr's friend, Samuel Swartwout, were arrested in New Orleans and taken to Washington for interrogation. Charged with treason, they were quickly freed when Chief Justice John Marshall ruled that no treason had been committed because the two had not actually levied war against the United States.

The Secretary of the Navy sent a letter ordering navy officials in New Orleans to "intercept and if necessary destroy" any boats under Burr's command. At that time, Burr had just left Nashville, heading down the Cumberland River. In early January, Wilkinson learned that Burr supposedly had several thousand men ready to join his expedition in Natchez, and martial law was declared in New Orleans. In fact, Blennerhassett later wrote, "I do not believe that the number of persons engaged for Burr has ever amounted to five hundred," and of those, some were men whose only plan was to colonize Burr's Bastrop Grant lands.[45]

Back at The Oaks in South Carolina, Theodosia and Joseph Alston could only guess about the progress of her father's plans. Because they had left the Blennerhassetts before the loss of the boats and the looting of the mansion, they probably did not know how precarious their chances were of ever achieving their dreams of a Mexican empire.

It was probably better that Theodosia did not know the truth or how rapidly her father's power was deteriorating. Leading his small flotilla in one of the bateaux, Burr and a handful of associates went ashore near Bayou Pierre, north of Natchez. His host for the night was Judge Peter Bruin, who showed Burr a January 6 edition of the Natchez *Mississippi Messenger*, which declared that Secretary of War Dearborn had ordered the arrest of the "Burr conspirators." It reprinted Wilkinson's self-serving translation of the cipher letter attributed to Burr (but written by Dayton).[46] Burr saw that his expedition was doomed. He and his men floated several miles downstream, where they beached their boats and hid their weapons. He surrendered to Mississippi authorities on January 14, 1807, with the assurance that he would be given the full protection of the law.

In Washington, a small town near Natchez, Burr was bound over to a grand jury and released after his friend, Col. Benejah Osmun, a New Jersey native and owner of Windy Hill Manor near Natchez, posted a $5,000 bond. He spent the next week as the guest of Osmun and several wealthy Natchez-area planters. On February 4, the grand jurors not only acquitted Burr of any wrongdoing but also vilified the authorities who, they said, had wrongfully maligned and harassed him.

Windy Hill Manor

Enraged, the judge ignored the jury's verdict, ordered Burr's bond forfeited, and demanded that Burr personally appear before him. Burr did a quick reality check and went into hiding. The judge immediately declared him a fugitive from justice, despite the fact that the grand jury had acquitted him of all charges. In his final act on the Mississippi, Burr demonstrated the generosity that typified the way he treated his military comrades. He divided all of the expedition's boats and supplies among his followers and told them to head directly to the Bastrop lands, where he authorized them to stake out claims. Some of them, including Harman Blennerhassett, were later arrested and freed, but Blennerhassett was re-arrested and sent to Richmond, Virginia, to stand trial for treason.

By the first week of February 1807, numerous stories of Burr's supposedly treacherous plans had reached the east. In an effort to further undercut Burr, Jefferson had written South Carolina governor Charles Pinckney that Alston—then Speaker of the South Carolina House of Representatives—was a participant in Burr's "unlawful enterprise."[47] Alston felt sufficiently threatened that he wrote a public letter to Pinckney denying everything that Jefferson knew was factual. Alston's letter was a brazen attempt to distance himself from the Burr fiasco and build a firewall between him and his father-in-law's legal problems. The letter, which Alston soon came to regret, laid himself wide open to claims of perjury—something that Harman Blennerhassett would later try to use to his advantage.

In his letter, Alston claimed to have no knowledge of any planned attack on New Orleans. He asked the rhetorical question, "Can it be supposed that a man like himself, descended from a family which has never known dishonor, happy in the affection and esteem of a large number of relations and friends, possessed of an ample fortune, and standing high in the confidence of his fellow citizens—could harbor, for an instant, a thought injurious to the country which was the scene of these blessings?"[48]

Alston then crossed over the line from protest to outright falsehood when he stated that he and Theodosia did not accompany Burr on the trip. Then Alston went on to deny that he himself had been a part of Burr's 1806 Mississippi trip, stating that "I have been ever since the adjournment of the legislature peaceably directing the plowing my rice-fields, and preparing my lands for the ensuing crop." Testimony in Burr's future trial in Richmond would soon demonstrate that Alston's letter to Pinckney was designed solely to distance himself from Burr's odious shadow and protect Alston's interests in his native state. Pragmatic man that Burr was, he never condemned Alston for his act of self-preservation.

In the summer of 1807, Blennerhassett was clearly concerned that Burr could not, or would not, cover his debts, and looked to Alston for assurances that he would make good his promises to back the debts if Burr did not pay. The replies from Theodosia and Joseph provide insights into the complex and delicate relationship between the Alstons and the Blennerhassetts just before the trial and demonstrate the forces that would soon turn their strained relationship bitter. From The Oaks on June 22, 1807, Joseph Alston wrote to the Blennerhassetts in Natchez:

You perceive from the very first word I have written that I address you with the same feelings with which

we parted [September 1806]. There are certain expressions in your letter of April last, which if you recollect,
you must acknowledge are not calculated to conciliate:
they spring, however, so manifestly from a zealous
attachment to Col: Burr, & a misapphehension of my
feelings, that they have produced none of those sensations, which under different circumstances, they would
not have failed to excite. I pass them over, too, the more
readily, as I am persuaded, from your temper, the
moment of discovering your error, will be the moment
of regret at having indulged it.— Suffer me, then, to
assure you, I have inflicted none of those wounds upon
my 'friends or relatives,' which you apprehend.— Col.
Burr feels that he has not the smallest ground of resentment against me—he is perfectly satisfied—nor does
there exist the shadow of that animosity between us
that you deprecate. The fact is, from not having a view
of the whole ground, you have judged precipitately
& erroneously. Of my error in giving faith to the letter
attributed to Col. Burr by Gen. Wilkinson [the July 1806
"cipher letter"] I have long been satisfied from several
quarters—nothing but the shape, apparently so unques-
tionable, in which it came, could have gained it credit
with me for a moment. These things, however will
shortly be put to rights.—As soon as the trial now pend-
ing at Richmond is over, the event of which, I am persuaded, can not but be favorable, Col: Burr will be with
us—a letter from him of the 12th Inst. announces health,
spirits & confidence.

Your letter was received at the beginning of the
present month, & but for the necessity of ascertaining
the intentions of Col: Burr upon the subject of it, should
have been acknowledged immediately. I forwarded it
to him directly, & have just heard from him. He informs
me that the bill-holders have instituted no suit against
you, but are at present expecting payment from him;
that he has hope of shortly effecting an arrangement,

by which he shall be able to meet the bills himself—
which, of course, will relieve you, & render a reference
to me unnecessary. He adds that a gentleman, as agent
for him, was to set out, in a few days, for the Western
Country, thro' whom you should hear further & more
amply on the subject.— These expectations of Col: B. I
trust will be accomplished: I have this day written him,
making certain offers, which I hope will facilitate them:
but should they unfortunately fail, I shall certainly
consider myself bound both in honor & justice to fulfill my engagement to you. The total failure of my
crops, caused by the storm of last fall, has occasioned
me a temporary embarrassment; but should your re-
imbursement devolve upon me, I shall cheerfully make
any arrangement for a settlement which may prove
satisfactory.

The troubles & vexations you have undergone; the
dreadful solicitudes & painful situation so long endured
by your amiable family; have my liveliest sympathies.
The energy of mind which distinguishes Mrs. Blennerhassett has had a painfully ample field for exertion; but
the storm is past, & better moments I trust are about to
arrive.— Of the friendly attentions & unremitting hos-
pitalities received from you during our tour through
the Western Country, allow me to assure you of my
grateful recollection. Were it within the scope of prob-
abilities, I need not tell you how much pleasure the presence of yourself & family at the Oaks would give us.
Tender, I pray you, to Mrs. Blennerhassett my profound
& most friendly respects.[49]

Given the mean-spirited treatment his father-in-law was
then suffering, Alston added the postscript, "It is so customary
at this time to publish extracts from every letter in which the
name of Col: Burr happens to be mentioned, that I was about
to observe to you that you will readily perceive without the
observation, that it is not meant for the same purpose, but

merely for your own perusal. J.A." This letter was dictated to Theodosia, as Joseph was unwell at the time. She then added her own postscript:

> Having acted as amanuensis [transcriptionist] for Mr. Alston I now beg leave to speak for myself, & enquire after the health of Mrs. Blennerhassett; her fortitude has, I hope, supported her through the troubles of the [word overwritten] winter,—may they be the last she has ever to en[dure]. I wrote to her last autumn, but I suppose my letter h[as not reached] her—the fulfill-ment of our mutual promise of corresponding, would afford me real pleasure; for it will, now be the only means of supporting a friendship, which, I flatter myself, commenced in conformity of sentiment & sin-cerity; but, whatever may be the length of our separa-tion, or discontinuance of intercourse, the happy days I spent on the Ohio, & the character of Mrs. B. will remain indelibly impressed on the mind of her friend & admirer, T.B. Alston.[50]

On February 18, Burr and his guide, Chester Ashley, fell into the hands of the law at Wakefield, near the Tombigbee River in what is now Washington County, Alabama. There, Burr was arrested, taken downriver to Fort Stoddart, and handed over to federal authorities. In late March, prisoner Burr, six heavily armed "husky civilians," and two soldiers started their 1,000-mile ride through the wilderness to Washington.[51] The guards knew that popular sentiment was on Burr's side, and they were watchful for anyone who might try to free him. Nicholas Perkins, who had met Burr at Wakefield and turned him in to the authorities to claim a $2,000 federal reward, was one of the guards.

They were particularly wary when they crossed the Georgia border into South Carolina, where Joseph Alston's wide ac-quaintance would have been especially problematic for the guards. They changed their guard formation to place two men in front of Burr, two men behind, and two on either side. They carefully remained on side roads and skirted all major settlements, but often got lost. However, their worst fears were realized when they reached the small village of Chester, South Carolina, about sixty miles north of Columbia. As they passed by George Kennedy's tavern[52] on the top of the hill in the village, music was playing inside, and the customers were having a fine time dancing and milling about outside. Burr seized the opportunity, jumped off his horse onto a large rock outside the tavern and cried to the astonished citizens, "I am Aaron Burr, under military arrest, and claim the protection of the civil authorities."[53]

Nicholas Perkins dismounted, guns drawn, and ordered Burr to remount. When the other guards cocked their pistols, the tavern guests ran inside to escape the danger. Burr refused

The Lewis Inn, near Chester, South Carolina

to remount. Not wanting to shoot his valuable prisoner, Perkins dropped his guns, "and being a man of prodigious strength and the prisoner a small man, seized him round the waist and placed him in the saddle."[54] Thomas Malone, another of the guards, took the reins of Burr's horse, and they rapidly continued on their way before the astonished residents of Chester could react.

Burr wept as his captors led him away, leaving behind them a thoroughly bewildered crowd. It was the first time anyone had ever seen Aaron Burr cry. In sympathy with his prisoner's frustration, Malone wept with him.[55]

That night the escort party stopped for the night at Lewis's Inn at what is now known as Lewis's Turnout, about seven miles past Chester. Burr was placed in an upstairs bedroom, but, according to local historian Lucille McMaster, he "conspired

with the girl who served his supper to help him escape."[56] Burr
made it downstairs to the living
room below, where a guard was
sleeping by the fire. He awoke,
wrestled Burr to the ground,
and alerted his colleagues. Burr
spent the rest of the night under heavy guard on a wooden
bench at the inn.[57] To prevent
another escape attempt, the es-
corts purchased a carriage and
kept Burr inside it for the rest of
the trip.[58]

When the guard detail
reached Fredericksburg, Virginia, they found orders redi-
recting them to Richmond. Had
it not been for his military escort,
no one in Richmond would have

*"Burr's bench"
from Lewis's Inn*

recognized the former vice president of the United States. Burr
was dressed in the same disguise he used to make his escape
from Windy Hill Manor. He wore the shabby clothing of a
boatman, which consisted of an old blanket coat; coarse, cop-
peras-dyed cloth trousers, held up by a leather strap, with a
tin cup suspended on the left and a scalping knife on the right;
and a dirty, old, wide-brimmed beaver hat, once white, with
a wide, flopping brim.[59] In addition, his face hadn't felt a
razor for over a month.

On March 26, 1807, Burr was led to a room in the Eagle
Tavern. He was fifty-one years, one month, and ten days old,
a federal prisoner, soon to stand trial for treason. Theodosia
had already suffered the loss of her mother and her health
and was still under the pall cast by Burr's duel with Hamilton.
Her father's trial was yet another heavy affliction.

The day after his arrival in Richmond—the first time he
had been permitted to possess pen and paper since his arrest—

he wrote a brief, businesslike note to Theodosia. "My military escort having arrived at Fredericksburgh on our way to Washington, there we met a special messenger, with orders to convey me to this place. Hither we came forthwith, and arrived last evening. It seems that here the business is to be tried and concluded," he wrote. "I am to be surrendered to the civil authorities to-morrow, when the question of bail will be determined. In the mean time I remain at the Eagle tavern."[60]

Theodosia's response required no deliberation. She immediately made plans to join her father in Richmond. She did not arrive there until the end of July, however, and her ill health may have delayed her. On April 26, 1807, a month after his arrival, Burr wrote to her, "Your letters of the 10th and those preceding seemed to indicate a kind of stupor; but now you rise into phrensy [frenzy]. Another ten days will, it is hoped, have brought you back to reason. It ought not, however, to be forgotten that the letter of the 15th was written under a paroxysm of the toothache."[61] Burr went on to compare his situation to the immortals of old who were martyrs to their noble causes. "You have read to very little purpose if you have not remarked that such things happen in all democratic governments. Was there in Greece or Rome a man of virtue and independence, and supposed to possess great talents, who was not the object of vindictive and unrelenting persecution?"[62] The stress of her father's predicament must have weighed heavily on the frail shoulders of his daughter, who had recently turned twenty-four.

The trial was a spectacle unlike anything the nation had ever seen. Burr, a founding father, and the former Vice President of the United States, stood accused of treason—plotting to induce the secession of the western states—and of the lesser crime of conspiring to plan the invasion of a friendly country. The judge was John Marshall, Chief Justice of the United States Supreme Court, a man now regarded as the greatest justice in American history. Burr's defense team consisted of Luther Martin; William Paterson, Burr's mentor, who served as lead counsel; and Edmund Randolph. Martin, a native of New Jersey and a graduate of the College of New Jersey, was Paterson's friend. Randolph was a respected Virginian who had served as U.S. attorney general and secretary of state. The attorneys for the prosecution were Charles Lee, former U.S. attorney general, and William Wirt, a future presidential candidate. Behind the scenes was the puppetmaster of the prosecution, President Thomas Jefferson, author of the Declaration of Independence, who relished the thought of seeing Burr get his comeuppance.

On March 30, Burr appeared before Chief Justice Marshall and a federal grand jury, whose job it was to determine if sufficient evidence existed to bind Burr over for trial. The prosecution argued that he should be tried for treason. Burr strenuously objected, painting an innocent picture of his activities, and complained bitterly about the treatment he had received from the government since he left Blennerhassett Island. Jefferson was stunned when Marshall ruled on April 1 that the prosecution had failed to make a case for treason but bound him over for trial on the "high misdemeanor" charge of planning the invasion of Mexico.

Shortly thereafter, Burr was moved from the small tavern to more spacious quarters in the Virginia State Penitentiary. The women of Virginia saw to it that Burr received new clothes appropriate to his station in life, and even the jailer treated him with uncommon courtesy. As Burr told it in a letter of July 3, "I have three rooms in the third story of the penitentiary, making an extent of one hundred feet. My jailer is quite a polite and civil man—altogether unlike the idea one would form of a jailer. You would have laughed to have heard our compliments the first evening," he wrote to Theodosia.

The Virginia State Penitentiary at Richmond

"*Jailer*. I hope, sir it would not be disagreeable to you if I should lock this door after dark.

"*Burr*. By no means, sir; I should prefer it, to keep out intruders.

"*Jailer*. It is our custom, sir, to extinguish all lights at nine o'clock; I hope, sir, you will have no objection to conform to that.

"*Burr*. That, sir, I am sorry to say, is impossible; for I never go to bed till twelve, and always burn two candles.

"*Jailer*. Very well, sir, just as you please. I should have been glad if it had been otherwise; but, as you please, sir."

The citizens of Richmond kept his larder well provisioned, he wrote to Theodosia. "While I have been writing different servants have arrived with messages, notes, and inquiries, bringing oranges, lemons, pineapples, raspberries, apricots, cream, butter, ice, and some ordinary articles."[63]

He wrote to Theodosia on July 6, "If you come I can give you a bedroom and parlour on this floor [of the penitentiary]. The bedroom has three large closets, and it is a much more commodious one than you ever had in your life." Burr then showed that he still kept his daughter on a short leash when he instructed her, "Remember, no agitations, no complaints, no fears or anxieties on the road, or I renounce thee."[64]

On July 24, a few days before the trial got underway, Burr wrote to her, "I may be immured in dungeons, chained, murdered in legal form, but I cannot be humiliated or disgraced. If absent you will suffer great solicitude. In my presence you will feel none, whatever may be the malice or power of my enemies, and in both they abound."[65] Theodosia and her family arrived the next week and moved into a house close to the prison furnished by Burr supporters. He referred to his own quarters on the third floor of the state penitentiary as "my townhouse."

Jefferson had his agents scour the entire West to secure witnesses for the prosecution. Their testimony did not please Burr, who wrote of them on June 24, "Out of fifty witnesses who have been examined before the grand jury, it may be safely alleged that thirty at least have been perjured."[66] General Wilkinson, "the alpha and the omega of the prosecution," arrived to testify on June 15. On June 24, the grand jury returned indictments against Burr for treason and high misdemeanor. After accepting Burr's plea of not guilty to both charges, the court adjourned until August 3.[67]

Two weeks earlier, Blennerhassett had reached Lexington, Kentucky, where he was promptly arrested, indicted for treason by a grand jury, and packed off to Richmond by David Meade, a marshal for the Kentucky District, with an armed guard of five men.[68] In his journal, the dapper and undaunted Irishman wrote that the guards, "vied with each other all the way in emulating the exertions of that excellent young man, David Meade, to promote my ease."[69]

From Natchez, on August 3rd, Margaret Blennerhassett wrote to her husband that she had just learned of his arrest, which "afflicts and mortifies me." She asked to "assure Col. Burr of my warmest acknowledgments for his and Mrs. Alston's kind remembrance, and tell him to assure her that she has inspired me with a warmth of attachment that never has, nor ever can diminish while I live. I wish him to urge her to write to me: a letter from her now would be most acceptable."[70]

Blennerhassett took over Burr's old quarters at the tavern, where he wrote, "I am lodged in a suite of commodious apartments, affording me a walk of forty paces in length, lately occupied by Col. Burr, who has been removed to another house [the penitentiary], under guard, for the more convenient intercourse with his counsel during his trial.... I was not half an hour here when I had a lively note from Col. Burr, a present of tea, sugar, and cakes from Mrs. Alston, and a visit from Alston."[71]

During the trial, Burr and the Alstons were on cordial terms with the Blennerhassetts, but Harman wrote to Margaret expressing great fears about their finances. With the mansion sacked, he feared the sale of it might not bring in as much money as they would need. "It is truly painful to me," he wrote, "to tell you to expect nothing from the Island," noting that "Alston is endeavoring to raise money here to meet all the demands, the success of which I shall learn to-day or to-morrow, but little [to] depend upon. On failure of this, he, Alston, will assume the whole, payable one-half a year from next January [1808], the remainder the January following, with interest. The impossibility, he declares, to raise money in Carolina, by sale or mortgage, and his having fewer negroes than his estates require, make this the best arrangement he can make; but which, I fear, will not be accepted.... Alston talks confidently of Burr's recovering his demands upon the Government, to the amount of $50,000. This event would be prosperous, indeed, but I have little faith in it."[72] Sadly, when Blennerhassett ran out of funds, and Alston could not cover Blennerhassett's claims against him, the relationship soured and then turned hostile.

The trial was held in the Hall of the Virginia House of Delegates, and it began on August 3 to a packed house. By August 15th, the jury selection was complete. District Attorney Hay delivered the opening statement for the prosecution two days later and called William Eaton, Commodore Truxton, and the Blennerhassetts' gardener, Peter Taylor.

Taylor described a conversation he had with the master of Blennerhassett Island. Blennerhassett said, "I will tell you what, Peter, we are going to take Mexico, one of the finest and richest places in the whole world." Taylor recounted that Blennerhassett had said that Colonel Burr would be King of Mexico, and Mrs. Alston, daughter of Colonel Burr, was to be the Queen of Mexico whenever Colonel Burr died. He said that Colonel Burr had made fortunes for many in his time, but none for himself; but now he was going to make something for himself.[73]

Throughout the trial, Theodosia radiated confidence as she sat in the courtroom every day, her husband at her side. She showed the world that she was as proud of her father in Richmond as she had been the day that he was inaugurated Vice President of the United States. "There is nothing in human history that is more touching than her devotion during this ordeal," wrote an early Blennerhassett historian.

"Beautiful, intelligent far beyond the average women of her time, she was the center of admiration throughout the entire trial. When all the world doubted, she still believed in him, and stood bravely, unswervingly at his side, notwithstanding the stain it must leave on her. She brought with her little Gamp, who was ever a delight to his grandfather, and went about Richmond making valuable friendships by her sweet gentleness of manner."[74]

After the prosecution tried to make a case that an invasion force had been assembled on Blennerhassett Island in 1806, Burr objected that he could not be held responsible because he was a hundred miles downstream when it happened. In a decision that infuriated Jefferson, "Marshall ruled that Burr could not be found to have committed treason based on the events at Blennerhassett's Island, saying that 'If those who perpetrated the fact be not traitors, he who advised them [Burr] cannot be a traitor.'" Marshall subsequently excluded all testimony "elsewhere and subsequent to the transactions on Blennerhassett's Island." This blow ended the prosecution's hopes. On September 1, the case went to the jury, who returned the verdict: "We of the jury say that Aaron Burr is not proved to be guilty under this indictment by any evidence submitted to us. We therefore find him not guilty."[75]

The chief justice proposed that Burr and Blennerhassett each be freed on $3,000 bail, with each to stand trial in Ohio. The prosecution declined to press the matter, and the second charge was dismissed on technical grounds. Burr was a free man again, and on Monday, September 1, 1807, Blennerhassett wrote in his journal, "This day at 11 o'clock a.m. ended my captivity, which lasted fifty-three days." One of his Wood County friends posted bond for his bail for charges still pending in Ohio, but he was never summoned to trial. As soon as Theodosia heard the good news about her father, she wrote a close friend, probably her half-brother's wife, Frances Prevost:

I have just this moment received a message from court, announcing to me that the jury brought in a verdict of acquittal, and I hasten to inform you of it, my dear, to allay the anxiety which, with even more of your usual sweetness, you have expressed in your letter of the 22nd of July. It afflicts me, indeed, to think that you should have suffered so much from sympathy with the imagined state of my feelings; for the knowledge of my father's innocence, my ineffable contempt for his enemies, and the elevation of his mind have kept me above any sensations bordering upon depression. Indeed, my father, so far from accepting sympathy, has continually animated all around him; it was common for desponding friends, filled with alarm at some occurrence, terrified with some new appearance of danger to fly to him in search of encouragement and support, and to be laughed out of their fears by the subject of them. This I have witnessed every day, and it almost persuaded me that he possessed the secret of repelling danger, as well as apprehension of it. Since my residence here, of which some days, and a night, were passed in the penitentiary, our little family circle has been a scene of uninterrupted gaity. Thus you see, my lovely sister, this visit has been a real party of pleasure. From many of the first inhabitants, I have received the most unremitting and delicate attentions, sympathy, indeed, of any that I have ever experienced.[76]

Burr was angry because the jury had seemed to suggest that they might have convicted him had they been able to consider all the evidence. But the verdict was sufficient to end the trial in his favor. Nevertheless, he stood disgraced for the second time in three years and would never again be chosen to fill a role of public service.

A free man with a black cloud hanging over him, Burr remained unvanquished. Years later, after hearing news of the Texas Revolution, he told a friend with great relish, "There! You see? I was right! I was only thirty years too soon. What was treason in me thirty years ago, is patriotism now."[77]

Three years earlier, when the duel with Hamilton ended all his career hopes in the East, Burr looked west and followed his star in that direction. Now both halves of the nation were closed to him, and Mexico had slipped out of his grasp. Burr was a man without a country. Undaunted, he turned his eyes across the Atlantic, envisioning, with a certainty only Burr's mind could muster, that in Europe, things could not possibly go as badly as they had for him in America. The confirmation was not long in coming.

CHAPTER EIGHT

The Expatriate's Daughter

Through all this bitter time the daughter's love
Failed not nor wavered, but a steadfast flame
It shone the brightest in that darkest hour
When all men thought him fouled with treason's stain.

—Alexander T. Ormond

A s the British mail packet *Clarissa Ann* rocked gently at
its New York wharf on the evening of June 6, 1807,
Mr. G. H. Edwards spent the evening in earnest conversation with his daughter, Mary Ann. Edwards was preparing to leave the next day for an extended stay abroad, and so
they passed the evening exchanging warm assurances of hope,
reassurance, and affection, for Mary Ann could not travel with
him. Edwards told his daughter of the elaborate code systems
the two would use to correspond, for Edwards knew he was
constantly being watched.

Mr. Edwards was not among the twenty-six passengers who
were on board the *Clarissa Ann* when she prepared to make
weigh the next morning. It was only at the last minute that he
stepped off a rowboat that had brought him to the ship as she
was waiting for a fair wind. He quickly took up his residence
in the one third of a small stateroom for which he had paid
sixty guineas.[1] On June 7, 1808, Edwards wrote in his journal,
"At 11 A.M. went on board [the] pilot-boat.... Set sail." On June

9, he cleared New York Harbor and was on his way. It was the last time the father and daughter would ever see each other again.

As with all things Burrian, the picture was not what it appeared to be. Only the captain of the *Clarissa Ann* knew that the name "Mr. G. H. Edwards" was the alias Burr had used to slip out of the country unnoticed by the law, his enemies, and creditors. And "Mary Ann Edwards?" Her real name, of course, was Theodosia.[2]

Burr's acquittal in the treason trial did little to solve his many pressing problems, other than to eliminate the possibility of his spending half a lifetime behind bars in his Richmond, Virginia, "town house." After the trial, Burr was surrounded by well-wishers and a long line of creditors. Harman Blennerhassett, reduced to poverty and extreme distress by the aftermath of the Burr affair, dogged him for weeks, trying to get some assurance that Burr would make good on his financial promises. Sadly, when Burr finally granted him an audience, it was to grill poor Blenny for European contacts, not to make arrangements to pay what he owed.

Burr, having played all his Mexican empire cards in the United States, now looked to England or France to find backing for "X", which was the code name he assigned to his Mexican plan. Burr spared no effort to pull strings and cover every bet the moment he arrived in England. When he filled out his alien arrival declaration on August 10, 1808, he noted that he was a citizen of the United States, but that "The undersigned was born within the King's allegiance and his parents British subjects."[3]

Theodosia had been his rock during the trial, but the emotional toll was heavy. In its aftermath, she felt the social chill that had descended over Burr and his small family. After his trial ended in Richmond, he remained there until December. He used the time to plan his trip to England, where he proposed to push his plan for overthrowing Mexico.[4] During February and March of 1808, Burr resided incognito in Baltimore, then traveled in April to New York. He scurried from the house of one friend to another, seeking to avoid arrest for his debts and the outstanding warrants for his arrest in New York and Ohio. Much of the time in New York he stayed with his old friend, Samuel Swartwout. Just before he departed, Burr borrowed some money from Mr. & Mrs. Anthony Bowrowson, former servants at Richmond Hill. The Bowrowsons wisely took as security his remaining possessions: crates of personal and household effects, including his portraits. Burr never repaid the debt, and in 1849, his cousin, Judge Odgen Edwards, recovered many—but not all—of the paintings.[5]

In April and May he traveled back and forth between New York and New Jersey, keeping a low profile, residing only with close-lipped friends to keep one step ahead of his ill-wishers.

Just before he sailed, Burr tasked Theodosia to carry out a ruse to confuse his enemies before and after his clandestine departure. He directed Theodosia to leak false information to the New York newspapers after the ship had sailed, to the effect that on a certain day, Burr, with one Frenchman and two Americans or Englishmen, had passed through a designated place on his way to Canada, and that Mrs. Alston passed through the same day to Saratoga for her health.[6] Thus Aaron Burr, once the top legal lion of New York and Vice President of the United States, smuggled himself out of New York, disguised by secrecy, frequent moves, a false name, and ruses perpetrated by his daughter.

In the weeks before he took ship for his self-imposed European exile, Theodosia's health was again taking a turn for the worse. She turned twenty-five years of age just two weeks after her father sailed for England. About the time that her father left for England, Joseph Alston purchased land in the hilly South Carolina Upcountry near Greenville, South Carolina. In 1810 he had thirty slaves on the property, suggesting that it was being used for both farming and as a summer home. Theodosia found life in the Upcountry quite boring. She wrote to her husband from Rocky River Springs, South Cariolina, on June 22, 1809, the day after her twenty-sixth birthday, "I do not believe that you will spend the summer here— there is no society, to relieve the want of occupation— a life of all others the most irksome to an active mind.— Suppose we botanize to pass away time.— Bring your little volume of botanical dialogues, they have a very respectable reputation— though supposed to take place merely between a mother & her daughters— They will do for me at all events.— I should like to analise these waters—look in Fourevoy, vol. 4, & see whether it will be in our power."[7] Alston had hoped that the change of scenery might comfort Theodosia, but her medical problems were far too advanced for that. While Burr was in England, being entertained as the former vice president, Theodosia's health was steadily declining.

On October 3, 1808, Theodosia wrote a detailed history of her medical problems to her friend and physician, Dr. William Eustis. Using the third person out of modesty, she described how her failed health could be traced back to the prolapsed uterus resulting from the difficult delivery of her son, Aaron Burr Alston, in 1802. She went on to list the frequent discharge of offensive fluids, which resulted from severe and recurring uterine infections, and a panoply of pain attacks accompanying her irregular menstrual periods. She noted an apparent recovery in 1806, but a relapse in 1807, which brought her intense pain when her meager menstrual flow started. For the eighteen months prior to her letter, her womb, she said, was "obstructed." In January 1808 "she had a slight attack of the inflammatory rheumatism, for the first time she had ever felt any rheumatic complaint. Shortly after this disappeared, your ill fated patient met with a severe fall which injured the spine so much that for several days she was stiffened from head to foot, & and confined & bed three months— at this time she took little nourishment except tea; for two months nothing else. April brought another physician, & a new form of treatment; she then took daily doses of steel dissolved in vitriolic acid, & Peruvian bark mixed with Eanella Alba, & twice a week pills of Aloes and Rhubarb."[8]

In June 1808 she went back to the spa at Ballston and bathed there for two months, but found that the waters "increased her nervous complaints, without relieving any others."

Returning to New York, she consulted Dr. David Hosack, Hamilton's physician at the duel. He recommended mercury, but Theodosia was afraid of it. A French physician advised frequent warm baths and a diet of rennet or lime juice, whey, water, roast meat, a few vegetables, and very little fruit, tea, coffee, chocolate, porter, or wine. She followed his advice until September, when "her sore mouth, for it had never been quite well, became highly inflamed, the stinging to be come as violent as ever."[9]

The unrelenting pain and misery ultimately affected her mind. She wrote Eustis, "The most violent affections have tormented her during the whole of the last eighteen months—hysteric fits, various colors & flashes of light before her eyes, figures passing around her bed, strange noises, low spirits, & worse, much worse than all, periods of inconceivable irritability & impatience—the attention can not be kept awake to a long sentence in conversation, the memory is impaired, & there is a sense of stupor almost mounting to absolute folly at times."[10]

In addition to severe infections, Theodosia was probably harboring a large and growing cancerous uterine tumor. She was desperate for medical advice that would help her rather than hurt her. She concluded her letter with a plea to her trusted friend, Eustis. "Let me entreat, then, that you will read this letter, if possible, more than once with patience, & give me your candid opinion, as well as your advice on the subject. You will have perceived that except drinking the Ballston waters, no system has been pursued with any constancy; this proceed from a want of faith in the opinions of all I have consulted about myself—be assured that your most trifling injunctions shall be adhered to rigidly. Unremittingly I feel now as if the end of my troubles were approaching."[11] Sadly, there was nothing Eustis could do.

Theodosia and Gampy spent the winter of 1808 at Pelham with Frederick Prevost, worrying about the possibility of war with England, and still secure in the hope that she would sometime assume the throne of Mexico. Believing that war might be imminent, Theodosia wrote to her father, "Vessels in Boston are said to be ready laden, and armed to brave all opposition, if their departure should meet with any [British embargo]. It is generally believed that we shall have trouble very soon. Thank God I am not near my [Mexican] subjects; all my care and real tenderness might be forgotten in the strife, for no doubt the flames of civil war would soon spread in that direction."[12]

By the end of the month, she had heard from Burr that the British were cool to his plans. From New York on October 30, 1808, she wrote to him, "You are well and happy, but X is abandoned! This certainly was inevitable, but I cannot part with what has so long lain near my heart, and not feel some regret, some sorrow. No doubt there are many other roads to happiness, but this appeared so perfectly suitable to you, so complete a remuneration for all the past; it so entirely coincided with my wishes relative to you, that I cherished it as my comfort, even when illness scarcely allowed me any hope of witnessing its completion."[13]

While Theodosia was overwhelmed with pain from her multiple afflictions, her father was in England, enjoying a seemingly unending stream of hospitable invitations to wine, dine, dance, and share companionship both in public and between the sheets. His jocular, coded journal, full of witticisms, allusions, and spatterings of poor French, Swedish, and German, was kept chiefly as an amusement for Theodosia, but also as a historical record of where he visited and who he conversed with. It portrays a well-known former vice president of the United States, more welcomed than shunned, making every effort to interest the British government in his Mexican plan—and accomplishing nothing.

Ultimately, Burr ran out of money, and about the same time, the British government, finding him more of a nuisance than an asset, declared him *persona non grata*. On April 4, 1809, "Mr. Kirby," the name Burr was then living under to avoid his latest collection of creditors, was arrested and offered a passport to any country that would take him. He departed for Sweden, and then traveled on to Denmark and Germany, where he spent the last half of 1809.

In Copenhagen, Theodosia made a strong impression (although *in absentia*) on the Danish artist, Karl Frederick von Breda. Burr had taken his copy of the "traveling Vanderlyn" portrait of Theodosia to von Breda to be retouched, varnished, and framed. "'Good God,' says he, 'pardon the freedom; but can any man on earth be worthy of that woman? I know how to estimate her. Such a union of delicacy, dignity, sweetness, and genius I never saw. Is she happy?'"[14]

No, Theodosia was not happy. Her health was in shambles, her father was wandering through Europe with no visible means of support and no way to return home without risking arrest or jail for his debts, and her husband was preoccupied with his planting and his role as speaker of the South Carolina State House of Representatives. A letter from Gottenburg (Göteborg), Sweden dated October 13, 1809—the first she had received in five months—gave her some hope that Burr might return soon, but that did not come to pass.

Theodosia was continually amazed with the apparent ease with which her father shouldered his many burdens and survived so many stinging arrows with never a complaint. She wrote, "I witness your extraordinary fortitude with new wonder at every misfortune. Often, after reflecting on this subject, you appear to me so superior, so elevated above all other men; I contemplate you with such a strange mixture of humility, admiration, reverence, love, and pride, that very little superstition would be necessary to make me worship you as a superior being: such enthusiasm does your character invite in me. When I afterward revert to myself, how insignificant do my best qualities appear. My vanity would be greater if I had not been placed so near you; and yet my pride is our relationship. I had rather not live than not be the daughter of such a man."[15]

Theodosia had turned twenty-six that summer of 1809 and spent much of her little available strength trying to make it possible for Burr to return. Just after her birthday, she wrote to her old friend, Dolley Madison, now the First Lady and wife of President James Madison, asking for her to intercede with her husband and to get him to clear the legal obstacles to Burr's return.

"You may perhaps be surprised at receiving a letter from one with whom you have had so little intercourse for the last few years," Theodosia wrote, "but your surprise will cease when you recollect that my father, once your friend, is now in exile; and that the President only can restore him to me and to his country." Theodosia then revealed that she was writing without the knowledge of her husband, but stated, "If it be an error, attribute it to the indiscreet zeal of a daughter whose soul sinks at the gloomy prospect of a long and indefinite separation from a father almost adored, and who can leave nothing unattended, which offers the slightest hope of procuring him redress. What indeed would I not risk once more to see him, to hang upon him, to place my child upon his knee, and again spend my days in the happy occupation of endeavoring to anticipate his wishes."[16]

So that her husband would not learn of her request for Mrs. Madison's intervention, she asked her to send her reply not to The Oaks, but in care of Frederick Prevost in Pelham. Their former friendship notwithstanding, Burr's stained reputation had permeated all of Washington, and Theodosia's eloquent plea was tactfully declined. On September 12, 1809, Theodosia wrote to Frederick Prevost, "The long expected answer from Mrs. Madison was such as reason & experience unmixed with hope might have led us to suppose it. She expresses great affection for me, calling me her 'precious friend,' pays me some compliments badly teared; & regrets that Mr. M[adison] finds it impossible to gratify my wishes &c."[17]

On August 2, 1809, while Burr was in Sweden, Natalie Sumter was in Washington, preparing for her husband's diplomatic posting to Brazil. Overwrought with concern at the failed health of her almost-sister, Natalie wrote a breathless and nearly unpunctuated letter to her friend, Mary Hooper, in Stateburg:

> I told you yesterday how distressed I was about Mrs.
> Alston—she has been very sick as well as Burr [Gampy]
> since she was with us she could not see from one eye

she has such inflammation in her face she said her
soul was harrowed from what she heard of her father—her husband was not with her—nor did she
know when he was coming or if he was coming at
all—I am going to tell Mrs. Huger as much as I want
the family to know by Mrs. Huger that is how much
she is respected here—that the report here is that they
have separated & that she inspires more respect & interest than him & that for his own importance he ought
to be with her—I can hardly believe though he means
to discard her & has lost his affection for her it cannot
be, I am sure I never was more mistaken in a man if it
is—do tell me what is said with you. I have not written yet to Bartow Prevost he can do no good at present,
if it is true her father is deranged I hope she will be
able to have him with her & nurse him it will be her
only consolation—the only thing I am afraid of is if
she hears this when she is at the springs by herself sick
is that she will die, sometimes I think of writing Mr.
Alston but I don't know what to do I write often to
her & try to keep up her courage.[18]

Burr, the wandering conspiratorial genius, left Germany for
France in 1810. When he arrived in Paris, he was thrilled to
learn that his young former protégé, John Vanderlyn, was
searching for him in the city. From February 1810 until September 1811, the two were nearly inseparable. They breakfasted,
lunched, and dined together; went to social and sporting events;
toured the countryside; and relished each other's company at
every possible moment. Burr recorded all of these details in his
journal, along with virtually every other detail of his daily life.
Burr was a doer, not a thinker, and it was his doings, unvar-
nished, that he dutifully logged into his journal almost every
day. Considering that he was keeping the journal for Theodosia,
and that he regularly sent her portions of it, it is profoundly
strange that in it he recorded virtually all of the numerous sexual
encounters he had with prostitutes while in Europe.

Burr's financial straits were so severe that he often could afford only a potato for breakfast or lunch, yet often, when he had to choose between buying food or renting sex, he chose sex. "There are few more scandalous records of erotic adventure anywhere, and the tone of the whole implies the image of Theodosia looking over his shoulder when he wrote it," noted one reader of his journal.[19] His European journal writings beg the question, *why* was Burr sharing every lurid detail of his sex life with his daughter?

"It will probably surprise the reader that a father should write and preserve such a record for his daughter," wrote the Rev. Gardner Spring to Burr's biographer, Matthew Davis, in 1838 as the *Journal* was about to be published. Spring's father, the Rev. Samuel Spring, had served with Burr at Québec during the war, and wanted to see him before the elder Spring left the city. The father and son spent an evening with Burr, a description of which the son shared with Davis. In discussing Burr's journal, Spring said, "It must be remembered, however, that the perfect unreservedness with which the author of the diary wrote to his daughter was part of the system, be it erroneous or not, on which her education and their intercourse had been conducted. It was his theory…that female education should in no respect differ from that of young men; and that, between parent and child, there should be the same frankness and candour of demeanour and conversation as between two friends of equal age. The theory may have been most unfounded," Spring wrote, "and yet he may be excused for adhering to it, or in spite of it, [because it produced] such a model of purity, intelligence, and loveliness as Theodosia Burr Alston."

Back on the American side of the Atlantic, Harman Blennerhassett was making life as miserable for Joseph Alston as Burr had for Blennerhassett. Since the trial, Blennerhassett had not been able to obtain so much as a dollar from either Burr or Alston. Blennerhassett claimed that his association with Burr had cost him $50,000: $12,500, which Alston had paid, and an additional $37,500, evidently for collateral damages, namely compensation for the loss of his mansion and island after it had been sacked by the militiamen and his neighbors in the 1807 fiasco.

Blennerhassett was blunt about his intentions if Alston did not pay. He threatened the publication of a tell-all book which would expose Alston as a financial underwriter and first-tier participant in the Mexican plan, and a perjurer as well for having publicly denied his involvement, active participation, and Ohio River travel to Governor Pinckney. The blackmail threat would be withdrawn and Blennerhassett would withhold publication of the book and its revelations about Alston's involvement if Alston paid him the $37,500. He wrote to Alston:

> To you, however, it belongs to say whether they shall remain shrouded within the sanctuary of your own breast, or stalk forth the heralds of the private treason and public *perjury* they will proclaim infallibly to the honest Democratic electors of South Carolina, who would thence remove you from the chair of their assembly with a different kind of zeal from that through which they placed you in it. Yes, sir, I submit it to your discretion, to keep concealed from your friends and from your country that led you to take part in our confederacy, which you pledged yourself to back with all your property, worth, as you stated, 200,000 guineas [about $1,000,000], to join and support us at New Orleans, at the head of 2,000 to 3,000 men, to leave with me, besides your oral and written guarantee of indemnity for all my losses, a private cipher, the inscrutable of our correspondence, afterward, to commit the *shabby treason* of deserting from your parent by affinity, and your sovereign in expectancy; and then, finally, in your letters to your Governor, to vilify your father-in-law, and perpetuate an open perjury by publicly denying all privity [knowledge] or connection with his views or projects.[20]

With war and a British embargo imminent, the value of Alston's rice crop had plummeted, and even if he had been willing to succumb to Blennerhassett's blatant extortion plot, he didn't have the means to do so. Alston never paid, but Blennerhassett never published.

Burr and Paris were a perfect match for one another, save for one thing: poverty. Unlike his artist friend, Vanderlyn, he did not have a portable trade and had no way to earn money. This left him at the financial mercy of friends old and new, from whom he borrowed at every opportunity, but he often was forced to sell his last remaining possessions—including books and trinkets he had purchased for Theodosia and little Gampy—just to keep body and soul together.

All chances for the success of "X" in France were doomed by Burr's reputation in government circles there. The French minister to the United States wrote that Burr was obsessed with "money, intrigue, and fame," and that "he will plot wherever he is," but probably did not have "the necessary boldness to execute his plans." Burr tried several plans of business that would bring in some money, but all proved impracticable. The American community in Paris shunned him, and he wrote to Theodosia, "My affairs are stagnant. I have no other prospects but that of starving in Paris."[21] Sensing that the political and financial climate in France was hopeless, Burr sought and obtained a passport to return to America. On July 20, 1811, Burr departed Paris for Amsterdam, where he ran into yet another obstacle: the captain who had offered him passage to the United States now wanted more money. Burr had to sell off yet more of his personal treasures to comply with the extortion. When his ship, the *Vigilant*, finally set sail, and Burr felt it possible to breathe a sigh of relief, what should appear in view but a British warship, ordering the *Vigilant* to heave to and prepare to be boarded! Burr soon found himself back in England, where he was forced to wait until the captain could get clearance to sail. In order to pay for a room, Burr was forced to sell off even more of the precious books and gifts he had bought for Theodosia and Gampy.

Ultimately, Burr was forced to seek another master who would carry him back. A Captain Porter, of the *Aurora*, agreed to furnish him passage, and Burr adopted the alias Adolphus Arnot. John Reeves, a friend of Burr's at the British Foreign Office, was able to get him a passport in that name. After a relatively quiet voyage of thirty-nine days, Mr. A. Arnot, sporting whiskers and a wig, arrived in Boston on May 4, 1812. The timing of his arrival was fortunate, because two weeks later, England declared war on the United States, and Burr's ship might well have been captured.

When he again reached dry land, Burr's pockets were empty, his spirits were low, and he was wary and uncertain of the reception he would receive.[22] His first contact was not encouraging. A former college-mate from Princeton snubbed him, and Burr was forced to sell two of his most valuable books to Dr. John Kirkland, president of Harvard College, to have enough money for his transportation to New York.[23]

In Gotham, Burr immediately sought out his closest friend, Samuel Swartwout, but he was not home. That night, unable to find an inn with space for him, Burr slept in a flophouse. The last entry he made to Theodosia in his European journal reads, "Being already dressed, I rose, paid for my lodgings 12 cents, and sailed out to 66 Water street, and there had the luck to find Sam. alone. He led me immediately to the house of his brother Robert, and here I am, in the possession of Sam.'s room in Stone Street, in the city of New York, on this 8th day of June, *anno dom.* 1812, just four years since we parted at this very place." Burr was fifty-six years old; Theodosia was two weeks shy of turning twenty-nine, and Gampy had just turned ten. He immediately sent a letter to her, telling of his return, and of the joy he would experience when he reunited with his daughter and grandson. Unknown to Burr and Theodosia, the most chaotic and tragic part of their lives was about to begin.

CHAPTER NINE

The Voyage of the Patriot

Then from a Southern port set sail, she braved
The grisly horrors of an unknown sea.
                                   —Alexander T. Ormond

B y the fall of 1812, Theodosia's life was full of dark shadows. She was weak in spirit, emaciated from ten years
of recurring medical problems, profoundly depressed
by the long separation from her father, and deep in grief from
the recent death of her son, Aaron Burr Alston, from a summer fever. From Debordieu Island on July 12, 1812, she wrote
to Burr, "There is no more joy for me. The world is a blank. I
have lost my boy. My child is gone for ever. He expired on the
30th of June. My head is not now sufficiently collected to say
anything further. May Heaven, by other blessings, make you
some amends for the noble grandson you have lost.[1]

A month later, Theodosia was still forlorn and in deep
despair. "Alas! my dear father," she wrote, "I do live, but
how does it happen? Of what am I formed that I live, and why?
Of what service can I be in this world, either to you or any
one else, with a body reduced to premature old age, and a
mind enfeebled and bewildered? Yet since it is my lot to
live, I will endeavor to fulfill my part, and exert myself to my
utmost, though this life must henceforth be to me a bed of
thorns."[2]

Inspired solely by the impending return of her beloved father after four years of foreign exile, Theodosia yearned to reunite with him in New York. As a loving husband, Joseph Alston would have done anything to console his physically ravaged and emotionally drained wife. Although he supported the New York reunion, he had logical reservations about the timing and physical toll of such a dangerous trip. First of all, he could not accompany Theodosia. As a brigadier general in command of the state militia, Alston could not leave South Carolina on private business while the War of 1812 was underway and his state was under direct attack by the enemy. On July 26, 1812, a month after the death of his son, he wrote to Burr, "We have not been able to form any definite plan of life. My present wish is that Theodosia should join you, with or without me, as soon as possible. My command here, as brigadier-general, embarrasses me a good deal in the disposal of *myself*. I would part with Theodosia reluctantly; but if I find myself detained here, I shall certainly do so. I not only recognise your claim to her after such a separartion, but change of scene and your society will aid her, I am conscious, in recovering at least that tone of mind which we are destined to carry through life with us."[3]

On December 10, 1812, he had been elected governor by a razor-thin margin.[4] This doubled the impossibility of him escorting Theodosia north. Given her health, her depression, and the preparations necessary for her impending trip, it is unlikely that Theodosia, although she was now officially the First Lady of South Carolina, even attended her husband's inauguration or visited Columbia during December 1812.

Traveling by land or by sea were Theodosia's only two options to reach New York. By land meant riding in Joseph Alston's family carriage, a rough and wearying two-week trip for a debilitated woman. However, Theodosia's health was not the sole deciding factor. Regarding Joseph Alston's family coachman, she wrote, "He is a great drunkard, and requires the presence of a master."[5] Hence, land travel was not an option.

Traveling by sea was extremely hazardous but promised a relatively brief five- or six-day passage with somewhat less discomfort. The first danger was the possibility of her ship being captured by the British fleet and being sailed off to a British port as a prize of war. This was no idle threat. Powerful British warships were patrolling the Atlantic coast, raiding North Carolina coastal settlements and South Carolina plantations with impunity. In 1812, a dozen British warships blockaded Charleston harbor where, on October 14, 1812, they took eight American vessels as prizes.[6]

Numerous other hazards loomed large. Foul weather at sea posed a problem. The weather was often severe off the Atlantic coast in January. In addition, pirates and privateers were active in Carolina waters. Furthermore, should the ship run aground, the fate of any surviving passengers and crew would almost certainly fall into the hands of the "wreckers," coastal residents whose livelihood depended on salvaging the cargo and any useful materials such as fittings or wood cast up on the shores of North Carolina's treacherous Outer Banks, the famous "graveyard of the Atlantic."

By late fall, Theodosia had overcome her husband's protective arguments. She obtained his reluctant consent to travel by sea to New York to "draw strength and hope from the source that had never failed her—her father's inspiring presence."[7] Theodosia and her father had been separated for four years, "and now their common desire was to seek solace in each other's company."[8] She hardly had the strength to travel, but she wrote to her father, "I have been reading your letter over again. I am not insensible to your affection, nor quite unworthy of it, though I can offer nothing in return but the love of a broken, deadened heart, still desirous of promoting your happiness, if possible. God bless you."[9]

Because of her advanced illness, exhaustion, and depression, Burr persuaded Dr. Timothy Ruggles Greene, an old Revolutionary War friend and business associate from Boston, to undertake the dangerous mission: travel to South Carolina and then accompany Theodosia back to New York by sea.

Greene traveled south by land and arrived in South Carolina on November 28, 1812.[10]

He initially received a cool reception from Alston, who was miffed that Burr had apparently shown so little confidence in his ability to provide for Theodosia's safety.[11] From Charleston, on December 7, 1812, Greene wrote to Burr, "I arrived here from New-York on the 28th ult. [of last month], and on the 29th started for Columbia. Mr. Alston seemed rather hurt that you should conceive it necessary to send a person here, as he or one of his brothers would attend Mrs. Alston to New-York. I told him you had some opinions of my medical talents; that you had learned your daughter was in a low state of health, and required unusual attention, and medical attention on her voyage; that I had torn myself from my family to perform this service for my friend. He said that he was inclined to charter a vessel to take her on. I informed him that I should return to Charleston, where I would remain a day or two, and then proceed to Georgetown (S.C.) and wait his arrival."[12]

Practicality quickly displaced pride, as Alston knew that he could not accompany Theodosia himself. Although he told Greene that he could have sent one of his brothers to accompany her, his siblings were probably saddled with their own service obligations to the militia. Greene tactfully defused the situation by assuring Alston that Burr's sole concern was Theodosia's health and that his medical competence—limited though it was—and his age (47), which rendered him exempt from military service—made him the logical choice to be the escort.

From Georgetown on Tuesday, December 22, 1812, Greene wrote to Burr, "I have engaged passage to New-York for your daughter in a pilot-boat that has been out privateering, but has come in here, and is refitting merely to get to New-York. My only fears are that Governor Alston may think the mode of conveyance too undignified, and object to it; but Mrs. Alston is fully bent on going. You must not be surprised to see her very low, feeble, and emaciated. Her complaint is an almost incessant nervous fever. We shall sail in about eight days."[13] The term "privateer" designated that the *Patriot* was a private ship that had been authorized by the government to carry guns and attack British merchant ships. With only three to five cannon at the most, she would never have taken on a British warship.

According to local tradition, Theodosia, accompanied by Joseph, Dr. Timothy Greene, and one or more servants, walked from the Alston house at The Oaks to their boat landing on Oaks Creek and were rowed to Georgetown via the Waccamaw River on Wednesday, December 30, the day before her departure. That evening, a farewell reception was said to have been held in Theodosia's honor in the Mary Mann house in Georgetown.[14] The event has been described by some as "a ball in her honor." However, it is unlikely that the planters would hold "a ball" for a woman with a prolapsed uterus and re-curring uterine infections—and possibly dying of cancer. If held at all, the event was more likely to have been a warm farewell gathering in honor of the respected First Lady of South Carolina, the wife of one of their most prominent neighbors, and a woman setting off on a risky voyage during wartime.

The *Patriot* was set to sail around noon the next day, so it makes sense that Theodosia and her traveling party would have overnighted in Georgetown prior to the voyage. However, there is no record of their activities on the night of the 30th, so exactly what happened that evening remains open to speculation.

Alston gave Burr a detailed description of the ship that Theodosia would soon board for her trip to New York. The *Patriot*, a schooner used as a pilot boat, was commanded by Capt. William Overstocks, with the aid of an old New York pilot named Samuel Coon as sailing-master. The vessel had dismissed her crew and was returning home with her guns dis-mounted and stowed below decks.[15] The ship had seen service as a privateer, Alston wrote, and "had been sent by the gov-ernment last summer in pursuit of Commodore Rodger's squadron." Alston chose the *Patriot* because of "her reputed excellence and swiftness in sailing, [which] would ensure a passage of not more than five or six days."[16]

According to the research done by archaeologist James L. Michie, the *Patriot* was a sixty-three-foot, shallow-draft coastal schooner with a beam of seventeen feet, eight inches; was six feet, eight inches deep; and displaced about sixty-eight inches—less that six feet—of water. The one-year-old ship, a square-sterned schooner, had a single deck, two masts, and a tuck bow and was enrolled (registered) on November 9, 1811. The ship was probably built in Catskill, New York by Richard Hill, master carpenter, and sponsored by James Flinn, John White, David Torry, and Samuel Coon, all New York City residents. In an 1811 New York City directory, James Michie found Samuel Coon, occupation "pilot," and Capt. William Overstocks, occupation "mariner." Neither man appears in city directory listings after 1812. Thus, the ship would have been piloted by one of its owners and commanded by a fellow New Yorker, both of whom disappear from the New York residential records after the *Patriot* was lost.[17]

The *Patriot's* log or passenger and cargo manifest have not survived, but reasonable assumptions can be made about who and what was on board when the ship sailed from Georgetown. The senior officers were the two New Yorkers, Capt. Overstocks and Mr. Coon. Crewmembers were either seasoned hands from previous privateering missions or several sailors recruited from Georgetown. According to a veteran contemporary sailor, sailing a boat this size would only require "two men and a boy." The *Patriot*, fitted out as a privateer with cannon on board, probably carried a somewhat larger crew, but Overstocks, Coon, and two additional adult seamen would have been sufficient to sail her, cannons stowed, with or without a cabin boy.

The passenger list included Theodosia Burr Alston and Dr. Timothy Greene. In addition, Theodosia's French maid is said to have accompanied them, and her cook may also have been aboard. Both servants would have wanted to return to New York to see their northern friends and families again.[18] It has never been suggested or documented that any other passengers or animals were aboard the *Patriot* on this voyage.

Theodosia's personal baggage would have consisted of trunks containing her clothing, jewelry, toiletries, and cosmetics. In addition, she was carrying the carefully sealed tin boxes containing her father's personal and professional papers, which she had safeguarded while he was in Europe.[19]

The ship was traveling with her guns stowed below deck so that it might pass for a civilian vessel rather than a privateer warship.[20] An Alston descendant stated that the ship's cargo included barrels of Joseph Alston's rice, which were to be sold in New York to help defray the cost of the voyage.[21] If so, the heavy barrels of rice would have served to further conceal the cannons.

Many years later, tales appeared saying that Theodosia had "a white and a black dress" with her, along with "the Burr family silverware, which she was returning to her father."[22] Another put a "little black and tan dog" aboard.[23] Statements were also made that the *Patriot's* master "probably painted out her name,"[24] that the ship was "richly laden with the proceeds of her raids," and that Theodosia carried with her a painting to give to her father as a welcome-home gift, but there is no documentary evidence to support any of these allegations.[25]

On Thursday, December 31, 1812, Theodosia, one or more of her servants, her husband, and Dr. Greene are said to have stepped from a dock at the foot of Cannon St., fronting on the Sampit River, into a small boat. From there, they were rowed to the *Patriot*, which was anchored at the mouth of Winyah Bay, Georgetown's harbor.

Aboard the *Patriot*, Joseph kissed the love of his life and said goodbye, climbed back down into the rowboat, and was carried back to Georgetown. "I parted with our Theo. near the bar about noon on Thursday, the last of December," he wrote to Burr two weeks later.[26] As painful as the parting was for the loving couple, the weather seemed auspicious for a safe voyage. "The wind was moderate and fair," he wrote.[27] Theodosia, her maid, and Dr. Greene settled into the main cabin for what they hoped would be an uneventful voyage.

Captain Overstocks ordered the crew to weigh anchor and hoist the sails. The breeze quickly filled the canvas, and the

Patriot sailed off to meet its destiny. The captain guided her around the tip of North Island, tacked to port, steered a north-east course fairly close to shore, and slipped out of view behind the wax myrtles that grew wild on the beach.

Theodosia was twenty-nine years, five months, and ten days old. Since the election of her husband as governor, she had been First Lady of South Carolina for barely three weeks. Few people ever got to meet her in her official role as the governor's wife, for after she left Georgetown on December 31, 1812, Theodosia, her fellow passengers, the crewmen, and the *Patriot* were never seen again.

Two weeks passed without the desired good news announcing Theodosia's safe arrival in New York. As the days passed, Joseph Alston and Aaron Burr's nervous concerns deepened into genuine fear, and fear soon became despair. Both men went to bed each night tortured by the possibility that Theodosia was gone forever, but heartened by the possibility that if a wreck had occurred, some of the *Patriot's* passengers might have been rescued by a passing ship and taken to a foreign destination. Then Theodosia might, a week, a month, a year from then, re-appear from some distant port.

From the state capital, Columbia, on January 15, 1813, Alston wrote to Theodosia in care of her father in New York, hoping their letters would cross in the mail. "Another mail, and still no letter! I hear, too, rumors of a gale off Cape Hatteras the beginning of the month! The state of my mind is dreadful. Let no man, wretched as he may be, presume to think himself beyond the reach of another blow. I shall count the hours till noon to-morrow. If I do not hear then, there will be no hope till Tuesday. To feelings like mine, what an interval! May God grant me one word from you to-morrow. Adieu. All that I have left of heart is yours. All my prayers are for your safety and well-being."[28]

Four days later, he wrote to her again. "Forebodings! wretched, heart-rending forebodings distract my mind. I may no longer have a wife; and yet my impatient restlessness addresses her a letter. To-morrow will be three weeks since our separation, and not yet one line. Gracious God! For what am I reserved?"[29]

From Columbia, Alston wrote to Burr on January 19, 1813. The tone of his letter suggested that Alston might have been holding Burr at fault to some degree for having required the trip. "To-morrow will be three weeks since, in obedience to your wishes, Theodosia left me. It is three weeks, and not yet one line from her. My mind is tortured.... [The *Patriot's*] reputed swiftness in sailing inspired such confidence of a voyage of not more than five or six days, that the three weeks without a letter fill me with an unhappiness—a wretchedness I can neither describe nor conquer. Gracious God! Is my wife, too, taken from me? I do not know why I write, but I feel that I am miserable."[30]

Alston's search for relief from the guilt he must have felt for having let his sick wife make the voyage is understandable, but the trip was virtually unstoppable. The magnetic attraction between Burr and his daughter was so intense that either would have gladly risked death to make it happen. Theodosia's grief was as inconsolable as her physical pain was intense. Joy was no longer possible for her. Only seeing her father again could possibly give her any hope or comfort. On January 31, a month after Theodosia's departure, Alston again wrote to his father-in-law, this time from Charleston:

> A call of business to this place occasioned your letter of the 20th not to be received till this morning. Not a moment is lost in replying to it. Yet wherefore? You ask me to relieve you of your suspense. Alas! it was to you I looked for similar relief. I have written to you twice since my letter of December 29. I can add nothing to the information then given.... I have been the prey of feelings which you only can imagine. When I turned from the grave of my boy I deemed myself no longer vulnerable. Misfortune had no more a blow for me. I was wrong. It is true, I no longer feel, I shall never feel as I was wont; but I have been taught that there was still one being in whom I was inexpressibly interested. I have in vain

endeavored to build upon the hope of long passage. Thirty days are decisive. My wife is *either captured or lost!*[31]

Poseidon, it seemed to all, had claimed yet another precious prize. Nevertheless, in those desperate times, both Alston and Burr held onto any scrap of hope. The vessel was sound, hardly a year old. Perhaps the storm had blown her out to sea. Maybe a ship had rescued the passengers and transported them to some foreign port, from which Theodosia would soon return. Perhaps a British warship had captured the *Patriot* and its crew. If so, word would eventually reach home. Burr sent letters of inquiry to officials in ports from New York to the Caribbean, all to no avail. No one, it seemed, had any news about Theodosia or her ship. Oddly enough, the historical record preserves no proof that either Burr or Alston made inquiries along the North Carolina coast—the place where the *Patriot* was most likely to have been lost.

The nature of his high office and the customs of the time required that Alston remain stoic in public. He tried to hide his grief and carry on the business of state without wavering, but emotionally, he was a shattered man. By the end of another month, Alston had given up all hope. On February 25, 1813, he wrote to Burr:

Your letter of the 10th, my friend, is received. This assurance of my fate was not wanting. Authentic accounts from Bermuda and Nassau, [both British colonies] as late as January 30, connected with your letter from New-York of the 28th, had already forced upon me the dreadful conviction that we had no more to hope. Without this victim, too, the desolation would not have been complete. My boy—my wife—gone, both! This, then, is the end of all the hopes we had formed. You may well observe that you feel severed from the human race. She was the last tie that bound us to the species. What have we left? In surviving the 30th of June [when Gampy died]

I thought I could meet all other afflictions with ease,
yet I have staggered under this in a manner that I am
glad had not a witness. Your letter of January 28 was
not received till February 9. The Oaks, for some months
visited only at intervals, when the feelings the world
thought gone by were not to be controlled, was the asylum I sought. It was there, in the chamber of my wife,
where every thing was disposed as usual; with the
clothes, the books, the playthings of my boy around me,
that I sustained this second shock, doubled in a manner
that I could not account for. My son seemed to have
been reanimated, to have been restored to me, and to
have just perished again with his mother. It was the
loss of both pressing upon me at the same moment.

Should it be my misfortune to live a century, the
30th of June and the 10th of February [when Burr's letter arrived suggesting her fate] are so impressed upon
my mind that they will always seem to have just
passed. I visited the grave of my boy. The little plans
we had all three formed rushed upon my memory.
Where now was the boy? The mother I cherished with
so much pride? I felt like the very spirit of desolation.
If it had not been for a kind of stupefaction and confusion of mind which followed, God knows how I should
have borne it. Oh, my friend, if there be such a thing
as the sublime of misery, it is for us that it has been
reserved.

You are the only person in the world with whom I
can commune on this subject; for you are the only person whose feelings can have any community with mine.
You knew those we loved. With you, therefore, it will
be no weakness to feel their loss. Here, none knew them;
none valued them as they deserved. The talents of my
boy, his rare elevation of character, his already extensive reputation for so early an age, made his death regretted by the pride of my family; but, though certain
of the loss of my not less admirable wife, they seem to

consider it like the loss of an ordinary woman. Alas! they know nothing of my heart. They never have known anything of it. Yet, after all, he is poor actor who cannot sustain his little hour upon the stage, be his part what it may. But the man who has been worthy of the heart of *Theodosia Burr*, and who has felt what it was to be blessed with such a woman's, will never forget his elevation."[32]

In January 1813, two strong men—Burr and Alston—lost their spark of life. For weeks after Theodosia's departure from Georgetown, Burr walked the docks of New York, searching the bustling harbor for good news. A collateral descendant, Charles Burr Todd, wrote "His symbol, which he loved occasionally to stamp upon the seal of a letter, was a rock in the tempest-torn ocean, which neither wind nor wave could move. But his firm and manly nature, which no danger or reverse nor any of the previous circumstances of life had been able to shake, was near giving way."[33] Burr had suffered six major life blows: the stillbirth or death of three children, the death of his first wife, the disgrace of the duel with Hamilton, the collapse of his western adventure, the public spectacle of his trial for treason, the death of his only grandson, and now, the loss at sea of his beloved daughter.

Burr considered her possible fates. The *Patriot* was wrecked in a hurricane and sank with all hands aboard. The ship was boarded by pirates, who robbed and killed the passengers and scuttled the ship. The crew had mutinied. The ship had run aground and been looted by wreckers on the Outer Banks. The ship was captured by British warships and the passengers taken prisoner. Perhaps to put his own mind to rest, he chose to believe that Theodosia had been lost in a natural disaster—or that she might somehow still be alive.

Burr had supposedly been told by the *Patriot's* owner that the officers and crew never planned to sail for New York but instead had returned to privateering, which is to say, state-sanctioned piracy. This may have sparked Burr to write on March 29, 1813, that Theodosia might have been cast off "on shore in some West-indian Island or on some part of South America," and might still find her way home.[34] About that same time, he wrote to "Kate," probably his late wife's cousin, Mrs. Catherine Bartow Howes, "My hope is that the vessel may have been taken and carried into Bermuda...but indeed I am wretched, and the utter impossibility of doing anything for her relief or my own makes me still more so," Burr wrote. "When or how this dreadful suspense will terminate, God only knows."[35]

When bloody pirate stories started to appear which suggested that the *Patriot's* crew had been murdered and Theodosia had been carried off, Burr's reaction was vehement and immediate. "No, no," said Burr to a friend who mentioned the rumor, "she is *dead*. She perished in the miserable little pilot-boat in which she left Charleston [Georgetown].[36] Were she alive, all the prisons in the world could not keep her from her father. When I realized the truth of her death, the world became a blank to me, and life then lost all its value.'"[37] For the rest of his life, only the broken-hearted shell of Aaron Burr walked the streets of New York.

But what about the British fleet offshore? The *Patriot* would have been a valuable war prize for the British. According to a statement first published on April 6, 1902, Captain Overstocks allegedly carried a letter from Governor Alston, addressed to the admiral of the British fleet patrolling the waters of the North Carolina coast, asking "the chivalrous British" to give the *Patriot* and his sick wife safe passage.[38] This major piece of new information was furnished by Jacob Motte Alston, Theodosia's great nephew by marriage. It was published as "The True Story of Her Death At Sea," in the *New York Times Saturday Review of Books*, May 31, 1902. He said of the *Patriot*:

> The boat was deemed safe and seaworthy, and for ballast carried tierces of rice to defray expenses in New York, and so the heart-broken mother, accompanied by several of her devoted servants, who refused to be left behind, sailed away forever from her Southern home, beloved by all who knew her. The captain of the vessel

carried with him a letter from Governor Alston to the British Admiral, requesting under the circumstances a safe permit through the fleet to New York. The non-arrival was, of course, a source of great anxiety, which became more intense as weeks and months passed; but for long and weary months all hope had not expired. The war was now over, Governor Alston had died, and no truthful intelligence had been received of the pilot boat or Theodosia till General Thomas Pinckney, a near connection of the family in Carolina, met at a dinner party in London the Admiral of the fleet already alluded to, who stated to him 'that the letter of Governor Alston had been received and read to him and the request promptly granted, but that a very violent storm had arisen during the night and the fleet was scattered, and doubtless the pilot boat and all on board were lost.' This was the first reliable information which had been received, and the family accepted it as absolutely true."[39]

Alston's detailed, heartfelt story was taken as the gospel truth and repeated by every subsequent writer, historian, and biographer for nearly a hundred years. His story about the letter of safe passage and the *Patriot's* encounter with the British fleet held sway until 1998, when South Carolina archaeologist James L. Michie started looking for proof that the *Patriot* had, indeed, been stopped and then released by the British. What he learned radically changed the history of Theodosia's last hours.

Michie commissioned a comprehensive search of the British Admiralty records to locate the logbooks of the warships that were patrolling the North Carolina coast during the period when the *Patriot* was lost. "If Theodosia had been stopped by Admiral Warren or any other British ship," Michie wrote, "the captain would have recorded the event, especially considering that her husband was governor of South Carolina and her father was a former vice president. Furthermore, if a storm had been responsible for her death, then details of the storm would be recorded in the ships' logs."[40]

Research revealed that several British warships were patrolling the North Carolina coast between December 30, 1812, and January 5, 1813. Their mission was straightforward: intercept every foreign ship and force it to heave to for inspection. "If the ship had legitimate business with America and operated under a license, it was searched to verify its cargo and then was allowed to proceed. If contraband was found, the ship was either scuttled by cutting a hole through the bottom, or was escorted to Bermuda to be sold."[41] All the details would be recorded in the warship's logbook.

Of the warships known to have been operating off the North Carolina coast during the first days of January, Michie's researcher was able to locate logbooks for the H.M.S. *Poicitier, Acasta, Tartarus, Sylph, Aeolus,* and *Sophie.* Although they stopped many ships during the critical time period, there was no mention of the *Patriot* or the names Theodosia Burr Alston, or Timothy Greene. Furthermore, the ship alleged to have stopped the *Patriot*, Admiral Warren's flagship, the H.M.S. *San Domingo*, "was anchored in Bermuda at the beginning of Theodosia's voyage and did not depart until the morning of January 4, six days after she sailed for New York." Clearly, if Admiral Warren was in Bermuda outfitting his ship when the storm hit the Carolina coasts, he could not have intercepted the *Patriot*, and, based on the other ships' logs, she was not stopped by any other British warship under his command.[42]

Although the logbooks negated Jacob Motte Alston's claims about the *Patriot* being stopped and then allowed to proceed through the British fleet, the same books confirmed accounts of a terrible storm which began off the Carolina coast late on Saturday afternoon, January 2, 1813, and continued well into Sunday. "The events and savagery of the storm are well recorded in the logs," Michie found. "The gale was so severe that the warships furled and reefed most of their sails. Nevertheless, the ferocity of the storm striped off top-gallant yards and masts, snapped rigging, and tore out chain plate bolts from the hull."

The *Patriot* must have been hugging the North Carolina coast at the time. Michie plotted its likely position as just North of Cape Hatteras when the gale was at its fiercest. "If the ship managed to escape this battering, which continued until midnight, it then faced near hurricane-force winds in the early hours of Sunday. Given this knowledge, the *Patriot* probably sank between 6 p.m. Saturday and 8 a.m. Sunday."[48]

Aaron Burr was fifty-seven at the time of Theodosia's disappearance, and for some time, he remained completely stoic, never expressing his feelings in words or actions. There was probably never a day in the rest of his life when Burr did not think fondly of his daughter, but physical reminders brought him more pain than his heart could bear. When at last he accepted the implications of her absence, "he quietly put out of sight every object which was peculiarly associated with her, every thing which her tasteful hands had made or adorned, every thing that had once been hers."[44]

Although Burr lived for an additional twenty-three years, his heart died in those anguishing first months of 1813. He continued to conduct a successful law practice but was generally shunned by New York's polite society. In the last decade of his life, few on the streets of the great metropolis even recognized him. In 1830, he suffered a slight stroke but recovered.

Aaron Burr, aged 78

In 1833, at the age of 78, he married Madame Eliza Jumel, the notorious mistress, later wife, and then widow of Stephen Jumel, a French merchant with a considerable fortune. The Burr-Jumel union quickly soured, due chiefly to Burr's lavish spending of his new wife's money. She filed for divorce the next year, citing infidelity. In 1834, he suffered another stroke, which rendered him immobile. Burr was ultimately cast upon the charity of Mrs. Newton, an old friend. He died at the Continental Hotel, Port Richmond, Staten Island, New York, on September 14, 1836.[45] Ironically, that was also the date that Madame Eliza Jumel Burr's divorce was granted.[46]

The members of Princeton's Cleosophic Society, of which Burr had been a member, along with members of the faculty, students, alumni, a military band, and the Mercer Guards, escorted his coffin to his grave in the President's Lot at the university, where he had wished to be buried.[47] As a distinguished officer in the revolution and former Vice President of the United States, he was buried with full military honors next to his father and grandfather.

᭦ᔆᔆ᭦

After Theodosia's death, Joseph Alston, deep in grief, tried to regroup his physical energies to find the strength to carry out his duties as South Carolina's new governor. He successfully coped with a crisis over control of the state militia during the war, overcame allegations that he had gained his office through corruption, and was forgiven by his peers for having given Burr money to finance his nefarious western schemes.

Those financial arrangements had included Alston pledging his "whole property to forward and support" the Burr-Blennerhassett-Alston Mexican empire scheme, together with Alston's special assurances to reimburse Blennerhassett for "all contingent losses of a pecuniary nature" that he might suffer. The beleaguered Blennerhassett tried unsuccessfully to collect $15,000 from Alston in 1811. In April 1813, just a few months after Theodosia's death, Blennerhassett was back—this time with a second threat to publish his exposé if Alston did not pay him the money Blennerhassett claimed was due him for his roles in the conspiracy. "My losses...I estimate at $50,000, of which his Excellency [Governor Alston] has already reimbursed, I believe, $12,500, and it is very probable nothing short of the publication of my book, hitherto postponed only by sickness, will bring me any part of the balance so long sought in vain from his honor and engagements. [Alston's] well earned election to the chief executive office of his state and your return from Europe will...render the publication more effective.... I would still agree to accept ... $15,000...and of course withhold the book, which is entitled *A Review of the Projects and Intrigues of Aaron Burr, during the years 1805, 6, 7, including therein as parties or privies, Thos. Jefferson, Albert Gallatin, Dr. Eustis, Gov. Alston, Dan. Clark, Generals Wilkinson... exhibiting original documents and correspondence hitherto unpublished, compiled from the notes and private journal kept during the above period by H. Blennerhassett, LL.B.*"[48]

There is no record that Joseph Alston made the payment. A rambling, bumbling, and pitifully myopic book—claiming to be an expanded version of the ominous autobiographical "smoking gun" Blennerhassett had threatened Burr with in 1813—was eventually published in 1864 after Blennerhassett's death. By that time, Burr and Blennerhassett were both ancient history, and few took any interest in the book.

Joseph Alston completed his term of office in November 1814, an emotionally depleted man who had never recovered from the loss of his son and wife. After leaving the governorship, Joseph's life force quickly drained away. Burr tried to galvanize him in 1815 by urging him to support a national effort to draw Andrew Jackson—who had entertained Burr so warmly at his home during his first trip down the Mississippi—into the presidential race. Burr urged, "It is time that you manifested that you had some individual character—some opinion of your own—some influence to support that opinion—Make them fear you and they will be at your feet—thus far they have reason to believe that you fear them.... Emerge from this state of nullity—You owe it to yourself—You owe it to me—You owe it to your Country—You owe it to the memory of the dead."[49]

Alston was too ill and depressed to reply. In fact, he had been unable to attend the fall session of the South Carolina legislature. On February 16, Alston wrote Burr that he had not "the spirit, the energy, the health necessary to give practical effect to sentiment. All are gone. I feel too much alone, too entirely unconnected with the world, to take much interest in anything."[50] Severely ill, and deeply in debt from depressed markets for his rice, Alston slipped into a spiraling depression.[51] Seven months later, on September 10, 1816, at the age of 37, he died. His obituary notice in the *South Carolina Gazette* read, "Died at his father's house in King Street on the 10th instant of a lingering complaint, General Joseph Alston, aged 38 years, former governor of S. Carolina."

Joseph was interred next to his son in the ancient family burying ground at The Oaks. His tombstone reads "Sacred to the memory of Joseph and Theodosia Burr Alston and of their son Aaron Burr Alston. This last died June, 1812, at the age of ten years and his remains are interred here. The disconsolate mother perished a few months after at sea, and on the 10th of September, 1816, died the father, when little over 37 years of age, whose remains rest here with the son's.... He met death with the same fortitude as his ancestor [his grandfather, Joseph Allston] from whom he derived his name and this estate, and which is to be found only in the good, hoping to rejoin those whose loss had left in his heart an aching void, that nothing on earth could fill."[52]

Joseph Alston and his father-in-law were not the only ones to grieve Theodosia's death. Perhaps it was her intense emotional bond with Natalie Sumter that reached across the thousands of miles to Rio de Janeiro, where Natalie was living with her husband, Thomas, the U.S. Minister Plenipotentiary to Portugal, whose government was then exiled in Brazil. On October 11, 1813, months after Theodosia's disappearance but well before she heard the news, Natalie had dark premonitions and feared for her friend's life. "Some time I fear she is crazy, thus I think she'll die," she wrote to Mary Heron Hooper, a friend in Stateburg. Then, toward the end of her letter, she stated simply, "I think she must be dead."[53] She was right.

Ultimately, it was Theodosia's friend, Margaret Blennerhassett, who wrote her epitaph. It took the form of a soulful poem, "On a Lady Who Was Supposed to have Suffered Shipwreck":

> To wake up with the early dawn,
>   And hail the coming day;
> To ramble o'er the dewy lawn,
>   With hearts then young and gay.
> Was ours.— ah! what a soul was thine,
>   Shade of departed worth!
> Never did cultur'd nature shine
>   More pure upon this earth!
> For thine was every outward grace,
>   With every virtue fraught;-
> Thy bosom was a resting place,
>   For love not to be bought.
> But thou art gone,—with thee is fleed
>   All hope again to find
> Another that like thee could shed
>   Peace o'er the woe-worn mind.
> And now I wander all alone,
>   Nor heed the balmy breeze,
> But list the ring-dove's tender moan,
>   And think upon the seas.
> The wind that rushes through the wood,
>   Has swept the fatal waves;-
> Far-far beneath the briny flood
>   Deep-deep in ocean's caves
> Thou liest?-ah! no—thou art not there,
>   Thou soar'st in amber bright,
> Perhaps e'en now, in tender care,
>   Thy looks on me may light![54]

CHAPTER TEN

Fates Worse Than Death: The Pirate Stories

> But the ill-fated bark that bore her forth
> Was lost, and whether shipwrecked by the storm
> It sank; or, victim of more cruel fate,
> Was taken by some murderous pirate craft,
> Will ne'er be known.
> —Alexander T. Ormond

B elieving that Theodosia met her death by drowning during a hurricane in the frigid waters of the Atlantic was cold enough comfort for Aaron Burr and Joseph Alston, but their anguish only increased in the years to come. Within weeks of her disappearance, a continuous stream of rumors and stories sought to account for Theodosia's mysterious disappearance. As each new tale appeared, it stirred a fresh round of interest in Theodosia—and pain in the hearts of the two men who loved her most. Each new telling of her life and tragic death added a layer of speculation, often at the expense of known facts about her life. The rule that seemed to guide many of the authors of the pirate stories, ghost tales, and novels that followed Theodosia's death was simple: "Never let the facts get in the way of a good story."

During the nineteenth century, newspaper readers were titillated every decade or so with lurid stories of Theodosia's alleged fate, including deathbed confessions of former pirates who had captured the *Patriot* and killed all aboard. The first novel based on her appeared in 1872. From then until the present day, romance novelists have mined the basic facts of her life, spinning off fanciful tales about alleged—but undocumented—love affairs and her death at the hands of bloodthirsty pirates.

Within a century after her death, the life of the real Theodosia—who had held discourses with presidents and Indian chiefs, served as confidential advisor to the man who plotted amazing international intrigues, and who rose above agonizing pain while caring for a young child—had been lost. In less than a hundred years, the flesh-and-blood woman had been replaced by an amalgamated literary character and morphed into an icon of popular culture who was more fiction than fact.

To understand how the brilliant, complex, and active woman of the early nineteenth century was transformed into a helpless pawn and victim of pirates, it helps to start with the earliest recorded tales of her fate, work forward in time, examine each story, and see how the accounts mutated with each new telling.

The most credible and best documented of all the pirate stories was the first to surface. An article in the June 23, 1820, edition of the *New York Advertiser*[1] (reprinting the same from the *Mercury Advertiser*) reported that on August 29, 1819, Jean Desfarges, captain of the two-gun privateer *Bravo*; his first mate, Robert Johnson; and their crew lost a battle with two U.S. revenue cutters, the *Louisiana* and the *Alabama*, in the Caribbean waters off the Dry Tortuga Islands. Desfarges surrendered after a fight, and the U.S. warships captured his ship, one of his prize ships, and the pirate crews of both. The captain and his first officer were tried and sentenced to death.

Soon thereafter, it became public that in addition to common piracy, the two had confessed to a "case of peculiar atrocity": the murder of Theodosia Burr Alston and the crew of the *Patriot*. In 1939, naval historian Stanley Faye wrote in *The Louisiana Historical Quarterly*, "Jean Desfarges and Robert Johnson had been sailors aboard the pilot-boat-built schooner *Patriot*, in which Theodosia Burr Alston had sailed from Charleston [sic] for New York. Two or three days in fair weather the *Patriot* had coasted northward. Then, at night, Desfarges and Johnson overpowered the passengers and crew, confined all below decks, stood in towards land and scuttled the schooner. With all valuables they could find they put off to shore in a small boat. Behind them the *Patriot* sank. To no dry death the fearless Theodosia went down. Two murderers, held together in fearful companionship, together kept during eight years a fearful secret."[2] The publication of this story must certainly have twisted the knife of agony in Aaron Burr's heart.

Two details of the story do not agree with known fact: the *Patriot* departed from Georgetown, not Charleston (a major error of fact in many of the alleged pirate stories), and the weather did not remain fair for three days. However, the story merits serious consideration because the self-confessed murderers, Desfarges and Johnson, were captured by a U.S. government revenue cutter, admitted their crimes to U.S. officials, were tried and convicted by a U.S. circuit court judge, and were executed on board a U.S. Navy warship in the Mississippi River. Although many of the "pirates-killed-Theodosia" stories that were to follow were intriguing, they all suffered from a major credibility flaw that this story does not: lack of documentation.[3]

One malicious and ludicrous story blamed Burr's own reputation as a womanizer for Theodosia's death. "A correspondent informed one South Carolina newspaper [*The Carolina Spartan*] of his passion for the wife of the *Patriot*'s captain. To keep the seaman from thwarting his designs, the story went, 'Burr corrupted his sailors to mutiny and destroy him.' That ship was supposedly the *Patriot*. Unfortunately, because the plan could not be carried out until the ship's return voyage to New York, Mrs. Alston became a victim of her father's scheme. 'Her fate was an awful retribution upon her abandoned father,' concluded the writer. Thus, the evil Burr had unwittingly planned his own daughter's murder, and poetic justice had been done."[4]

Twenty years after Theodosia's disappearance, *The Mobile Commercial Register* was supposed to have printed the following statement in its May 23, 1833, edition. The quote was furnished by William L. Stone, of Mt. Vernon, New York, to the *New York Sun* of August 27, 1904. He was supposedly the son of Col. William L. Stone, "a very intimate friend of Aaron Burr."[5]

It appears from the statement of a respectable merchant of Mobile that a man died in that city recently who confessed to his physician [Dr. Alex Jones] on his dying bed that he had been a pirate and helped to destroy the vessel and all the crew and passengers, on which Mrs. Alston had embarked for New York. He declared, says this gentleman, that after the men were killed, there was an unwillingness on the part of every pirate to take the life of Mrs. Alston, who had not resisted them or fought them, and therefore they drew lots who should perform the deed, as it had to be done. The lot fell on this pirate, who declares that he effected the object of putting the lady to death by laying a plank along the edge of the ship, half on it and half off, or over the edge, and made Mrs. Alston walk on that plank till it tilted over into the water with her. The dying pirate requested his physician to make this story public, but his surviving family will not permit or consent that the name of the deceased should be known. [6]

This is the first of the pirate stories to claim that Theodosia was made to "walk the plank." This dramatic detail, first alleged in 1833, would appear in virtually every other Theodosia-*Patriot*-pirate story and novel to appear for the next 170 years. However, the lack of any critical details, such as names, dates, places, weather, or ship descriptions makes it impossible to put much faith in this story. In addition, the entire romantic concept of pirates making their victims "walk the plank" is almost completely a creation of fiction writers, not history. Joseph Schwarzer, director of the Graveyard of the Atlantic Museum in Hatteras, North Carolina, noted that walking the plank was a rare occurrence. "In all of recorded piracy," he said, "there's maybe one instance." Schwarzer also pointed out another obvious problem with plank walking: aboard a ship, spare wood is scarce. "Dispatching a large number of captives on an unsecured plank would use up a lot of wood," he aptly observed.[7]

Thirty-seven years after Theodosia's disappearance, another pirate's deathbed story came to light. Two tellings of this tale agree on the main points. As the story goes, in 1850, Benjamin "Old Frank" Burdick, an old sailor and then an occupant of the Cass County Poorhouse in Cassopolis, Michigan, confessed that the act which caused him the most remorse during his life was having participated in making Theodosia Burr Alston walk the plank. He claimed to be a crewmember of the ship (never named) that had captured her vessel. When told she must walk the plank, she supposedly asked for a few minutes alone to prepare herself for her Maker. "She came forward when her time had expired," the story goes, "dressed beautifully in white, the loveliest woman I had ever seen. Calmly she stepped upon the plank. With eyes raised to the heavens and hands crossed reverently upon her bosom, she walked slowly and firmly into the ocean, without an apparent tremor. 'Had I refused to perform my work, as I wish with all my heart I had, my death would have been sure and certain,' the pirate said.[8] The Burdick story combines the basic element of the 1820 story, adds the "walking the plank" element, and introduces two new details: Theodosia was "dressed in white" and walked the plank with her "hands crossed reverently upon her bosom."

Burdick's admission sheds no light on the details of Theodosia's disappearance. He never provided the name of the pirate ship or its captain nor did he give the name of his victim's ship, describe its passengers and crew, or say anything else about it. The story was never officially recorded nor was it told under oath. Nevertheless, deathbed statements are compelling evidence, and such statements have often been enough to convict or free accused murderers in a court of law.

Mrs. Stella E.P. Drake, the indomitable Burrite researcher who forwarded the story to *The Washington Post* on July 27, 1879, underscored the gravity of Burdick's statement. "It seems to me, when an old man, bemoaning his life, filled with sin, makes such a confession, without any provocation whatever than the unburdening of his soul during his preparation for another life—for death came soon after—that there must be truth in this statement."[9] As much as some might like this belief to be universally true, however, just as many deathbed confessions are fantasy, born of senile dementia, loneliness, and regret.

One of the most unusual tales to explain Theodosia's fate revolves around the story of Capt. Octave Chauvet and the *Vengeance*, his ten-gun former English brig that had been captured by his colleague, master pirate Alexander Lafitte, and assigned to him. For two years, starting in 1810, Chauvet and the *Vengeance* preyed on Spanish ships off the Mexican coast and Cuba. When suitable prey proved hard to find, Chauvet headed up the Atlantic coast, looking for fresh opportunities.

According to the storyteller, "Upon reaching the Carolina coast near Charleston, a lookout sighted a fast schooner, struggling in heavy seas. For two days, the storm-weary *Vengeance*, with shortened sails, plowed through heavy seas, eventually overtaking the three-gun American privateer *Patriot*, bound for New York. Believing his prey to be a rich prize, Chauvet immediately ordered the *Vengeance's* decks cleared for action. The *Patriot* had sailed from Georgetown, So. Caro., on New Year's Day with an unusual cargo for a warship. She carried two passengers, Timothy Green [sic] and his charge, Mrs. Theodosia Burr Alston, the wife of the governor of South Carolina. The beauteous socialite carried with her the valuable Burr family silverware, which she was returning to her father, Aaron Burr, in New York. The *Patriot* fought like a trapped tiger, killing and maiming several aboard the *Vengeance*, but the outgunned vessel refused to surrender.

Eventually, the battle ended after the *Patriot* was boarded, and its crew were slaughtered with small arms and cutlasses.

"AS THE PIRATES REACHED THE DECK, THEODOSIA GRASPED A CUTLASS."

The schooner's desks were littered with the dead and dying, whom Chauvet cast overboard. After all booty, including the attractive Mrs. Alston and her silverware were transferred to the *Vengeance*, Chauvet then burned the defeated schooner. For days Mrs. Alston fought off Chauvet's drunken and amorous advances. She was later found dead in her cabin, either murdered by the captain or a suicide from strychnine. Among her possessions were many expensive dresses, each monogrammed 'T.A.,' and a valuable gold locket with the inscription, 'To My Wife Theodosia,' and containing a tintype of her deceased son Gampy." Chauvet himself was killed in August 1818, when the *Vengeance* was attacked by a large Spanish cruiser. While being overhauled in Galveston Bay, the ship caught fire and sank in Galveston Harbor.[10]

This story has several problems. If the *Vengeance* intercepted the *Patriot* at sea, the *Patriot* would have immediately been forced to heave to, as she was sailing with her guns stored below deck, and they could not have been remounted for action. Theodosia's death at the hands of a murderous pirate is conceivable, but if she met her fate through suicide by strychnine, where did the strychnine come from? The final problematic element is the statement that a gold locket was found containing a "tintype" of her son, Aaron Burr Alston, known to her and her father as "Gampy." Although miniature paintings were common in Theodosia's time, tintypes (ferrotypes) did not come into common use in Charleston until the Civil War era, nearly fifty years after Theodosia's death.[11] Hence, in 1813, she could not have possessed a locket containing a tintype.

Then there was the Norfolk tale. On an unstated date, two criminals were executed in Norfolk, Virginia, after having confessed to making Theodosia walk the plank.[12] Citing an undated "article of news just now going the rounds" in the Pennsylvania *Enquirer*, Charles Burr Todd, a Burr family historian, told the tale of a sailor, who had recently died in Texas, confessing on his deathbed "that he was one of the crew of mutineers who, some forty years ago, took possession of a brig on its passage from Charleston [sic] to New York, and caused all the officers and passengers to walk the plank.... The dying sailor professed to remember [Theodosia] well, said she was the last to perish, and that he never forgot her look of despair as she took the last step from the fatal plank."[13] Why he didn't remember sailing from Georgetown is not known.

What is undoubtedly the most exotic and least plausible of all the pirate stories comes from an anonymous author whose apocryphal tale was found on the Internet in 2002.[14] Although it contains numerous factual errors, it is nevertheless morbidly interesting because of its lurid claims. It alleges that Theodosia was indeed captured by pirates and ultimately died after being chained naked to the bulkhead of a ship that was destroyed by an 1816 hurricane on the Texas coast.

As the story goes, the mouth of the San Bernard River, near Galveston Island, Texas, was a favorite rest-and-recuperation spot for pirates. The storyteller stated that it was also the home of the Karankawa Indians, who were said to have "used cannibalism in their ceremonial rituals." Their massive chief wore a large gold locket around his neck. "Inside the locket was a miniature painting of a handsome young man and a small boy. Engraved across the back of the locket was a single word: 'Theodosia.' When he was later asked where he got the locket, he said it was given to him by his 'white wife.' When he was asked where he got a white wife, he said she was given to him by the Great Storm, and the gods quickly took her away."

The unnamed author of the story believes that a hurricane that hit the Texas coast in 1816 was the one the chief referred to. The chief said that after the storm, he came across the wreckage of a ship, lying half in, half out of the San Bernard River. Aboard he found drowned crewmembers—and a "small, ghostlike form of a mature white woman," who was barely alive. After freeing her from the wreckage, the chief gave her water and she revived. The story continues:

> She said she was the daughter of a great chief of the white men, but that the great chief was badly misunderstood by his people and had to leave his country. She was also the wife of a governor of a large state. Some time before, perhaps three winters—maybe more—she got on a great boat similar to the one that lay wrecked a few yards away to go visit her father. The first boat was attacked by the one that was now wrecked. Her boat

was burned and all on board, except herself, were murdered. She had been kept, naked and chained, as a slave to the crew of the wrecked boat ever since. Then she gave the warrior her gold locket and told him that if he ever met white men who spoke English, he was to show it to them and tell them the story. The Karankawa said she then began to sing softly to herself until she fell asleep. She died a short while later.

When the woman died, the warrior buried her in the sand along the river's bank, digging her grave with broken pieces of the wrecked ship. He then covered the grave with a broken door from the wreck. Today, no man knows where that grave lies, although there have been attempts to find it.... Without the missing locket, however, it is impossible to prove that the 'white wife' of the Karankawa Indian warrior was Theodosia Burr Alston, only daughter of Aaron Burr, Vice-President of the United States. But if untrue, just who was the mystery woman of the San Bernard?[15]

Yet another ex-pirate came forward to claim the dubious honor of having helped execute the *Patriot*'s crew and passengers. His name was Canfield, and in 1896, his story was published in *A Secret of the Sea*, by Cornelia Mitchell Parsons, a great-granddaughter of Dr. Timothy Ruggles Greene, who had accompanied Theodosia on her fatal voyage. Canfield's tale differs from the others because he stated that the ship (unnamed, as was the pirate captain) that captured the *Patriot* sailed from Georgetown.

'Twas on December the twenty-ninth, 1812, [sic] when the Patriot sailed. I, with some of the sailors from our vessel, was loungin' around the wharf, lookin' curiously at the great chests that Mrs. Alston was takin' away with her. Some said they were packed with family plate and jewels. After the *Patriot* sailed, our captain ordered us aboard our own vessel, we also soon set sail. We kept close in the wake of the *Patriot*. When off Cape Hatteras we opened fire and attacked her. The fight was short. We boarded her, made the captain and crew walk the plank, and all the passengers, all but Mr. Green and Mrs. Allston.... When it came their turn, Tom Brown, one of the sailors, was ordered to come forward and tip the plank. Mr. Green was to go first. He was a fine lookin' gentleman, very courtly. He begged the captain to spare his life, sayin' his wife and children needed him. But our captain was a hard, wicked man. He swore a fearful oath, then ordered Mr. Green to step on the plank. This he did without a murmur. He took off his watch, which, with a few papers, he handed to Tom Brown, askin' him to send them to his wife, givin' her address. Kneelin' down, Mr. Green prayed for his family, for the lady in his charge, and for the souls of his murderers. Then solemnly he repeated the words, 'Lord Jesus, into thy hands I commit my spirit.' I can't ever forget the way he said it. A nod from the captain, and Tom Brown tipped the plank. There was a splash, and all was over."[16]

Other permutations of Theodosia's folktale-filled afterlife also appeared. In 1910, a story by J. A. Elliott, of Norfolk, Virginia, surfaced. As his story goes, "in the early part of 1813, the dead body of a young woman, with every indication of refinement, drifted upon the shore of Mr. ——, at Cape Charles...on the sea coast of Virginia.... She was buried on the farm of the gentleman who found her, and has remained there unidentified and undisturbed the past ninety-seven years."[17]

Another variation, the "Tale of the Female Stranger," was published in the October 1928 issue of *The Mentor*, a popular womens' magazine. In 1816, it related, "a veiled lady, frail, slight, graceful," came ashore from a passing packet boat at Alexandria, Virginia, with a companion. The mysterious couple was driven to the city's best hotel, Gadsby's Tavern. Her escort gave no names when checking in, and the lady never lifted her veil. The woman soon took sick and died. The local physician who attended her never knew her name. She was buried in St. Paul's Episcopal graveyard, where her tombstone reads, "To the memory of a Female Stranger, Whose mortal sufferings terminated on the 11th day of October, 1816, aged 25 years, 8 months." In 1816, Theodosia would have been thirty-three years old, not twenty-five. The legend was based upon the assumption that "from 1813 to 1816 Theodosia lived on some tropic isle under the protection of a pirate captor."[18]

One of the more fantastic of the long series of ex-pirate confession stories was published in Theodosia's second home: South Carolina. This time, the pirate was allegedly none other than actor-dramatist John Howard Payne, who in 1823 wrote the lyrics for the immortal song, "Home, Sweet Home." Writing in the magazine section of Charleston's *News and Courier*, Foster Haley claimed that documents he found in the State Archives in Mobile, Alabama, stated that Payne's pirate ship "had captured the *Patriot* after a bloody one-sided battle that ended with the surrender by Captain Overstocks and what was left of the crew. The pirates murdered every one of them," Haley wrote, "including a woman who was obviously a noblewoman or a lady of high birth.... Who she was meant little to the ruffians, declared Payne. She was blindfolded and forced to walk the plank just as were the others."[19] Haley never identified or cited the documents which allegedly formed the basis for his story, which contained nothing new except the attribution to John Howard Payne.

But the ultimate version of this story was yet to appear. It was reported by R. J. Cannady and published in the same newspaper on August 4, 1963. Cannady tells the story advanced by Col. Justus Dane, a wealthy New Yorker who "spent a lifetime in research on Theodosia Burr Alston."[20] Cannady wrote that Dane "was at Aaron Burr's bedside when he died, and kept a picture of Theodosia in his safe. A romanticist, Dane wrote to a friend, 'I have never married, but if I had been at any time during my life fortunate enough to have met a counterpart of Theodosia Burr, I should have thrown myself at her feet, and wooed her even more persistently than did that persistent young man, Joseph Alston."

According to Colonel Dane's description of the *Patriot*'s last days (much of which was strikingly similar to the story, "Jean Baptiste's Brass Cannon"), when the weather turned fierce, Captain Overstocks steered south, heading for Cuba to avoid the storm. The next morning, the *Patriot* was allegedly intercepted by *La Vengeance*, captained by the bloodthirsty pirate, Thaddeus Boncourt. When Overstocks told her of their imminent fate, Theodosia—against the orders of the captain, Dane says—ordered the *Patriot's* cannon to be mounted, after which Theodosia personally aimed the cannon, lit the fuse, and scored a direct hit on the pirate ship. This, we suppose, was a reflection of her upbringing as the equal of a man.

It was all to no avail. Boncourt's pirates swarmed the ship and murdered everyone but Theodosia. The pirate took her back to *La Vengeance*, where she was given every courtesy, food, and even champagne. Finding pen and paper, plucky Theodosia "hastily penned a letter to her father in French, and one to her husband, Gov. Alston, in English, describing in brief detail all that had occurred since the Patriot had left Charleston [sic] harbor." She then found a small file, cut off her wedding ring, and placed the two letters and the severed ring in a champagne bottle.

When Boncourt returned to the cabin, he gave Theodosia two options. Plan "A" was to marry him and live in luxury in France, where he had "securities, money, and jewels totaling over a million dollars." He also planned to reform his behavior and cease the pirate trade and was willing to wait to see if he could awaken love in her heart. Plan "B" was straightforward: walk the plank and die immediately. Theodosia, who was no one's fool, asked for time to consider the options.

During the night, *La Vengeance* collided with a British warship. While Boncourt, dragging Theodosia along with him, tried to escape in a small boat, the captain of the warship shot and killed him and mortally wounded Theodosia. "Her body fell into the sea, her long, dark tresses floating on the water." The captain lamented that he had inadvertently killed a woman, and her body was given a formal burial at sea. Somehow during the melee, the champagne bottle containing Theodosia's letters dropped into the ocean.

The bottle was later found by a fisherman, in whose family—cursed for eternity by a total lack of curiosity, it seems—the bottle remained unopened for fifty years. A traveler purchased it, opened it, recognized the contents, and sold it to a New York collector. "Col. Justus Dane, who purchased the contents of the champagne bottle, displayed his evidence to friends on rare occasions, but at his death the journal could not be located, thus leaving room for skepticism," wrote Canaday.[21]

No trace of the letters or the ring have been found, but that is no coincidence. The entire *La Vengeance* / Thaddeus Boncourt / letters-and-wedding-ring-in-a-champagne bottle story was identical in virtually every detail to the ending of Charles Felton Pidgin's well-known 1901 romantic novel, *Blennerhassett*. Whether Pidgin got the story from Dane or Dane from Pidgin is not known, but a historical account of Theodosia's fate, it certainly wasn't.

By the end of the nineteenth century, the "pirate motif" had become an integral part of Theodosia's literary persona. But as Gamaliel Bradford wrote in 1923, "It does not require mythical pirates, who drowned her, to complete the tragedy."[22]

CHAPTER ELEVEN

Literary Kudzu

*Burr's love for his child, and her love for him,
is nowhere duplicated in the realm of poetry and romance.*
— George E. Clark, 1904

It was only a matter of time before all the newspaper and magazine accounts of Theodosia's tragic life and mysterious death captured the attention of writers of fiction. Fifty-nine years after she vanished, the first overtly fictional tale of her life—as opposed to those accounts filled with speculation but billed as fact—appeared. The 492-page work was titled *Fernando De Lemos: Truth and Fiction: A Novel* and was published in New York by G.W. Carleton in 1872. Its author was Charles Etienne Arthur Gayarré. A New Orleans lawyer, judge, politician, historian, essayist, dramatist, and novelist, he had studied law in Philadelphia and returned home to begin his legal practice in 1829. Gayarré's masterwork was the four-volume *Histoire de la Louisianne*, published between 1854 and 1866.

His novel drew upon his intimate knowledge of Louisiana folklore. It related a fictional deathbed confession by Dominique You, a pirate crony of Jean Lafitte, who allegedly admitted to finding the *Patriot* off Cape Hatteras, "dismantled by the storm." "After killing all the crew," said Dominique You, "my men rushed down below and brought up to the deck a woman of surpassing beauty, deadly pale, but showing no other signs of terror. She looked at us with a sort of serene haughtiness, which was truly wonderful." After saving Theodosia from being raped by the crew, You nevertheless made her walk the plank. "She stepped on it and descended into the sea with graceful composure," Gayarré wrote, "as if she had been alighting from a carriage. She sank, and rising again, she, with an indescribable smile of angelic sweetness, waved her hand to me as if she meant to say: 'Farewell, and thanks again'; and then sank forever."[1] Why, save for a sudden attack of dementia, Theodosia would smile and wave warmly in thanks to the man who was in the process of killing her was not explained.

By the middle of the nineteenth century, hundreds of newspaper articles and magazine stories about Theodosia's life and tragic fate had appeared. They thrilled and inspired thousands of women, a good number of whom named daughters after her. That was the case with a little girl who was born Theodosia Burr Goodman in Cincinnati, Ohio, on July 29, 1885. When she took up acting in silent films, she chose Theda Bara (an anagram for "Arab Death") as her screen name. After her 1915 role as "the vamp" in director Frank Powell's "A Fool There Was," she went on to become one of the most successful, glamorous, inaccessible, and mysterious actors in Hollywood.

In the 1890s, a poet found inspiration in Theodosia's life. According to folklorist Eric Hause, young Robert Frost came to Kitty Hawk, North Carolina, in 1894. Suffering from acute depression, he chose the solitude of the vast expanses of open beach to get away from the pressures of life. "One night," Hause wrote, "he crossed over the Kitty Hawk beach and walked with a member of the local lifesaving crew on patrol. The patrolman told him Theo's story, and it moved him deeply. Years later, he would recount the experience and her tale in one of his lesser-known poems, 'Kitty Hawk.'"[2]

> *Did I recollect*
> *how the wreckers wrecked*
> *Theodosia Burr off this very shore?*
> *'Twas to punish her*
> *but her father more.*

The first novel about Theodosia to reach readers in large numbers was Charles Felton Pidgin's 1901 tale, *Blennerhassett, or The Decrees of Fate, A Romance Founded Upon Events of American History*. The novel, handsomely illustrated by Charles H. Stephens, was a success, and it inspired a sequel, *The Climax; or, What Could Have Been*, which appeared a year later. Pidgin, a devoted Burrite, was councilor-in-chief of the Aaron Burr Legion in Boston and exchanged information with his fellow Burr enthusiasts, who included art collector John E. Stilwell.

In *Blennerhassett*, Pidgin has Theodosia's ship, the *Patriot*, with a crew of fifteen and twelve passengers, turn south because of a hurricane, after which it was boarded by pirates from Capt. Thaddeus Boncourt's ship, *La Vengeance*. Theodosia orders the crew to put up a fight, and she personally fires a cannon at the approaching pirates. Grasping a cutlass, she cuts off the hand of one brigand. The *Patriot* is scuttled, and ten survivors are taken to Boncourt's ship. All but Theodosia are forced to walk the plank. Boncourt offers to spare her life if she will live with him in Cuba. She agrees to do so if he will give up pirating and drinking. They slip off the ship near Cuba, only to have their skiff discovered. Boncourt is killed. Theodosia is wounded, dies, and is buried at sea. It was at about this point, the dawn of the twentieth century, that the concept of Theodosia's tragic death at the hands of pirates became part of the public's perception of her.

For the second half of the twentieth century, a romantic historical novel entitled *My Theodosia* reigned as the primary portrait of the woman who was Aaron Burr's prodigy daughter and Joseph Alston's soulmate. Its author was Anya Seton Chase, a native of New York City. Her father, Ernest Thompson Seton, was a naturalist and writer. Her mother, Grace Gallatin Seton, was a leading suffragist and also a writer and was a descendant of Albert Gallatin, the nation's second secretary of the treasury. Seton was educated by tutors, studied at a private school in New York, and attended Oxford University but did not graduate. Although she wished to become a physician, she instead married twice, reared three children, and

"BECAUSE, THEODOSIA . . . . . I LOVE YOU."

took up writing romance novels under her maiden name, Anya Seton.

My Theodosia, her first such novel, was published in 1941. She went on to write a dozen more, one of which, *Green Darkness* (1972), remained on the *New York Times* bestseller list for six months. Seton was praised for the period detail that she incorporated into her stories, and she attracted a large, enthusiastic, and extremely loyal audience. She classified herself as a "bio-graphical" novelist, rather than "historical," saying, "I have a passion for facts, for dates and for places. I love to recreate the past, and to do so with all the accuracy possible. This means an enormous amount of research, which is no hardship. I love it."[3] A prominent reviewer wrote of her, "Unlike some other authors in her subfield of romance, [Seton] does not take short cuts or distort the historical record; instead she spins her tale within the limits of the known."[4] The reviewer must have been referring to Seton's later work because the characterization does not apply to *My Theodosia*.

As a romance novel, *My Theodosia* was enormously success-ful and captured the hearts of three generations of readers. In-deed, most women of the present era who have heard of Theodosia first met her through Seton's novel. In the preface, the author states, "While this story is a fictional interpretation of Theodosia's life, I have tried to be historically accurate in every detail."[5] She failed on a massive scale. Not only did she not achieve accuracy, she mis-stated well-known facts about Theodosia's southern experience and Joseph Alston, while sanitizing the life of Theodosia's northern-born father. Seton's novel deserves close scrutiny because of the powerful effect it had on shaping America's perception of Theodosia and Jo-seph Alston for half a century.

Promotional material for *My Theodosia* claimed, "In recon-structing Theodosia's life, [Seton] traveled extensively and stayed for some weeks in South Carolina." During her southern sojourn, she had the extreme good luck to discuss local history and culture with Genevieve Chandler, a descendant of several generations of Georgetown rice planters. Chandler was the perfect source for the northern-born Seton, as she was both a child of the Deep South and a respected folklorist by training. A few years earlier, during the Great Depression, Chandler had been selected by the W.P.A. as one of the writers charged with a profound responsibility: to record the oral histories of the last of the remaining former slaves, whose ages were great and whose numbers were dwindling rapidly. Later, Chandler served for twenty-eight years as staff historian and docent at Brookgreen Gardens, where Theodosia and Joseph Alston's plantation, The Oaks, is located. When Seton met her, Chandler was undoubtedly the world's foremost living authority on southern coastal folklore, rice plantation life and culture, The Oaks, the Alston / Allston family, and Theodosia's southern experience.

The novelist seems to have learned nothing about South Carolina folklore and customs from her southern mentor. *My Theodosia* reflects near-total ignorance of the realities of plantation life and culture as experienced by either black or white South Carolinians. By the fourth chapter of *My Theodosia*, it is clear that Seton loathed and despised every aspect of the South, its history, and its culture. Seton's descriptions of Gov. Joseph Alston and his family, slaves, homeland, and heritage, are both arrogantly patronizing and patently inaccurate. Not only was *My Theodosia* a distortion of factual information readily available to any researcher of her time, it was also racist and venomously anti-southern.

Seton's characterizations of Joseph Alston were uniformly pejorative and seemed designed to evoke disgust and pity. She described the affluent plantation owner and future governor of South Carolina as having "A pompous air about him; he looked arrogant and humorless." She pictured him as "of medium height and heavy-set, a circumstance which his bright plum-colored suit did nothing to conceal. It seemed stuffed to bursting across his broad back. His hair was black and cut short à la Brutus; it clustered on his round head in tight curls. Theo thought instantly of a bust of the Emperor Tiberius that she had once seen in a Philadelphia drawing room: 'the same thick neck, low forehead, and full, disdainful mouth.'"[6] In fact, the miniature portrait of Alston that was donated in 1945 to Amherst College shows a fashionably dressed upper-class man with relatively long, curly hair and a small, pleasant smile.

In his actions, manners, and outlook, Seton's Joseph Alston was a coarse, uncouth, unlettered, slow-witted, boorish, dull, awkward, insecure, easily upset, boring, ponderous, ill-tempered oaf. As a suitor, he was portrayed as capable of expressing his emotions only when drunk, and as a lover on his wedding night, he was presented as a clumsy, inept sexual failure, who evoked not passion but maternal pity from his new bride. As if that weren't enough, Seton pictured him bullying a frail and dying Theodosia in the hours before she is to set sail for the planned reunion with her father. "His rantings, his puny commands could not reach her," Seton wrote.

Seton also portrayed Alston as unrelentingly derisive and abusive of his slaves, whom she had him kick and call "niggers." In reality, that term was seldom used in South Carolina by upper-class planters before the Reconstruction era, which did not arrive until a full fifty years after Joseph Alston's death in 1816. The 1940s, the period when Seton was writing this novel, was not known for its social enlightenment concerning African-Americans. Perhaps that is why Seton projected existing racist stereotypes of the World War II era onto both Joseph Alston and Theodosia.

Seton wrote, "She [Theodosia] tried to copy Joseph's air of affable condescension, wondering how in the world he ever told one black face from another. Each seemed to have the identical assortment of protruding lips around enormous white teeth, slate-black skin, and rolling eyes." Speaking of the children of the Alston slaves, Seton wrote, "Seven nigger wenches at the plantation had produced healthy brats—fertile niggers were mighty good assets."[7] On the other hand, Seton ignored the fact that Theodosia grew up among slaves in Aaron Burr's slave-owning New York family. Nor did she mention that it was black servants and cooks who kept the Richmond Hill mansion humming just outside the New York City limits or that Burr was the descendant of generations of New York and New England slaveowners.

In matters of culture, Seton painted Joseph Alston as both ignorant and disdainful of art, dance, and foreign languages. Nothing could have been further from the truth. Alston was part of the top one-half of one percent of the South Carolina plantation aristocracy. His large family traveled widely throughout the Western world and had variously studied or mastered French, Italian, Greek, and Latin. The Alstons were well educated, and some of the men graduated with distinction from the best universities of the United States and England. Indeed, both Joseph Alston and Aaron Burr had attended Princeton.

In matters of art, the various Alstons visited Europe's most important cities, art galleries, museums, and historic sites. Joseph's neighbor and cousin, Washington Allston, was a nationally famous painter. Joseph's family patronized the finest portrait and landscape artists of two continents. They regularly hosted elaborate soirées in the ballrooms of their homes; produced and consumed the finest foods; imported the finest European wines for their cellars and wine garrets; shopped in the best stores in Charleston, Boston, New York, and abroad; and patronized the finest spas and resorts in both the North and the South. In addition, they entertained numerous American presidents and European dignitaries in their homes.

Seton portrayed Joseph Alston's family as believers in mystic Gullah conjuring. Only someone ignorant of the religious orthodoxy of the southern plantation aristocracy would have been so naïve as to think that a high-born, well educated Episcopalian family such as the Alstons would have believed in the hags, haints, and other superstitions of their slaves.

Had she done even cursory library research, Seton could have found copious information about Joseph and his well-known family in *The Allstons and Alstons of Waccamaw,* which had been printed in 1936, five years before her novel appeared. She would also have found Elizabeth Waties Alston Pringle's respected and well-known *Chronicles of Chicora Wood,* a detailed story of life on the Alston plantations, which was published in New York in 1922. Both books would have been readily available to her through the Alston family, Genevieve Chandler, and Brookgreen Gardens when she visited the Waccamaw—not to mention the New York Public Library.

Burr himself does not come off much more accurately in Seton's tale. She was quick enough to acknowledge a dalliance with a "Little Sally Martin," whom she portrayed as "an occasional physical necessity," but ignored all the women that Burr bedded before, during, and after his first marriage. Furthermore, she haughtily pronounced that "brothels offended his fastidiousness," despite the fact that while in Paris, Burr recorded numerous dalliances with whores in the private journal he kept for Theodosia. That journal, published in 1837, would have been available to her from a New York library.

In all, New Yorker Seton found everything about the South to be primitive, distasteful, or threatening. She was even intimidated by its ubiquitous Spanish moss, which so many visitors find beautiful, evocative, or seductively romantic.

Genevieve Chandler's daughter, author Genevieve Chandler Peterkin, reported that her mother felt that Seton had discarded everything Chandler tried to impart about the South and had "re-invented southern history." Furthermore, she said that Chandler "resented very much" the distortions of the history of the Alstons and South Carolina plantation life and culture. According to Peterkin, Seton told Chandler, "Oh, I'm just writing this for the movies."[8] Chandler felt betrayed, and the Alston descendants believed that Joseph Alston had been seriously maligned by the book. They prepared to sue Seton for slander but ultimately chose not to do so, for fear of giving the book more publicity.

Seton's wholesale trashing of the South and its people, black and white, appears to have been the product of northern elitist prejudices against the rural South, which were strong in the 1940s. Oddly enough, all that most women—even southern women—remember about Seton's novel is that it was a good romance story. It was so good, indeed, that the extent to which it maligned southerners and their culture has been largely forgotten.

No other Theodosia-based novel ever matched *My Theodosia* in popularity. However, a second Theodosia novel was also published in 1941. Anne Colver wrote *Theodosia, Daughter of*

Aaron Burr for the juvenile fiction market. Her novel was a simple, unquestioning, uncontroversial tale designed for adolescents. Through its dreamy portrayal of masculine father and husband stereotypes, Colver soft-pedaled Burr's duel with Hamilton, Joseph Alston's involvement with Burr's Western Conspiracy, and Theodosia's involvement with anything except love and adoration for horses, her girlfriend Natalie, her father, and her husband.

In 1950, Nova Scotia native Cyril Harris, a descendant of Loyalists displaced by the American Revolution, wrote *Street of Knives*, which was set on the Ohio River in 1806. There we find Theodosia "arrogant and as devoted to her father as he was to himself," says the author. Also accompanying Burr was a twenty-two-year-old frontiersman called Hugh Shadwell. The fictional Shadwell was a literary stand-in for one of Aaron Burr's several illegitimate children.

Theodosia learns of Shadwell's ancestry during the course of the story and resents him for it. She is not at all interested in having any kind of relationship with him that is not necessary to maintain her position of importance next to her father. At one point, Theodosia and her husband conspire to have Shadwell removed from Blennerhassett Island. Although Burr ejects Shadwell to pacify the Alstons, he charms his son back into his Grand Plan after the Alstons are out of earshot. Joseph Alston is portrayed as aware of the details of the Mexican conspiracy, as a financier of the scheme, and as an apathetic, unambitious ne'er-do-well of a son-in-law.

Theodosia is portrayed as being aware of, and deeply involved in, her father's Mexican plans. She is not seen as a victim but more as a vindictive co-conspirator in her father's schemes and as a jealous daughter bent on keeping her bastard half-brother from becoming close to Burr. *Street of Knives* made no serious pretense of historical accuracy and sought only to tell a dramatic and romantic tale.

Although other Theodosia-based novels have since appeared, the last major controversy about her in the twentieth century came in Gore Vidal's 1973 bestseller, *Burr: A Novel.*

Vidal's exceptional research and sophisticated understanding of the players he wrote about is apparent. The novel centers on Burr, not Theodosia, but historians know Vidal best for his introduction of the previously mentioned "incest motif" into the great scholarly Burr debate.

A wide variety of ghost stories added to the mystery of Theodosia. They included tales about appearances of her apparition in such places as a New York tavern; Huntington Beach, South Carolina (near her plantation, The Oaks); and Bald Head Island, North Carolina.

Novels and ghost stories are one thing, but they tended to obscure Theodosia's life rather than reveal it. Theodosia's official introduction into the national non-fiction hall of fame came when she was the only woman included in James Parton's 1868 volume, *Famous Americans of Recent Times*. Other notables who were profiled in the book included intellectual, religious, political, and business titans such as Henry Clay, Daniel Webster, John C. Calhoun, Henry Ward Beecher, Commodore Cornelius Vanderbilt, and John Jacob Astor. Theodosia's sketch, written by Parton, Burr's first serious biographer, was adapted from a story he had originally written for the August 1864 edition of *Harper's New Monthly Magazine*.

Over the course of the next three decades, newspapers and magazines published snippets of Theodosia lore, but it was not until 1901 that Virginia Tatnall Peacock devoted a full chapter of her collective biography, *Famous American Belles of the Nineteenth Century*, to a thoughtful and comprehensive overview of Theodosia's life.

The first major attempt to rebuild a literal image of Theodosia came at the hands of Charles Felton Pidgin. After writing his two previously mentioned Theodosia-based novels, he published a non-fiction book, *Theodosia: The First Gentlewoman of Her Times*, in 1907. Pidgin dedicated the rambling, hodgepodge collection of Theodosia lore to "The young women graduates of advanced institutions of learning in America and Foreign Lands."

Other writers added their non-fiction pieces of the Theodosia puzzle in the early twentieth century. In 1912, Edith

Tunis Sale emulated the Victorian literary tradition with a sketch of Theodosia that emphasized her filial devotion. In 1924, Meade Minnigerode, who had been half of the writing team (with Samuel H. Wandell) that produced the two-volume biography, *Aaron Burr*, authored an extensive, illustrated biographical sketch of Theodosia for the September 6, 1924 issue of the *Saturday Evening Post*. This mass-circulation magazine immediately revitalized her image. The next year, Minnigerode honored Theodosia by including her with three prominent men (Stephen Jumel, William Eaton, and Edmond Charles "Citizen" Genêt) in his book, *Lives and Times: Four Informal American Biographies*. In 1929, famed Columbia University professor Mark Van Doren published *The Correspondence of Aaron Burr and His Daughter, Theodosia*, a collection of letters primarily culled from those published nearly a century earlier by Matthew L. Davis. This disappointing volume included only a cursory, four-and-a-half-page introduction and provided little, if any, insight into the documents it reproduced.

By the 1950s, interest in Theodosia was waning. A 1954 *Fate* magazine article—with its portrayal of Theodosia as a Hollywood starlet on the cover—carefully explored the story of the mysterious Nag's Head portrait (which will be discussed in detail in the next chapter), but until the end of the twentieth century, only a handful of scholarly articles kept Theodosia's flame flickering.

In 1953, Dorothy Valentine Smith's "An Intercourse of the Heart" explored forty of Theodosia's little-known letters in the *New York Historical Society Quarterly*. Twenty years later, Dr. Ronald Ray Swick's 1975 article, "Theodosia Burr Alston," in *The South Atlantic Quarterly*, provided readers with a reliable and insightful overview of her nearly forgotten life. Theodosia received a scholarly shot in the arm in Suzanne Burr Geissler's 1976 Ph.D. dissertation entitled "The Burr Family, 1716-1836." Unfortunately, few people ever get to read doctoral dissertations, and by the last decade of the twentieth century, Theodosia and Joseph Alston had, for all practical purposes, been forgotten. Their renaissance was

TRUE STORIES OF THE
STRANGE AND THE UNKNOWN

FATE
ANC
MAGAZINE

June 1954 **35¢**

THE STRANGE DISAPPEARANCE OF THEODOSIA BURR

Theodosia's public image in 1954

sparked not by a writer but an archaeologist and his series of research papers.

1992 was a banner year for Theodosia and Joseph Alston because it marked the start of archaeological research at Brookgreen Gardens. For years, archaeologist James L. Michie had dreamed of finding the site of Theodosia and Joseph's house,

The Oaks. Funded by grants from the Friends of Brookgreen
Gardens, he and a team of five paid assistants and additional
volunteers worked for seven weeks, cutting more than seven
miles of transects and digging more than 900 holes, and were
successful in locating the site of the house.

Since Theodosia's death in 1813, numerous fragments of her
story have been presented by dedicated researchers for almost
200 years. No one has ever tried to assemble the whole puzzle
to tell the full story of her life until now. This book is my attempt
to pull all the pieces together into a coherent biography of this
intriguing, complex woman. Given her fascinating life and
mysterious death, Theodosia Burr Alston will undoubtedly be
the wellspring of many more articles, novels, biographies, and
dissertations well into the future. But anyone who tries to
solve the mystery of Theodosia's disappearance will also have
to solve the mystery of the Nag's Head portrait, a captivating,
enigmatic painting that has been the center of controversy
for nearly a century and a half.

CHAPTER TWELVE

The Mystery of the
Nag's Head Portrait

Her eyes speaketh softness and love
But discretion with a sceptre setteth on her brow.
—The sayings of a Chinese philosopher

Fifty-six years after Theodosia's disappearance, the most enduring enigma surrounding her fate came to light. In 1869, Dr. William Gaskins Pool, a well-known and highly respected physician of Elizabeth City, Pasquotank County, North Carolina, acquired an evocative 14 ½-inch x 17 ½-inch oil painting on a wooden panel that he spent the rest of his life trying to authenticate as being a portrait of Theodosia Burr Alston. The picture soon came to be known as the "Nag's Head" portrait, named after the place on the beach of North Carolina's Outer Banks where it was allegedly found.

Since the day it was discovered, stories about the painting and the efforts undertaken to authenticate it have made it a legend among art historians. If it were indeed a portrait of Theodosia, it would be the only piece of physical evidence known to have survived her voyage on the *Patriot*. And if that were true, the portrait would help answer many other questions about her death.

Dr. Pool's history of the Nag's Head portrait revolves around the following scenario: the *Patriot* did not sink in the Atlantic but instead ran aground (with or without the intervention of pirates) and was wrecked near Kitty Hawk, just south of Nag's Head on North Carolina's Outer Banks, in

The Nag's Head portrait

the first days of January 1813. There, the ship was looted and the portrait found by local scavengers known as "wreckers."

The wreckers were a shadowy, ragtag group of residents of the Outer Banks—the barrier islands that fence the coast of North Carolina. Their livelihood depended on salvaging anything useful from the hulls of ships cast up—or lured onto—the shores of the "Graveyard of the Atlantic." When the wreckers found a grounded ship, surviving passengers were often killed. Within a matter of weeks, the entire wreckage of a ship could totally disappear. For the wreckers, disposing of all traces of a sixty-seven-foot coastal schooner like the *Patriot* would have been easy work.

Dr. Pool obtained the portrait in 1869 in payment for medical services provided to a Mrs. Mann, an impoverished wrecker's widow who lived near Nag's Head. Pool was never certain whether the story she gave was true or complete. His daughter, Mrs. Anna L. Overman, sent a detailed, notarized description of the portrait's discovery to author Charles Felton Pidgin in 1904.[1] Both Pidgin and Mrs. Overman were devoted Burr partisans who hoped that historians would "yet pry open the sealed vaults wherein there are treasures of data, and reveal to the world that Aaron Burr was not a traitor, a murderer, nor a terror to the morals of humanity." Mrs. Overman's sworn letter stated:

> In the summer of 1869, my father took his family to Nag's Head in search of sea breezes, so grateful after the parching suns of Pasquotank.... He was called professionally to the "banker" woman, Mrs. Mann. To all appearances, as they kept no exact dates, she was about 70 years old. I accompanied my father,[2] and entering her rude house, constructed mostly of timbers from wrecks, and thatched with reeds and oakum, our attentions were attracted to a beautiful picture hanging against the rough wall, in dimension 18 x 20 inches, of a beautiful young woman about twenty-five years of age. The house was not clean, and the rafters and portrait were festooned with cobwebs of many seasons. Questioning Mrs. Mann very closely concerning her strange possession, these are the facts she told:
>
> Some years before her marriage (which, however, was not entered into by legal form) to her first husband, one Tillett,[3] a pilot boat came ashore near Kitty Hawk, two miles up the beach, north; her sails were set and the rudder fastened. Tillett, with other bankers, boarded her. Not a soul was on the boat. They found

in the cabin the table set for breakfast; for this they gave the reason that the berths were not yet made up and the cabins were in disorder, yet there was no trace of blood to indicate a scene of violence. From this wreck they brought many things, but so many years had elapsed that she said she knew of nothing left except that Tillett, her husband, gave to her. She had an old black trunk opened and showed us two soft black silk dresses and a lovely black lace shawl. The dresses were certainly the apparel of a gentlewoman, small of physique. The dresses were very full skirts gathered into a low-cut bodice, with short sleeves.... The contents of an old beaufet [sic] also exposed to our view a vase of wax flowers under a glass globe, and a shell beautifully carved in the shape of a nautilus. These were all the relics in her possession that had survived the ravages of many years. My father questioned her closely concerning the details and dates. She said it was before she was married to Tillett, when the English were fighting us on the sea. She knew it was when there was a war, because the wreckers had booty from war vessels, and she had heard the summer folks say so....

My father calculated the dates to tally. In 1869 she was certainly 70 years old. This would make her fourteen in 1813. She said she was married to Tillett when she was a young girl—more than likely when she was sixteen. The bankers, even today, are most singular in their habits, and generally marry, though now by legal and sometimes church service, at fifteen and sixteen. My mother, Mary Savina Pool, examined the dresses and said they were homespun silk. Certainly, I had never seen anything like them. Remarkably well preserved for the long time, but as the banker woman said, they had stayed in the trunk and were aired only on state occasions, possibly half a dozen times since her marriage with Tillett.

The coloring of the portrait, though very much worn, is still very good. The hair is tinged with auburn, eyes piercing black,[4] lips and cheeks pink. The dress is white. This handiwork of a master is painted on wood, and the mysterious beauty of the face seems to speak from a strange, invisible source, 'Will you doubt me more?' It is held in what was once a plain gilt frame, with but a small, beading on the inner edge, those handsome gilt nails having but once, when in the search for some obscure name to prove its identity, been taken from the setting. A tarnished brass ring on the upper edge, by which it may be suspended, completes this most interesting relic from the abandoned vessel."[5]

Over the next few years, a few additional details came to light. Mrs. Mann's first name was said to be Polly; her first husband's full name was Joseph Tillett; and the date of the wreck was said to be January 1813.

A newspaper article in the Elizabeth City, North Carolina *Economist* dated July 31, 1888, stated that the newspaper's editor, Col. R. B. Creecy, was introduced to Mrs. Stella E. P. Drake, a fourth cousin Burr descendant.[6] Mrs. Drake was in town to visit The Eyrie, the Pool's plantation near Elizabeth City, to examine the Nag's Head portrait. Mrs. Drake stated that "When a little girl my mother used to rock me to sleep, telling me a wonderful tale of pirates and how they had caused Theodosia Burr to walk the plank to a fearful death beneath the waves of the ocean. Time and time again she told the story. I never tired of it. Repetition made it almost real."[7] Mrs. Drake was to become one of the most enthusiastic Burrite supporters and researchers of the Nag's Head portrait.

Col. Creecy went on to say that he had known about the existence of the portrait prior to its discovery by Dr. Pool. "We have been familiar with that painting for many years," he wrote, "long before it had come into possession of Dr. Pool and it had been indelibly impressed upon our memory."[8]

Creecy's statement lends credibility to Dr. Pool's story that he acquired the portrait from Mrs. Mann.

Dr. Pool was quickly struck by the apparent matches between the known facts about Theodosia's disappearance and Mrs. Mann's stated origins of the Nag's Head portrait. The date of the first appearance of the portrait (January 1813) corresponded with the date that Theodosia and the *Patriot* disappeared (just after December 31, 1812). The place of the wreck matched multiple reports (and, later, solid documentation) of a severe storm off the North Carolina coast shortly after the *Patriot* departed from Georgetown. There were no other ships reported lost at the time that the *Patriot* disappeared (and allegedly washed up) at Nag's Head. The portrait was that of an affluent woman of about Theodosia's age, dressed in clothing appropriate to Theodosia's station in life. No one has ever come forward to claim that the Nag's Head portrait was someone other than Theodosia.

The first printed record of the Nag's Head portrait story appeared in 1878, when Col. John Hill Wheeler addressed the North Carolina Historical Society.[9] He stated that he had recently seen a portrait owned by Dr. Pool of Elizabeth City, North Carolina, "which purported to represent Aaron Burr's daughter."[10] Mrs. Stella E. P. Drake, then a young girl, read about Wheeler's report and wrote the to the editor of the *Washington Post*. She related to the newspaper the 1850 tale of "Old Frank Burdick" being one of the pirates who made Theodosia walk the plank, a story that had been passed down from her grandmother and mother. The *Post* printed Mrs. Drake's letter about "Old Frank" on July 27, 1879. Shortly thereafter, the *New Orleans Democrat* consolidated the story of the pirate with the story of the portrait, and the two stories, co-joined, were accepted as part of Theodosia's "history." "From that day on," Mrs. Drake wrote, "I resolved that I would see this portrait of Theodosia Burr."

Mrs. Drake told *The Washington Post* that she had visited the home of the late Dr. Pool and viewed the Nag's Head portrait. She compared it to engravings copied from the 1802

John Vanderlyn profile portrait of Theodosia, which was published in volume two of Matthew L. Davis's *Memoirs of Aaron
Burr, With Selections From His Correspondence* (1838), and the
H. Wright Smith engraving of the 1802 John Vanderlyn profile
portrait, reproduced in James S. Parton's *The Life and Times of
Aaron Burr* (1858). To most viewers, these three portraits look
like three different women, but Mrs. Drake "was convinced
that the portrait was in truth a likeness of Theodosia Burr
Alston."[11]

Over the next half-century, numerous Burr family members pronounced the Nag's Head portrait to be that of
Theodosia, and as many Alston family members disagreed. Two
things united both proponents and opponents of the portrait's
authenticity: all of them held strong opinions, but none could
produce any physical or documentary evidence to support their
claims. The unsigned, undated portrait itself offered few clues.
As one New York newspaper put it, "The uncertainty about
her death forms one of those curious lapses of history which
are rich in rumor, but seemingly lacking in authenticated fact."[12]

As the story was retold, the details changed. In one version,
one of the silk dresses that Tillett gave his wife was black, the
other, white, which contradicted the sole eyewitness account
by Anna Overman. A 1901 retelling of the tale by Alexander
Quarles Holladay, LL.D., based on a conversation with Dr.
Pool's elderly widow, stated that the cabin of the foundering
ship appeared to have been looted.[13]

On June 4, 1895, the Nag's Head portrait story appeared in
the *New York World* and the *Philadelphia Record*. The storyteller this time was the former rector (not named) of Trinity
Episcopal Church, Elkton, Maryland. About 1902, he visited
the widow of Dr. Pool, who told him the story of the portrait.
In this re-telling, two new story elements appeared—something
quite common in oral history. The priest stated that Theodosia
"took with her, as a present to her father, a beautiful painting
of herself." On close examination, this statement seems to be
an attempt to retrofit the existing facts with an undocumented
assumption made decades after the initial discovery. The other

new wrinkle was that when the bankers reached the foundering ship, "the only living thing aboard was a little black and tan dog."[14] Both of these assertations quickly became attached to the portrait and reported as "fact," despite the absence of any documentation.

The lack of hard evidence was not due to any lack of work by Dr. Pool. He spent the rest of his life trying to authenticate the Nag's Head portrait as that of Theodosia Burr Alston. He, and later, his daughter, Anna, sent photographs of the portrait and letters of inquiry to Burr and Alston family members far and wide in an attempt to find people who had seen Theodosia before her death and might be able to authenticate the portrait.

In 1912, Edith Tunis Sale, the author of *Old Time Belles and Cavaliers*, which reproduced the Nag's Head portrait, stated, "Photographs of the portrait were sent to Mrs. Stella Drake Knappin, Charles Burr Todd, [Mrs. Sale herself], and many other descendants of the Burr family, all of whom pronounced it the likeness of Theodosia. Later, when several of the Burr connection visited Dr. Pool for the purpose of verifying the painting, with one accord they pronounced it that of their lamented relative."[15] The "pronouncements" all shared a single flaw: not a single one of the pronouncers had ever seen Theodosia alive.

Mrs. Sale's desire to claim the Nag's Head portrait as being the likeness of Theodosia clouded her presentation of the facts. The Burr descendants were not, in fact, as unwavering in their opinion as she stated. In his 1902 book, *The True Aaron Burr: A Biographical Sketch*, Charles Burr Todd, who was familiar with several authenticated portraits of Theodosia, and who visited the Pool home in 1889,[16] wrote that he "once recognized a marked resemblance, although he would hesitate confidently to pronounce it a portrait of that lady."[17]

While the Burr descendants generally accepted the Nag's Head portrait as a likeness of Theodosia, the members of the Alston family—the last ones to see her—did not. Mrs. Marie A. Matthew, a Burrite supporter of the authenticity of the Nag's

Head portrait, wrote to Charles Pidgin with regret, "I sent photographs to several members of the Alston family, and I was amazed when I received no responsive favor in its behalf."

In 1878, a letter from Dr. Pool arrived at the home of Mrs. William Bull Pringle, the Miles Brewton House in Charleston, South Carolina. Born Mary Motte Alston in 1803, she was the youngest daughter of Col. and Mrs. William Alston of The Oaks. Mary was Joseph Alston's youngest sister, born two years after Joseph married Theodosia. She was only nine years old when her sister-in-law disappeared, but by 1878, when Mary was 75, she was the last surviving member of the Alston family who had ever seen Theodosia alive. Dr. Pool enclosed an 8-inch by 10-inch glossy photograph of the Nag's Head portrait with his letter and asked Mary Pringle if she could authenticate the picture as being of Theodosia.[18] His letter read:

> Dear Madam: I enclose you a photo of the painting I believe to be a portrait of Mrs. Alston. It has been sent to many of the relatives of Colonel Burr in New York and elsewhere, who all see in it a strong resemblance, but as none living there recollect to have ever seen Theodosia, they cannot say positively if it was her. We are fortunate and happy to have found in you one who knew Mrs. Alston and who now has a vivid recollection of her appearance. Be so good, after carefully examining it, to give me your impression and views. The history of this painting makes it almost certain that it is of Theodosia. The wife of Dr. Wheeler, the historian of North Carolina, the daughter of the painter, [Thomas] Sully, pronounced it to be clearly of her, as do also other artists who have seen it. Yours respectfully, W.G. Pool.[19]

On August 6, 1878, Mary Pringle wrote back to Dr. Pool, "I do remember her beautiful eyes, and the eyes in the picture are really beautiful."[20] However, Mary Pringle said nothing to confirm that the Nag's Head portrait was that of Theodosia. The Burrites were now on the defensive, for Mary Pringle—the only living person who had personally seen Theodosia—could not authenticate the painting.

A generation later, on May 24, 1915, Charles Burr Todd wrote to Mary Pringle's eldest granddaughter, Susan Pringle Frost, enclosing another photograph of the portrait and asking for information about it. Todd wrote, "Accept please a photo I had made of the oil portrait which was found in a deserted pilot boat off Nag's Head, N.C., in the winter of 1812.... We—members of the Burr and Edwards families—think it a portrait of Theodosia."[21] Miss Frost's response is unknown.

Since its discovery in 1869, art historians have been unable to positively identify the Nag's Head portrait. Two major problems stand in the way. First, other than the story that Mrs. Mann told to Dr. Pool and his daughter, Anna, there is no conclusive documentary or physical evidence that any ship's wreckage was found near Nag's Head in January 1813 or that such wreckage was the *Patriot*. Second, the portrait bears no identifying marks to indicate the name of the subject, the name of the artist, or the date or place where it was painted.

Dr. Pool died in March 1887, resolute in his beliefs but without having accomplished his goal of positively identifying the portrait or its painter. His daughter did not have any better luck. Over the years, the portrait changed hands many times before reaching its final home in the Lewis Walpole Library of Yale University in Farmington, Connecticut. With the portrait came a typed sketch of its provenance. A brass plaque attached to the frame states that it portrays Theodosia Burr Alston and was painted by John Vanderlyn. The plaque notwithstanding, there is no physical or documentary evidence that the woman is Theodosia Burr Alston, and it seems certain that John Van-derlyn did not paint—indeed could not have painted—the picture. A perfect enigma, the legendary Nag's Head portrait remains an unsolved mystery to this day. The following is an attempt to lay down all the the known facts, define the chain of custody, explore the mysteries, and answer some crucial questions.

The portrait starts out in a total void. On an unknown date, in an unknown place, this portrait of an unidentified, well-dressed, upper-class white woman, aged between twenty-five and thirty years old, with dark brown eyes and dark, curly auburn hair, was painted in oils on a wooden panel by an unidentified but highly skilled portrait artist, most likely in the early years of the nineteenth century.

Prior to 1869, Col. R. B. Creecy, editor of the Elizabeth City *Economist*, recalled seeing the Nag's Head portrait in the residence of Mrs. Polly Mann, the widow of Joseph Tillett, a Nag's Head wrecker. In 1869, Dr. William Gaskins Pool, of Elizabeth City, North Carolina, stated that he acquired the portrait as compensation for medical services provided to a Mrs. Mann, "an elderly woman aged about 70," of Nag's Head. It hung in his plantation home, The Eyrie, near Elizabeth City, where it was said to have sustained some fire damage when the house burned.[22]

The first extensive description of the story was contained in the June 1878 commencement address made by North Carolina historian Col. John H. Wheeler to the Historical Society of North Carolina during commencement week of the University of North Carolina at Chapel Hill.[23]

In 1887, Dr. Pool's daughter, Anna L. Pool Overman, wife of John Pool Overman, inherited the portrait upon her father's death. It was hanging in her Elizabeth City home in 1912.[24] Anna Overman sold it to the William Macbeth Gallery in New York City in 1913.[25] That same year, the gallery sold the portrait to Herbert Lee Pratt, a Glen Cove, Long Island, art collector, who owned it as of 1928, when it was reproduced in Dr. John E. Stillwell's *History of the Burr Portraits*. Pratt bequeathed a collection of his artwork (which included the miniature portrait of Joseph Alston on page 111) to Amherst College, in Amherst, Massachusetts. At some point after 1928, and before his death in 1945, Pratt sold the Nag's Head portrait back to the William Macbeth Gallery.[26]

In 1936, the portrait was exhibited at a meeting of the North Carolina State Art Society in Raleigh, North Carolina.

Robert Macbeth, then owner of the Macbeth Gallery, told the society that he had acquired the portrait from Dr. William Pool.[27] In fact, Macbeth purchased it not from Pool but from Pool's daughter.

Annie Burr Jennings, of Fairfield, Connecticut, purchased the painting in 1936 from the Macbeth Gallery.[28] Her niece, Annie Burr Auchincloss Lewis (the wife of art collector Wilmarth S. Lewis), inherited the portrait upon her aunt's death in 1939.[29] In February 1966, the portrait was reproduced in *American Heritage* magazine, where it was noted as being from the "collection of Wilmarth S. Lewis."[30] Lewis bequeathed his library and its collections to Yale University in 1979. Since that time, the portrait has been in the collection of the Lewis Walpole Library of Yale University.[31]

Proof that the Nag's Head portrait is a likeness of Theodosia Burr Alston rests upon the answers to a number of challenging and interlocking questions. Is Mrs. Mann's story about how she acquired the portrait credible? Is Dr. Pool's story about how he acquired the portrait credible? Would Theodosia likely have commissioned such a portrait? If so, where and when was it painted, and who was the artist? Does the portrait resemble any authenticated paintings of Theodosia? Was the portrait aboard the *Patriot* when she sailed for New York? What was the actual fate of the *Patriot* and its passengers? Does the painting harbor any physical evidence that discloses information about its origins? We will examine these questions in order.

Did Mrs. Mann, formerly the teenaged common-law wife of a Nag's Head wrecker receive the beautiful portrait (and perhaps other scavenged goods, such as two dresses) from her husband, Joseph Tillett, in January 1813? If so, did the booty come from the wreckage of the *Patriot*? There is no proof that it happened this way, but the story is consistent with the lifestyle of the wrecker families. In addition, newspaper editor R. B. Creecy and Dr. Pool, both respected men in their community, state that they saw the portrait hanging in Mrs. Mann's beachfront house.

Dr. Pool stated that he acquired the portrait from Mrs. Mann in 1869 in return for medical services rendered. His witness was his daughter, who visited Mrs. Mann's house "many times." R. B. Creecy further corroborates his story. Pool spent the rest of his life searching for factual information about the portrait. He never attempted to sell the painting, so there was no profit motive to taint his story. In short, there is no good reason to question Dr. Pool's account of how he acquired it from Mrs. Mann.

On her fatal voyage, Theodosia was headed for a long-awaited reunion with her father. It would have been quite logical and appropriate for a loving daughter to commission a portrait of herself as a gift for her father. Burr was in European exile from June 1, 1808 to June 7, 1812. If the portrait were to be a gift to her returning father, it would logically have been created then, and probably in the latter part of the period. Art collector Stillwell proposed that the portrait was painted in the spring of 1812, when Theodosia was nearing the age of 29.[32] The face in the Nag's Head portrait fits that age. At that time, she was anticipating the imminent return of her father, but the death of her son had not yet occurred. However, it is more likely that the portrait was painted a year or two earlier, as the woman in the portrait looks rosy-cheeked and healthy, whereas by 1812, Theodosia, for years in poor health, was described as "very low, feeble, and emaciated."

It is quite unlikely that the portrait would have been painted after young Aaron Burr Alston died (June 1812), for, as Stillwell correctly observed, "from that time she sank into such a state of apathy that any thought of the portrayal of her sick forlorn body would never have occurred to her, nor would an act so mundane have appealed to her."[33]

If this sick—and probably dying—woman, who could not travel any great distance without pain, commissioned a portrait to be painted, then one must ask, "Who painted it, and where?"

Stillwell speculated that "local talent, the best available, no doubt, was requisitioned." But what local talent was available at the time? Theodosia divided her time between The

Oaks and other Alston plantations near Georgetown and cosmopolitan Charleston, fifty miles to the south. The portrait is obviously the work of a highly skilled professional portrait painter. Indeed, it is so striking that only one of the best painters in the country could have produced it. If we define the period of creation as 1808-1812, the years of Burr's exile, and if we assume that since she was seriously ill, and her trips north during her father's exile were for the restoration of her rapidly deteriorating health, then the portrait was probably painted in South Carolina.

In her adoptive state, only two locations offer possibilities: nearby Georgetown, reachable from The Oaks in an hour or two by carriage or small boat, or Charleston, a two-day trip by carriage or coastal schooner. It is unlikely that the artist lived in or near Georgetown, since, in 1808-1812, it was little more than a small coastal village, and few skilled portraitists worked there except during brief visits.[34]

For Theodosia, the only nearby place of sufficient size to attract artists with the talent and skill level necessary to produce the Nag's Head portrait was Charleston. Samuel F. B. Morse, one of the foremost portraitists to work in Charleston, noted in 1819, "the city fairly swarms with painters." The vibrant, wealthy city attracted a number of acknowledged portrait masters during the first two decades of the nineteenth century, as well as a larger number of others who did not have the talents of the best-known painters or visited only briefly. So, if Charleston was the place where the Nag's Head portrait was painted, then who was the artist?

Joseph Alston's kinsman, Washington Allston (1779-1843), a skilled romantic painter of ambitious religious and allegorical subjects (and friend of John Vanderlyn), has been suggested as a possibility. Allston was born on the Waccamaw River and graduated from Harvard, where he composed music and wrote poetry. In May 1801, he and his fellow artist, Edward Greene Malbone, departed for London, where Allston studied under Benjamin West. He returned to America in 1809 and departed again in 1811, with the young Samuel F. B. Morse in tow.

Allston remained in Europe until 1818, when he returned, settled in Boston, and worked until his death in 1843. Thus, Allston, who was in the United States from 1809 till 1811 and would have met Theodosia, is a possible candidate for being the Nag's Head portraitist.

Washington Allston's talented student, Samuel F. B. Morse (1791-1872), was a favorite of the Georgetown planters. His patron was John Ashe Alston, Joseph's brother, and he worked in Charleston. Between 1818 and 1820, Morse painted two regal portraits of Col. and Mrs. William Alston, Theodosia's in-laws. But during the period in question, young Morse—not yet an artist—had recently graduated from Yale (1810), and he immediately traveled abroad to London, where he studied under Washington Allston until 1815. His youth and inexperience removes Samuel Morse from the list.

According to a 1954 telling of the Nag's Head portrait tale, "Dr. Pool also carried a photograph of the painting to Washington and showed it to Colonel John H. Wheeler, author of *Historical Sketches of North Carolina*. Mrs. Wheeler, daughter of Thomas Sully, a famous painter who once painted Queen Victoria, spoke up: 'It is strikingly like one I have in my possession; let me show you.' The likeness of Theodosia Burr produced by Mrs. Wheeler compared identically with Dr. Pool's picture."[35] This seems to suggest that Sully was the painter.

Sully, a masterful and prolific romantic portraitist who painted the alluring portrait of Theodosia's young niece, Mary Motte Alston Pringle, between 1842 and 1845 in Philadelphia, also painted Mary's parents, Col. and Mrs. William Alston.[36] However, Sully settled in Philadelphia in 1807, traveled in England in 1808-1810, and returned to Philadelphia in 1810. Sully, in Philadelphia, would probably have been out of reach for the failing Theodosia, even if the portrait were made in 1811 or 1812. Nevertheless, based on the quality of the work and the possibility that Theodosia might have been well enough to travel, Sully is at least a possibility.

Two other skillful and popular Charleston artists might have been sought to do the job. Charles Fraser (1782-1860), a favorite with the Lowcountry rice planters, and Edward Greene Malbone (1777-1807) recorded the likenesses of some of Charleston's most esteemed citizens, including many of the Alston clan. Fraser worked in the city his entire life, and Malbone was there from December 1800 through part of 1801 and returned in December 1805 for several months before contracting tuberculosis. However, both Fraser and Malbone specialized in miniatures, not full-size portraits, and for that reason must be scratched from the list. This exhausts the roster of major artists known to be in Charleston between 1808 and1812, leaving as possible candidates Washington Allston and Thomas Sully.

In his 1928 survey of portraits of Aaron Burr and Theodosia, art collector John E. Stillwell simultaneously attributed the Nag's Head portrait to two different artists. On page 62 of his treatise, he first states, "Local talent, the best available, no doubt, was requisitioned." On the next page, he tells us that Vanderlyn "probably arrived in America [from Europe] in July, 1811, and must have visited The Oaks, Governor Alston's South Carolina home, where he painted another portrait of Theodosia [the Nag's Head portrait or a profile portrait in a black dress] [37] which rivals, in excellence and beauty, the one of her that he painted in 1802."[38] The problem words are "probably" and "must have." Both indicate that Stillwell was relying solely on conjecture and had no documentation whatsoever for his guesswork. Vanderlyn's undocumented attribution as painter of the Nag's Head portrait was inherited by the portrait's current owner, the Lewis Walpole Library, when they accessioned the portrait. At that time, the portrait bore an impressive brass plaque that stated unequivocally, "Theodosia Burr Alston. 1775 John Vanderlyn 1852. 'The Nag's Head Portrait'."

Vanderlyn was, indeed, devoted to Burr, who had sponsored his work and commissioned several portraits of himself and Theodosia. However, Vanderlyn left the United States for Europe in 1803. While in exile during between 1808 and 1812, Burr traveled with a rolled-up Vanderlyn portrait of

Theodosia, which the artist retouched while the two were in Paris together. We can be certain that Vanderlyn was in Paris from February 16, 1810, when Burr arrived, until Burr departed the city in July 1811, as he and Vanderlyn saw each other almost every day during that period.

Research by Vanderlyn art experts and the author show conclusively that Vanderlyn did not set foot on American soil between May 1803 and June 1815, two-and-a-half years after Theodosia's death.[39] Consequently, he could not have painted the Nag's Head portrait—or any other portrait in America during that time. The "traveling Vanderlyn" of Theodosia, which the artist retouched while Burr was in Europe, could not have been the Nag's Head portrait, for it was painted on canvas and the Nag's Head portrait is painted on a wooden panel. Vanderlyn did work in Charleston for two years in 1822 and 1823, but that was a decade after Theodosia's death. He also returned briefly in 1836. However, his unbroken residence in Europe between 1803 and 1815 rules him out as the creator of the Nag's Head portrait. Indeed, his uninterrupted presence in Europe for this period rules out his creation of any other portraits in the United States during this period.[40]

In 1928, Stillwell wrote, "Whether the *Patriot* simply foundered during the violent January gale of 1813, or whether she succumbed to the attack of buccaneers, or whether 'the bankers' or land pirates completed what the gale or sea pirates started, may remain a matter of speculation, but there is interwoven with her loss the history of a stranded vessel from which was recovered a portrait of an attractive young woman supposedly Theodosia Burr Alston."[41]

If beauty is in the eye of the beholder, then so is resemblance. A gnawing problem facing those who try to authenticate the Nag's Head portrait is that it doesn't bear an unmistakable resemblance to any of the known portraits of Theodosia. But, by a quixotic twist of fate, that alone doesn't disqualify it from being a portrait of Theodosia. As the perverse luck of this mystery would have it, no two of the authenticated original portraits of Theodosia bear a strong resemblance to each other. Nevertheless, some of the authenticated portraits do share several common characteristics: black or very dark brown eyes; curly, dark auburn hair; a somewhat plump, rounded fullness of the jawline; and the shape of the subject's left ear canal.

The Nag's Head portrait—and the c. 1801 miniature on the cover of this book—exhibit all of these essential characteristics. The clothing is appropriate to Theodosia's status in life and to the time period (1808-1812) during which the portrait was supposedly painted. Further, the age of the woman in the Nag's Head portrait (25 to 30 years) matches Theodosia's age between 1808, when she was 25, and 1812, when she was 29. Like fingerprints, ear shapes are unique but can be deceiving if viewed from different angles. There is a strong resemblance in the ear shape of the 1802 Vanderlyn and the ear in the Nag's Head portrait. On the other hand, portrait artists pay the most attention to the details and shape of the subject's eyes, nose, mouth, hair, and overall shape of the face. Ears get less attention and may or may not be rendered as carefully. For that reason, the ears in the various Theodosia portraits are not a strong indicator of a match unless the similarity is striking.

There is no known inventory of what items Theodosia took aboard the *Patriot* for what was probably to be a six-month trip. Clearly, her baggage would have included a number of trunks containing clothing, cosmetics, jewelry, and some cash. From Burr himself we know that she was carrying a large quantity of his papers sealed in tin boxes. It is also perfectly logical—but completely undocumented—that she may have carried a gift (such as a portrait) for the father she had not seen in four years. Therefore, any statement that she took a portrait on board is pure undocumented speculation.

Since there is no proof that the *Patriot*'s passengers and crew were ever seen or heard from again after December 31, 1812, they must have met one of four possible fates:

1. They were captured by a British warship. If a British warship had taken the *Patriot* in good condition, a prize crew would have sailed her off to a British port. The passengers and crew would have been treated as official prisoners of war and would have been formally repatriated in exchange for British prisoners at the end of the war. If the *Patriot* had been captured in damaged condition, the ex-privateer would have been set afire or scuttled. However, no British Admiralty records record either fate, and Theodosia, the daughter of a former U.S. vice president, would certainly have been documented and repatriated had she been imprisoned. Hence, this theory must be discarded.

2. The ship was destroyed in a severe storm. The ship sank unnoticed at sea, and all on board drowned. In this scenario, the one accepted by Aaron Burr and Joseph Alston, the *Patriot* ran into a gale and went down without having been seen by anyone from the time she departed from Georgetown and until her ultimate fate. This scenario is logical and fits all the known facts. However, it argues against the authenticity of the Nag's Head portrait, which would have gone down with the ship if it had been onboard. There is the slight possibility that the portrait might have floated ashore when the ship sank, but no one has ever suggested that the portrait simply washed up on the beach.

3. The *Patriot* was captured by pirates, who killed all aboard. In this version, the *Patriot* was boarded by pirates (or the crew and passengers were overpowered by mutineers), who murdered everyone and then looted and scuttled the ship. This is consistent with the 1820 Jean Defarges / Robert Johnson crew mutiny story described earlier. Alternatively, if pirates had been discovered by an American or British warship while pillaging the pilot boat, and the brigands had already killed those on board, they would have fled and left the *Patriot* adrift. If pirates did capture and scuttle the *Patriot*, this again argues against the authenticity of the Nag's Head portrait, which would have gone down with the ship, for pirates had little interest in art. If buccaneers killed the passengers and set the *Patriot* adrift, the schooner, with the portrait, if aboard, might have washed ashore, thereby setting the stage for the last of the possible scenarios.

4. The ship was wrecked on the Outer Banks. The authenticity of Theodosia Burr Alston being the subject of the Nag's Head portrait hangs on this theory alone: that the *Patriot*—whether or not it was boarded by pirates and whether or not the British fleet ever saw it—was for, some reason, wrecked on the beaches of the Outer Banks near Nag's Head, North Carolina. There, bankers allegedly looted the wreck and disposed of any survivors, and one banker saved the portrait and gave it to his fiance'e. This is the "Nag's Head portrait / Joseph Tillett / Mrs. Mann / Dr. Pool" scenario.

Regardless of which scenarios one may choose to discount, two nagging pieces of negative evidence remain. First, if the Nag's Head portrait is *not* of Theodosia Burr Alston, then whose face is it? It has been more than a century since a picture of the painting was first published. Since then, tens of thousands of copies of the painting have appeared in numerous newspapers, magazines, and books. Yet over that considerable period of time, no one has ever come forward to claim that the Nag's Head portrait is someone *other* than Theodosia Burr Alston.

Second, no notice ever appeared in newspapers or other known historical record that any *other* ship was lost at the same time—early January 1813—and place—near Nag's Head—where the wrecked ship containing the portrait was said to have been found by Mrs. Mann's husband. This lack of conflicting evidence proves nothing—as nothing can be proven solely on the basis of negative evidence—but it does serve to strengthen the argument that the Nag's Head portrait might be that of Theodosia.

A writer who had admired the portrait in the first years of the twentieth century wrote, "What a story it might tell! What a mystery it might lift could the veil of silence be withdrawn!"[42] Is the Nag's Head portrait that of Theodosia Burr Alston? There are only two possible answers.

Yes, it is Theodosia. This requires accepting the "Mrs. Mann / Dr. Pool" story of its origins. But doing so would still not explain anything else about the fate of the *Patriot* or its crew and passengers in January 1813. It would also tell us nothing about the identity of the artist or the place or date of the creation of the portrait.

No, it is not Theodosia. It is someone else: a case of mistaken identity, attributed to Theodosia because of the lack of documentary evidence, inadequate or faulty research, or misassumption or misrepresentation by one or more owners or researchers. This also does not establish the identity of the artist or the date or place of its creation.

Can either verdict currently be made with authority? No. A good deal of persuasive circumstantial evidence exists to support the "Mrs. Mann / Dr. Pool" theory. However, the lack of any hard physical or documentary evidence makes it impossible to declare beyond a reasonable doubt that the Nag's Head painting is or is not a portrait of Theodosia Burr Alston or to determine who painted it or where and when it was painted. There is no proof that such a portrait was even taken aboard the *Patriot*, and no one other than the late Mrs. Mann can account for its whereabouts between 1813 and 1869.

Any future authentication will have to rest upon new physical evidence (such as the presence of sea salts in the wooden panel) from the scientific study of the painting itself; from from detailed comparisons with the work of likely artists; or from documentary evidence not currently available to researchers.

Theodosia's life was filled with enormous promise, great potential, Spartan courage, a warm heart, and a powerful will to live. If Burr's Mexican scheme had succeded, what would have happened had Theodosia become Empress of Mexico? And would young Aaron Burr Alston have turned into the intellectual prodigy and mighty Mexican monarch his grandfather planned him to become?

As it was in 1869, the Nag's Head portrait remains, as does Theodosia's disappearance itself, a perfect enigma: one that is likely to tantalize, inspire, and frustrate historians for many years to come. But ultimately, Theodosia's legacy always revolves around the question, "What if...?"

~∽∾~

Source Notes

PREFACE

1. William K. Bixby, ed., *The Private Journal of Aaron Burr, reprinted in full from the original manuscript in the library of Mr. William K. Bixby, of St. Louis, Mo., with an introduction, explanatory notes, and a glossary. In two volumes* (Rochester, N.Y.: The Genesee Press, 1903).

CHAPTER 1: Good Stock, Deep Roots

1. Theodosia Bartow was born "toward the end of 1746": Milton Lomask, *Aaron Burr* (New York: Farrar, Straus, Giroux, 1979, 2 vols.), I:65.

2. Mary-Jo Kline, ed., *Political Correspondence and Public Papers of Aaron Burr* (Princeton, N.J.: Princeton University Press, 1983, 2 vols.), I:lxvi; also Lomask, I:99.

3. Lomask, I:99.

4. Lomask, I:lxvi.

5. Lomask, I:98-99; also Walter Flavius McCaleb, *The Aaron Burr Conspiracy* (New York: Wilson-Erickson, Inc., 1936), 68.

6. Lomask, I:5.

7. Charles Felton Pidgin, *Theodosia: The First Gentlewoman of her Time* (Boston: C.M. Clark Publishing Co., 1907), 71.

8. In early branches of her family tree, Sarah's surname was sometimes spelled Pierrepont.

9. Pidgin, *Theodosia*, 12. If taken literally, he would have us believe that his daughters averaged six feet in height!

10. Pidgin, *Theodosia*, 16.

11. Pidgin, *Theodosia*, 18.

12. Pidgin, *Theodosia*, 24.

13. Pidgin, *Theodosia*, 17.

14. Pidgin, *Theodosia*, 25.

15. Herbert S. Parmet and Marie B. Hecht, *Aaron Burr: Portrait of an Ambitious Man* (New York: The MacMillan Co., 1967), 7.

16. Pidgin, *Theodosia*, 97, citing Jeremiah Eames Rankin, editor, *Esther Burr's Journal* (Washington, D.C.: Woodword & Lothrop, 1903). The Rev. Dr. Rankin, former president of Howard University, which published his book, was intimately familiar with the family's history.

He describes himself as the "author and editor" of the journal. He wrote it as if in her voice, but it reads more like a male-authored late nineteenth-century literary work than the personal journal of a mid-eighteenth-century woman. Pidgin said diplomatically that "whether the solid basis for the diary is large or small, the material is handled with great ingenuity."

17. Pidgin, *Theodosia*, 86.

18. Pidgin, *Theodosia*, 79, citing Franklin Bowditch Dexter, *The Literary Diary of Ezra Stiles* (New York: Scribners, 1901), vol. II.

19. Pidgin, *Theodosia*, 80.

20. Pidgin, *Theodosia*, 95.

21. Pidgin, *Theodosia*, 95.

22. Pidgin, *Theodosia*, 74.

23. The letter was dated July 20, 1752. Pidgin, *Theodosia*, 87.

24. Pidgin, *Theodosia*, 97.

25. Pidgin, *Theodosia*, 96.

26. Pidgin, *Theodosia*, 88-89.

27. Throughout this book, Aaron Burr's sister, Sarah Burr, who married Tapping Reeve, will be called Sally for the purpose of clarity, as she was seldom addressed as Sarah by friends and family. George E. McCracken, "Who Was Aaron Burr?" *The American Genealogist*, #158, vol. 40, no. 2 (April 1964), 65-70.

28. Lomask, I:3.

29. James Parton, *The Life and Times of Aaron Burr*, (Boston and New York: Houghton Mifflin, enlarged edition, 1892, 2 vols.), I:50; also Parmet and Hecht, citing Josephine Fischer, "The Journal of Esther Burr," in *The New England Quarterly*, III:300.

30. Pidgin, *Theodosia*, 81.

31. Lomask, I:18, and Parton, *Theodosia*, I:47, citing Esther Burr to Jonathan Edwards, November 2, 1754, A.B. Jennings Collection, Yale.

32. Lomask, I: 66.

33. Henry Bischoff, "Theodosia Bartow Prevost Burr at The Hermitage," *Ourstory: Journal of the New Jersey Council for History Education*, vol. 6, no. 1, (Fall 2000), 14.

34. Pidgin, *Theodosia*, 121.

35. Pidgin, *Theodosia*, 119, 124, citing W. Jay Mills, *Historic Houses of New Jersey* (Philadelphia: Lippincott, 1902), 151-152.

36. Henry Bischoff, "Theodosia Bartow Prevost Burr at The Hermitage," 14.

37. Charles Burr Todd, *The True Aaron Burr: A Biographical Sketch* (New York: A.S. Barnes & Co., 1902), 11-12.

38. Lomask, I:686.

39. Henry Bischoff, "Theodosia Bartow Prevost Burr at The Hermitage," 14.

CHAPTER 2: Reverend Burr's Son

1. Timothy Edwards, the sixth child of the Rev. Jonathan Edwards, was born in Northhampton, Massachusetts, on July 25, 1738, married Rhoda Ogden (1742-1822) on September 25, 1760, in Elizabethtown, New Jersey, and died on October 28, 1813, at Elizabethtown. McCracken, 65.

2. George E. McCracken, "Who Was Aaron Burr?" *The American Genealogist*, vol. 40, no. 2 (April 1964), 65, citing *New Jersey Wills*, 3:48.

3. Parmet and Hecht, 12.

4. James Parton, *The Life and Times of Aaron Burr* (Boston and New York: Houghton Mifflin Co., enlarged edition, 1892), I:52.

5. "Aaron Burr," United States Senate. Official biography online at http://www.senate.gov, May 3, 2002.

6. Parmet and Hecht, 13.

7. Parton (1892), I:52.

8. Parton (1892), I:52-53.

9. Pierpont Edwards (1750-1826), the son of Rev. Jonathan and Sarah (Pierpont) Edwards of Northampton, Mass., graduated from Princeton College 1768 and saw active service in the Revolutionary War. He became an eminent lawyer in Connecticut. Edward Hooker, *The Descendants of Rev. Thomas Hooker, Hartford, Connecticut, 1586-1908*, (Rochester, N.Y.: E.R. Andrews Printing Co., 1909), 90.

10. Parton (1892), I:53.

11. Parton (1892), I:53.

12. Parton (1892), I:54.

13. Parton (1892), I:55.

14. Arnold A. Rogow, *A Fatal Friendship: Alexander Hamilton and Aaron Burr* (New York: Farrar, Straus and Giroux, 1999), 55.

15. Parmet and Hecht, 13, citing "On Dancing," Duer Collection, Historical Society of Pennsylvania.

16. Parton (1892), I:56.

17. Parton (1892), I:56.

18. Parton (1892), I:56.

19. Tapping Reeve (1744-1823) founded The Litchfield Law School, America's first law school (1774) whose graduates included Aaron Burr, South Carolina's John C. Calhoun, and 130 members of Congress. An endowed chair at the University of Connecticut School of Law is named in his honor. He served as a volunteer in the revolution and eventually was named Chief Justice of the Connecticut Supreme Court.

20. McCracken, 65-66.

21. Parmet and Hecht, 1-16; "Aaron Burr," U.S. Senate official biography.

22. Matthew L. Davis, ed. *Memoirs of Aaron Burr, With Selections From His Correspondence* (New York: Harper & Brothers, 1837 & 1838), I:45

23. Parton (1858), 626.

24. Parton (1858), 681.

25. Pidgin, *Theodosia*, 44.

26. Parton (1892), I:62-63.

27. Oliver H. Leigh., ed., *Letters to His Son. On the Fine Art of Becoming a Man of the World and a Gentleman.* By the Earl of Chesterfield (New York: M.W. Dunne, 1901), i.

28. Richard N. Côté, *Mary's World: Love, War, and Family Ties in Nineteenth-century Charleston* (Mt. Pleasant, South Carolina: Corinthian Books, 2000), 113.

29. Parton (1892), I:63.

30. Parmet and Hecht, 16.

31. Parmet and Hecht, 18.

32. Parton (1892), I:64-65.

33. Kline, II:1223.

34. Parmet and Hecht, 20, citing AB to Sarah Reeve, September 18, 1775, Park Family papers, Yale.

35. Parmet and Hecht, 21, citing AB to Sarah Reeve, September 18, 1775, Park Family papers, Yale.

36. Rogow, 55, 297n4

37. Parmet and Hecht, 22.

38. Parmet and Hecht, 32.

39. For a detailed description of Prevost's military service, see Edward G. Williams, "The Prevosts of the Royal Americans," *in The Western Pennsylvania Historical Magazine,* January 1973, 1-38.

40. Edward G. Williams, "The Prevosts of the Royal Americans," 14-15.

41. The early days of The Hermitage are described in Henry Bischoff, "The Hermitage: An Historical Overview," *Ourstory: The Journal of the New Jersey Council for History Education,* vol. 6, no. 1 (Fall 2000), 11-13. A detailed biographical sketch of Aaron Burr's first wife may be found in Bischoff's article, "Theodosia Bartow Prevost Burr at The Hermitage, *ibid,* 14-17. George Washington's visit to The Hermitage is detailed in Alec J. Hurst's "George Washington Stepped Here," *ibid,* 18-19.

42. Pidgin, *Theodosia,* 134; Lomask, I: 65.

43. Henry Bischoff, "Theodosia Bartow Prevost Burr at The Hermitage," *Ourstory: The Journal of the New Jersey Council for History Education,* vol. 6, no. 1 (Fall 2000), 15.

44. Augustine Frederick Bartow Prevost was named after his uncle, General Augustine Prevost. He was a successful lawyer. Aaron Burr and his wife often used his home, known as "The Shrubbery," in Pelham, N.Y., as a summer retreat from the heat of New York City.

45. John Bartow Prevost was an attorney. He served in the New York State legislature and was appointed a Supreme Court justice in New Orleans, Louisiana Territory, by Thomas Jefferson in 1803.

46. Parton (1892), I: 134.

47. Pidgin, *Theodosia*, 124.

48. Alec J. Hurst, "George Washington Stepped Here: July 10-14, 1778," *Ourstory: Journal of the New Jersey Council for History Education*, Vol. 6, no. 1 (Fall 2000), 18-19; also Lomask, I:65.

49. James Monroe to Theodosia Bartow Prevost, in Jonathan Daniels, *Ordeal of Ambition: Jefferson, Hamilton, Burr* (Garden City, New York: Doubleday & Co., 1970), 46-47.

50. Parton (1892), I:103.

51. Lomask, I:64.

52. Lomask, I:65.

53. Lomask, I:70.

54. Bischoff, "Theodosia Bartow Prevost Burr at The Hermitage," 16.

55. Edmund Clarence Stedman, "Aaron Burr's Wooing," in *Harper's New Monthly Magazine*, October 1887, 666-667.

56. Parton (1892), I:120.

57. William Paterson to AB, March 18, 1779, in Pidgin, *Theodosia*, 140.

58. Parton (1892), I:122.

59. Parmet and Hecht, 50-51.

CHAPTER 3: Courtship and Courtrooms

1. Lomask I:69, 73.

2. Parmet and Hecht, 53, citing Thaddeus Burr to AB, August 12, 1780, in Burr Miscellaneous Mss., New York Public Library.

3. Lomask, I:71, citing Theodosia Bartow Prevost to Sally Reeve, June 16, 1780, Burr Family Papers, Yale.

4. Mrs. Theodosia Prevost, Litchfield. Conn., to AB, May 1781, in Davis, *Memoirs*, I:227.

5. Williams, "The Prevosts of the Royal Americans," 16.

6. Voltaire was the pen name of François Marie Arouet (1694-1778), a French poet, dramatist, satirist, and historian.

7. TBP, Litchfield, Conn., to AB, February 12, 1781, in Davis, *Memoirs*, I:224-225.

8. AB, Ruritan, N.J., to Major R. Alden, February 15, 1781, in Davis, *Memoirs*, I:222.

9. TBP, Litchfield, Conn., to AB, May 1781, in Davis, *Memoirs*, I:226.

10. AB to TBP, December 5, 1781, in Davis, *Memoirs*, I:233.

11. TBP, Litchfield, Conn., to AB, May 1781, in Davis, *Memoirs*, I:226.

12. AB, Albany, N.Y., to Chief Justice Richard Morris, October 21, 1781, in Davis, *Memoirs*, I:231.

13. Davis, *Memoirs*, I:240.

14. Lomask, I:79.

15. Williams, "The Prevosts of the Royal Americans," 16.

16. Pidgin, *Theodosia*, 120.

17. Williams, "The Prevosts of the Royal Americans," 17.

18. AB to TBP, December 6, 1781, in Davis, *Memoirs*, I:234-235.

19. The Hermitage today incorporates the 18th-century house where Aaron Burr married Theodosia Prevost. The National Historic Landmark was remodeled and enlarged in 1847-48 to the designs of architect William H. Ranlett. Today the picturesque Gothic Revival house is a museum.

20. Parmet and Hecht, 56. The source is not furnished. Parton, I:138 states that the minister was the Rev. David Bogart, of the Dutch Reformed Church, but this is an error. Neither Parton nor Davis gives the place. Wandell and Minnigerode, I:97 publish the text of the license: "I do hereby certify that Aaron Burr of the State of N. York Esqr. and Theodosia Prevost of Bergen County, State of N. Jersey widow were by me joined in lawful wedlock on the second day of July instant, Given, under my hand and seal this 6th day of July 1782. B'n Ven Der Linde." They speculate that the wedding place was The Hermitage. Pidgin, 126, stated that the records of the Dutch Reformed Church at Paramus had been destroyed by fire, "so that it is impossible to determine whether Burr was really married there or not," and gives the testimony Mr. W. C. Rosencrantz, a former owner of The Hermitage, whose grandmother was of one of the bridesmaids, to establish the place of the ceremony as the parlor of the Hermitage. Dr. Henry Bischoff, Director of Historical Studies, The Hermitage, concurs, and wrote that "the marriage took place at The Hermitage on July 2, 1782."

21. Wandell and Minnigerode, I:98-99 (also Lomask, I:81), citing a letter from Theodosia Prevost Burr, Albany, to Sally Reeve, Paramus, N.J., c. July 9, 1782, New Jersey Historical Society.

22. Henry Bischoff, "Theodosia Bartow Prevost Burr at The Hermitage,"14.

23. Parton, "Theodosia Burr," *Harper's New Monthly Magazine*, August, 1864, 294.

24. TPB, Albany, N.Y., to AB, August 14, 1783, in Davis, *Memoirs*, I:246-247.

25. Parton (1892), I:139.

26. Edith Tunis Sale, *Old Time Belles and Cavaliers* (Philadelphia: J.B. Lippincott Co., 1912), 248.

27. Parton (1892), I:142.

28. Eugene Didier, in Lomask, I:86.

29. AB, Jane's in the Mountains [N.Y.?], May 1785, in Davis, *Memoirs*, I:259.

30. The "situation of my house" refers to her advanced pregnancy. TPB, New-York, to AB, April 1785, in Davis, *Memoirs*, I:260.

31. AB, Chester, N.Y., to TPB, May 12, 1785, in Davis, *Memoirs*, I:261.

32. AB, n.p., 9 o'clock at night, 19th May 1785, in Davis, *Memoirs*, I:264.

33. Abbé Gabriel Bonnot De Mably, *Observations Sur Le Gouvernement Et Les Loix Des Etats-Unis D'Amerique* (Observations on the Government

and Laws of the United States of America). Various editions were published in French and English starting in 1784.

34. AB, n.p., to TPB, May 22, 1785, in Davis, *Memoirs*, I:266-267.

35. TPB, New-York, to AB, May 22, 1785, in Davis, *Memoirs*, I:268.

36. TPB, New-York, to AB, September 25, 1785, in Davis, *Memoirs*, I:271.

37. TPB, New-York, to AB, August 1786, in Davis, *Memoirs*, I:275.

38. AB, Albany, August 1786, to TBA, in Davis, *Memoirs*, I:276.

39. Lomask, I:100.

40. Lomask, I:99.

41. TPB, New-York, to Tapping Reeve, Litchfield, Conn., August 3, 1788, in Pidgin, *Theodosia*, 169-170; also Lomask, I:99.

42. Kline, I:182n4.

43. AB, Chester [N.Y.], to TPB, Friday, May 1785, in Davis, *Memoirs*, I:255.

44. AB, Philadelphia, to TPB, Saturday, April 1785, in Davis, *Memoirs*, I:252-253.

45. TPB, New-York, to AB, May 22, 1785, in Davis, *Memoirs*, I:253-254.

46. TPB, New-York, to AB, May 1785, in Davis, *Memoirs*, I:256.

47. Parton, James S., "Theodosia Burr," *Harper's New Monthly Magazine*, vol. 29, issue 171 (August, 1864), 295.

48. AB, Albany, N.Y., to TPB, April 1785, in Davis, *Memoirs*, I:254.

49. AB, Chester, N.Y., to TPB, May 1785, in Davis, *Memoirs*, I:257.

50. Parmet and Hecht, 61. In 1800, New York's slaves comprised 3.5% of its population. In South Carolina, slaves made up 42.3% of the population.

51. Parmet and Hecht, 61.

52. Lomask, II:403-404.

53. Davis, *Memoirs*, I:318.

54. Davis, *Memoirs*, I:288.

55. Lomask, I:144.

56. TPB to AB, July 23, 1791, in Davis, *Memoirs*, I:328.

57. AB, to TPB, December 21, 1791, in Davis, *Memoirs*, I:328.

58. AB, New-York, to Jacob De Lamater, October 30, 1792, in Davis, *Memoirs*, I:358.

59. Daniels, 129.

60. Daniels, 130.

61. Parmet and Hecht, 87, citing Luss Ms., Burr Additional Papers, Princeton.

62. Ray Swick, *An Island Called Eden: The Story of Harman and Margaret Blennerhassett* (Parkersburg, West Virginia: Blennerhassett Island Historical State Park, 2000), 37.

63. Daniels, 48.

64. Parmet and Hecht, 88, citing Rebecca Blodgett to AB, December 28, 1823, Burr Papers, New-York Historical Society.

65. Parmet and Hecht, 88.

66. TPB, New-York, to AB, May 22, 1785, in Davis, *Memoirs*, I:268.

67. TPB, New-York, to AB, November 1787, in Davis, *Memoirs*, I:277-278.

68. TPB, Pelham, N.Y., to AB, July 23, 1791, in Davis, *Memoirs*, I:299.

69. AB, Claverack, to TPB, June 27, 1791, in Davis, *Memoirs*, I:291.

70. TPB, Pelham, N.Y., to AB, July 23, 1791, in Davis, *Memoirs*, I:298-299.

71. Dorothy Valentine Smith, "An Intercourse of the Heart. Some Little-Known Letters of Theodosia Burr," *New York Historical Quarterly*, 1953, II:42.

72. Theodosia B. Burr, n.p., to Dear Brother [Frederick Bartow], Pelham, New York, October 20, 1792, Burr-Purkitt Family Papers, Washington University Libraries, St. Louis, Missouri.

73. Janet Todd, *Mary Wollstonecraft: A Revolutionary Life* (New York: Columbia University Press, 2000).

74. "Mary Wollstonecraft," online at http://www.philosophy pages.com/ph/woll.htm April 15, 2002.

75. Jone Johnson Lewis, "A Vindication of the Rights of Woman: Mary Wollstonecraft," online at http://womenshistory.about.com/library/weekly/aa092099.htm, March 3, 2002.

76. Mary Wollstonecraft, *An Historical and Moral View of the Origin and Progress of the French Revolution and the Effect it has Produced in Europe* (London: Joseph Johnson, 1794).

77. AB, Philadelphia, February 16, 1793, to TPB, in Davis, *Memoirs*, I:363.

78. Robbie L. Alford, "Theodosia Burr Alston," in Historic Georgetown County Leaflet Number 1 (Georgetown, S.C.: The Rice Museum, 1975), 1.

79. The copy, by an unknown artist, appears in John E. Stillwell, *The History of the Burr Portraits. Their Origin, Their Dispersal and Their Reassemblage* (N.p.: privately printed, 1928), 84.

80. Swick, "Theodosia Burr Alston," 499.

81. Parton (1858), 651,

82. Rogow, 90.

83. Parmet and Hecht, 64.

84. TPB, New-York, to AB, August 28, 1785, in Davis, *Memoirs*, I:269.

85. AB, Westchester, to TB, October 8, 1792, in Davis, *Memoirs*, I:317-318.

86. AB, Philadelphia, to TPB, February 8, 1793, in Davis, *Memoirs*, I:361-362

87. AB, Philadelphia, to TPB, February 15, 1793, in Davis, *Memoirs*, I:362.

88. AB, Philadelphia, to TB, February 24, 1794, in Davis, *Memoirs*, I:365.

89. AB, Philadelphia, to TB, December 16, 1793, in Davis, *Memoirs*, I:366.

90. AB, Albany, to TB, January 4, 1799, in Davis, *Memoirs*, I:397-398.

91. Ronald Ray Swick, "Theodosia Burr Alston," in *The South Atlantic Quarterly*, vol. 74, no. 4 (Autumn 1975), 496.

92. Swick, "Theodosia Burr Alston," 496, citing Harman Blennerhassett, Jr.'s account of the Burr Conspiracy, Blennerhassett Papers, Library of Congress.

93. Mr. St. Aivre: a dancing teacher.

94. TPB to AB, July 2, 1791, in Davis, *Memoirs*, I:293-294.

95. Dorothy Valentine Smith, II:42.

96. Parton (1858), 201.

97. TPB to AB, July 3, 1791, in Davis, *Memoirs*, I:295

98. Parmet and Hecht, 63.

99. Parmet and Hecht, 63, citing TPB to AB, July 16, 1791, A.B. Jennings Collection, Yale.

100. AB, Albany, to TPB, July 17, 1791, in Davis, *Memoirs*, I:296.

101. "I have the pleasure to tell you, my dear Frederick that I am very much better, & that my face will not be quite so much scared [sic] as was expected." Theodosia Bartow Prevost Burr, to A. J. Frederick Prevost, East Chester, October 30, 1789, Burr-Purkitt Family Papers.

102. AB, Albany, to TPB, October 28, 1789, in Davis, *Memoirs*, I:290-291.

103. Kline, 150-151, quoting AB to Benjamin Rush, August 20, 1793, Burr Family Papers, Yale.

104. AB, Philadelphia, to TPB, December 24, 1793, in Davis, *Memoirs*, I:367.

105. AB, Philadelphia, to TB, February 13, 1794, in Davis, *Memoirs*, I:374.

106. AB, Philadelphia, to TB, February 13, 1794, in Davis, *Memoirs*, I:374.

107. AB, Philadelphia, to TB, January 16, 1794, in Davis, *Memoirs*, I:374.

108. Daniels, 128.

109. Kline, I:182n3, citing *Papers of Aaron Burr*, 3:545, New Haven Colony Historical Society, New Haven, Connecticut.

110. Daniels, 130.

111. Pidgin, *Theodosia*, 133.

112. Parton (1892), I:162.

CHAPTER 4: The Mistress of Richmond Hill

1. TPB mentioned "Louisa," who could have been Anna Louisa Bartow Prevost or Mary Louisa Bartow Prevost. TPB, Pelham, N.Y., to AB, July 23, 1791, in Davis, *Memoirs*, I:298.

2. AB, New-York, to TB, January 5, 1795, in Davis, *Memoirs*, I:386.

3. Pidgin, *Theodosia*, 207.

4. Pidgin, *Theodosia*, 207.

5. Pidgin, *Theodosia*, 210.

6. Thomas Tisdale, *A Lady of the High Hills: Natalie Delage Sumter* (Columbia, S.C.: University of South Carolina Press, 2001), 15.

7. Abigail Adams, Richmond Hill, N.Y., to Mrs. Shaw, September 27, 1789, in Pidgin, *Theodosia*, 211.

8. Daniels, 53.

9. Meade Minnigerode, "Theodosia Burr, Prodigy," *The Saturday Evening Post*, September 6, 1924, 11.

10. TB, Pelham, N.Y., to A.J. Frederick Prevost, October 20, 1792, in Pidgin, *Theodosia*, I:182.

11. Meade Minnigerode, "Theodosia Burr, Prodigy," 11.

12. Pidgin, *Theodosia*, 210.

13. AB, Philadelphia, to TB, March 31, 1794, in Davis, *Memoirs*, I:378.

14. Tent wine: from Spanish, *tinta, or vino tinta*. A deep red wine, similar to Madeira, chiefly from Galicia or Malaga in Spain. When aged, it resembled a tawny port.

15. AB, Philadelphia, to TB, February 13, 1794, in Davis, *Memoirs*, I:376.

16. AB, Albany, N.Y., to TB, February 11, 1799, in Davis, *Memoirs*, I:204.

17. AB, Philadelphia, to TB, August 4, 1794, in Davis, *Memoirs*, I:380.

18. In March 2002, this watch was sold at auction by Butterfield's, San Francisco, for $4,250.

19. Stillwell, 8.

20. AB, New-York, to TB, Philadelphia, January 5, 1795, in Davis, *Memoirs*, I:385. The history of the portraits of Aaron Burr and Theodosia is as controversial as the two people themselves. It is complicated further by the fact that the copying of portraits of one painter by another was and is still common. This often leads to confusion as to which is the original and which the copy. Dr. John E. Stillwell claims that the portrait published in Wandell and Minnigerode's 1925 biography, *Aaron Burr*, is the original Stuart, prior to its cleaning and restoration, and that the photograph he published in 1928 is the same painting of Theodosia, after cleaning. Stillwell was mistaken. The "before cleaning" picture is, in reality, a painted copy of the original Stuart "after cleaning." An examination of photographs of the two paintings reveals significant differences that cleaning cannot account for. The "cleaned" Stuart published in 1928 by Stillwell, opposite page 44, then owned by Miss Annie Burr Jennings, shows a girl with a sweet smile, large eye pupils centered in their sockets, looking towards the right. It also shows a soft shadow from her head on the table to her left that supports two books. That painting is the Stuart original, donated in 1947 to the Yale University Art Gallery by Oliver B. Jennings, in memory of Miss Annie Burr Jennings. The portrait published in the 1925 *Aaron Burr*, opposite page 128, also cited as being owned by Miss Annie Burr Jennings, is quite different, and must be an artist's painted copy of the original Stuart. Its caption reads, "Theodosia Burr. From the original portrait by Stuart in

the possession of Miss Annie Burr Jennings, now reproduced for the first time." This painting shows the face of a tired, slightly depressed, forty-ish-looking woman trapped in an eleven-year-old body. Her dull eyes are placed to the left of center in their sockets, looking directly at the viewer. Her mouth is firmly closed, with no hint of a smile, and she has thinning hair with locks sticking out not found in the Stuart original. It also shows a heavy shadow from her head on the table to her left that supports the two books. The change in expression, position of the eye pupils, and thinning of the hair cannot be accounted for by any kind of cleaning work that might have been performed. The caption, "*From* the original portrait by Stuart" clearly suggests that the published photograph in *Aaron Burr* is of a painting *copied from* the Stuart, not a photograph *of* the original Stuart portrait. This is confirmed by the 1928 publication of the copy in Minnie Kendall Lowther's *Blennerhassett Island in Romance and Tragedy*. There it was labeled, "*From* Stuart Portrait. *Original* owned by Annie Burr Jennings." Italics mine: RNC.

21. Pidgin, 19.

22. These Burr slaves in New York are noted in Davis, *Memoirs*, I & II, *passim*; Kennedy, 189; and Gamaliel Bradford, *Wives* (New York: Harper & Brothers, 1925), 111.

23. Peggy Gartin, New-York, to Honoured Master [AB], December 3, 17, and 29, 1801 and January 12, 1802, in Davis, *Memoirs*, I:403-405.

24. AB, Bristol, N.Y., to TB, September 14, 1795, in Davis, *Memoirs*, I:394.

25. Thomas Tisdale notes that in the biography of Natalie's mother, authored by La Comtesse H. De Reinach-Foussemagne, titled *La Marquise de Lage de Volude* (Paris: Perrin et Cie, Libraires-Editeurs, 1908), the governess was referred to as Madame Senat, rather than de Senat, a name treatment normally accorded only to members of the nobility. In his letters, Europhile Burr referred to her as " Madame de S.," "Madame De Senat, or "Madame de Senat." The latter form will be used here. After her arrival in New York, Nathalie de Lage de Volude soon anglicized her name to Natalie de Lage. That spelling is used here.

26. The given names of Madame de Senat and her daughter have been lost. For a detailed biography of Nathalie de Lage de Volude, see Thomas Tisdale, *A Lady of the High Hills: Natalie Delage Sumter* (Columbia, South Carolina: University of South Carolina Press, 2001).

27. Tisdale, 9.

28. Tisdale, 10.

29. Sister M. Ignatia Gavaghan, O.L.M., *Nathalie deLage Sumter: A Dedicated Life of Faith* (Sumter, S.C.: The Sumter County Historical Commission, 1984), 13.

30. Dr. William Eustis (1753-1825) was a Harvard graduate and Revolutionary War physician. A strong anti-Federalist, he met Burr in

New York, where they became close friends, then returned to his home in Massachusetts. Rogow, 197, citing microfilm of AB, November 1795, to William Eustis, Burr Papers, New-York Historical Society.

31. AB, Washington, February 27, 1802, to TBA, Davis, *Memoirs*, II: 180.

32. Lomask, I:195.

33. AB, Philadelphia, to TB, September 17, 1795, in Davis, *Memoirs*, I:387.

34. AB, Bristol, N.Y., to TB, September 14, 1795, in Davis, *Memoirs*, I:386.

35. Mrs. Penn, a married woman, was retained as Theodosia's governess after the death of Theodosia Bartow Prevost Burr. She remained in that role for some time, well after the arrival of Madame de Senat, whose role was chiefly that of teacher.

36. AB, Albany, N.Y., to TB, August 4, 1794, in Davis, *Memoirs*, I:380.

37. AB, Albany, N.Y., to TB, August 4, 1794, in Davis, *Memoirs*, I:381-382.

38. AB, Albany, N.Y., to TB, August 18, 1794, in Davis, *Memoirs*, I:383.

39. AB, Philadelphia, to T.B., December 21, 1794, in Davis, *Memoirs*, I:384.

40. James S. Parton, "Theodosia Burr," *Harper's New Monthly Magazine*, vol. 29, issue 171 (August, 1864), p. 295.

41. Pidgin, Theodosia, I:178, citing Grace Greenwood (Mrs. S. J. Lippincott), *Gleanings From An Old Scrapbook, Containing Sketches of Yankee Life and Character* (date and publisher unknown, mid-19th century).

42. AB, Troy, N.Y., to T.B., August 21, 1794, in Davis, *Memoirs*, I:384.

43. AB, Philadelphia, September 17, 1795, to TB, in Davis, *Memoirs*, I:388.

44. AB, Bristol, N.Y., to TB, September 14, 1795, in Davis, *Memoirs*, I:386.

45. Pidgin, *Theodosia*, I:218.

46. Roger G. Kennedy, *Burr, Hamilton and Jefferson: A Study in Character* (Oxford and New York: Oxford University Press, 2000), 240.

47. Parmet and Hecht, 114-115.

48. William Leete Stone, *Life of Joseph Brant-Thayendanegea: Including the Border Wars of the American Revolution* (New York: Alexander V. Blake, 1838), I: 455.

49. Parmet and Hecht, 113-115.

50. Parmet and Hecht, 115-116.

51. AB, Philadelphia, February 28, 1797, to TB, No. 30 Partition-Street, New-York, February 28, 1797, in Stone, I:456. Witbeck, who lived in upstate New York, was an early friend of Burr's and a fellow land speculator.

52. Stone, II:456.

53. Pidgin, *Theodosia*, I:220.

54. Stone, II:456-457. Stone cites as the source of Theodosia's report to her father conversations Stone had with Burr. "The Colonel was anxious that this letter from his daughter should be found among his papers," Stone noted, "but Mr. Davis, his biographer, after diligent search, has not discovered it—nor has he been able to find the correspondence between Brant and Colonel Burr." These papers may have been among those destroyed when Theodosia and the *Patriot* were lost at sea.

55. Virginia Tatnall Peacock, *Famous American Belles of the 19th Century* (Philadelphia: J.B. Lippincott Co., 1901), 30.

56. Swick, "Theodosia Burr Alston," 498, citing John Davis, *Travels of Four Years and a Half in the United States of America During 1798, 1799, 1800, 1801, and 1802* (1803; reprinted New York: Henry Holt, 1909), 26.

57. Swick, "Theodosia Burr Alston," 498. The younger Blennerhassett was a son of Harman Blennerhassett, a co-conspirator in Burr's "Western conspiracy" of 1805-1807.

58. Charles R. King, ed., *The Life and Correspondence of Rufus King* (New York: G. P. Putnam's Sons, 1896), III:459.

59. Rogow, 195, citing microfilm of Burr Papers, New-York Historical Society.

60. Daniels, 204.

61. Daniels, 228.

62. Pidgin, *Theodosia*, 223.

63. Kenneth C. Lindsay, *The Works of John Vanderlyn: From Tammany to the Capitol* (Binghampton, N.Y.: University Art Gallery, State University of New York, Binghamton, 1970), 3.

64. Salvatore Mondello, "John Vanderlyn," in *The New-York Historical Society Quarterly*, vol. LII, no. 2 (April 1968), 40. The record is unequivocally clear that at no time between 1803 and 1815 did Vanderlyn set foot in the United States. This crucial fact has been overlooked by those who have attributed to Vanderlyn portraits painted in America during this period.

65. Daniels, 234.

66. Daniels, 367.

67. Parmet and Hecht, 151.

68. Parmet and Hecht, 153.

69. AB, Albany, to TB, January 26, 1800, in Davis, *Memoirs*, I:401-402.

70. Palmetto plutocrat: Daniels, 204. Walter B. Edgar and N. Louise Bailey, eds., *The Biographical Directory of the South Carolina House of Representatives*, volume IV (1791-1815), pp. 32-35.

71. Like almost everything else associated with Theodosia, this portrait of her husband has elements of mystery. The accession records at Amherst College, Amherst, Massachusetts describe it as an oval miniature, 2" x 2-5/8", in a gold frame. The back was blue glass, with a braid of hair insert and the initials JA in gold. The miniature was acquired by

Amherst in 1945 from the estate of Herbert L. Pratt, who stated that it had been purchased from "the family of William Temple Alston of Georgetown, S.C." No "William Temple Alston" is known to have lived in South Carolina, and "Temple" is neither a given nor a family name ever associated with the Alstons. Platt attributed the miniature to Edward Greene Malbone (1777-1897), who visited Charleston in 1800, 1801, and 1805. Several notes in the Amherst College accession records question the attribution to Malbone and whether or not it was a portrait of Joseph Alston. However, the miniature of Theodosia on the cover of this book has been attributed to Malbone by competent authority, and seems to be contemporaneous with this Joseph Alston miniature. This suggests that the two miniatures may have once been a matched set, perhaps painted for Aaron Burr at the time of the 1801 wedding, but only future research can determine that. Some of these questions might have been subject to resolution had the portrait not been destroyed by fire at Amherst in 1947. Only a copy photograph at the Frick Art Reference Library survives of the Joseph Alston miniature.

72. For a detailed description of Pierpont's experiences as a teacher in the employ of Col. William Alston, see Richard N. Côté, *Mary's World: Love, War, and Family Ties in Nineteenth-century Charleston* (Mt. Pleasant, S.C.: Corinthian Books, 2000), 40-45.

73. "Autocratic": E. S. Thomas, *Reminiscences of the Last Sixty-Five Years....* (Hartford, Conn., 1840), II:71-73. An unidentified member of the Alston family, evidently unaware of the existence of this miniature, wrote to Charles F. Pidgin in 1895, "It is a subject of great regret to his relatives that they have no likeness of him. The only one ever taken was in a large family group, which was stolen from the residence of one of his brothers during the Confederate War." Pidgin, *Theodosia*, 230.

74. George C. Rogers, Jr., *History of Georgetown County*, (Columbia, S.C.: University of South Carolina Press, 1970), 316.

75. Walter B. Edgar and N. Louise Bailey, eds., *The Biographical Dictionary of the South Carolina House of Representatives*, volume IV (1791-1815), pp. 32-35.

76. He refers to the "Cataline conspiracy," in which Lucius Sergius Catalina, a Roman politician, governor of Africa, and conspirator in the time of Julius Caesar, plotted to murder Roman consuls because he was denied a consulship based on unfounded allegations of misconduct. Acquitted, Catalina later ran again for a consulship, was defeated by his political opponent, Cicero, and plotted an unsuccessful political revolt to gain power. Parmet and Hecht, 154, citing Henry Cabot Lodge, ed., *The Works of Alexander Hamilton* (New York: G. P. Putnam/Knickerbocker Press, 1904), X:387.

77. Parmet and Hecht, 153-154, citing AB to William Eustis, August 10, 1800, Massachusetts Historical Society.

78. Parmet and Hecht, 155; Daniels, 205.

79. Parmet and Hecht, 155.

80. TB, New-York, to JA, January 13, 1801, in Davis, *Memoirs*, I:423-424.

81. TB, New-York, to JA, January 13, 1801, in Davis, *Memoirs*, I:424.

82. Joseph Alston may well have "finished his college education" by the time he was seventeen, but his studies consisted of two years at the College of Charleston, one at Princeton, and a degree from neither.

83. The short "manuscript poem of my own," authored by Matthew L. Davis and inserted at this place in his book, has been deleted.

84. Here again, Alston was again more enthusiastic than candid. The author of this book, a New Englander by birth and a twenty-five-year South Carolina Lowcountry resident by choice, could not help but chuckle when reading Alston, who had never visited Vermont, referring to sub-tropical Charleston, with its 90+ degree and 90+ percent humidity summers, referred to as the "Montpelier of the South." In fact, virtually all of the planters who could afford to do so fled Charleston in the muggy, disease-ridden summers for cooler, healthier places in the North Carolina mountains; for the spas of New England; for northern seashore resorts, such as Newport; or for Europe.

85. Anthony Q. Devereaux, *The Rice Princes: A Rice Epoch Revisited* (Columbia, S.C.: The State Co., 1973), v.

86. JA, Charleston, S.C., to TB, December 28, 1800, in Davis, *Memoirs*, I:424-433.

87. TB, Poughkeepsie, N.Y., to JA, January 24, 1801, in Davis, *Memoirs*, II:145.

88. Parmet and Hecht, 163

89. AB, New-York, to JA, January 15, 1801, in Davis, *Memoirs*, II:144.

90. Parmet and Hecht, 168-169.

CHAPTER 5: The Yankee Belle

1. Swick, "Theodosia Burr Alston," 500.

2. Walter B. Edgar and N. Louise Bailey, eds., *The Biographical Directory of the South Carolina House of Representatives*, IV:32-33.

3. Rogow, 194, citing Charles R. King, ed., *The Life and Correspondence of Rufus King* (New York: G.P. Putnam's Sons, 1896), III:459.

4. Swick, "Theodosia Burr Alston," 500, citing Charles Moore, *The Family Life of George Washington* (Boston and New York: Houghton and Mifflin, 1926), 165.

5. Minnie Kendall Lowther, *Blennerhassett Island in Romance and Tragedy* (Rutland, Vermont: The Tuttle Publishing Co., 1936, 157-158.

6. The description comes from the 1945 accession records of this 2" x 2-5/8" miniature at the Mead Art Museum of Amherst College.

7. The latest proof of their relative status was evidenced by archaeologist James L. Michie, who wrote in 1994, "we were asked to investigate

the property [The Oaks, now located on the property of Brookgreen Gardens] with an emphasis on finding and excavating Theodosia's house." Theodosia was still the charismatic half of the couple, which is why Michie did not write "Joseph and Theodosia's house."

8. AB, Albany, to TBA, February 17, 1801, in Davis, *Memoirs*, II:145.

9. AB, Washington, to TBA, March 8, 1801, in Davis, *Memoirs*, II:146.

10. AB, New-York, to TBA, April 5, 1801, in Davis, *Memoirs*, II:149.

11. Tisdale, 32.

12. Tisdale, 34.

13. Tisdale, 38.

14. Tisdale, 48.

15. TBA, Clifton, to AB, November 8, 1803, in Davis, *Memoirs*, II:244.

16. Jacob Motte Alston, "Random Recollections of an Inconspicuous Life," typescript, 1890, pp. 16-17. Miles Brewton House collection.

17. Alston, "Random Recollections," 16-17.

18. It is not known whether the Alstons owned property or constructed a beach house on Sullivan's Island (both are possible but undocumented) or merely visited there while staying in Charleston.

19. Swick, "Theodosia Burr Alston," citing Knapp, *Aaron Burr*, 195.

20. Parmet and Hecht, 170.

21. AB, New-York, to TBA, April 15, 2002, in Davis, *Memoirs*, II:148.

22. Parton, *Life of Aaron Burr*, 298.

23. AB, New-York, to TBA, March 29, 1801, in Davis, *Memoirs*, II:148.

24. AB, New-York, to TBA, April 29, 1801, in Davis, *Memoirs*, II:150.

25. TBA, Charleston, to AJF Prevost, June 10, 1801, Washington University Libraries, St. Louis, Missouri.

26. James L. Michie, *The Oaks Plantation Revealed: An Archaeological Survey of the Home of Joseph and Theodosia Burr Alston, Brookgreen Gardens, Georgetown County, South Carolina*. Research Manuscript 4. (Conway, S.C.: Waccamaw Center for Historical and Cultural Studies, Coastal Carolina University, 1993), p. 10.

27. The house in which he was born remains to be documented. Joseph would not have been born at the Miles Brewton House, for Colonel Alston did not acquire it until after 1791, when he married his second wife, Rebecca Brewton Motte.

28. Alston, "Random Recollections," 5-6.

29. Frederick Law Olmsted, *A Journey in the Seaboard Slave States, With Remarks on their Economy* (New York: Dix & Edwards, 1856), 419.

30. Obituary of Colonel Alston.

31. Jacob Motte Alston, "Random Recollections," 8.

32. Côte, 32-33.

33. Côté, 75-77.

34. "Journal of Josiah Quincy, Jr., 1773," in *Journal of the Massachusetts Historical Society*, 49:446-447.

35. Côté, 20-21.

36. David Duncan Wallace, *South Carolina: A Short History* (Columbia, S.C.: The University of South Carolina Press, 1961), 350-351.

37. Virtually all of the details about The Oaks presented here come from the work of James L. Michie, Associate Director, Waccamaw Center for Historical and Cultural Studies, Coastal Carolina University, Conway, S.C., as published in a series of research papers more fully listed in the bibliography. Additional details and context came from an ongoing exploration of Theodosia's life by the author and Mr. Michie conducted by telephone and correspondence between 1991 and 1994.

38. Michie, Research Manuscript 4 (1993), 1.

39. "Journal of Josiah Quincy, Jr., 1773," in *Proceedings of the Massachusetts Historical Society*, 49:453.

40. Susan H. McMillan, research assistant to James L. Michie, noted that based on the number of nails found at The Oaks, Michie concluded that the house was likely a 1½-story structure similar to another Waccamaw River plantation named, coincidently, "Richmond Hill." See James L. Michie, *Richmond Hill Plantation, 1810-1868: The Discovery of Antebellum Life on a Waccamaw River Rice Plantation* (Spartanburg, S.C.: The Reprint Company, 1990).

41. Michie, Research Manuscript 7 (1995), 7.

42. James L. Michie, *Revealing the Past: The House of Theodosia Burr Alston*, p. 2.

43. Michie, Research Manuscript 5 (1994), 57- 61

44. The garret at The Oaks is noted in Davis, *Memoirs*, II:439.

45. The 1820 census for Georgetown District showed 1,830 whites and 15,773 blacks. Wallace, *Short History*, 710.

46. Rogers, *History of Georgetown County*, 339, 524.

47. "By a Carolinian" (Edward Jenkins Pringle), *Slavery in the Southern States* (Cambridge, Massachusetts: John Bartlett, 1852). For a complete description, see Côté, *Mary's World*, 144-147.

48. Much of the information presented here about South Carolina plantation life and culture and the Alston family was drawn from Côté, *Mary's World: Love, War, and Family Ties in Nineteenth-century Charleston*.

49. Mary Motte Alston Pringle and Rebecca Brewton Pringle, Beneventum Plantation, Georgetown District, to John Julius Pringle, aboard the USS *Concord*, February 27, 1842. John Julius Pringle Collection, South Carolina Historical Society, Charleston, S.C.

50. Jane Pringle, Greenfield Plantation, to MMP, c/o Smith & Coffin, Charleston, December 1, 1845. Mitchell-Pringle Papers, South Carolina Historical Society, Charleston, S.C.

51. AB, Washington, to TBA, December 6, 1803, in Davis, *Memoirs*, I:250.

52. AB, New-York, to The Hon. William Eustis, Boston, June 24, 1801, in Kline, II: 599.

53. Dwight Whalen, *Lovers Guide to Niagara Falls* (Niagara Falls, Ontario: Horseshoe Press, 1990), 3.

54. Kline, II:599, citing Papers of Aaron Burr, New-York Historical Society, 4:1063.

55. Elizabeth McKinsey, *Niagara Falls: Icon of the American Sublime* (New York: Cambridge University Press, 178-179.

56. AB, New-York, to TBA, August 20, 1801, in Davis, *Memoirs*, II:152.

57. AB, New-York, to Thomas Morris, September 18, 1801, in Davis, *Memoirs*, II:153.

58. "John Vanderlyn," online at http://www.niagaracc.suny.edu/homepags/Knechtel/vanderlyn.html April 5, 2002.

59. Lindsay, 56.

60. Lindsay, 56.

61. Stone, II: 457.

62. Kennedy, 240.

63. AB, New-York, to TBA, August 20, 1801, in Davis, Memoirs, II:152.

64. TBA, Dumfries, Va., to AJF Prevost, New Rochelle, New York, October 1, 1801, Washington University Libraries, St. Louis, Missouri.

65. Kline, II:599.

66. AB, New-York, to TBA, November 3, 1801, in Davis, *Memoirs*, II:155.

67. Stone, II:438.

68. AB, New-York, to TBA, November 9, 1801, in Davis, *Memoirs*, II:157.

69. AB, New-York, to TBA, November 9, 1801, in Davis, *Memoirs*, II:156.

70. AB, New-York, to TBA, November 20, 1801, in Davis, *Memoirs*, II: 159-160.

71. JA, Columbia, to TBA, Emmett Collection, New York Public Library, courtesy Blennerhassett Island Historical State Park.

72. AB, New-York, to JA, December 13, 1801, in Davis, *Memoirs*, II:162-163.

73. AB, New-York, to JA, February 2, 1802, in Davis, *Memoirs*, II:170.

74. AB, Washington, to TBA, January 16, 1802, in Davis, *Memoirs*, II:168-169.

75. AB, Washington, to TBA, January 22, 1802, in Davis, *Memoirs*, II:170.

76. Parmet and Hecht, 183, citing TBA to Frances Prevost, March 24, 1802, Burr Papers, New-York Historical Society.

77. The Republic of the Seven Isles (the Ionian Islands, also knows as the Eptánisos), are strung out along the west coast of Greece. Owned in the 1790s by Venice, they were coveted by Napoléon.

78. AB, New-York, to TBA, December 8, 1801, in Davis, *Memoirs*, II:162.

79. AB, Washington, to TBA, February 2, 1802, in Davis, *Memoirs*, II:172.

80. AB, Washington, to TBA, February 23, 1802, in Davis, *Memoirs*, II:177-178.

81. AB, Washington, to TBA, March 4, 1802, in Davis, *Memoirs*, II:181.

82. AB, Washington, to JA, March 8, 1802, in Davis, *Memoirs*, II:184.

83. The 1802 Vanderlyn portrait of Theodosia was probably executed solely in New York, where she could have sat for him during her trip that year. It is unlikely that the painter, who was already severely overworked, could or would have made the trip to South Carolina that Burr had suggested.

84. AB, Washington, to TBA, April 5, 1802, in Davis, *Memoirs*, II:195.

85. Revolutionary War heroine Rebecca Brewton Motte (1738-1815), was the mother-in-law of Col. William Alston's second wife, Mary Brewton Motte. Her rice plantation, Eldorado, was situated on the Santee River in Georgetown District, a half-day's ride south of Clifton. AB, Clifton [Plantation, Georgetown District, S.C.], to TBA, May 3, 1802, in Davis, *Memoirs*, II:196-197.

86. Charleston *Times*, May 14, 1802.

87. Sources differ on the date of Aaron Burr Alston's birth in 1802, which has been stated as May 22, May 29, "mid-May," and "the third week of May." There was no mention of the event in the Charleston newspapers; no date carved on his tombstone at The Oaks; and no date was recorded by Burr's early biographers, Knapp, Davis, or Parton; or by Theodosia's biographer, Pidgin.

88. Parmet and Hecht, 183, citing JA to TBA, August 22, 1802, Simon Gratz Collection, Historical Society of Pennsylvania.

89. TBA, New-York, to JA, June 24, 1802, in Davis, *Memoirs*, II:200-201.

90. Tonka beans: fragrant, black, nutlike seeds of the tonka bean tree from South America. They were used in perfumes and medicines, to add flavor to tobacco snuff, and as a substitute for vanilla.

91. TBA, New-York, to JA, June 26, 1802, in Davis, *Memoirs*, II:203.

92. TBA, New-York, to Natalie de Lage, July 5, 1802, in Davis, *Memoirs*, II:205.

93. TBA, New-York, to JA, June 28, 1802, in Davis, *Memoirs*, II:204.

94. Lomask, I:328-329, citing TBA to Frances Prevost, July 18, 1802, Burr Papers, New-York Historical Society.

95. Lomask, I:329.

96. AB, New-York, to JA, September 8, 1802, in Davis, *Memoirs*, II: 211.

97. TBA, New-York, to JA, September 30, 1802, in Davis, *Memoirs*, II:212.

98. TBA, New-York, to JA, September 3, 1802, in Davis, *Memoirs*, II:207-208.

99. TBA, New-York, to JA, October 30, 1802, in Davis, *Memoirs*, II:213.

100. AB, New-York, to JA, November 5, 1802, in Davis, *Memoirs*, II:215.

101. AB, New-York, to TBA, December 4, 1802, in Davis, *Memoirs*, II:215.

102. TBA, Clifton, to AB, March 17, 1802, in Davis, *Memoirs*, II:220-221.

103. TBA, Washington, to AB, October 16, 1803, in Davis, *Memoirs*, II:241-242.

104. TBA, Lumberton, to AB, October 29, 1803, in Davis, *Memoirs*, II:243-244.

105. Lomask, I:197-198.

106. TBA, Clifton, to AB, November 8, 1803, in Davis, *Memoirs*, II:244.

107. AB, Washington, to TBA, December 6, 1803, in Davis, *Memoirs*, II:249-250.

108. AB, New-York, to TBA, March 28, 1804, in Davis, *Memoirs*, II: 281.

109. AB, New-York, to TBA, November 7, 1803, in Davis, *Memoirs*, II:245.

110. AB, Washington, January 17, 1804, to TBA, in Davis, *Memoirs* II: 268.

111. AB, New-York, May 8, 1804, to TBA, in Davis, *Memoirs*, II:287.

112. AB, Washington, to TBA, December 4, 1803, in Davis, *Memoirs*, II:247.

113. AB, New-York, June 11, 1804, to TBA, in Davis, *Memoirs*, II:288.

114. TBA, Clifton, to AB, December 10, 1803, in Davis, *Memoirs*, II:252.

115. Tisdale, 54-57; Gavaghan, 21-23.

116. This was the traditional time period for the planters' "summer migration," when they departed their plantations for cooler, healthier climates. AB, Washington, January 5, 1804, to Natalie Delage Sumter, in Davis, *Memoirs*, II:272.

117. That his garret was stocked with wine showed that Burr enjoyed Madeira, which could be stored warm or hot.

118. By "Ada," Burr was referring to a "dah," the Gullah term for a black nursemaid. AB, New-York, April 25, 1804, to TBA, in Davis, *Memoirs*, II:283-284.

119. AB, Washington, to TBA, January 3, 1804, in Davis, *Memoirs*, II:266.

120. AB, New-York, May 1, 1804, to TBA, in Davis, *Memoirs*, II:285.

CHAPTER 6: The Clouds of Weehawken

1. AB, Washington, to TBA, June 24, 1804, in Davis, *Memoirs*, II:289-290

2. Theodosia either carried out this destruction request, or the potentially harmful letters in question survived but went down with her on the *Patriot*, or Burr's biographer, Matthew Davis destroyed them, for few letters meeting this description have survived.

3. These letters in the "blue boxes" may have ultimately been consigned to Theodosia as part of the collection sealed inside the "tin boxes," which also went down with her on the *Patriot*.

4. "Put" was a common name for a carriage horse.

5. "Clara," a woman who evidently had South Carolina ties, remains unidentified.

6. AB, New-York, to TBA, July 10, 1804, in Davis, *Memoirs*, II:322-323.

7. AB, New-York, to Joseph Alston, July 10, 1804, in Davis, *Memoirs*, II:325-326.

8. AB, New-York, July 10, 1804, to Joseph Alston, in Davis, *Memoirs*, II:324-326.

9. Parmet and Hecht, 209.

10. Mark O. Hatfield, with the Senate Historical Office, *Vice Presidents of the United States, 1789-1993* (Washington: U.S. Government Printing Office, 1997), 31-44; online as "Aaron Burr (1801-1809)," at http://www.senate.gov/learning/stat_vp3.html, May 5, 2002, citing Robert Troup to Rufus King, May 6, 1799.

11. Parmet and Hecht, 159.

12. Everett Somerville Brown, ed., *William Plumer's Memorandum of Proceedings in the United States Senate, 1803-1807* (New York: MacMillan, 1923, 74-75.

13. Parmet and Hecht, 173, citing AB to William Eustis, April 28, 1801, Massachusetts Historical Society.

14. Hatfield, "Aaron Burr," citing Mary-Jo Kline, "Aaron Burr as a Symbol of Corruption in the New Republic," in *Before Watergate: Problems of Corruption in American Society* (New York: Columbia University Press, 1978), 69-76; Parmet and Hecht, 168-193.

15. Hatfield, "Aaron Burr," citing Dumas Malone, *Jefferson the President, First Term, 1801-1805* (Boston: Little, Brown & Co., 1970), 123-124.

16. Buckner F. Melton, Jr., *Aaron Burr: Conspiracy to Treason.* (New York: John Wiley & Sons, Inc., 2002), 38.

17. Parmet and Hecht, 202, citing Harold C. Syrett and Jean G. Cooke, eds., *Interview in Weehawken: The Burr-Hamilton Duel* (Middletown, Conn.: Middletown University Press, 1960), 45.

18. Parmet and Hecht, 202.

19. Rogow, 237, citing Harold C. Syrett et al., *The Papers of Alexander Hamilton* (New York: Columbia University Press, 1961-1980), 26:619.

20. Melton, 45.

21. Melton, 45-46, citing Everett Somerville Brown, ed., *William Plumer's Memorandum of Proceedings in the United States Senate, 1803-1807* (New York: The Macmillan Co., 1923), 517-518.

22. Melton, 46, citing Alexander Hamilton to Robert G. Harper, February 19, 1804, *The Hamilton Papers*, 26:192.

23. Rogow, 55, 239; Daniels, 383.

24. Rogow, 239, citing Gertrude Atherton, *The Conqueror: A Dramatized Biography of Alexander Hamilton* (New York: Frederick A. Stokes, 1902), 509, 535.

25. Robert Hendrickson, *Hamilton* (New York: Mason/Charter, 1976), 2 vols.

26. Gore Vidal, *Burr: A Novel* (New York: Random House, 1973), 271-272.

27. Rogow, 240, citing a personal communication between himself and Vidal.

28. Lomask, I:160; Rogow, 240.

29. Rogow, 48, 240.

30. Patricia Love, Ph.D., *The Emotional Incest Syndrome: What to Do When a Parent's Love Rules Your Life* (New York: Bantam Doubleday Dell, 1991).

31. The series of Burr's letters and Hamilton's replies preceding the duel may be found in Davis, *Memoirs*, I:293-321 and elsewhere.

32. Lomask, I:352-353.

33. Henry Adams, *History of the United States During the Administrations of Jefferson and Madison* (Chicago: University of Chicago Press, 1967).

34. Parmet and Hecht, 214.

35. William K. Bixby, *The Private Journal of Aaron Burr* (Rochester, New York: The Genesee Press, 1903), I:vi-vii.

36. Parton, II:13-14.

37. AB, New-York, to Joseph Alston, July 13, 1804, in Davis, *Memoirs*, I:327.

38. Pidgin, *Theodosia*, 267.

39. Kline, II:886.

40. AB, Philadelphia, to TBA, August 3, 1804, in Davis, *Memoirs*, II:331.

41. AB, Philadelphia, to TBA, August 11, 1804, in Davis, *Memoirs*, II:332.

42. AB, St. Simonds, to Charles Biddle, Esqr., Philadelphia, September 1, 1804, in Kline, II:894.

43. AB, St. Simon's, to TBA, August 31, 1804, in Davis, *Memoirs*, II:333-335.

44. AB, St. Simon's, to TBA, August 31 and September 1, 1804, in Davis, *Memoirs*, II:333-335.

45. Peter Yates was "my now valet," a "black boy purchased last fall" (1803). AB, probably Savannah, to TBA, Tuesday, October 2, 1804, in Davis, *Memoirs*, II:344.

46. Tisdale, 74.

47. AB, Washington, to JA, November 5, 1804, in Davis, *Memoirs*, II:349.

48. AB, Richmond, to TBA, October 31, 1804, in Davis, *Memoirs*, II:348.

49. Lomask, I:368-369.

50. On November 17, 1804, Burr wrote to Theodosia, "Leave off the vice-president, &c., in the direction of your letters. Let it simply be A.B. or Colonel B. Tell Mari so." Davis, *Memoirs*, II:351. It is not known whether this signified that Burr was considering resigning at that time.

51. Anthony Merry, Philadelphia, to Lord Harrowby, August 6, 1804, in Kline, II:891-892.

52. AB, Washington, to TBA, March 10, 1805, in Davis, *Memoirs*, II: 359-360.

53. Maria Alston (b. 1778), Joseph's older sister, married first Sir John Nisbet and then Dr. John Murray.

54. Charlotte Alston (1785-1817), his younger sister, married South Carolina Governor John Lyde Wilson and survived Joseph by one year.

55. Catherine Brown, her half-sister.

56. Frederic Bartow Prevost, her half-brother.

57. Sally Burr Reeve, Aaron Burr's sister, who married Tapping Reeve.

58. Peggy Gallatin, a slave at Richmond Hill.

59. TBA, n.p., to JA, August 6, 1805, in Davis, *Memoirs*, II:439-441.

CHAPTER 7: Codeword: Emperor

1. Lomask, II:141.

2. William H. Safford, *The Blennerhassett Papers* (Cincinnati: Moore, Wilstach & Baldwin, 1864), 66.

3. Lomask, II:6.

4. Lomask, II:13.

5. Lomask, II:32-33.

6. AB, Philadelphia, to JA, March 22, 1805, in Davis, *Memoirs*, II:364-365.

7. AB, Philadelphia, to TBA, March 29, 1805, in Davis, *Memoirs*, II:365.

8. For a more detailed summary of Burr's "Western adventure," see Kline, II:919-925. For a book-length treatment, see Buckner F. Melton, Jr., *Aaron Burr: Conspiracy to Treason*.

9. AB, Pittsburgh, to TBA, April 30, 1805, in Davis, *Memoirs*, II:368.

10. Swick, *An Island Called Eden,* 16.

11. Melton, 74.

12. Melton, 75.

13. Norris F. Schneider, *Blennerhassett Island and the Burr Conspiracy* (Columbus, Ohio: The Ohio Historical Society, 1966),

14. Swick, *An Island Called Eden*, 28.

15. Swick, *An Island Called Eden*, 28-29.

16. John Dos Passos, "The Conspiracy and Trial of Aaron Burr," *American Heritage*, XVII, No. 2 (February, 1966), 71.

17. AB, Lexington, Kentucky, to TBA, May 23, 1805, in Davis, *Memoirs*, II:370.

18. AB, Lexington, Kentucky, to TBA, May 23, 1805, in Davis, *Memoirs*, II:371.

19. TBA, n.p., to Joseph Alston, August 6, 1805, in Davis, *Memoirs*, II: 439-442.

20. Lomask, II:75.

21. Lomask, II:82.

22. Pidgin, *Theodosia*, 273.

23. Dos Passos, 73.

24. Lomask II: 39.

25. Dos Passos, 74.

26. Safford, 118.

27. Lomask, II:112.

28. The detailed analysis performed by Dr. Mary-Jo Kline and her staff at the New-York Historical Society on the ciphered "smoking gun" letter may be found in Kline, II:986-987.

29. Kline, II:987.

30. Swick, *An Island Called Eden*, 40.

31. Swick, *An Island Called Eden*, 40.

32. Parton, II:59-60.

33. Lomask, II:120.

34. TBA to Frederick Prevost, August 18, 1806, Burr-Purkitt Family Papers.

35. Swick, "Theodosia Burr Alston," 503, citing TBA to Frederick Prevost, August 18, 1806, Burr-Purkitt Family Papers.

36. Lomask, II:137.

37. Lomask, II:125.

38. Schneider, 20.

39. Lomask, II:135.

40. Lomask, II:131.

41. Parton, II:66.

42. Lomask, II:132.

43. Morris B. Belknap, Marietta, Ohio, to Timothy E. Danielson, Brimfield, October 11, 1806, in William Eaton to James Madison, U.S. Secretary of State Letters in Relation to Burr's Conspiracy, Acc. 748, Library of Congress.

44. Schneider, 22.

45. Safford, 182.

46. Lomask, II:214-215.

47. Daniels, 366.

48. Parton, II:356.

49. Joseph and Theodosia Alston, The Oaks, to Harman Blennerhassett, Natchez, Mississippi, June 22, 1807, Blennerhassett Island Historical State Park archives; also Safford, 255-257.

50. Joseph and Theodosia Alston, The Oaks, to Harman Blennerhassett, Natchez, Mississippi, June 22, 1807, Blennerhassett Island Historical State Park archives; also Safford, 257.

51. Lomask, II:223-224.

52. The name of the tavern was provided through the courtesy of W.L.D. "Bill" Marion, Esq., of Chester, South Carolina, and his mother, Ann Davidson Marion.

53. Safford, 225.

54. Safford, 225.

55. Lomask, 224-2125; Lowther, 47-48.

56. Lucille McMaster, "How Aaron Burr's Escape Was Foiled," in the *Atlanta Journal and Constitution,* May 7, 1961.

57. The "Aaron Burr Bench" is now preserved at the Chester County Historical Society Museum, Chester, South Carolina.

58. "Perkins returned [to Chester] and purchased a gig." Safford, 226.

59. Lomask, II:222; Lowther, 41.

60. AB, Richmond, to TBA, March 27, 1807, in Davis, *Memoirs,* II:405.

61. AB, Richmond, to TBA, April 26, 1807, in Davis, *Memoirs,* II:405

62. AB, Richmond, to TBA, April 16, 1807, in Davis, *Memoirs,* II:405.

63. AB [Richmond penitentiary], to TBA, July 3, 1807, in Davis, *Memoirs,* II:409.

64. AB [Richmond penitentiary], to TBA, July 6, 1807, in Davis, *Memoirs,* II:410.

65. AB [Richmond penitentiary], to TBA, June 24, 1807, in Davis, *Memoirs,* II:408.

66. AB [Richmond penitentiary], to TBA, June 24, 1807, in Davis, *Memoirs,* II:408.

67. "The Treason Trial of Aaron Burr," a succinct summary of the trial by Professor Douglas Linder of the University of Missouri- Kansas City School of Law, may be found online at http://www.jurist.law. pitt.edu/trials21.htm.

68. Safford, 270.

69. Safford, 274.

70. Margaret Blennerhassett, Natchez, August 3, 1807, to Harman Blennerhassett, in Safford, 273.

71. Safford, 274.

72. Safford, 278-279.

73. Linder, "The Treason Trial of Aaron Burr."

74. Lowther, 62.

75. Linder, "The Treason Trial of Aaron Burr."

76. Lowther, 64-65. The letter may have been written to her close friend and sister-in-law, Frances Ann Bartow, in Pelham, N.Y.

77. Linder, "The Treason Trial of Aaron Burr."

CHAPTER 8: The Expatriate's Daughter

1. Parton, II:162.

2. Pidgin, *Theodosia,* 282; Bixby, I:1.

3. Bixby, I:3.

4. Davis, *Journal,* I:9.

5. Lomask, II:296; Stillwell, 3.

6. Parton, II: 163; Van Doren, 239.

7. TBA, Rocky River Springs, S.C., to JA, June 22, 1809, Emmett Collection, New York Public Library.

8. TBA, New Rochelle, N.Y., to William Eustis, Boston, October 3, 1808, Aaron Burr and Burriana Autographs and Documents, C.P.G. Fuller Collection, Portfolio III, Box 2, Item 15, Princeton University Library.

9. TBA, New Rochelle, N.Y., to William Eustis, Boston, October 3, 1808, *ibid.*

10. TBA, New Rochelle, N.Y., to William Eustis, Boston, October 3, 1808, *ibid.*

11. TBA, New Rochelle, N.Y., to William Eustis, Boston, October 3, 1808, *ibid.*

12. TBA, Pelham, N.Y., to AB, December 5, 1808, in Matthew L. Davis, *The Private Journal of Aaron Burr, During His Residence of Four Years In Europe* (New York: Harper & Brothers, 1858, 2 vol.) I:115.

13. TBA, New-York, to AB, October 31, 1808, in Davis, *Journal*, I:72.

14. Davis, *Journal*, I:249.

15. TBA to AB, in Parton (1858), frontis.

16. Todd, *The True Aaron Burr*, 68-70.

17. TBA to Frederick Prevost, September 12, 1809, Burr-Purkitt Papers.

18. Natalie Sumter, Washington, to Mrs. Mary Hooper, Stateburg, S.C., August 2, 1809, in Daniels, 389-390.

19. Bradford, *Wives*, 116.

20. Safford, 535-536.

21. Parmet and Hecht, 322.

22. Lomask, II:357.

23. Lomask, II:357.

CHAPTER 9: The Voyage of the *Patriot*

1. TBA, Seashore [S.C.] to AB, July 12, 1812, in Mark Van Doren, ed., *Correspondence of Aaron Burr and His Daughter, Theodosia* (New York: Covici-Friede, Inc., 1929), 339 (not included in Davis, *Memoirs*).

2. TBA, Seashore [S.C.] to AB, August 12, 1812, in Van Doren, 339-340.

3. JA to AB, July 26, 1812, in Van Doren, 343-344.

4. "Joseph Alston," *Biographical Directory of the South Carolina House of Representatives*, IV (1791-1815): 32-35.

5. TBA, Seashore [S.C.] to AB, August 12, 1812, in Van Doren, 339-340.

6. Wallace, *History of South Carolina*, II: 389.

7. Parton, I: 247.

8. Swick, "Theodosia Burr Alston," 504.

9. TBA, Seashore [S.C.], to AB, August 12, 1812, in Van Doren, 340.

10. Greene says he arrived in Charleston, which suggests a sea voyage, as tiny Georgetown was not a frequent destination for southbound ships. If, as some writers have suggested, he came by land, it would have been odd for him to have passed through Georgetown

without stopping, as Charleston lies two days' carriage ride past the Alston home at The Oaks, which lies ten miles north of Georgetown.

11. Parmet & Hecht, 329.

12. Davis, *Memoirs*, II:428.

13. Davis, *Memoirs*, II:428.

14. Georgetown historian, Patricia Davis Doyle, a native of Georgetown, graduate of the University of South Carolina, and owner of the Mann-Doyle Mansion on Front St. (built 1770) where the event is supposed to have taken place, does not believe the "old rumor" of a ball and has not been able to find any documentation to support it.

15. JA, Columbia, to AB, January 19, 1813, in Van Doren, 345-346.

16. JA, Columbia, to AB, January 19, 1813, in Van Doren, 345-346.

17. James L. Michie, "Theodosia! Some Facts Relating to the Last Days of Theodosia Burr Alston and the *Patriot*," *Carologue*, Summer 1998, pp. 16-20. Michie was former associate director of the Waccamaw Center for Historical Studies of Coastal Carolina University and associate principal investigator and program director of the South Carolina Institute of Archaeology and Anthropology, University of South Carolina. He directed the excavation of Joseph and Theodosia's home, The Oaks, now part of Brookgreen Gardens.

18. "Several of her devoted servants," per Jacob Motte Alston, New York Times *Saturday Review of Books*, May 24, 1902).

19. Burr's papers "sealed in tin boxes": Parton, II: 398-400, citing an article in the *New York Evening Post* "in the early part of 1858." Burr's first biographer, Samuel L. Knapp, confirmed that the papers were lost with Theodosia when in 1835 he wrote, "It is necessary that the memoirs of Colonel Burr should be written in his lifetime, as a great portion of his papers were lost with his daughter, on her passage from Charleston [sic], South Carolina, to New-York, to visit her father." Knapp, viii. The editors of *Political Correspondence and Public Papers of Aaron Burr*, I:xxx, state that "Burr left a trunk containing many of his more important manuscripts with his daughter, Theodosia Alston. This trunk was lost when Mrs. Alston met her tragic fate."

20. Guns stowed below deck: per Timothy Greene.

21. "Tierces of rice": per Jacob Motte Alston, *New York Times Saturday Review of Books*, May 24, 1902; "laden with casks of rice to defray her expenses": Jacob Motte Alston, "Random Recollections of an Inconspicuous Life," 17.)

22. W.T. Block, citing the *Galveston Daily News*, 1875-1907.

23. Minnigerode, *Lives & Times*, 142.

24. "Probably painted out her name": Minnigerode, *Lives & Times*, 142.

25. Minnigerode, *Lives & Times*, 142

26. JA, Columbia, to AB, January 19, 1813, in Davis, *Memoirs*, II:430.

27. JA, Charleston, S.C., January 31, 1813, to AB, in Van Doren, 345-346.

28. JA, Columbia, S.C., January 15, 1813, to TBA, in Davis, *Memoirs*, II: 428.

29. JA, Columbia, S.C., to TBA, January 19, 1813, in Davis, *Memoirs*, II: 429.

30. JA, Columbia, to AB, January 19, 1813, in Van Doren, 345-346.

31. JA, Charleston to AB, January 31, 1813, in Van Doren, 346-347.

32. JA, n.p., to AB, February 25, 1813, in Davis, *Memoirs*, II:430-432.

33. Todd, *The True Aaron Burr*, 54.

34. Parmet & Hecht, p. 330, citing AB to unknown, March 29, 1813, Wetmore Papers, Yale.

35. Wandell and Minnigerode, II:298-299.

36. Parton was mistaken. The *Patriot* departed from Georgetown.

37. Parton, II: 248.

38. Jacob Motte Alston first recorded the "letter to the Admiral" statement in an 1890 typescript memoir, "Random Recollections of an Inconspicuous Life," 17. His 1902 letter to *The New York Times* is the first published source for this information. Burr's early biographers, Davis (1837) and Parton (1857), never mentioned it, but post-1902 writers, including Pidgin (1907), Wandell & Minnigerode (1927), Schachner (1961) Parmet & Hecht (1967), Daniels (1970), and Lomask (1982), accepted the statement at face value.

39. Pidgin, *Theodosia*, 393-394.

40. James L. Michie, "Theodosia!" 18.

41. James L. Michie, "Theodosia!" 18.

42. James L. Michie, "Theodosia!" 18, 20.

43. James L. Michie, "Theodosia!" 18.

44. Parton II: 248-249.

45. Schachner, 515.

46. Schachner, 515.

47. Burr's interment ceremony: http://mondrian.princeton.edu/CampusWWW/Companion/burr_aaron_jr.html.

48. Parton, II: 368-369.

49. AB to JA, November 15, 1815. *Burr Papers*, pp. 1165 ff.

50. JA to AB, February 16, 1816. *Burr Papers*, p. 1169n.

51. Michie, Research Manuscript 4, 18, citing JA, January 25, 1815, to Charles Biddle, Princeton University Library, Aaron Burr and Burriana Autographs and Documents, Portfolio III, Box 2, Item 2.

52. Pidgin, 356.

53. Daniels, 405; Tisdale, 88.

54. Margaret Blennerhassett, *The Widow of the Rock and other Poems, by a Lady* (Montreal, Quebec, Canada: R.V. Starhawk, Printer, 1824, 50-52.

CHAPTER 10: Fates Worse Than Death

1. A search of newspapers held by U.S. libraries in 2002 revealed none with copies of the *New York Advertiser* for this date, but in 1971, Dr. Ray Swick obtained a photocopy of the newspaper article from the

American Antiquarian Society, Worcester, Massachusetts, which he kindly loaned me.

2. Stanley Faye, "Privateersmen of the Gulf and Their Prizes," *Louisiana Historical Society Quarterly*, 1939, 1083-1084.

3. Faye cites the New York *Mercantile Advertiser*, June 23, 1820.

4. Parmet and Hecht, 330-331, citing "newspaper clippings," in the New York Public Library. Schachner, 500, also dismissed the tale as "odious," named the newspaper [the *Carolina Spartan*] but failed to give the publication date.

5. Pidgin, *Theodosia*, 359, 398-399. Neither Lomask nor Kline makes any mention of a William L. Stone.

6. I searched the microfilm of *The Mobile Commercial Register and Patriot* for Thursday, May 23, 1833, and found no stories relating to this subject.

7. "Theodosia's Fate Still Subject of Debate," in *The Virginian-Pilot* and *The Ledger-Star*, Norfolk, Virginia, August 10, 2001; also telephone interview with Mr. Schwarzer, May 7, 2002.

8. Pidgin, *Theodosia*, 365.

9. Pidgin, *Theodosia*, 366.

10. This story is contained in W. T. Block's online article, "A Tale of Jean Baptiste's Brass Cannon," at www.wtblock.com/wtblockjr/jean.html on November 19, 2001. The article cites the *Galveston Daily News* of January 4, 1875; March 6, 1893; March 3, 1907; "and other papers." This author did not find any reference to Theodosia or the *Patriot* in the named issues of the *Galveston Daily News*.

11. As regards the photographic history and use of tintypes in Charleston, I am again indebted to Charleston's Jack Thomson, author of *Charleston At War* (Thomas Publications, 2000).

12. Dr. Alexander Jones of Mobile, Alabama, stated in a letter dated July 19, 1825, and published in various places, including the Charleston *Courier*, August 3, 1835, that one of the two men executed was named Foster, and that "He was without family, and kept a grog shop... He was an illiterate man, and probably never read anything on the subject," noted Milton Lomask, author of *Aaron Burr*, in a letter to Dr. Ray Swick, November 12, 1979. Courtesy Dr. Ray Swick.

13. Todd, *The True Aaron Burr*, 73-74.

14. "Mysterious Theodosia," online at www.theoutlaws.com/table2c.htm on December 29, 2001. Neither the author nor the source of the story was given or could be obtained.

15. Online at http://www.theoutlaws.com/people3.htm on June 26, 2002.

16. Cornelia Mitchell Parsons, *A Secret of the Sea* (New York: J.S. Ogilvie Publishing Co., 1896), 128-130.

17. Edward R. Outlaw, Jr., and Louise Greenleaf Outlaw, *Old Nag's Head* (Norfolk, Virginia: Liskey Lithograph Corp., 1956), 27; also Wandell and Minnigerode, II:300.

18. Genevieve Wimsatt, "Was She Theodosia Burr? The Tale of the 'Female Stranger,'" in *The Mentor* (Springfield, Ohio: The Croswell Publishing Co.), October 1928, 30-31.

19. "A Lady Vanishes," in Adi-Kent Thomas Jeffrey, *The Bermuda Triangle* (New York: Warner Paperback Library, 1975), 55-56.

20. Dane's name is not mentioned in any of the standard works on Burr by Parton, Pidgin, Wandell and Minnigerode, Schachner, McCaleb, Lomask, or Kline.

21. R.J. Cannaday, "The Mystery of Theodosia Burr," in *The News and Courier* (Charleston, S.C.), August 4, 1963, 6-C.

22. Bradford, *Wives*, 92. The portrait labeled "Theodosia Burr" opposite page 94 of Bradford's book bears no resemblance to any known image of Theodosia, and is obviously from a much later period.

CHAPTER 11: Literary Kudzu

1. Pidgin, *Theodosia*, 364.

2. Eric Hause, "The Outer Banks: The Fate of Theodosia Burr," online at www.coastalguide.com/packet/theodosiaburr.htm on November 3, 2001.

3. *Contemporary Authors Online*. The Gale Group, 2000. Reproduced in *Biography Resource Center*. Farmington Hills, Michigan: The Gale Group, 2001. http://www.galenet.com/servlet/BioRC.

4. *Contemporary Authors Online*. The Gale Group, 2000. Reproduced in *Biography Resource Center*. Farmington Hills, Michigan: The Gale Group, 2001. http://www.galenet.com/servlet/BioRC.

5. Anya Seton, *My Theodosia* (New York: Grossett & Dunlap, 1941), v.

6. Seton, 39.

7. Seton, 141.

8. Interviews by the author with Genevieve Chandler Peterkin and Alberta Quattlebaum, February 18 and 21, 2002.

CHAPTER 12: The Mystery of the Nag's Head Portrait

1. February 22, 1904, in Pidgin, *Theodosia*, 422-426.

2. Anna Overman later stated that she visited Mrs. Mann's house with her father "many times." Pidgin, *Theodosia*, 390.

3. The Tilletts were well-known Outer Bankers in nineteenth-century North Carolina. Outlaw, passim.

4. The eyes in the Nag's Head portrait are, in fact, very dark brown. The rest of the description is accurate, but the "plain gilt frame, with but a small, beading on the inner edge" has been replaced with one more elegant.

5. Pidgin, *Theodosia*, 422-425. The Nag's Head story also appears in the *Philadelphia Times* of February 20, 1880, and elsewhere.

6. Outlaw, 55.

7. Pidgin, *Theodosia,* 385

8. Pidgin, *Theodosia,* 384.

9. John Hill Wheeler, a well-known North Carolina historian, was the author of *Historical Sketches of North Carolina* (1851) and *Reminiscences and Memoirs of North Carolina and Eminent North Carolinians* (1884).

10. Pidgin, *Theodosia,* 387.

11. *The Economist,* Elizabeth City, N.C., July 31, 1888, in Pidgin, *Theodosia,* 385.

12. Arthur C. Mack, in the *New York Times Saturday Review of Books,* per Pidgin, *Theodosia,* 382.

13. Pidgin, *Theodosia,* 379-380.

14. Pidgin, *Theodosia,* 377.

15. Sale, 256.

16. Dr. Pool died in 1887, and the portrait was inherited by his daughter, who lived in his former home in Elizabeth City, N.C., at the time.

17. Todd, *The True Aaron Burr.* 76.

18. Pidgin, *Theodosia,* 394.

19. Pool's letter is part of the Alston-Pringle-Frost Collection at the South Carolina Historical Society, Charleston, S.C. The photograph is part of the Miles Brewton House collection.

20. Pidgin, *Theodosia,* 417-418.

21. Charles Burr Todd, Toy House, Washington Crossing, Titusville, N.J., May 24, 1915, to Miss Susan P. Frost, Charleston, S.C. Alston-Pringle-Frost Collection, South Carolina Historical Society. The letter was accompanied by a high-quality copy photograph of the Nag's Head portrait.

22. Pidgin, *Theodosia,* 389.

23. John H. Wheeler, "Sketch of the Life and Character of Aaron Burr and His Daughter Theodosia Burr Alston, Delivered before the Historical Society of the State of North Carolina at the Annual Commencement of the University at Chapel Hill on the 6th day of June, 1878. The speech was reprinted in part in "'Nag's Head' Portrait of Theodosia Burr is Exhibited for First Time in North Carolina," in the Georgetown (S.C.) *Times,* December 25, 1936.

24. Sale, 257.

25. Lewis Walpole Library provenance records for the "Nag's Head Portrait." Copies of the accession and provenance records, and a color copy of the portrait, were made for the author in January 2002.

26. Lewis Walpole Library provenance records.

27. John Harden, "The Disappearance of Theodosia Burr," *Fate Magazine,* June 1954, 25.

28. Lewis Walpole Library provenance records.

29. Lewis Walpole Library provenance records.

30. Dos Passos, 8.

31. Lewis Walpole Library provenance records, also letter from Dr. Maggie Powell, Lewis Walpole Library, May 30, 2002.

32. Stillwell, 61. Kenneth C. Lindsay, who researched the exhibition catalog, *The Works of John Vanderlyn, From Tammany to the Capital* (University Art Gallery, State University of New York at Binghamton, 1970), p. 129, wrote of Stillwell, "For information concerning the Burr portraits we are indebted to and burdened by the basic study by Dr. Stillwell. The data he obtained from people living in the 1880s is valuable, indeed, it is the sole source of information for some of the Burr portraits; but his conclusions are sometimes insupportable." The speculations and statements Stillwell made about the Nag's Head portrait exemplify this problem.

33. Stillwell, 61.

34. The ebb and flow of artists through the South Carolina Lowcountry was surveyed in Anna Wells Rutledge, *Artists in the Life of Charleston* (Columbia, S.C.: University of South Carolina Press, 1940; reprinted, with a new preface by John Morrill Bryan, 1980).

35. Harden, 24.

36. The Sully portrait of Mary Motte Alston Pringle hangs in the south parlour of the Miles Brewton House in Charleston; those of Col. and Mrs. Alston hang in Charleston's Gibbes Museum of Art.

37. In 1940, Charleston art historian Anna Wells Rutledge also attributed the "1809-1811" portrait of Theodosia (profile facing left, black dress, sheer lace collar, at the New-York Historical Society) to Vanderlyn. Rutledge presented no explanation for the attribution and may simply have accepted what the N.Y.H.S. had been told—probably by Stillwell—about its origins. The attribution of this portrait to Vanderlyn has been challenged. See *Artists in the Life of Charleston*, 175, figure 17.

38. Stillwell, p. 62.

39. State University of New York at Niagara Falls. "John Vanderlyn," online at http://www.sunyniagara.cc.ny.us/homepags/Knechtel/vanderlyn.html; also Kenneth C. Lindsay, *The Works of John Vanderlyn, From Tammany to the Capital* (University Art Gallery, State University of New York at Binghamton, 1970.

40. Dr. William T. Oedel, Associate Professor of Art History at the University of Massachusetts, Amherst, who wrote his Ph.D. dissertation on the works of John Vanderlyn, stated to the author that "several portraits thought to represent Theodosia Burr Alston have been attributed to Vanderlyn solely on the basis of the relationship between artist and subject and not for sound historical or stylistic reasons. The only portraits I accept as authentic are: the small unfinished, damaged (and unsatisfactory) oil on paper at the Senate House in Kingston (c. 1796, Stillwell, opp. p. 48); the engraving after Vanderlyn (location of Vanderlyn's original unknown) by Saint-Mémin (1797, Stillwell, opp. p. 50); the canvas at Yale (finished in December 1802; an oil copy by ? of the Yale portrait is in Stillwell, opp. p. 52); and a copy of that painting

in a private collection (c. 1811, location not known to this author). Two other portraits (one on enamel) mentioned in the correspondence are unlocated." Oedel specifically questioned the Vanderlyn attributions of the "1809/1811" painting of Theodosia (bust profile, facing left, high forehead, black dress, standing transparent lace collar, in Stillwell, opp. p. 56) at the New-York Historical Society and the Nag's Head portrait at the Lewis Walpole Library of Yale University (Stillwell, opp. p. 59).

41. Stillwell, 60.

42. Sale, 258.

Bibliography

MANUSCRIPTS

Alston Family Papers, 1735-1957. Library of Congress, Manuscript Division, Washington, D.C.

Alston, Jacob Motte. "Random Recollections of an Inconspicuous Life," 1890. Typescript, Miles Brewton House Collection, Charleston, South Carolina.

Alston-Pringle-Frost Collection, South Carolina Historical Society, Charleston, South Carolina.

Burr Family Papers, 1750-1853. Yale University Library, New Haven, Connecticut.

Burr-Purkitt Family Papers. Washington University Libraries, St. Louis, Missouri.

Emmett Collection, New York Public Library.

Geissler, Suzanne. "The Burr Family, 1716-1836." Ph.D. dissertation, Graduate School of Syracuse University, 1976.

Harman and Margaret Blennerhassett Papers, Blennerhassett Island Historical State Park archives, Parkersburg, West Virginia.

John Julius Pringle Collection, South Carolina Historical Society, Charleston, South Carolina.

Mitchell-Pringle Papers, South Carolina Historical Society, Charleston, South Carolina.

Oedel, William. "John Vanderlyn: French Neoclassicism and the Search for an American Art." Ph.D. dissertation, University of Delaware, 1981.

Slack Research Collections, Dawes Memorial Library, Marietta College, Marietta, Ohio.

PUBLISHED SOURCES: NON-FICTION

Abernethy, Thomas Perkins. "Aaron Burr in Mississippi," in *Journal of Southern History*, vol. XV, no. 1 (February 1949), 9-21.

Adams, Henry. *History of the United States During the Administrations of Jefferson and Madison*. Chicago: University of Chicago Press, 1967.

Alford, Robbie L. "Theodosia Burr Alston," in *Historic George-town County Leaflet Number 1*. Georgetown, South Carolina: The Rice Museum, 1975.

Alston, Elizabeth Deas. *The Allstons and Alstons of Waccamaw*. Privately printed, 1936.

Alston, Jacob Motte. "Theodosia Burr: The True Story of Her Death At Sea," in *The New York Times Saturday Review of Books*, May 24, 1902.

Bischoff, Henry. "The Hermitage: An Historical Overview," in *Ourstory: Journal of the New Jersey Council for History Education*, vol. 6, no. 1, (Fall 2000), 11-13.

Bischoff, Henry. "Theodosia Bartow Prevost Burr at The Hermitage," in *Ourstory: Journal of the New Jersey Council for History Education*, vol. 6, no. 1, (Fall 2000), 14-17.

Bixby, W. K. *The Private Journal of Aaron Burr, Reprinted in Full from the Original Manuscript in the Library of W. K. Bixby, of St. Louis Missouri, with an Introduction, Explanatory Notes, and a Glossary*. Rochester, New York: The Genesee Press, 1903. 2 vols.

Blennerhassett, Margaret. *The Widow of the Rock, and Other Poems. By A Lady*. Montréal, Québec, Canada: R.V. Starhawk, Printer, 1824.

Bradford, Gamaliel. *Wives*. New York: Harper & Brothers, 1925.

Brown, Everett Somerville, ed. *William Plumer's Memorandum of Proceedings in the United States Senate, 1803-1807*. New York: MacMillan, 1923.

Buckner, Melton F., Jr. *Aaron Burr: Conspiracy to Treason*. New York: John Wiley & Sons, Inc., 2000.

Cannaday, R. J. "The Mystery of Theodosia Burr," in *The News and Courier* (Charleston, South Carolina), August 4, 1963, 6-C.

Daniels, Jonathan. *Ordeal of Ambition: Jefferson, Hamilton, Burr*. Garden City, New York: Doubleday & Co., 1970.

Davis, Matthew L., ed. *Memoirs of Aaron Burr, With Selections From His Correspondence*. New York: Harper & Brothers, 1837 and 1838. 2 vols.

Davis, Matthew L., ed. The *Private Journal of Aaron Burr, During His Residence of Four Years in Europe; With Selections From His Correspondence*. New York: Harper & Brothers, 1858. 2 vols.

Davis, Richard Beale, ed. *Jeffersonian America: Notes on the United States of America Collected in the Years 1805-6-7 and 11-12 by Sir Augustus John Foster, Bart*. San Marino, California: Huntington Library, 1954.

"Death of Aaron Burr," in *The New Yorker*, September 17, 1836, p. 414.

Devereaux, Anthony Q. *The Rice Princes: A Rice Epoch Revisited.* Columbia, South Carolina: The State Co., 1973.

Dos Passos, John. "The Conspiracy and Trial of Aaron Burr," in *American Heritage*, February 1966, 4-9, 69-84.

Faye, Stanley. "Privateersmen of the Gulf and Their Prizes," in *Louisiana Historical Quarterly*, 1939, 1012-1094.

Gavaghan, Sister M. Ignatia. *Nathalie DeLage Sumter: A Dedicated Life of Faith.* Sumter, South Carolina: The Sumter County Historical Commission, 1984.

Harden, John, "The Strange Disappearance of Theodosia Burr," in *Fate*, June 1954, 20-25.

Harrison, Margaret Hayne. *A Charleston Album.* Rindge, New Hampshire: Richard R. Smith Publisher, Inc., 1953.

Hatfield, Mark O., with the Senate Historical Office. *Vice Presidents of the United States, 1789-1993.* Washington: U.S. Government Printing Office, 1997.

Hendrickson, Robert. *Hamilton.* New York: Mason/Charter, 1976. 2 vols.

Hurst, Alec J. "George Washington Stepped Here: July 10-14, 1778," in *Ourstory: Journal of the New Jersey Council for History Education*, vol. 6, no. 1 (Fall 2000), 18-19.

"Joseph Alston," in *Biographical Directory of the South Carolina House of Representatives, IV (1791-1815):* 32-35.

Kennedy, Roger G. *Burr, Hamilton, and Jefferson: A Study in Character.* New York: Oxford University Press, 1999.

King, Charles R., ed. *The Life and Correspondence of Rufus King.* New York: G. P. Putnam's Sons, 1896. 6 vols.

Kline, Mary-Jo and Joanne W. Ryan, eds. *The Political Correspondence and Public Papers of Aaron Burr.* Princeton, New Jersey: Princeton University Press, 1983. 2 vols.

Knapp, Samuel L. *The Life of Aaron Burr.* New York: Wiley and Long, 1835.

Lindsay, Kenneth C. *The Works of John Vanderlyn: From Tammany to the Capital.* Binghamton, New York: University Art Gallery, State University of New York, Binghamton, 1970.

Lomask, Milton. *Aaron Burr: The Years from Princeton to Vice President, 1756-1805.* New York: Farrar, Straus and Giroux, 1979.

Lomask, Milton. *Aaron Burr: The Conspiracy and Years of Exile, 1805-1836.* New York: Farrar, Straus and Giroux, 1982.

Love, Patricia. *The Emotional Incest Syndrome: What to Do When a Parent's Love Rules Your Life.* New York: Bantam Doubleday Dell, 1991.

Lowther, Minnie Kendall. *Blennerhassett Island in Romance and Tragedy.* Rutland, Vermont: Tuttle Publishing Co., 1936.

McCaleb, Walter Flavius. *The Aaron Burr Conspiracy.* Expanded edition with introduction by Dr. Charles A. Beard. New York: Wilson-Erickson, Inc., 1936.

McCracken, George E. "Who Was Aaron Burr?" *The American Genealogist,* vol. 40, no. 2 (April 1964), 65-70.

McKinsey, Elizabeth. *Niagara Falls: Icon of the American Sublime.* New York: Cambridge University Press, 1985.

McMaster, Lucille. "How Aaron Burr's Escape Was Foiled," in the *Atlanta Journal and Constitution,* May 7, 1961.

Michie, James L. *Richmond Hill Plantation, 1810-1868: The Discovery of Antebellum Life on a Waccamaw River Rice Plantation.* Spartanburg, South Carolina: The Reprint Company, 1990.

Michie, James L. *The Excavation of Joseph and Theodosia Burr Alston's House Site, The Oaks Plantation, Brookgreen Gardens, Georgetown County, South Carolina.* Research Manuscript 5. Conway, South Carolina: Waccamaw Center for Historical and Cultural Studies, Coastal Carolina University, 1994.

Michie, James L. "Theodosia! Some facts relating to the last days of Theodosia Burr Alston and the *Patriot,*" *Carologue* (South Carolina Historical Society), Summer 1998, 16-20.

Michie, James L. *The Oaks Plantation: Additional Discoveries Related to the Managerial Complex and the Architecture of Joseph and Theodosia Burr Alston's House Site, Brookgreen Gardens, Georgetown County, South Carolina.* Research Manuscript 7. Conway, South Carolina: Waccamaw Center for Historical and Cultural Studies, Coastal Carolina University, 1995.

Michie, James L. *The Oaks Plantation Revealed: An Archaeological Survey of the Home of Joseph and Theodosia Burr Alston, Brookgreen Gardens, Georgetown County, South Carolina.* Research Manuscript 4. Conway, South Carolina: Waccamaw Center for Historical and Cultural Studies, Coastal Carolina University, 1993.

Michie, James L. *The Oaks Plantation Rice Mill, Brookgreen Gardens, Georgetown County, South Carolina.* Research Manuscript 9. Conway, South Carolina: Waccamaw Center for Historical and Cultural Studies, Coastal Carolina University, 1996.

Mills, W. Jay and John Rae. *Historic Houses of New Jersey*. Philadelphia: J.B. Lippincott, 1904.

Minnigerode, Meade. *Lives and Times: Four Informal American Biographies*. New York: G.P. Putnam's Sons, 1925.

Minnigerode, Meade. "Theodosia Burr, Prodigy, An Informal Biography," in *The Saturday Evening Post*, Sept. 6, 1924, 10-11, 174, 177-178, 181-182, 185-186.

Mondello, Salvatore. "John Vanderlyn," in *The New-York Historical Society Quarterly*, vol. LII, no. 2 (April 1968), 161-183.

Olmstead, Frederick Law. *A Journey in the Seaboard Slave States, With Remarks on their Economy*. New York: Dix & Edwards, 1856.

Outlaw, Edward R., Jr. and Louise Greenleaf Outlaw. *Old Nag's Head*. Norfolk, Virginia.: Liskey Lithograph Corp., 1956.

Parmet, Herbert S., and Marie Hecht. *Aaron Burr: Portrait of an Ambitious Man*. New York: Macmillan Press, 1967.

Parsons, Cornelia Mitchell. *A Secret of the Sea*. New York: J. S. Ogilvie Publishing Co., 1896.

Parton, James S. *Famous Americans of Recent Times*. Boston: Ticknor and Fields, 1868.

Parton, James S. *The Life and Times of Aaron Burr*. New York: Mason Brothers, 1858.

Parton, James S. *Life and Times of Aaron Burr*. Enlarged edition. Boston: Houghton Mifflin, 1892. 2 vols.

Parton, James S. "Theodosia Burr," in *Harper's New Monthly Magazine*, vol. 29, issue 171 (August 1864), 293-305.

Peacock, Virginia Tatnall. *Famous American Belles of the 19th Century*. Philadelphia: J.B. Lippincott Co., 1901.

Pidgin, Charles Felton. *Theodosia: The First Gentlewoman of Her Times; the Story of her Life, and a History of Persons and Events Connected Therewith*. Boston: C. M. Clark Publishing Co., 1907.

Rankin, Jeremiah Eames, ed. *Esther Burr's Journal*. Washington, D.C.: Woodword & Lothrop, 1903.

Ravenel, Mrs. St. Julien. *Charleston, The Place and the People*. New York: The MacMillan Company, 1929.

Rogers, George C., Jr. *A History of Georgetown County*. Columbia, South Carolina: University of South Carolina Press, 1970.

Rogow, Arnold A. *A Fatal Friendship: Alexander Hamilton and Aaron Burr*. New York: Farrar, Straus and Giroux, 1999.

Roosevelt, Theodore. *The Winning of the West: Louisiana and Aaron Burr*. N.Y.: The Current Literature Publishing Co., 1906.

Rutledge, Anna Wells. *Artists in the Life of Charleston*. Columbia, South Carolina: University of South Carolina Press, 1940; reprinted, with a new preface by John Morrill Bryan, 1980.

Safford, William H. *The Blennerhassett Papers, Embodying the Private Journal of Harman Blennerhassett, and the Hitherto Unpublished Correspondence of Burr, Alston, Comfort Tyler, Devereaux, Dayton, Adair, Miro, Emmet, Theodosia Burr Alston, Mrs. Blennerhassett, and Others, Their Contemporaries; Developing the Purposes and Aims of Those Engaged in the Attempted Wilkinson and Burr Revolution; Embracing also the First Account of the "Spanish Association of Kentucky" and a Memoir of Blennerhassett, by William H. Safford*. Cincinnati: Moore, Wilstach, & Baldwin, 1864.

Sale, Edith Tunis. *Old Time Belles and Cavaliers*. Philadelphia: J.B. Lippincott Co., 1912.

Schachner, Nathan. *Aaron Burr: A Biography*. 1937; reprinted New York: A. S. Barnes & Co., 1961.

Schneider, Norris F. *Blennerhassett Island and the Burr Conspiracy*. Columbus, Ohio: The Ohio Historical Society, 1966.

Smith, Dorothy Valentine. "An Intercourse of the Heart: Some little-known letters of Theodosia Burr," in *New York Historical Society Quarterly*, 1953, 40-53.

Stedman, Edmund Clarence. "Aaron Burr's Wooing," in *Harper's New Monthly Magazine*, October 1887, 666-667.

Stillwell, John E. *The History of the Burr Portraits. Their Origin, Their Dispersal and Their Reassemblage*. N.p.: privately printed, 1928.

Stone, Col. William Leete. *The Life of Joseph Brant-Thayendanegea, Including the Border Wars of the American Revolution and Sketches of the Indian Campaigns of Generals Harmar, St. Clair, and Wayne*. Cooperstown, New York: various publishers, 1838 and 1844. 2 vols.

Swick, Ray. *An Island Called Eden: The Story of Harman and Margaret Blennerhassett*. Parkersburg, West Virginia: Blennerhassett Island Historical State Park, 2000.

Swick, Ronald Ray. "Theodosia Burr Alston," in *The South Atlantic Quarterly*, vol. 74, no. 4 (Autumn 1975), 495-506.

"Theodosia's Fate Still Subject of Debate," in *The Virginian-Pilot and The Ledger-Star*, Norfolk, Virginia, August 10, 2001.

Thomas, Ebeneezer Smith. *Reminiscences of the Last Sixty-Five Years....* Hartford, Connecticut: Tiffany and Burnham, 1840. 2 vols.

Todd, Charles Burr. *The True Aaron Burr. A Biographical Sketch*. New York: A. S. Barnes & Co., 1902.

Todd, Janet. *Mary Wollstonecraft: A Revolutionary Life.* New York: Columbia University Press, 2000.

Van Doren, Mark, ed. *Correspondence of Aaron Burr and His Daughter Theodosia.* New York: Covici-Friede, 1929.

Wallace, David Duncan. *South Carolina: A Short History.* Columbia, South Carolina: University of South Carolina Press, 1951.

Wandell, Samuel H. and Meade Minnigerode. *Aaron Burr.* New York: G.P. Putnam's Sons, 1927. 2 vols.

Wimsatt, Genevieve. "Was She Theodosia Burr? The Tale of the 'Female Stranger,'" in *The Mentor* (Springfield, Ohio: The Croswell Publishing Co.), October 1928, 30-31.

Wollstonecraft, Mary. *A Vindication of the Rights of Woman: With Strictures on Political and Moral Subjects.* London: J. Johnson, 1792; reprinted in 1989 by Prometheus Books, Amherst, N.Y

Whalen, Dwight. *Lover's Guide to Niagara Falls.* Niagara Falls, Ontario, Canada: Horseshoe Press, 1990.

Williams, Edward G. "The Prevosts of the Royal Americans," in *The Western Pennsylvania Historical Magazine,* January 1973, 1-38.

PUBLISHED SOURCES: FICTION

Colver, Anne. *Theodosia: Daughter of Aaron Burr.* New York: Holt, Rinehart & Winston, 1941.

Harris, Cyril. *Street of Knives.* New York: Little, Brown & Co., 1950.

Johnson, Mary. *Lewis Rand.* Illustrated by F. Yohn. New York: Houghton Mifflin, 1908.

Pidgin, Charles Felton. *Blennerhassett or The Decrees of Fate, A Romance Founded Upon Events of American History.* New York: Grosset & Dunlap, 1901.

Pidgin, Charles Felton. *The Climax: Or What Might Have Been.* Boston: C.M. Clark, 1902.

Seton, Anya (Anya Seton Chase). *My Theodosia.* New York: Grosset & Dunlap, 1941.

Vidal, Gore. *Burr: A Novel.* New York: Random House, 1973.

PUBLISHED SOURCES: ONLINE

Block, W.T. "A Tale of Jean Baptiste's Brass Cannon," online at http://www.wtblock.com/wtblockjr/jean.htm on November 19, 2001.

Brigham, David R., Laura K. Mills, and Philip Klausmeyer. "John Vanderlyn," online biography at the Worcester Museum of Art, Worcester, Mass., at http://www.worcesterart.org/Collection/Early_American/Artists/vanderlyn/biography/index.html, online on February 3, 2002.

Hause, Eric. "The Outer Banks: The Fate of Theodosia Burr," online at http://www.coastalguide.com/packet/theodosiaburr.htm on November 3, 2001.

Lewis, Jone Johnson. "A Vindication of the Rights of Woman: Mary Wollstonecraft," online at http://womenshistory.about.com/library/weekly/aa092099.htm on March 3, 2002.

Linder, Douglas, "The Treason Trial of Aaron Burr," online at http://www.jurist.law.pitt.edu/trials21.htm on June 10, 2002.

"Mysterious Theodosia," online at http://www.theoutlaws.com/people3.htm on June 26, 2002.

Acknowledgments

My work on this biography of Theodosia was made immensely more fruitful because of the generous support I received from a large number of Burrian and Theodosian scholars and researchers, a number of whom had devoted most of their professional life to aspects of Theodosia's life. To them I owe thanks for enriching this story and helping me tell it accurately. Any errors of omission or commission are, of course, solely my own doing and will be corrected in the next printing if brought to my attention.

Dr. Ray Swick, State Historian, at Blennerhassett Island Historical State Park, in Parkersburg, West Virginia, provided so much material and intimate knowledge of Harman and Margaret Blennerhassett's interactions with Burr and the Alstons during the "Burr Conspiracy" that I came to think of him more as an incarnation of the fascinating couple than a mere interpreter of their lives.

At The Hermitage, in Ho-Ho-Kus, New Jersey, where Aaron Burr married Theodosia's mother, Theodosia Bartow Prevost, T. Robins Brown, Executive Director, Friends of The Hermitage, Inc., and Dr. Henry Bischoff, Director of Historical Studies, graciously provided pictures, details, and precious insight into the life of Theodosia's parents. Alec J. Hurst, whose Theodosia and Aaron Burr research spans decades, and who donated his research to The Hermitage, also provided much-needed and timely information and guidance.

From Joseph K. Schwarzer, II, Executive Director of the Graveyard of the Atlantic Museum in Hatteras, North Carolina, and from Helen Wilson, I learned a great deal about the wreckers of the Outer Banks and the fact that pirates forcing their victims to "walk the plank" is more myth than reality.

To Margaret K. Powell, Librarian, and Marielle Mudgett-Olson, Research Assistant at The Lewis Walpole Library of Yale University in Farmington, Connecticut, I owe thanks for a high-precision color photographic copy of the Nag's Head portrait and copies of their accession and provenance records, both of which were used to try to solve the ultimate Burr/Alston art mystery: who is the woman in the portrait, and who painted the picture? In addition, Dr. William T. Oedel, Professor of Art History at the University of Massachusetts at Amherst, and Dr. Kenneth C. Lindsay, retired Professor of Art History at the State University of New York at Binghamton, both authorities on the work of John Vanderlyn, graciously took the time to review my research. At the Senate House Museum in Kingston, New York, Deana Preston, Archivist and Curator, helped me understand the intricacies of John Vanderlyn's work and travels. David R. Brigham, Laura K. Mills, and Philip Klausmeyer provided additional Vanderlyn information through their online biography of the artist, courtesy of the Worcester Art Museum, Worcester, Massachusetts.

It took the combined efforts of the staffs at four institutions to locate the likeness of Joseph Alston, which burned in a 1947 fire at Amherst College. There, Daria D'Arenzo, Head, Archives and Special Collections, and Stephen Fisher, Registrar, Mead Art Museum, combed their accession records for information. The clues they gave me led me to Barbara Bernard and Andrea Gibbs at the National Gallery of Art. They guided me to Mariko Iida at the Frick Art Reference Library, who located and provided me with a copy of the only existing copy photograph of the destroyed miniature. My search for a portrait of Mary Wollstonecraft, Aaron Burr's educational role model for his daughter, went quickly because of Anna Sheppard, Picture Librarian at The Tate Picture Library in London. Monique Crine at Butterfield's, San Francisco, made it possible to use their picture of Aaron Burr's pocket watch, which they auctioned in 2002.

As usual, my colleagues in South Carolina gave unstintingly of their time to help me blaze a trail through the

Theodosian wilderness. First among them is James L. Michie, the tireless archaeologist who excavated the physical record of The Oaks. I am also indebted to his hard-working and loyal assistant, Susan H. McMillan of Conway, for her own insights into what they uncovered at The Oaks. I am also grateful for the support of the management and staff at Brookgreen Gardens, who are now the owners and caretakers of The Oaks and who provided financial support and encouragement for Jim Michie's archaeological digs there.

In Georgetown, Katrina P. Lawrimore, Museum Director of the Kaminski House Museum, and James A. Fitch, Executive Director of The Rice Museum, helped me understand coastal watercraft, the *Patriot,* and the hazards of navigating Winyah Bay in the early 1800s. I am grateful to Alberta Quattlebaum, president of the Georgetown Chapter, National Society of Colonial Dames in the State of South Carolina, and "Sister" Genevieve Chandler Peterkin, daughter of historian/ folklorist Genevieve Chandler, for the details of Anya Seton Chase's visit to South Carolina. Georgetown historian Patricia Davis Doyle shared her knowledge of the city and its rice rivers (known in the Lowcountry as "holy water"), and I could have never fathomed the intricacies of property ownership in the rice country without the help of Agnes Leland Baldwin, grande dame of McClellanville and South Carolina's foremost authority on colonial Lowcountry land records. I am also grateful to Lucille Vanderbilt Pate for the opportunity to visit Prospect Hill plantation house, and to Raejean and Franklin D. Beattie, the gracious stewards of Hopsewee Plantation on the North Santee.

In the Holy City, as Charleston is known to its natives, many people and institutions shared their knowledge and resources. Chief among them was poet-screenwriter-novelist Rose Moore Tomlin, whose willingness to search, find, and share Theodosia material was an enormous help. Jane and Daniel Heyward Hamilton, Jr., had the c. 1801 miniature of Theodosia restored and graciously permitted me to use it in this book. Other aides included Thomas A. Tisdale, author of

A Lady of the High Hills: Natalie Delage Sumter; the photographic history expertise of Jack Thomson; Lynn Todd's knowledge of French; and Mary Giles' assistance with art history. As always, the staff of the Historic Charleston Foundation's magnificent Edmondston-Alston House, which cares for a number of Theodosias's books, was helpful, and one of their docents, Phyllis J. Fulmer, helped me research Joseph Alston's life. Finally, Ashton and Lavonne Phillips graciously invited me to tour their—and Theodosia's—beautiful townhouse at 94 Church Street. The Charleston County Library system, especially the Mt. Pleasant Regional Library, and the Greenville County Library, all gave unstintingly of their time and skills, as they have so many times in the past.

At the Lower Cape Fear Historical Society, Wilmington, North Carolina, Executive Director Catherine Myerow directed me to folklorists such as John Golden, who knew local versions of the Theodosia ghost and pirate stories. From Chester, South Carolina, W. L. D. "Bill" Marion shared local Burr lore and provided fine photographs. And in Mt. Pleasant, Alejandro Alvarez and Andrés Betancourt were always there to help type, file, sort, fold, and send. Ken Westdyk and Coralee Cummings also contributed, as did family historians Norris Taylor, Kimball G. Everingham, James Reid Hancock, and Neal Friedman.

Finally, at Corinthian Books, Senior Editor Diane Anderson carried out the bulk of the heavy editorial work, with the assistance of Dr. Elizabeth Burnett, the able editor of my previous biography, *Mary's World.* The proofreading and indexing benefited greatly from the keen eyes of Jennifer Corley, Margaret Grace, Michelle Adams, and Georgianne Frances Batts. Dwain Skinner's maps, Steve McCardell's typesetting. Rob Johnson's design, and Tip Atkeson's color separations all contributed to the book's design and readability.

Illustration Credits

In the listings below, RNC stands for the collection of the author, Richard N. Côté. All other sources are described in full.

Cover: Theodosia Burr Alston, c. 1801, miniature watercolor on ivory, attributed to Edward Greene Malbone, from the collection of Mr. David Heyward Hamilton, Jr., a great-great-great-grandson of William and Mary Brewton Motte Alston.

Flyleaf: Theodosia Burr, about 13 years old, by Charles Balthazar Julien Fevret de Saint-Mémin, 1796, from Virginia Tatnall Peacock, *Famous American Belles of the Nineteenth Century* (1901), also at The Corcoran Gallery of Art, Washington.

Chapter 1: Good Stock, Deep Roots. Rev. Aaron Burr, from Samuel H. Wandell and Meade Minnigerode, *Aaron Burr* (1927); Rev. Jonathan Edwards, steel engraving, artist unknown, RNC; Sarah (Pierpont) Edwards, wife of the Rev. Jonathan Edwards, artist unknown, from Charles Felton Pidgin, *Theodosia* (1907); and The Parsonage of the First Presbyterian Church, Newark, New Jersey, drawing by John Rae, from W. Jay Mills, *Historic Houses of New Jersey* (1904).

Chapter 2: Rev. Burr's Son. Nassau Hall, Princeton, New Jersey, 1764, from *An Account of the College of New Jersey, 1764;* Tapping Reeve, from *Harper's New Monthly Magazine,* March 1877; George Washington, engraved by J.C. Buttre after a painting by Gilbert Stuart, RNC; Benedict Arnold, engraver unknown, from Samuel H. Wandell and Meade Minnigerode, *Aaron Burr* (1927); A view of Quebec in 1775, engraver unknown, from *Harper's New Monthly Magazine,* in Samuel H. Wandell and Meade Minnigerode, *Aaron Burr* (1927); The Hermitage, in Ho-Ho-Kus, New Jersey, photograph courtesy

Friends of The Hermitage, Inc., and the New Jersey Division of Parks and Forestry; and "Aaron Burr's Wooing," poem by Edmund Clarence Stedman, illustration by Howard Pyle, engraved by J. Tinkey, from *Harper's New Monthly Magazine*, October 1887.

Chapter 3: Courtship and Courtrooms. Alexander Hamilton, engraved by Johnson, Fry, & Co., New York, 1861, after an original painting by Alonzo Chappell, RNC; Mrs. James (Dorothea "Dolley" Payne Todd) Madison, engraved by D. Appleton & Co., New York, 1856, after a painting by Gilbert Stuart, RNC; Aaron Burr as a young lawyer, by Charles Balthazar Julien Fevret de Saint-Mémin, National Portrait Gallery of the Smithsonian Institution; and Mary Wollstonecraft, by John Opie, c. 1797, courtesy The Tate Gallery, London, 2002.

Chapter 4: Mistress of Richmond Hill. The Richmond Hill Mansion, from *Harper's New Monthly Magazine*, in Samuel H. Wandell and Meade Minnigerode, *Aaron Burr* (1927); Aaron Burr's pocket watch, c. 1792, 88: courtesy Butterfield's, San Francisco; Theodosia Burr, about eleven years old, by Gilbert Stuart, 1795, from John E. Stilwell, *The Burr Portraits* (1928), now at the Yale University Art Gallery; Natalie de Lage de Volude, about 13 years old, by Charles Balthazar Julien Fevret de Saint-Mémin, c. 1796, The Corcoran Gallery of Art, Washington; Theodosia Burr, about 13 years old, by Charles Balthazar Julien Fevret de Saint-Mémin, 1796, from Virginia Tatnall Peacock, *Famous American Belles of the Nineteenth Century* (1901), also at The Corcoran Gallery of Art, Washington; Theodosia as a teenager, engraver unknown, after a portrait by John Vanderlyn, 1796, RNC; Joseph Brant Thayendanegea, about 1776, from *London Magazine*, July 1776, courtesy Library of Congress; Aaron Burr in 1802, engraver unknown, after a painting by John Vanderlyn, 1802, from James L. Parton, *Life and Times of Aaron Burr*, vol. I (1892); Theodosia Burr Alston in 1802, engraved by H. Wright Smith, c. 1857, after a painting by John Vanderlyn, 1802, RNC; and Joseph Alston, about 1800-1810, attributed to Edward Greene Malbone, courtesy of the Mead

Art Museum of Amherst College; copy photograph courtesy of the Frick Art Reference Library, New York.

Chapter 5: The Yankee Belle. Theodosia Burr Alston, c. 1801, watercolor on ivory, attributed to Edward Greene Malbone, collection of Daniel Heyward Hamilton, Jr.; "The Castle" on Debordieu Island, S.C., photographer unknown, from Elizabeth Deas Allston, *The Allstons and Alstons of Waccamaw* (1936); The arms of William Alston of Clifton plantation, Miles Brewton House collection; Col. William Alston, of Clifton Plantation, copy of a miniature, artist unknown, Miles Brewton House collection; Mary Brewton Motte Alston, oil on canvas, by Edward Savage, 1792, Miles Brewton House collection (original now at the Gibbes Museum of Art, Charleston, S.C.); The Miles Brewton House, Charleston, 1920s postcard by Lanneau's Art Store, Charleston, RNC; Alston Rice Plantations on the Waccamaw Peninsula, map by Dwain Skinner for RNC; Niagara Falls, engraved from a sketch by an unknown artist by J. C. Buttre, published in New York by R. Martin, RNC.

Chapter 6: The Clouds of Weehawken. The scene of the duel, overlooking New York City, engraved by Lossing Barritt, from James S. Parton, *The Life and Times of Aaron Burr* (1858); and The duel, as imagined by an early illustrator, artist unknown, possibly from *Harper's New Monthly Magazine*, RNC.

Chapter 7: Codeword: Emperor. Aaron Burr, about 1805, artist unknown, engraved by Enoch G. Gridley, RNC; Gen. James Wilkinson, artist unknown, National Portrait Gallery, Smithsonian Institution; Burr's Theatre of Operations, 1805-1807, map by Dwain Skinner for RNC; Blennerhassett Island, as sketched in 1858 by Lizzie Forbes, courtesy Blennerhassett Island Historical State Park; The Blennerhassett Mansion, from an 1850 print after a c. 1840s painting by Marietta, Ohio artist, Sala Bosworth, courtesy Blennerhassett Island Historical State Park; Harman Blennerhassett, miniature on ivory, artist unknown, painted in London, c. 1796, courtesy Blennerhassett Island Historical State Park; Margaret (Agnew) Blennerhassett, miniature watercolor on ivory, artist unknown, probably

painted in Montréal, early 1820s, courtesy the Missouri His-
torical Society, St. Louis; Margaret Blennerhassett on the
Marietta Trail, engraver unknown, courtesy Blennerhassett
Island Historical State Park; Margaret Blennerhassett's flight
from the Island, engraver unknown, courtesy Blennerhassett
Island Historical State Park; Windy Hill Manor, postcard, c.
1920-1930, The Albertype Co., Brooklyn, N.Y., RNC; The
Lewis Inn, near Chester, South Carolina, photograph by W.
L. D. "Bill" Marion; "Burr's bench" at Lewis's Inn, (now in
the Chester County Historical Society Museum), photograph
by W. L. D. "Bill" Marion; and The Virginia State Penitentiary at Richmond, engraver unknown, courtesy Blennerhassett Island Historical State Park.

Chapter 9: Voyage of the *Patriot*. Aaron Burr, age 78,
engraved by E. G. Williams & Bro., New York, after a painting by James Vandyke, RNC.

Chapter 10: The Pirate Stories. "As the pirates reached the
deck, Theodosia grasped a cutlass," from James Felton Pidgin, *Blennerhassett, or, The Decrees of Fate* (1901), illustration
by Charles H. Stephens.

Chapter 11: Literary Kudzu. "Because, Theodosia....I Love
You," from James Felton Pidgin, *Blennerhassett, or, The Decrees
of Fate* (1901), illustration by Charles H. Stephens; *Fate* magazine cover, June 1954.

Chapter 12: The Mystery of the Nag's Head Portrait. The
Nag's Head portrait, alleged to be of Theodosia Burr Alston,
oil on wooden board, by an unknown artist, courtesy of the
Lewis Walpole Library of Yale University, Farmington, Connecticut.

Index

The following abbreviations are used: TBA for Aaron Burr's daughter, Theodosia Burr, later Theodosia Burr Alston; JA for Joseph Alston; ABA for their son, Aaron Burr Alston; AB for Aaron Burr; TBP for Theodosia Bartow Prevost Burr, Burr's first wife; HB for Harman Blennerhassett; and MB for Margaret Blennerhassett.